Native American Estate

Native American Estate

The Struggle over Indian and Hawaiian Lands

Linda S. Parker

University of Hawaii Press
Honolulu

94 93 92 91 90 89   5 4 3 2 1

Library of Congress Cataloging-in-Publication Data

Parker, Linda S. (Linda Sue), 1949–
  Native American estate : the struggle over Indian and Hawaiian
lands / Linda S. Parker.
    p.   cm.
  Bibliography: p.
  Includes index.
  ISBN 0–8248–1119–4
  1. Indians of North America—Land tenure.   2. Indians of North
America—Claims.   3. Hawaiians—Land tenure.   4. Hawaiians—Claims.
I. Title.
E98.L3P37   1989   89–4892
333.2—dc20   CIP

∞™ *The paper used in this publication meets the minimum
requirements of American National Standard for Information
Sciences—Permanence of Paper for Printed Library Materials*
ANSI Z39.48–1984

CONTENTS

PREFACE

WHILE a graduate student, I was intrigued by the fact that Hawaiians and American Indians have endured similar—as well as different—experiences as a result of western expansion. At the center stand the issues of land ownership and sovereignty. The U.S. government and its expansion-minded citizens have played a crucial, although not exclusive, role in the divestment of the indigenous peoples' land and dominion. This loss of land has continued into the twentieth century and to the present time. During the past two decades both Native Hawaiians and American Indians have fought through the dominant legal and political systems to protect or to regain possession of land and natural resource rights. These themes are the subject of this book. First written as a dissertation, it has been revised to incorporate many of the legal and political events that have occurred within the past decade.

Mere words cannot adequately express my deep appreciation for the guidance of the late Dr. Arrell M. Gibson. As scholar, mentor, and friend, Dr. Gibson helped me immeasurably throughout the preparation of the manuscript. I am also indebted to professors Sidney D. Brown, Russell D. Buhite, and H. Wayne Morgan of the University of Oklahoma, for their invaluable support while serving on my dissertation committee. Clare V. (Bud) McKanna, Jr., of San Diego State University contributed editorial comments on a more recent version of the manuscript. Appreciation is also extended to Professor Clifford Trafzer, chairman of American Indian Studies at San Diego State University, for his words of encouragement.

During preparation of the manuscript the College of Arts and Letters at San Diego State University provided typing assistance at a crucial time. I also want to express appreciation to the University of Oklahoma Graduate School for helping defray research expenses during the early stages of my research. The staff of the Archives of Hawaii, particularly Agnes Conrad, deserve commendation for the considerable assistance they provided in locating sources. And special thanks goes to Linda Delaney of the Office of Hawaiian Affairs for taking time from her busy schedule to discuss contemporary Native Hawaiian land issues.

1

Introduction: Perceptions, Philosophy, and Rationale

WHEN a nation with superior technology and a nativistic community come into contact, major conflict evolves from differing land tenure systems. This was the case when the imperial nations of Europe, and later the United States, encountered the native peoples of the American continent and the Hawaiian islands. Colonists claiming dominion over native peoples and their lands in the New World reflected the imperialistic mind-set of their age. They were committed to the exploitation of the New World's human and natural resources. Later, the new U.S. government implemented many aspects of Native American management that had been practiced by Great Britain. American justification for expropriating Indian land had its roots in European philosophy, theology, canon law, and international law derived from the rhetoric of the ancestral imperial nations. Americans formulated their own concepts to justify expropriation during the frontier movement in the early nineteenth century, and traders, settlers, and missionaries readily transferred them to Native Hawaiians and their lands.

The future relationship between the Old World settlers and the native inhabitants of the Western Hemisphere was thus to a large degree already determined at the time of contact. Christianity and classical philosophy helped form preconceived views of the New World peoples and the relation of Christian nations to them. European religious, ethical, and commercial standards provided the justification for conquest of native peoples and their territories in the New World. In the centuries following the European discovery of the Americas, various concepts were put forward to promote expansion, and all presumed the superiority of the Christian nations over heathen nations.

To justify the New World conquest European theologians and philosophers frequently referred to Aristotelian thought. The Spaniard Juan de Quevedo cited Aristotle's statement that some men were inferior by nature

1

to uphold the view that Indians were slaves by nature. Francisco de Vitoria denounced the idea that Indians were by nature subject to rule by others and incapable of self-rule. He believed they possessed sound minds and should not be slaves. Vitoria, however, interpreted Aristotle's teachings to mean that Indians "in their childish innocence" required protection from superior Christian nations. Thus, he too justified conquest for the Indians' good. Juan Ginés de Sepúlveda agreed with Quevedo and added that the New World peoples' customs and lack of individual ownership of land (title to Indian land was vested in the tribe) upheld the natural law of superiority of Christian nations over uncivilized non-Christian nations. Bartolomé de Las Casas charged that Sepúlveda did not understand Aristotle and maintained that few individuals were by nature slaves and claimed that Indians were rational. Fernando Vázquez de Menchaca accused his contemporaries of using Aristotle's theory of slavery to "cover wars with a cloak of justice," but the imperialist view that a Christian nation had a natural right to conquer Indians, use their labor, and exploit their lands prevailed.[1]

Theologians and philosophers also debated the moral and ethical responsibility to Christianize the Indians. Inseparable from this controversy was the idea of just wars. This concept evolved as justification for conquest, expansion, and later displacement of the Indians from their lands. St. Augustine first developed the idea that wars could be just if the objective was good, including the intention to avenge wrongs. Adding to this reasoning, Ambrose elaborated the moral obligation to correct or prevent injustices. Medieval theologians claimed that conquest was legitimate only if the war had been just. The Crusades divided the world into an antithetical view of right and wrong, as well as between the faithful and the infidel, and implanted the idea that wars of conquest waged in the name of Christianity were just. Later the doctrine evolved to justify world conquest.

After Pope Alexander VI assigned North America to Spain in 1493, debate ensued in the Spanish court over just wars and voluntary and forced conversion. The Spanish government directed its conquerors to read the *Requerimiento* to the Indians. If the Indians refused to acknowledge the Pope and the rulers of Spain as sovereigns, then the colonists would force them to accept the contents of the *Requerimiento*. The Laws of Burgos (1512) required that the Indians be treated humanely, but they could be coerced to accept conversion to the Christian faith. In 1529 Pope Clement VI in the bull *Intra Arcana* stated that Spanish officials could use force to convert the Indians. Vitoria denounced the application of force in Christianizing the Indians and rejected the belief that refusal to convert justified war. Vitoria did present another reason for a just war, which was adopted by the imperial nations in their relations with Indians. He argued that natural law and the law of nations allowed the Spanish to travel to the New World and to live there, as long as they did not injure the indigenous people. These two doctrines and divine law guaranteed the imperial nations the right to trade. If the Indians hindered the actualization of this right, then Europeans could go to war against them. Vitoria's concept provided justification for intervention and conquest.

Many philosophers and theologians in the late sixteenth century continued the debate regarding just wars. Francisco Suarez denounced the idea that failure to convert justified war, but he argued that the prevention of teaching the Gospel did justify war. An Italian, Alberico Gentili, agreed with Vitoria that religion or forced conversion did not excuse war and that the prevention of trade, which was part of the law of nations, justified war against Indians. Out of this debate emerged the moral and legal defense of intervention, conquest, and occupation of the New World.

European philosophers also debated the morality of appropriating Indian lands. Sir Thomas More provided justification for expansion in *Utopia* (1516). If the Utopians moved to an area with vacant lands and the native people refused to obey the new laws, then they must be driven from their lands. Continued resistance provided a just cause for war. The English philosopher presented an argument derived from what he called the law of nature dealing with the right to put land to its most efficient use. "When people holdeth a piece of ground void and vacant to no good or profitable use: Keeping others from the use and possession of it, which notwithstanding, by the law of nature, ought thereof to be nourished and relieved." The evolving idea of just war later became part of the American justification for expropriating Indian land.

Another European tenet known as the doctrine of discovery legalized appropriation of aboriginal lands. Under this concept, which was based on the law of nations, a Christian sovereign acquired exclusive jurisdiction over new territories discovered by his representative or subject. The moral or ethical right to hold title to these lands rested on preconceptions of the native inhabitants. Such expansion became legitimate when the Indians existed in a supposed state of barbarism and heathenism. According to this view, Indians, who were non-Christian and by European standards uncivilized, held no property rights and existed outside of the sanctions of morality and international law. By divine law the Christian imperial nations were superior and had the right to dominion and rule over non-Christian inhabitants and their territories.

Early Spanish treatment of American Indians had not accorded them any natural rights to property, but Vitoria rose to the Indians' defense, claiming that even savages had some natural rights. According to the professor of theology at the University of Salamanca, the Indians had "as much right to possess property as the Catholic peasants" and not even the

Pope could take away that right. Spanish laws slowly recognized limited natural rights of the Indians to occupied lands but not to unoccupied property. Spanish officials later developed a policy compensating the Indians for appropriated lands. The form of payment consisted of grants of unoccupied property or wastelands.

During the sixteenth century the English refused to recognize any property rights for the Indians. Title to the new territories rested in the sovereign because of the right of discovery, which encompassed the idea of possession. Following the pattern started in 1496 when Henry VII commissioned John Cabot "to conquer, occupy and possess" the lands of "heathens and infidels," Elizabeth I authorized Sir Humphrey Gilbert in 1578 and Sir Walter Raleigh in 1584 to seize the "remote heathen and barbarous land."[2]

Dutch expansion on the Atlantic seaboard forced the English colonists to resort to the doctrine of natural rights to secure their land claims. The Dutch West India Company instructed its agents in 1625 to obtain legal possession by purchasing Indian claims. Some English settlers thereafter followed the Dutch policy of acquiring written Indian deeds.

John Winthrop, the first governor of the Massachusetts Bay colony, believed that the land in America was legally wasteland because Indians had no natural rights to land that had not been acquired in accordance with English law. The Puritans recognized legal title only to those lands with deeds from the Massachusetts Bay Company. They did not acknowledge Indian title to any land claimed by the Crown. Deviating from the views of most English colonists, Roger Williams rejected the assumption of ownership of land by the sovereign based on the right of discovery. Williams thought that Indians held the only valid title to the land unless it had been extinguished through purchase. The threat of acquisition by others later persuaded Winthrop to purchase land from the Indians.

In the English colonies the practice of compensating Indians for their land coexisted with recognition of the doctrine of discovery. Most of the colonial governments restricted private transactions in Indian land, trade, and creation of reservations. Later the U.S. government incorporated such practices into its Indian policy.

In reality the European nations had to go beyond the right of discovery to claim new territory in North America. The claimant sovereign had to deal with de jure facts and not mere theory. The military power and numerical dominance of the Indians who had not yielded jurisdiction or sovereignty over the land, and the power of contending European nations for the same territory, forced the discovering nation to reconcile its de jure assumptions with the de facto situation. In the contest among imperial nations for land in the New World, the more conclusive claim came with actual possession or occupation. By 1580 England applied possession as the basis for its claim to new territories.

In dealing with the Indians, the European nations used negotiation, purchase, treaties, and compensation. English officials followed the same diplomatic usages in dealing with the Indian chiefs as in their relations with other sovereign states. This provided a de facto recognition of Indian hegemony. If the claims under the right of discovery had been legitimate, then it would not have been necessary to make agreements and treaties with the Indians. Although the rights of Indian land tenure never had equal status to European claims, the colonists did come to recognize that the claims could be extinguished or retained. This led to the acknowledgment of aboriginal use and occupancy. The right of discovery did not acknowledge any political status for the Indians; the treaty process provided the basis for the evolution of the concept of Indian title. Later the U.S. government would view Indian land tenure as consisting of use and occupancy.

Except in the lower Mississippi Valley where they farmed, the French usually did not appropriate Indian lands, although they did bring tribal territories under Gallic dominion. For the most part the French and Russians exploited the Indians in the fur trade. The Russians in Alaska extended dominion over the area but did not interfere to any great extent in the Indians' land tenure.

Since the right of discovery brought the new territories under the exclusive jurisdiction of the European sovereign, conflicting claims emerged. Emmerich de Vattel, a noted eighteenth-century international law figure, believed the doctrine of natural law should be applied. According to the Swiss jurist no nation "can exclusively appropriate to themselves more than they have occasion for, or more than they are able to settle and cultivate." This precept also justified the appropriation of the Indians' land; the Indians should not have more land than they actually used. Vattel further applied natural law to support the view that agriculture provided the highest level of economic pursuit. Most Europeans conceived of the Indians as nomadic hunters, which made them naturally inferior to the agricultural Christian nations. John Locke had maintained that agricultural peoples should force hunting peoples to transform their economy. This concept provided partial justification of appropriation during the eighteenth and nineteenth centuries.

Following the War of Independence the new U.S. government assumed title to Indian lands within its boundaries that had been claimed by the English. American leaders perpetuated the imperial management concept that evolved from British practice, and the U.S. government duplicated the central organization initiated under the Crown. The national government also assumed the exclusive right to extinguish Indian title, to regulate trade, and to negotiate treaties. During the period of confederation, the government claimed title to Indian lands based on the right of conquest. The Indians, however, had not been conquered during the Revolution, only temporarily subdued. When the tribes asserted their sovereignty over territory, the national government resorted to the British method of purchasing Indian title.

During the early years of independence a policy developed for the management of Indian affairs, largely through the influence of Thomas Jefferson and Henry Knox, secretaries of state and war, respectively. Knox and Jefferson believed that the Indians possessed the natural rights of man, and their right to the soil could be extinguished by the federal government by purchase or by just wars. As reflected in the Northwest Ordinance of 1787 and subsequent American policy, the U.S. government used the concept of just wars to justify appropriation of Indian lands. Jefferson drew from the right of discovery and the Indian right of use and occupancy and propounded the right of preemption. According to this concept, Indians had legal title to their lands but could alienate it only to the intruding imperial nation. As the Indians' power diminished, the strength of their claims correspondingly decreased. In 1823 the Supreme Court decision of *Johnson and Graham's Lessee v. McIntosh,* delivered by Justice John Marshall, enunciated the doctrine of discovery whereby the United States held the exclusive title to Indian lands. Indian title comprised the right of use and occupancy.

During the nineteenth century the federal government forced numerous Indian tribes to cede their lands and remove to the trans–Mississippi River region known as the Great American Desert. Some of the reasons used to justify the expropriation and exile included charges of Indian savagery and tribal paganism, and possession of a nonagricultural-based economy. These reasons had been used for centuries by imperial nations to justify conquest and appropriation of Indian lands.

Certainly, American views toward the Indians and their territories already had crystallized before the extension of the American frontier to the Hawaiian islands. American settlers largely applied their view of Indians and land ownership to Native Hawaiians. Both religious and commercial reasons motivated American expansion. After 1820 when American settler, missionary, and trader immigration increased and became the dominant segment of the foreign community in the islands, most of the new arrivals perceived the indigenous people to be uncivilized, lazy pagans. Americans considered their Christian, commercial, and agricultural lifestyle superior to the Hawaiian mode—their superior institutions gave them the right to expand. American residents believed that Native Hawaiians would become civilized only when they adopted allodial (freehold) tenure, used the soil according to Christian principles of commerce, and converted to Protestantism. Man's natural right to own private property and the Americans' ability to exploit the soil to its highest utility justified acquisition of Hawaiian lands. American belief in free exercise of commercial rights led to continual requests to their home government for warships to enforce their assumed prerogative to engage freely in trade, to own land, and to be secure in their property. Local native power forced American and European residents to accept the original Hawaiian land tenure system until they attained sufficient power and influence to change it. American intruders applied the same rhetoric and some of the methods to acquire Hawaiian lands as they had used to secure Indian lands. The relatively small landmass of the islands, especially those lands suitable for agricultural or pastoral purposes, intensified the contest for property. Although some differences did exist, the final outcome of American imperialism in Hawai'i resulted in the extension of American sovereignty and possession of most of the Native Americans' lands.

This study will compare American Indian and Native Hawaiian land tenure systems, rhetoric and methods of expropriation, and vicissitudes of the indigenous peoples under European and Anglo-American imperialism. It concludes with a survey of the Native Americans' attempts to regain land and restore or reaffirm fishing, hunting, and water rights.

2

Native Land Tenure Systems

ADAPTATIONS in institutions ultimately lead to modifications in a society's land tenure system. Such alterations result from changes occurring within a society, from contact with alien societies, or because of changes forced by intruders. To comprehend the degree of change in Native Hawaiian and American Indian landholding and use systems, which resulted from contact and conquest by Western imperial nations, one must examine these systems as they existed at the time of contact, as well as Native American views toward land.[1]

NATIVE HAWAIIAN LAND TENURE

Native Hawaiian and American Indian cultures were not static during the precontact period; they experienced significant alterations in the thousands of years before contact with European-Americans. In the six centuries before the visit of Capt. James Cook in 1778, Hawaiian society and culture changed dramatically. Hawaiians extended their settlements from scattered permanent habitations in windward valleys to the arid and marginal regions of the islands. The development of a large population base, intensive agriculture, and a complex hierarchy of chiefs resulted in rival chiefs competing for control of land through warfare and conquest during the few centuries before Cook's arrival.[1]

During the early nineteenth century, writers including missionaries and Native Hawaiian scholars described the traditional sociopolitical and land tenure system as resembling feudalism. These observations came more than fifty years after the first European visit. Because the influence of Western ideas had considerable impact on Hawaiian culture during the early years, the sources must be evaluated carefully. A twentieth-century scholar suggested that the described feudalistic system might not have been indigenous, but rather a product of economic and political contact with Western imperial powers. British agents, such as Capt. George Vancouver, had considerable influence in the early postcontact years, particularly in Kamehameha's unification of Hawai'i. Many Hawaiian leaders were anxious to please foreign dignitaries to gain access to Western trade goods. Impressed with the power of the foreigners and with a desire to raise economic stability in his own dominion, Kamehameha might have instituted certain features of a feudal system based upon a European model.[2]

Archaeological research has revealed that during the several centuries before Cook's visit the Hawaiians constructed large irrigation systems, dryland field complexes, and religious temples. The intensive agriculture and sophisticated public works imply a level of cooperation among the *maka'āinana* that was probably maintained by a hierarchy of chiefs and priests. These developments also suggest the increasing complexity of class stratification and the importance of warfare. Evidence for this social order is supported by the detailed genealogies, histories, and legends collected by nineteenth-century Hawaiian scholars. Certainly, the common cultivators were much farther from the chiefs than in the clan-based land tenure systems of most agricultural American Indians.[3]

Both Hawaiian and American Indian relationships with land and nature were steeped in the metaphysical. Native American attachment to land was a transcendental identification with nature that was reflected in their economic, religious, social, and political institutions.

Indians believed that a supernatural power (known as the Maker, Great Holy Force Above, Great Spirit, or by other names) gave land to his children to use forever and to preserve for the benefit of their descendants. They perceived the earth as their mother—the source of life. Mother Earth provided them with flora and fauna that furnished them food, clothing, and shelter. Indians respected the earth and nature in all its features, believing that they came from the earth and were a part of it.

Native Hawaiians also had a mystical relationship and a spiritual identification with the land upon which they lived and from which they derived their subsistence. The nature gods, *Lono* and *Kāne*, gave the land to the Hawaiians to use and enjoy its fruitful products. The very features, qualities, and forces of nature confronting the Hawaiians endeared them to their lands. This attachment appeared frequently in legends. The Hawaiians' closeness to the land was reflected in their religious rites and beliefs. Their belief in the gods of the sea, volcano, water, rain, and agriculture was an intrinsic part of their relationship with nature. Hawaiians dedicated their sons at the time of weaning to Lono, the fertility and agricultural god, and they prayed for his blessing at the dedication of a new dwelling. In honor of Lono they offered the first fruits of the harvest at the beginning and end of each year at the *Makahiki* festival. Both Hawaiians and

Indians treasured, respected, even revered the land, its ecological features, and its fertility, whereas Westerners viewed land and the forces of nature as obstacles to overcome and conquer.[4]

Concepts of private or absolute ownership of land did not exist among either Indians or Hawaiians. Ownership in fee simple that prevailed in Western societies entailed the privilege of use and the right of alienation. The former prevailed among Indians and Hawaiians, but the right of alienation existed only in a few instances and even then was highly restricted. The right of alienation carried no similarities to absolute ownership in the Western legal sense. Among the few Indian landholding groups that permitted alienation, this privilege only allowed for the transfer of land or its resources to members of the local group occupying the land, and in some instances only with the group's prior approval.

Hawaiians and Indians did not consider land a commodity to be sold or bought in the marketplace—they did not value land as a piece of real estate and placed no commercial value on it. Native Americans treasured land because its produce provided subsistence for life; they valued the fruits of the soil and not the land per se. Even Hawaiians' frequent wars of conquest for territory were fought primarily to gain lands valued for their produce. Fertile productive land increased the material welfare of the island chiefs, the *ali'i,* and this was a measure of their supremacy. Among the few Indian landholding units, such as the Yuma of California, that occasionally allowed the selling or buying of land, the value of the land rested upon its produce. Both Hawaiians and Indians usually ceased to possess a tract of land when they no longer used it for its resources. In a few instances Indians, including the Navajos, retained possession of a plot when they did not use it.[5]

Among Hawaiians, the right to use land and water continued only as long as both resources were utilized. If a commoner stopped cultivating his land or produced insufficient food, the ali'i revoked the tenant's tenure and removed him from the land. If the *konohiki,* the ali'i's land supervisor and lower chief, did not fulfill his duties of ensuring the fruitful exploitation of the land, the chief removed him from his position and rescinded his allotment of plots that the commoners cultivated for the konohiki's exclusive use. Similar rights of tenure related to the proper utilization of water for irrigation. Hawaiians believed the gods provided water as a free resource rightfully belonging to all who used it. The duty of every Hawaiian, ali'i and commoner alike, required that they aid in the construction of irrigation ditches. If they failed to perform this task, their right to the water was revoked. If a commoner did not exploit the water provided in the water system, then his right to use the water ceased. Water rights therefore depended on effective cultivation of the land, for in most cases water ensured the fruitful production upon which continued usufruct rested.[6]

The concept of inherited-use ownership of land prevailed to a certain degree among both Indians and Hawaiians. It covered both communal and nominal private holding of land by Indians—a common holding of land existed, but the composition of the landholding unit varied greatly. Among Indian groups the right of land use uniformly existed; the Indian inherited this privilege from Mother Earth, the tribe or largest landholding unit, or in some cases from his family. Among Hawaiians the concept of inherited-use ownership did not completely apply to the land tenure system. All Hawaiians possessed the right to use the land and its resources. The supreme chief, the *mōʻī,* merely held the land rather than owning it. The gods Kāne and Lono made him a trustee of the land. Land tenure, in theory, was transitory for all Hawaiians. Even the aliʻi held no permanency in their proprietorship and could be removed by conquest or at the will of a superior chief. Inheritance of land by aliʻi often did not exist. Aliʻi, however, frequently bequeathed land to their heirs, and some chiefs retained land within the family for generations. Families of tenant farmers, whose usufruct depended upon the satisfactory cultivation of the soil and continued favor of the aliʻi, usually lived upon their lands for generations. In actuality, the tenants inherited the right to continue using their lands.[7]

Although the aliʻi could revoke the makaʻāinana's tenure for any personal reason or for violation of customary laws, the tenant usually remained untouched by the frequent warfare waged for control of the land. The aliʻi sought to retain stability with those who tilled the soil and produced other products necessary for the subsistence and comfort of the aliʻi class and their warriors. The chiefs, moreover, needed the loyalty of the makaʻāinana in time of war. This allegiance was imperative to ensure that they would not align with an opposing chief and would continue producing food.[8] Since the mōʻī required the loyalty of the people in his district, the aliʻi usually were not overdemanding in their treatment of the makaʻāinana, at least according to the moral standards of their society. The aliʻi relegated the overseeing of the *ahupuaʻa,* an administrative land unit, to konohiki, who usually treated the commoners fairly. A chief would investigate the konohiki's relationship with the tenants if the annual tribute for the chief's needs or the produce from the *kōʻele,* fields specifically cultivated by the tenants for the exclusive use of the aliʻi, was insufficient. If the aliʻi found the konohiki maltreating the makaʻāinana, he removed the lower chief from his position. The aliʻi's dependence upon the commoners tended to protect the makaʻāinana from the capriciousness possible in such a system and provided them with some security in their tenure.[9]

Although the Native Hawaiian land tenure system possessed similarities with European feudalism, it also differed in several important aspects. In Hawaiʻi the commoners were not tied to the soil and they could freely move to a district controlled by a different chief. The makaʻāinana seldom obtained much advantage by transferring his loyalties to another chief. Occasionally a commoner simultaneously held plots under two different chiefs to protect himself in case of dispossession by one of the ali'i. As in European feudalism, commoners and lower chiefs owed tribute and labor; in contrast, the ali'i did not give reciprocal obligations to the maka'āinana and the commoners depended upon the ali'i's benevolence. A certain moral obligation, however, somewhat like the European noblesse oblige, was built into the system and custom decreed that the king should protect the property of the maka'āinana and carefully refrain from exacting excessive demands.[10]

The exactions required of the commoners were harsh by Western standards; under feudalism in England, France, and Germany "definite limits" were placed upon the demands of the lords. Ali'i could require unlimited produce and services. Rebelling or moving to another chief's lands provided some relief for commoners against harsh treatment. On a number of occasions, the maka'āinana revolted and killed or expelled exploitive chiefs.[11]

During the annual Makahiki festival the maka'āinana and ali'i offered tribute to the mō'ī. The priests, dressed in a physical representation of Lono, traveled along the entire seacoast of each island collecting tribute. The konohiki in control of the ahupua'a collected the manufactured goods consisting of feather mats, *tapa,* and produce of the soil at the altar erected at the boundaries of the ahupua'a. The king exacted heavier taxes from the larger districts. The mō'ī took the tribute, setting aside a portion for himself and his retainers and then allocating the remaining goods to the subordinate chiefs. Although the Makahiki was a religious festival, it also acknowledged the superior land rights of the ruling ali'i.[12]

The Hawaiian islands were delimited into geographic and administrative land units. A supreme chief, the mō'ī or *ali'i 'aimoku,* held the largest geographical division or *moku,* which was usually an island, as an independent kingdom. At the time of Cook's visit in 1778, a mō'ī claimed suzerainty on each of the four largest islands—Hawai'i, Maui, Kaua'i, and O'ahu. Some of these supreme chiefs also ruled over Ni'ihau, Lana'i, Moloka'i and Kaho'olawe. During an earlier period of Hawaiian history individual chiefs ruled over districts of an island so that a moku sustained several independent kingdoms simultaneously.[13]

The chiefdoms increased or diminished in size in accordance with the ambitions and abilities of the mō'ī and of competing junior relatives. Control and redistribution of land measured political supremacy and prompted frequent wars, especially in the seventeenth and eighteenth centuries. The paramount chief of an island or district held all the land under his jurisdiction, not as an individual, but by virtue of his office and as a trustee of the gods. A ruling chief obtained possession of the land either through conquest or inheritance. When a new mō'ī ascended to power by the former process, he customarily redistributed the land among his subordinate chiefs and followers, retaining some of the choice lands for his own use. This division generally resulted from the decisions of a grand council of chiefs or in later times, through the actions of the *kālaimoku,* the highest ruler's political and military administrator. The mō'ī usually did not allocate the larger districts to the highest chiefs to prevent them from obtaining sufficient power to overthrow his government. If the new distribution displeased any of the chiefs, they could acquiesce or revolt. Loyal followers of the new ruler often remained undisturbed in the holding of their lands. When a district chief died, the lands reverted to the mō'ī. Sometimes the paramount chief allocated the land to the designated heirs of the deceased ali'i or redistributed it to one of the other chiefs.[14]

The ali'i subdivided their lands to the charge of lesser chiefs, dependents, and konohiki. At the lower end of the allotment process, the maka'āinana received usufruct over their plots from the lower chiefs. Only the ali'i were concerned with obtaining possession of the land. Words from an ancient Hawaiian legend conveyed this idea: "Thou art satisfied with food, O Thou common man, To be satisfied with land is for the chief."[15]

Struggle among the ali'i for control of districts and ahupua'a intensified with the more economically valuable and populous lands. The ideal ahupua'a existed as a self-sustaining pie-shaped wedge with its base reaching from the coast to its apex at the center of the mountaintop. Often other ahupua'a intersected an ahupua'a and cut it off from the mountain or sea. The sizes of ahupua'a varied; some were of a standard dimension of 0.25 mile wide and several miles long. One mountain ahupua'a on Hawai'i comprised 300 square miles and another on O'ahu consisted of 40,000 acres. Some ahupua'a extended into the sea to include deep-sea fisheries. The monopolization of these deep-sea fisheries restricted the smaller ahupua'a to fishing along the shallow coastal waters. If breakers existed the ahupua'a stretched to them, and if not it extended 1.5 miles into the sea. Occasionally an ahupua'a did not reach to the sea, thereby barring its inhabitants from inshore fishing and compelling them to resort to deep-sea fishing.[16]

The people of an ahupua'a maintained rights to all the products within its boundaries: *taro,* bananas, coconuts, sugarcane, breadfruit, and sweet potatoes from the valleys; fish and seaweed from the sea; and timber, *pili* grass, and feathers from the forests. At times extension of exclusive rights to an individual to gather certain products of the ahupua'a, such as feathers, birds, animals, *koa* logs, or *wauke,* or to fish, restricted the privileges of the chiefs and commoners.[17]

Each of the ahupua'a had specific names and boundaries. Certain individuals within the community were trained to know the boundary lines

and were called upon to settle any disputes. Distinctive geographical char-
acteristics such as a ridge, depression, stream, the line of growth of a specific tree, grasses or herbs, or the location of a rock or a certain bird's habitat marked the boundaries of the ahupua'a. Altars erected for the purpose
of collecting tribute during the Makahiki festival also delimited the borders
of the ahupua'a on the seacoast. An ancient method of determining the
boundaries between hillside and valley ahupua'a consisted of rolling a
stone down the hillside. This method was used to demarcate the boundary
between the ahupua'as Kewalo and Kai-muohema. The land above the
position where the stone stopped was Kewalo and the property below was
Kai-muohema.[18]

The *'ili,* normally an oblong tract running parallel to the ahupua'a
boundaries and sometimes reaching to the sea, was the administrative land
unit next in size to the ahupua'a. Each 'ili had specific limits and names.
An ahupua'a usually was divided into 'ilis that varied in dimensions. Some
ahupua'a contained thirty to forty 'ili, although at times an ahupua'a did
not have any 'ili. Occasionally 'ili existed without being in an ahupua'a.
There were two main kinds of 'ili: the *'ili of the ahupua'a* and the *'ili kūpono.*
The former was a subdivision of the ahupua'a. Some of the 'ili included
most of the area of the ahupua'a; on Hawai'i, 90 percent of the ahupua'a
of Waimea consisted of the 'ili kūponos of Pu'ukapu and Waikaloi. The
chief of the 'ili kūpono owed allegiance in the form of service and tribute
directly to the mō'ī, but, unlike the chief of the 'ili of the ahupua'a, did
not have any obligation to the ali'i of the ahupua'a in which the 'ili
kūpono was located. Usually the high chief of the island gave the 'ili
kūpono to a chief from another ahupua'a to strengthen his own political
control of the area.

When a chief of an 'ili kūpono died, the tract reverted to the mō'ī, who
then reallocated the land but not necessarily to the designated heirs of the
former chief. When the mō'ī reassigned the lands of an ahupua'a in which
the 'ili kūpono was located, this did not affect the holdings of the chief of
the 'ili kūpono. Sometimes an 'ili contained several dispersed tracts that
were designated as *lele.* On O'ahu, the 'ili of Kānewai had a lele at Kāhala
on the sea and a taro lele in the valleys of Pālolo and Mānoa. Occasionally
the lele had separate names or the same appellation as that of the 'ili.[19]

The people living in an 'ili comprised the *'ohana,* a dispersed expanded
family related by blood, marriage, and adoption. Members of the 'ohana
residing on the seacoast and inland exchanged commodities. The entire
'ohana participated in the harvesting of *olonā,* a plant with strong sinuous
fibers, and its subsequent production into fishnets and lines. During the
Makahiki festival the konohiki levied the tribute on the 'ohana, and its
head, the *haku,* possessed the responsibility for gathering the taxes. The
ali'i also exacted offerings from the 'ohana preceding the commencement

of a war and when honoring the firstborn of the chiefs. The 'ili contained several *mo'o'āina*, a land unit farmed by extended family households. A tenant cultivated a field, the *kīhāpai*, for his own use.[20]

The maka'āinana cultivated two kinds of agricultural field systems. Irrigation farming predominated in the fertile valleys on the windward or rainy sides of the islands. These lands were built into terraces with stones and farmed for taro, a plant with a starchy, edible root. Some of these bottomland systems were very large and intensively worked. One irrigation ditch on Kaua'i spanned 3.7 kilometers.[21]

The dryland farming areas were located mainly on the leeward sides of Maui and Hawai'i and on some of the smaller islands, such as Kaho'olawe, that lie in the rain shadow of the larger islands. The sweet potato was the major crop grown by dryland farmers, although taro and sugarcane predominated in some areas. The early inhabitants of the islands probably practiced a form of dryland farming called shifting agriculture. This method consisted of clearing an area in the forest to farm, cultivating it, abandoning it to clear another garden, and allowing the original plot to remain fallow for ten to twenty years. As the population dramatically increased in pre-Cook Hawai'i the maka'āinana cultivated many of the gardens more intensely, shortening the fallow time to three or four years. In some areas the cultivation became permanent and the fields were marked by individual stone or earth boundaries. Commoners also constructed elaborate mounds and terraces for farming rougher terrain in the dryland field systems.[22]

Parallelling population growth in the two centuries before Cook's arrival, intensively worked wetland and dryland argicultural fields grew to occupy large areas of the islands. Growing demand for food, particularly protein nutrition, likely spurred the development of fish-pond technology. Among Pacific islanders, this form of aquaculture or fish farming was unique to Hawaiians. In the shallow bays around the islands commoners constructed walls made from coral and basalt that extended in a semicircular arc seaward from the shore to form enclosed saltwater ponds. Varying in size from one acre to five hundred acres, the ponds were primarily farmed for mullet and milkfish and served as a source of intensive food production. The ali'i controlled and valued the ponds as symbols of power and status.[23]

AMERICAN INDIAN LAND TENURE SYSTEMS

In contrast to Native Hawaiians, who had a uniform system of land tenure, American Indians practiced a variety of land tenure systems. Even within the same landholding group several systems of land tenure often prevailed.

Property rights frequently depended upon the types of subsistence: hunting, fishing, gathering, or farming. Indians usually held land in common, though the composition of the landholding unit varied. It consisted of either the tribe, tribelet, village, band, clan, lineage group, family, or nominally an individual. Frequently several units simultaneously held the land.

The nominal owner of the land often differed from the proprietor. In the Pacific Northwest a wealthy man of the village held title to the land, but the whole village or kinship group possessed the usufruct. Among many Indians, the tribe held the land while family units were the actual proprietors of individual plots.

The flora and fauna dominating an ecological area largely determined the main method of subsistence. The primary means of existence included hunting, gathering, farming, and fishing and normally more than one method characterized the overall economy of a particular landholding unit.

To a certain degree, the ecology of a locality determined the land tenure systems. A desert region such as the Great Basin with its widely scattered, scarce food sources necessitated small family groups having free access to a large area to obtain the food needed for survival. Exclusive, small tracts of land would have meant starvation for the band and family members.

The Great Basin tribes consisted of the Shoshoni linguistic family. The Shoshonis generally did not conceive of exclusive rights to land or its products and believed the resources were free for everyone to use. Most of the Shoshonis and many of the Northern and Southern Paiutes lacked a concept of band or village ownership of food areas and land. The main exceptions were the Northern Paiutes in Owens Valley, the Reese River Paiutes, some Southern Paiutes in Death Valley, and the Pahrump and Las Vegas villages. These bands possessed property rights in delimited hunting and seed territories. The Owens Valley Paiutes held exclusive claim to hunting, fishing, and seed-gathering rights within specific boundaries. A district headman determined when and where the members of the community would gather seeds. Some anthropologists maintain that families claimed exclusive rights to plots. Communal hunts were restricted to the district, while individual hunters could hunt anywhere. Some of the districts shared hunting, fishing, and seed rights in specific areas. Both the Owens Valley and Reese Valley Paiutes protected their territories against trespass. The Owens Valley deviation from the Shoshonian pattern of maintaining no exclusive property rights in food areas largely can be explained by the ecology of the area. It was a fertile, densely populated locality with permanent villages, and a small area provided the essential food resources. Some of the Southern Paiutes also held rights to exclusive use of some food areas. Although the Paiutes of Death Valley did not conceive of band ownership of food territories, individual families held cultivated land and mesquite, screw bean, and pine-nut plots. The Death Valley Paiutes did not claim exclusive use of other wild-seed and hunting areas. Families among the

Pahrump and Las Vegas villages in southern Nevada, eastern California, southern Utah, and northern Arizona held property rights in pine-nut groves, and these were inherited patrilineally. They freely invited, however, those whose crops had failed to participate in the seed harvest. Families did not claim other wild-seed areas and hunting territories. Families of the Saline Valley Shoshonis of eastern California possessed usufruct to pine-nut plots while neither the family nor band owned other food areas.[24]

In the Plateau region individuals usually did not hold exclusive rights to land or its resources and usufruct rested with the village, band, tribe, or in some cases the families. The tribes or bands held the more favorable fishing sites in common. Families, however, claimed special rights to certain rocks and fishing areas, and small groups held usufruct to improved hunting sites such as pitfalls, traps, and game fences, but the length of tenure has not been determined. The Nez Percé villages claimed special fishing sites, but the entire nation shared the more productive places. Band members fished, hunted, and gathered roots on the prairies surrounding the sheltered canyons where they lived during the winter. A village's territorial rights to these areas were recognized by other Nez Percé bands.[25]

A similar land tenure system existed among the Coeur d'Alene bands of Idaho and eastern Washington. Villages of the tribe held the land, rivers, and lakes in common. Each band chief directed the use of the area contiguous to the villages and determined when roots and berries would be gathered. The bands did not hold exclusive rights to the village locality, since other tribal members possessed the privilege to exploit this area. They had to notify the village chief, however, as well as follow his regulations for use of the resources. Even so, outsiders seldom utilized the village area of another band. The area distant from the villages was tribal territory and could be exploited freely by any of the tribal members.[26]

Like most other Plateau landholding groups, the Okanagon, Sanpoil, Colville, and Lake tribes of Washington each held land in common. Tribal members freely exploited the entire tribal territory, but one band normally did not use the land near the headquarters of another band without express permission.[27]

Tribelets of village communities in California existed as the typical autonomous political and landholding units. Probably about five hundred of these miniature tribes occupied aboriginal California. In southern California clans claimed the land and its resources. In dealing with the California culture area, anthropologists usually divide the Indians into approximately forty ethnic, nonpolitical units or tribes.

The tribelet held a distinct territory recognized by its members and surrounding tribelets and guarded its boundaries against trespass. These village communities usually extended utilization of food resources to visiting tribelets who secured permission.

Among at least half of the tribelets including the Patwin, Achumauei,

Yaki, Ipai, and Tipai, the community held the land and its resources in common with free use to all its members. Among the remaining tribelets the village, clan, family, or individuals simultaneously claimed exclusive rights to the land and its resources. Shasta families held exclusive rights to fishing sites and hunting places while claiming private use of tobacco plots for only one season. Among the Northern Yanas, tribelets held the land and families possessed usufruct to seed plots and fishing sites. Tolowa villages held the territory and families claimed acorn groves and salmon-fishing areas for fifteen miles inland from the coast. The Maidu villages possessed hunting and fishing sites, but other members of the community maintained the privilege of using the sites provided they obtained the proprietor's permission. These fishing places were inherited patrilineally. Similar to the Maidus, the Nisenan tribelets held the hunting and fishing grounds in common, and families controlled specific fishing places, oak groves, and certain trees. Each of the Southern Valley Yokut tribelets held land and food sources in common although in some areas, individual women controlled tracts abundant in seed. The Coast Miwok tribelets held the land, but families claimed exclusive right to certain trees, hunting areas, fishing spots, and clam-digging spots.[28]

Three Southeastern Pomo tribelets at Clear Lake held in common the land on which their villages were located. Plots of shore land belonged to individual families, who claimed exclusive gathering rights to acorns and other vegetable food. Common hunting privileges pertained to the entire tribelet territory, including the family tracts. Deer hunters refrained from hunting on other families' gathering grounds during the fall so they would not be suspected of gathering acorns. Highly developed concepts of exclusive family use of food sources prevailed in areas of dense population and abundant food, such as Clear Lake and some interior locales. Other Pomo tribelets recognized common rights to land and its resources, and a few of the tribelets shared hunting and gathering privileges in one another's territory.[29]

The Yurok had the most highly developed property rights of the California Indians; multiple forms of ownership prevailed among these tribelets. Families possessed certain fishing sites, oak groves, hunting grounds, and gathering places. Unclaimed food-source areas remained communal and were available for use by the entire village. Individuals and families could sell or buy fishing, gathering, and hunting rights to specific sites to or from other members of their community.[30]

Among other California Indians, particularly in southern California, clans or lineages held the land. The Cahuilla tribe was separated into clans that consisted of three to ten lineages. Clan members held their territory in common. The lineage possessed the area contiguous to the village and the clan controlled other land, which was divided into tracts used by the clan, families, and individuals. Among the Serrano, Luiseño, and Cupeño, clans also held the land. The members of a Luiseño village collectively used the resources of the territory—a village chief directed the exploitation of hunting and gathering areas. Individual families possessed usufruct over gardens, which were inherited patrilineally. Patrilocal families also claimed certain oak groves, plant areas, and tobacco plots. Cupeño clans held the more favorable areas of their nation's territory, and the region located between clan territories was freely used by all clan members. Every Cupeño could hunt throughout the entire territory claimed by the clans. Some lineages within the clan claimed separate lands.[31]

In the Pacific Northwest from northwestern California to Alaska, two overlapping concepts of property rights existed. The most profitable sites for subsistence were allocated. Nominally rich men of the village held title to the more favorable fishing, snaring, trapping, and gathering places. They granted permission to kinship groups—often the entire village—to exploit these areas, so actually usufruct rested with the community. The nominal owner retained the right to use the sites at the most favorable times. Some of the land remained common hunting grounds for the entire village. Among the Yuroks, individuals held private fishing sites and occasionally claimed them jointly with nonrelatives. The son inherited these fishing places from his father. Individuals could buy and sell fishing sites, although this right of alienation applied only to community members. The village built communal fishing weirs annually and usually allocated specific sections of the weirs to individuals. The Makah Indians of western Washington in the Cape Flattery locality held restricted areas contiguous to their villages. The outlying land remained free territory and other tribes came to the area to fish.[32]

In the western Arctic in present Alaska, Eskimos and Aleuts subsisted on caribou, moose, sea mammals, and fish. These peoples lived in small aggregations and did not claim defined territories. Patricentered families held exclusive usufruct for salmon and seal netting sites, as well as for inland hunting places or tracts. Patrilineal inheritance prevailed for salmon net sites.[33]

The food quest of the Athapaskan Indians of the Yukon subarctic in Alaska centered around fishing and hunting of caribou and moose. Moose hunting was international in some localities, while in other areas it was band centered. Kinship groups claimed exclusive rights to fishing sites.[34]

The Iroquois League before 1678 consisted of numerous Mohawk, Oneida, Onondaga, Cayuga, and Seneca villages situated in western New York. The Iroquois nation held nominal title to tribal territories. Villagers, however, possessed usufruct over the hunting land, fishing sites, berry patches, gardens, medicine plant areas, pigeon nesting sites, and sugar-bush areas contiguous to the village. Tribal members could hunt throughout the tribal territory. Kinship groups held usufruct over fishing sites, and maternal lineages held agricultural land. When the fertility of a village's land became exhausted and firewood and game became scarce, the entire village moved and at the new location the maternal lineage households received new plots of land. The Iroquois tribes allowed dislocated tribes to occupy and use tribal land, but title remained with the Iroquois.[35]

Some of the eastern agricultural Indians shared tribal hunting grounds with other tribes. Only the Powhatan and Delaware claimed restricted use of hunting territories. Among the Delaware a matrilineal group held the hunting land, whereas Powhatan men nominally held tracts of land that were probably used by their kinship group. Both fishing and hunting rights were included in these tracts of land.[36]

On the Atlantic coast in Virginia and eastern North Carolina, each family among the Algonkians possessed usufruct to its own garden plot. The village also held a town field and the entire community shared its produce. Each Indian cleared as much land as he wanted and the plot remained exclusively his as long as he cultivated it. If he abandoned the field, anyone could claim it. Title rested with the tribe.[37]

The Sac and Fox tribes of the upper Mississippi Valley held communal title to their land. Each season the tribal council designated certain areas for small groups to exploit. Their neighbors, the Winnebagoas, subsisted mainly on hunting; agriculture supplied secondary food sources. Each clan segregated and kinship groups held fields in common, with each family usually cultivating its own field.[38]

In the subarctic regions of the eastern and northern United States, the Algonkians' food quest largely involved hunting. Many of these tribes divided their lands into well-defined patrilineal family tracts. Much anthropological debate in the twentieth century has centered on whether this system had an aboriginal or postcontact origin. Current consensus maintains that small family hunting territories developed in the historic period largely in response to the fur trade.[39]

The Plains Indians subsisted by hunting large game, such as buffalo, elk, deer, and antelope. These hunters roamed the Plains in their food quest. A subculture included the Pawnee, Mandan, Hidatsa, Arikara, Assiniboin, Omaha, and southern Siouan tribes, which some anthropologists have described as Prairie tribes. These tribes differed from the buffalo-based Plains culture because their means of subsistence was derived from both farming and bison hunting.

Many of the Plains Indians organized into autonomous political units either on the band or tribal level. Some, including the Cree, divided into family units during the winter to enhance survival. The Plains tribes or bands did not claim a defined territory because they believed Mother Earth belonged to all mankind. The tribes or bands usually restricted their hunting to certain areas so they could preserve food sources for their exclusive use. If the food supplies within their territory became depleted the bands or tribes entered the domain of other groups, knowing that their trespass could lead to warfare. The Plains Indians believed food sources belonged to everyone. Some of the tribes or bands shared hunting grounds. No social unit smaller than the band or tribe among the primary Plains culture held usufruct.[40]

The subculture of the Prairie Indians allowed proprietor rights to small garden plots or wild-rice areas. The Omaha, Mandan, Gros Ventre, and Arikara tribes recognized usufruct in garden plots as long as the women used the fields. Nominally the women held the plots but the matrilineal kinship group cultivated the gardens, so in reality usufruct rested with the latter. If a family allowed a plot to remain uncultivated for a season anyone in the tribe could then claim it, because the tribe or band merely had loaned the plot to the cultivator. Clans among the Hidatsa tribe possessed definite property rights; when the proprietor of a garden plot died, the land reverted to the clan. In the wild-rice area around the Great Lakes, Indian families habitually returned to the same rice fields every year. Property rights pertained to the wild-rice beds rather than to the land.[41]

The agricultural tribes of the Southwest viewed the produce of the fields as the essential element in tenure rather than ownership of land. Among these tribes multiple forms of land tenure existed, and the landholding unit included the tribe, village, clan, family, and individual. Each pueblo existed as an autonomous political unit and consisted of numerous extended families. The village divided its agricultural land among the kinship groups, thus enabling each to possess proprietorship over its fields. Family plots were inherited bilineally.[42]

Among the Hopis the village, clan, and families held land. Each village allotted land to the matrilineal clans while retaining some tracts as village lands. The clan assigned fields to the maternal lineage segments, which lived in separate households. The women of the household held usufruct over individual plots and possessed the right of alienation subject to the approval of the clan or sib mother. Families and clans both possessed numerous dispersed fields in the village area to guard against families becoming destitute when fields flooded or were destroyed. To further insure against such disasters, the clan retained some of its fields from cultivation to assign them to families beset by ruined fields. The mother of the household gave plots to her daughters when they married. Upon the mother's death, any remaining fields usually descended to female relatives, mainly to daughters. If a man cleared former village wasteland, he assumed exclusive use of the plot as long as he cultivated it. Another villager could claim a field that fell into disuse, but he had to obtain permission from the original cultivator, who could reassert possession if he resumed farming the plot. Upon the death of the cultivator the field was transferred to a son or nephew; otherwise the field reverted to the village. The village or clan set aside land for political, ceremonial, and dancing societies. Village inhabitants maintained these fields and also cultivated the chief's land.[43]

Among the Navajos the first person, man or woman, who cultivated a plot established permanent possession even if the original cultivator or his descendants abandoned the field. Exclusive use, however, pertained only to agricultural produce and not to the natural vegetation, such as shrubs, trees, roots, and berries, or to springs that anyone could use freely. The land was inherited matrilineally. Anthropologists have described the Navajo land tenure system as one of inherited-use ownership.[44]

Similar to the Pueblos, the Pima land tenure consisted of village, family, and nominally individual possession. The men received allotted lands from the village. Even though women could not claim land they retained usage rights. The male head of the household held official possession of the land, but the entire family worked the plot and maintained usufruct. The family retained exclusive use to the agricultural products, trees, and bushes on their assigned land, but the vegetation on unassigned tribal land could be exploited by anyone. If a family required additional land, it applied to the village council.[45]

Among the agricultural tribes of the Southwest, kinship groups seldom claimed hunting territory. Chiricahua Apache bands, consisting of kinship groups, possessed hunting territories. The Pueblo hunting territory was controlled either by an entire pueblo or was international.[46]

The southeastern tribes—the Chickasaws, Cherokees, Creeks, Choctaws, and Natchez—were largely agricultural with hunting and gathering as secondary methods of subsistence. Each tribe claimed sovereignty over designated areas. Several of the tribes shared rights to certain hunting territories and also had specific tribal hunting areas. Even in the latter case, some tribes hunted on the other's territory without fear of punishment for trespass. A hunter could hunt anywhere on tribal territory outside the jurisdiction of the villages, which usually extended only beyond the contiguous limits consisting of scattered houses with garden plots. The Euchees, a Creek cognate, however, apparently claimed exclusive hunting territory.[47]

Each village held lands in common. The inhabitants, under the charge of a village overseer, communally cultivated the crops, which largely consisted of maize. Each cooperative garden, usually located on the outskirts of the village, was divided into family plots with artificial features, such as strips of grass and poles, marking the boundaries between plots. During the harvest season the woman of the household reaped the family plot in the town field and stored the produce in the family's private granary. Each family gave a portion of the crop to the village storehouse under the charge of the village chief. The food supply stored in the public granary provided food for village visitors, ceremonies, war parties, families whose granaries became depleted, and disaster relief.[48]

Each family held usufruct to a garden plot located by its house. Among the Creeks the garden plots were inherited matrilineally. A family could cultivate any amount of land and could claim the plot exclusively, as long as the plot was farmed. If the family abandoned the plot, any village member could assert usufruct.[49]

The Natchez assigned certain plots to the chiefs and designated other areas as sacred fields. The men worked the latter while all village members cultivated the chief's fields.[50]

In summary, the Indian and the Hawaiian valued land for its products rather than the land per se. They maintained a metaphysical relationship with the land and neither conceived of land in terms of absolute ownership. Inherited usufruct provides a more conclusive description of Indian land tenure than either communal, in common, or individual. Among the Hawaiian maka'āinana, inherited usufruct normally prevailed and occasionally applied to the ali'i class. Wars of conquest and the subsequent redivision of land frequently prevented the inheritance of land, especially among the chiefs of the Hawaiian islands.

3

Appropriation of the
Indian Landed Estate: Part I

Formulation of U.S. Indian Policy

THE U.S. government's relation with the American Indian has largely concerned the status of tribal territory and has resulted in the progressive reduction of the Indians' land base. Americans continuously clamored for additional land during their westward expansion. Usually the federal government negotiated with the Indians for land already occupied by frontiersmen. In the treaties the national government pledged that reduced tribal territories would remain forever in the possession of the Indians, but the seeming insatiable thirst of American settlers for land caused the United States repeatedly to break its pledges to the tribes. Even in the twentieth century the federal government has taken Indian lands held in trust or has instituted policies that ultimately led to alienation of Indian lands.

In the late eighteenth and for most of the nineteenth century, the U.S. government used two methods to appropriate Indian lands—treaties and military force. Federal officials often negotiated with the Indians for reduced tribal territory or for an exchange of lands in an unsettled area. Military conflict between Indians and the army frequently provided justification for taking land, because officially the Indians had committed either treason or rebellion against the United States. The army occasionally came to the aid of Indians when settlers invaded tribal territory, but usually it joined the frontiersmen in fighting the Indians. By recognizing the right of Indian tribes to make treaties, the U.S. government accepted the theoretical existence of Indian tribes as independent nations with sovereign character. Treaties were frequently used to institute new federal policies toward the Indians. Treaties also often sanctioned frontier expansion onto Indian lands as an *ex post facto* measure.

The United States essentially followed the British model in dealing with American Indians, although the founding fathers deviated from this course during the Confederacy. Thus, from 1783 to 1786 American leaders claimed Indian lands on the basis of the law of conquest. The participation of most of the eastern Indian tribes on the side of the British during the Revolutionary War provided justification for American demands that the Indians cede large portions of their land as war reparations. Demoralized as a result of the War of Independence, the northern and southern Indian tribes agreed to treaty provisions. By 1786 they had recovered and began to assert their claims to ownership of ceded lands and aggressively began to oppose settlement of these lands. American leaders discovered that their rationale for acquiring Indian lands failed in its application, because the Indians did not willingly accept the loss of their lands as reparations of war. Since the poverty-stricken American government could not afford to wage war against the Indians and because it desperately needed the income from the sale of lands acquired by the cession treaties, national leaders abandoned the principle of conquest and reverted to the British policy of purchasing land by token payment, thereby acknowledging the Indians' right to the soil.[1]

National leaders returned to the philosophy that the United States had acquired title to all land east of the Mississippi River based on the doctrine of discovery that they had inherited from the British. Thus Indian tribes merely possessed the right of occupancy on the lands they claimed. Based on this concept, U.S. leaders such as George Washington, Thomas Jefferson, and Henry Knox believed the national government should purchase the tribal right to the soil. They also espoused the view that just wars against the Indians permitted appropriation of Indian lands. These leaders formulated policy acknowledging Indian rights and protection of tribal land. Knox in particular sought a policy that would not stain the national honor.[2]

American officials believed that Indians would readily sell their lands and national expansion would proceed in a peaceful and orderly fashion. The Northwest Ordinance (1787) stated:

> The utmost good faith shall always be observed towards the Indians; their lands and property, shall never be taken from them without their consent; and, in their property, rights and liberty, they shall never be invaded or disturbed, unless in just and lawful wars authorized by Congress but laws founded in justice and humanity shall from time to time be made for preventing wrong being done to them, and for preserving peace and friendship with them.[3]

No matter how well-intentioned or humanitarian the official view, the national government lacked the means to control settlers' actions, few of

whom seemed to care about national honor or Indian rights. Frontiersmen, for the most part, saw Indians as obstacles to obtaining land, to westward expansion, and to economic development.

Rank-and-file Americans also held the European view that Indians
should not possess all of the land claimed by each tribe because they used
only a small portion of it. Americans also believed that land should be used
for farming and that nonagricultural tribes should be deprived of land that
held agrarian promise. Many reformers, missionaries, and national leaders
used morality to justify appropriating Indian land. They thought that Indians had a moral obligation to put land to its highest use and should
become farmers on small plots. Americans viewed private property as a sign
of civilization.[4] For the most part, the tribes held land in common and did
not conceive of land in terms of individual ownership.

Many officials, missionaries, and humanitarians believed that the federal
government should make an effort to "civilize" the Indians. They believed
that Indians should be encouraged to adopt farming, Christianity, European dress, and other aspects of Anglo culture.[5] Government policy and
missionary activity later reflected this attitude. Many American leaders
hoped to provide for peaceful territorial expansion by assimilating the Indians, who would then sell their lands so that American expansion could
proceed smoothly. Few Native Americans, however, willingly ceded their
land; most aggressively resisted. Although the United States had acquired
title to substantial tracts of Indian territory by the end of the eighteenth
century, it accomplished this largely through military force.

Thomas Jefferson supported the use of military force in the 1790s
against the Old Northwest tribes because of their insurgency, but he advocated other methods to acquire Indian land. He recommended that the
federal factory system be used to obtain Indian land; government traders
were encouraged to lead Indians into debt through generous extension of
credit; to pay their obligations the Indians would be forced to sell land. Jefferson also believed that many Indians would sell their land and move
westward as the settlement line approached their territory and destroyed
the game. He also supported assimilation as a way to acquire Indian land.
As Indians were absorbed into the white population, their land needs
would diminish. Until the War of 1812 these attitudes provided the basis
for U.S. Indian policy. Jefferson also entertained the idea of removing portions of some of the eastern tribes west of the Mississippi River.[6]

Early in the nation's history the concepts of right of conquest, doctrine
of discovery, treaty making, and military force played an important part in
dealing with Indian tribes. The United States reestablished peace with the
Iroquois Confederacy in 1784 at Fort Stanwix, New York. Most of these
tribes had sided with the British in the American Revolution and American
officials therefore claimed title to Indian lands in parts of western New

York, Ohio, and Pennsylvania by right of conquest. In the Old Northwest, conflict erupted after settlers moved into the territory guaranteed to the Indian tribes by the Northwest Ordinance of 1787. The frontiersmen demanded that the national army protect them as they expanded into the region above the Ohio River. After the army sent two unsuccessful expeditions into the area to bring peace, Gen. Anthony Wayne defeated the confederated Indians at Fallen Timbers in northwestern Ohio. Wayne forced the chiefs to cede about two-thirds of Ohio, a large part of Indiana, and other areas in the Old Northwest in the Treaty of Greenville (1795).[7]

From the beginning the national government tried to regulate Indian affairs and the transfer of aboriginal lands. In 1790 Congress passed the Trade and Intercourse Act, which required Indian land to be purchased only through federal treaties. Three years later Congress, in the second trade and intercourse law, required the presence of a U.S. commissioner at negotiations between individual states and tribes. Congress had to approve the treaties.[8]

Several states pursued independent policies in defiance of national rules. New York agents negotiated with the Oneidas for six million acres of tribal land, and for a large cession from the Onondagas and Cayugas. The state government persisted in its efforts to purchase Indian lands even after the U.S. government again guaranteed the lands of the Six Nations in the Treaty of Canandiagua in November 1794. Secretary of War Timothy Pickering and the U.S. agent to the Six Nations repeatedly told New York officials that the tribes' land rights could be extinguished only through treaties with congressional sanction. Federal officials informed the Iroquoian tribes and state officials that any other treaty would be deemed invalid. New York agents, however, negotiated cession treaties with the Cayuga, Onondaga, and Oneida tribes. During the eighteenth and nineteenth centuries, New York concluded more than two dozen treaties with the Oneidas. As late as 1890 state officials violated federal statutes by purchasing land from the Oneidas.[9]

Maine, Massachusetts, Connecticut, Rhode Island, and Georgia also violated the national directives. Massachusetts officials negotiated treaties with the Passamaquoddy and Penobscot tribes. After entering the Union in 1820, Maine assumed responsibility for these two tribes and within a few years Maine commenced its policy of selling and leasing Indian lands. In 1855 the Connecticut General Assembly authorized the sale of eight hundred acres owned in fee simple by the Pequots. The Rhode Island legislature enacted a series of statutes that removed land from the possession of the Narragansetts. In November 1786, Georgia authorities concluded a treaty with a small group of Creeks in which the Creek tribe ceded all its lands in Georgia east of the Oconee River.[10]

Soon after the Old Northwest cession in 1795, settlers invaded the

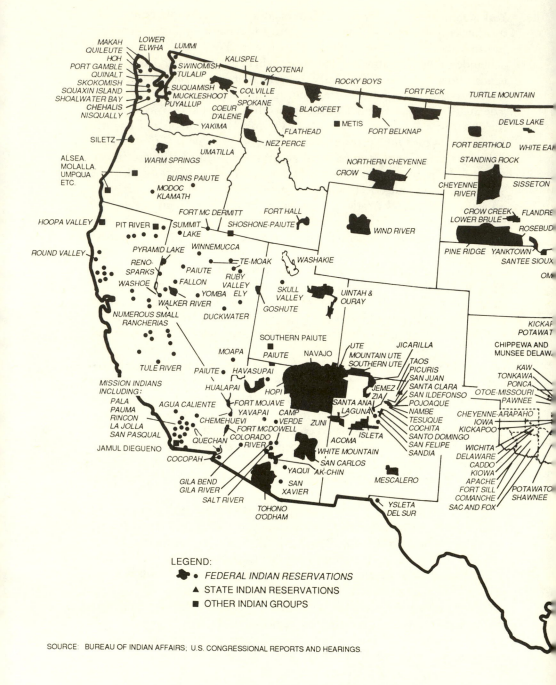

MAKAH
QUILEUTE
HOH
PORT GAMBLE
QUINALT
SKOKOMISH
SQUAXIN ISLAND
SHOALWATER BAY
CHEHALIS
NISQUALLY

LOWER
ELWHA
LUMMI

SWINOMISH
TULALIP
SUQUAMISH
MUCKLESHOOT
PUYALLUP

KALISPEL
KOOTENAI

SWINOMISH
COLVILLE
COEUR
D'ALENE
YAKIMA

SPOKANE

BLACKFEET

ROCKY BOYS

FORT PECK

TURTLE MOUNTAIN

METIS

FORT BELKNAP

DEVILS LAKE

FLATHEAD

NEZ PERCE

FORT BERTHOLD

WHITE EA

STANDING ROCK

SILETZ

ALSEA.
MOLALLA.
UMPQUA
ETC.

UMATILLA

WARM SPRINGS

BURNS PAIUTE

MODOC
KLAMATH

NORTHERN CHEYENNE
CROW

CHEYENNE
RIVER

SISSETON

HOOPA VALLEY

PIT RIVER

FORT MC DERMITT

SUMMIT
LAKE

FORT HALL

SHOSHONE-PAIUTE

WIND RIVER

CROW CREEK
LOWER BRULE

FLANDRE

ROSEBUD

ROUND VALLEY

PYRAMID LAKE

WINNEMUCCA

RENO-
SPARKS
WASHOE

PAIUTE

TE-MOAK

WASHAKIE

PINE RIDGE

YANKTOWN
SANTEE SIOUX

OM

FALLON

RUBY
VALLEY
ELY

YOMBA

SKULL
VALLEY

UINTAH &
OURAY

WALKER RIVER

NUMEROUS SMALL
RANCHERIAS

DUCKWATER

GOSHUTE

TULE RIVER

MOAPA

SOUTHERN PAIUTE

PAIUTE

NAVAJO

UTE
MOUNTAIN UTE
SOUTHERN UTE

JICARILLA

CHIPPEWA AND
MUNSEE DELAW.

KICKAP
POTAWAT

PAIUTE

HAVASUPAI

HUALAPAI

HOPI

TAOS
PICURIS
SAN JUAN
SANTA CLARA

KAW
TONKAWA
PONCA

MISSION INDIANS
INCLUDING:
PALA
PAUMA
RINCON
LA JOLLA
SAN PASQUAL

AGUA CALIENTE

FORT MOJAVE

YAVAPAI

CHEMEHUEVI

CAMP
VERDE

ZUNI

FORT MCDOWELL

JEMEZ
ZIA

SANTA ANA

SAN ILDEFONSO
POJOAQUE
NAMBE
TESUQUE
COCHITA

OTOE-MISSOURI
PAWNEE

CHEYENNE-ARAPAHO
IOWA
KICKAPOO

JAMUL DIEGUENO

QUECHAN

COLORADO
RIVER

LAGUNA

ACOMA

ISLETA

SANTO DOMINGO
SAN FELIPE
SANDIA

WICHITA
DELAWARE
CADDO
KIOWA
APACHE
FORT SILL
COMANCHE
SAC AND FOX

COCOPAH

GILA BEND
GILA RIVER

SALT RIVER

YAQUI

SAN
XAVIER

WHITE MOUNTAIN
SAN CARLOS
AK-CHIN

MESCALERO

POTAWATO
SHAWNEE

TOHONO
O'ODHAM

YSLETA
DEL SUR

LEGEND:

FEDERAL INDIAN RESERVATIONS

▲ STATE INDIAN RESERVATIONS

■ OTHER INDIAN GROUPS

SOURCE: BUREAU OF INDIAN AFFAIRS; U.S. CONGRESSIONAL REPORTS AND HEARINGS.

INDIAN LANDS AND COMMUNITIES

ED LAKE

NETT LAKE

GRAND PORTAGE

KEWEENAW BAY

LEECH LAKE
RED CLIFF BAD RIVER

OTTAWA AND CHIPPEWA

BAY MILLS
SAULT ST. MARIE

FOND DU LAC LAC COURTE- LAC DU
OREILLES FLAMBEAU

MILLE LAC
NITE ST. CROIX
LLS PRIOR LAKE

SOKAOGON
MENOMINEE

HANNAHVILLE
POTAWATOMI
ONEIDA
STOCKBRIDGE-
MUNSEE

VER SIOUX WINNEBAGO

BROTHERTON

ISABELLA
POTAWATOMI

MOHAWK

TONOWANDA
TUSCARORA
CAYUGA

ONEIDA

ONONDAGA
SENECA

NIPMUC

PEQUOT

WAMPANOAG

SCATICOOK
PAUGUSETT

NARRAGANSET

MOHEGAN
MONTAUK
SHINNECOCK
POOSEPATUCK

MALISEET

MICMAC

PASSAMAQUODDY

PENOBSCOT

SAC AND FOX
NNEBAGO

POGAGON
POTAWATOMI

MIAMI

SAC AND FOX
IOWA

WYANDOT

SHAWNEE
MIAMI
PEORIA
QUAPAW
SENECA-CAYUGA
WYANDOTTE

OSAGE
CHEROKEE
CREEK
SEMINOLE
CHOCTAW
CHICKASAW

AMHERST

MOOR
NANTICOKE
RAPPAHANOCK
UPPER MATTAPONI
MATTAPONI
PAMUNKEY
CHICKAHOMINY
HALIWA

PERSON COUNTY

CHEROKEE LUMBEE

COHARIE

CATAWBA

WACCAMAW

SUMMERVILLE

CHOCTAW

CHOCTAW

ABAMA-
OUSHATTA

CHOCTAW

CREEK

TUNICA

COUSHATTA

CHITIMACHA HOUMA

SEMINOLE

SEMINOLE

MICCOSUKEE
MICCOSUKEE

SEMINOLE

0   100   200   300   400   500 MILES

remaining Indian lands north of the Ohio River. A nationalistic Shawnee chief, Tecumseh, and his brother Tenskwatawa, opposed additional cessions and attempted to rally other Indian tribes into uniting and halting the continued sale of Indian lands. Tecumseh refused to accept land cessions made by weaker chiefs. He maintained that no tribe or individual could give away or sell any land because it was the common property of all tribes. Governor of Indiana Territory William Henry Harrison was determined to rid the region of Indians. When the War of 1812 erupted, Tecumseh joined the British in fighting the Americans. Harrison's troops killed Tecumseh and defeated the British at the Battle of Thames River in southern Canada in October 1813; with his death, Tecumseh's followers scattered. After the American victory the Indians lost their British allies, who had provided the key to effective resistance, and in a series of treaties quickly surrendered much of their remaining lands to the United States.[11]

Early U.S. Removal Policy

After the War of 1812 the federal government moved toward a policy of removing the Indian tribes west of the Mississippi River. This action started with the Old Northwest tribes. Settlers wanted the lands still occupied by the tribes and demanded the Indians removal. They justified their demands by claiming that the tribesmen had committed treason against the United States and therefore should be punished by cession of their lands. The Old Northwest tribes possessed little ability to resist American expansion, although a few bands of Kickapoos, Sac and Fox, and Winnebagoes resisted removal efforts. As late as 1832 Black Hawk, the Sac and Fox leader, resisted surrender of tribal lands in Illinois and removal to the trans-Mississippi region.[12]

Removal, a segregation policy, also affected the southeastern Indian nations, and their fate paralleled that of the Old Northwest tribes. After the American Revolution the U.S. government signed peace treaties with the southern tribes because most of them had sided with the British. Settlers eventually moved onto Indian lands and pressured the government to acquire additional territory from the Creeks and other tribes of the region. Angered by white expansion, a Creek faction, the Red Sticks, joined Tecumseh in his opposition to settler expansion. During the War of 1812 these insurgents aligned with the British. Red Stick raiders attacked settlements in Georgia and Alabama and killed several hundred American settlers. Gen. Andrew Jackson, aided by Creek and Cherokee regiments, defeated the Red Sticks at Horseshoe Bend in March 1814. At the Treaty of Fort Jackson (1814), the U.S. government forced the entire Creek

Nation to cede about two-thirds of its territory in Georgia and Alabama because one tribal faction had sided with the British.[13]

In 1818 troops under General Jackson invaded Spanish Florida to punish the Seminoles for harboring runaway slaves. One year later Spain ceded Florida to the United States. As a result of the First Seminole War, the United States forced the Seminoles to cede much of their land in Florida and to accept a reserve in the interior of the peninsula.[14]

Desiring to flee American settlement pressure, some tribal bands voluntarily moved west of the Mississippi. Kickapoos, Delawares, and Shawnees comprised the first immigrants, although Cherokee immigrants undertook the first substantial migration to the new Indian country. In the 1790s a band under the leadership of The Bowl moved to Arkansas, and in 1809 a group of Lower Cherokees joined them. In an 1817 treaty the Cherokees and the U.S. government formalized Cherokee possession of an area in northwestern Arkansas, where most of the immigrants resided, in exchange for ceding one-third of their lands in the East embracing tracts in North Carolina, Tennessee, and Georgia. Later in 1828 the U.S. government signed another treaty with the Cherokees in which they exchanged their lands between the White and Arkansas rivers for lands in present-day Oklahoma. They agreed to the exchange to escape the increasing number of American settlements springing up in the White and Arkansas river valleys. For the Cherokee land transactions to take place, the federal government negotiated treaties in 1808, 1818, and 1825 with the Osages for cession of their lands in present-day Missouri, Arkansas, and Oklahoma.[15]

Pressure by the U.S. government and white settlers also led a group of Choctaws to sign the Treaty of Doak's Stand in 1820 in which the tribe ceded a portion of its lands in Mississippi for lands in southwestern Arkansas Territory and Indian Territory. Title to the western land had been cleared in 1818 when the Quapaws concluded an agreement with the federal government ceding their lands between the Arkansas and Red rivers. In 1825 the Choctaw ceded their land in Arkansas Territory.[16]

Frontiersmen also had intruded into Creek territory and agitated for the tribes' land. A number of treaties with the U.S. government, including ones signed in 1818 and 1821, led to continued reduction of the Creek dominion. Concerned about their shrinking domain the Lower Creeks (under the leadership of Chief William McIntosh, a mixed-blood) agreed in 1825 to relinquish their lands in Georgia for a new home in Indian Territory. The Upper Creeks, led by Opothleyaholo, refused to sign the treaty until 1826 when they agreed to a removal treaty, the first Treaty of Washington. This agreement ceded only a portion of their lands in Alabama and Georgia in exchange for a new domain in Indian Territory. However, most of the Creeks wanted to remain on their ancestral lands and refused to move. During this period of voluntary removal, only a fragment of the Creeks, Cherokees, and Choctaws migrated to their western lands. Most of the tribal members remained on their ancestral lands in the South. Those Indians removing hoped to escape the continual encroachment by frontiersmen and harassment by state governments.[17]

The policy of forced segregation through removal or western exile that evolved in the early part of the nineteenth century received official sanction during the 1820s and in 1830. President James Monroe and Secretary of War James C. Calhoun formed the initial plan for relocating the eastern tribes. At first President John Quincy Adams tried to uphold the southern Indians' right to remain on their ancestral lands, but before leaving office Adams agreed that removal provided the only solution to the Indian problem. Almost every president had considered such a policy, but they always believed it should be voluntary. The decisive break came with the election of Andrew Jackson to the presidency in 1828. Jackson's policy led to forced removal sanctioned by treaties with the tribes surrendering their southern lands. Jackson's attitude reflected that of frontiersmen and southerners who believed that Indian residence in the eastern United States comprised an unnecessary obstacle to national growth and economic development. Jackson also thought that the Indians had only a "possessory right" to the land and thereby were subject to American sovereignty; he denied that Indian tribal governments could exist within a state or territory.[18]

The policy of segregation by removal reflected not only the desire of moving the Indians out of the path of westward expansion but also was consummation of the view held by some Americans that such a measure would benefit Indians. This attitude of morality urged that Indians must be removed west of the Mississippi River to save them from detrimental contact with Anglo-American civilization. Jefferson had proposed this idea as the basis for his consideration of Indian removal to the trans-Mississippi West. Frequently this view was mere rhetoric to disguise the desire for Indian lands. Wilson Lumpkin, a congressman and later the governor of Georgia during the removal period, rationalized predatory actions by Georgians against resident Indians on moral grounds. Lumpkin reasoned that the presence of squatters on Indian land would hasten removal. The Cherokees would be protected in their new western lands while they transformed from a state of "barbarism" to one of "civilization" and became acculturated.[19]

President Jackson argued that by removing west of the Mississippi the Indians, away from the influence of Euro-American civilization, would prosper. Since Americans wanted to justify the removal of the Indians, they adopted Jackson's rhetoric. They accepted the view that removal outside of the organized United States would save the Indian from destruction and that it provided the only humane alternative.[20]

Humanitarian Opposition to Forced Removal

During the early part of the nineteenth century, the vast expanse beyond Missouri was popularly viewed as the "Great American Desert," a region unfit for white habitation or survival. Many people therefore believed that American expansion would never extend west of Missouri; this belief supported the attitude that Indians would be safe and secure in their western lands. Jefferson and John C. Calhoun both held this view, and in 1825 Calhoun supported removal. William Clark, Superintendent of Indian Affairs at St. Louis, presented this view when he advised President Monroe that the federal government should be benevolent to Indians because they no longer posed a military threat; thus, they should be removed so they "could rest in peace." President Jackson presented a similar argument. Most Americans held this outlook and pro-Jackson forces used this reasoning in Congress during debate of Jackson's removal policy. A few men with more foresight argued that this policy would not work. Senator Theodore Frelinghuysen of New Jersey and Senator Edward Everett of Massachusetts, in objecting to Jackson's removal plan, maintained that Indian title to the land west of the Mississippi would not be secure since the United States would advance to the area before the end of the nineteenth century, especially if the region was as fertile as the proremoval forces argued in urging passage of the Indian Removal bill.[21]

A number of easterners in the 1820s and early 1830s supported the southern Indians' right to remain on their ancestral lands. These humanitarians, including members of the American Board of Commissioners for Foreign Missions and some abolitionists, stressed the obligation of the federal government to protect the Indians in their possession of aboriginal title as it had promised in treaties with the tribes. The humanitarians and anti-Jackson politicians who opposed the removal plan tried to defeat the measure in Congress. When this approach failed the antiremoval forces turned to the U.S. Supreme Court in an endeavor to safeguard the Indians' territorial rights.[22]

The Indians and their white supporters based their legal action on rights guaranteed by treaty and used Georgia's mistreatment of the Cherokees as a basis for their appeal to the Supreme Court. Settlers in Georgia as well as in other southern states harassed the Indians and carried out acts of depredations against them by burning towns, running off livestock, and squatting on Indian lands. State laws protected the frontiersmen in their activities by prohibiting Indians from testifying in court against whites. If the

Indians resisted militarily, frontiersmen summoned troops from frontier posts to put down the "Indian uprising." The southern states, following Georgia's precedent, extended state law over the tribes' territory and dissolved tribal governments. President Jackson refused to safeguard Indian rights.[23]

Cherokee Legal Attempts to Resist Removal

The anti-Jackson forces and humanitarians urged the Cherokees to take legal action and supported them in their appeals to the U.S. Supreme Court in the early 1830s. The Cherokees' legal maneuvering began in 1827 when they adopted a written constitution. This document proclaimed the Cherokees as an independent nation with complete sovereignty over tribal land in Georgia, North Carolina, Tennessee, and Alabama. Whereas the federal government previously had used tribal sovereignty as an excuse to obtain Indian land cessions, the Cherokees intended to use tribal sovereignty to prohibit future transactions. Since Georgia officials considered Indians mere tenants subject to the will of the state, they passed legislation extending state jurisdiction over the Indians' territory. To support their actions, Georgia officials referred to the 1823 *McIntosh* decision. On that occasion Supreme Court Justice John Marshall had stated that Indians held their land by "right of occupancy," which was subordinate to the "right of discovery" that the United States inherited from England.[24] The Cherokee Nation reacted by filing suit in the Supreme Court for an injunction to stop Georgia from interfering with the tribe's internal affairs. The Cherokees argued that the court must defend the tribe's legal right to its land and self-government since the federal government had long upheld these sovereign rights in treaties. The court in *Cherokee Nation v. Georgia* ruled that it did not have jurisdiction in the case because the Cherokees incorrectly sued as a foreign nation. Supreme Court Justice Marshall in the majority opinion described the Cherokees as a "domestic dependent nation" whose relationship to the federal government "resembles that of a ward to his guardian." Thus the Supreme Court ruled against the Cherokees' assertion of status as a sovereign nation. By holding that it did not have jurisdiction, the court avoided deciding the merits of the controversy.[25]

Although the Supreme Court's decision went against the Cherokees, they steadfastly continued to resist Georgia and President Jackson's demands for removal. In 1831 the Cherokees again appealed to the Supreme Court for relief from impositions by the state of Georgia. In December 1830 the Georgia legislature had passed an act that prohibited the presence of whites in Indian territory after 31 March 1831, without a license from the state. Georgia officials sought to exclude white missionaries residing among the Cherokees who, the Georgians believed, opposed removal. Two of the missionaries, Samuel A. Worcester and Elizur Butler, refused to obtain the permits, and the Georgia militia subsequently arrested the two men. The Cherokees petitioned the Supreme Court and the judiciary decided in their favor. In its decision, *Worcester v. Georgia,* the Court upheld the Cherokees' right of self-government, declared Georgia's extension of state law over the Indians unconstitutional, and ordered the immediate release of the missionaries. State officials refused to carry out the mandate. President Jackson allegedly remarked that "the decision of the supreme court has fell still born, and they find that they cannot coerce Georgia to yield to its mandate."[26]

Final Removal of the Five Civilized Tribes

The Cherokees' legal attempts to remain on their ancestral lands and to maintain tribal sovereignty followed earlier maneuvers by other southern tribes, including the Choctaws, Chickasaws, and Creeks, to resist the tide of settler encroachment. One strategy consisted of a policy of cooperation that included gradual cession of portions of tribal domains. During the War of 1812, the Five Civilized Tribes hoped that by remaining loyal to the United States they would be able to retain their land. The southern tribes also tried to coexist with settlers and to accept many Anglo-American ways and institutions. Some of the tribal members, especially the mixed-blood element, adopted large-scale farming, business, Western education, and American patterns of government in an attempt to win favor from their white neighbors and to be left alone. Rather than producing the desired results, these actions made the settlers jealous and had little effect on curbing the frontiersmen's lust for Indian land.

Another strategy used by some tribal members consisted of simply accepting removal to retain tribal sovereignty in their new territory and to escape harassment of frontiersmen. Choctaws, Chickasaws, and a mixed-blood faction of Cherokees, as well as bands of the tribes who had migrated west to new territories before 1830, followed this approach.

Resistance through additional legal endeavors, nonviolent refusal, or military action were other tactics tried by the Five Civilized Tribes. The Ross faction of the Cherokees, consisting mainly of full-bloods, employed both judicial means and peaceful obstinacy. The Creeks resisted by steadfastly staying on their eastern lands and by furious military action against encroaching Americans. The Seminoles, after provisionally agreeing to cede their eastern territory, for the most part refused to immigrate to Indian Territory. Those remaining fiercely resisted removal attempts by waging war against the U.S. Army in a conflict that lasted until 1842.

Some of the Seminoles remained in Florida. The military escorted to Indian Territory most of the Seminoles, Creeks, and Cherokees who took part in these last attempts to keep their homelands.

A few tribesmen continued to live in the South, but most of them immigrated to Indian Territory. The exodus of the Five Civilized Tribes resulted in a tremendous loss of life. Those who survived proceeded to restore their tribal governments and communities. Until the 1860s, they enjoyed prosperity and a largely peaceful life unhampered by white expansion.

During the Civil War the Cherokee, Creek, Seminole, Choctaw, and Chickasaw nations signed treaties of alliance with the Confederacy. Using this as an excuse for taking large sections of the Indians' territories, federal officials in 1866 forced the Five Civilized Tribes to cede the western half of Indian Territory to the United States as a form of war reparations. Federal officials planned to resettle Indians from Kansas, Nebraska, and the southern plains on this land.[27]

Final Removal of the Old Northwest Tribes

During the same period that the Five Civilized Tribes were being removed, the federal government forced the Old Northwest tribes to make additional land cessions and started them on a trail of numerous exiles to the trans-Mississippi West. American sympathy for the plight of the northern Indians did not arise as it had for the Five Civilized Tribes. Consequently, the northern Indians did not have humanitarian supporters to oppose federal acquisition of their lands. The federal government's policy toward the Old Northwest tribes consisted of making treaties for land cessions but without the excuse of military conflict. The tribes after 1815 possessed insufficient power to resist government demands and settler depredations. Poor organization among the tribes and reduction of tribal populations also added to the lack of strength for effective resistance. Actual removal west of the Mississippi River did not commence until after the inauguration of James Monroe as president in 1817. With the Indian Removal Act of 1830, forced migration beyond the Mississippi became a reality for the northern tribes as it had for the southern Indians. The government had removed most of the northern groups by 1845.

Emigration of the Old Northwest tribes marked the beginning of a long succession of tragic removals. After ceding their lands in the Great Lakes and Ohio region to the United States, the Sac and Fox, Delawares, Kickapoos and a few other groups were moved from reservation to reservation in Missouri, Iowa, and Kansas before finally receiving their last domain in present-day Oklahoma. Each time the federal government pledged that the new reservation would be the Indians' final home, but the insatiable demands of settlers pushed the Indians off their land, removing them to another reservation with the promise, never kept, that at last they had settled beyond the reach of aggressive frontiersmen. At the time of their removal to Indian Territory in the late 1800s, many of the Delaware and Sac and Fox elder tribesmen had experienced the ordeal of four removals. With each forced migration, the Indians succumbed to more illness, disease, death, white depredations, tribal disunity, tribal decimation, and demoralization. By the 1850s many of these former Old Northwest tribes lived on reservations in present-day Kansas and Nebraska. Other tribes also had been removed to the northern part of Indian Territory or had received reduced reservations in that area.

The Kansas-Nebraska Act

During the 1840s and 1850s Congress debated the opening of northern Indian Territory to white settlement. This action reflected the desires of frontiersmen, railroad officials, and such avid expansionists as Thomas Hart Benton of Missouri. The rush of westward immigration to the new territories of Oregon and California also played a vital role in the demand for opening of northern Indian Territory. Supporters of the Kansas-Nebraska Act argued that Kansas and Nebraska territories must be organized and opened to white settlement to connect the eastern part of the nation with the western part. They asserted that it was time to meet the demands of settlers who were waiting to migrate to northern Indian Territory and to sanction those frontiersmen who already had intruded on Indian lands. Advocates of the act claimed that the Indians' rights would be protected and that they could choose to remain in the newly organized territories.[28]

Voicing his opposition Volney Howard of Texas claimed that the settlers would soon surround the Indians, forcing them to become U.S. citizens or to sell their lands and migrate elsewhere. Opponents of the act pointed to earlier treaties that guaranteed Indians would have the lands forever and that their homes would remain outside the limits of any territory or state. Whether these supporters of Indian treaty rights solely reflected humanitarian intentions remains somewhat unclear, because supporters charged that their adversaries objected to the bill out of self-interest. Many of the outspoken critics represented Texas, who wanted the proposed transcontinental railroad to take a southern route through their state to retain the traffic of settlers moving to the western states and territories. Edward Everett, who had opposed earlier removal treaties consummated under Andrew Jackson, objected to the legislation. He reiterated a statement first articulated in 1830 that the Indians would never be safe from the thrust of westward expansion, and, if the act became law, then the United States must treat the Indians with much kindness. Most likely, the opposition to the opening of northern Indian Territory resulted from a combination of self-interest, humanitarian concern, and belief that the United States should uphold its treaty obligations.[29]

Proponents of the formation of Nebraska and Kansas territories obviously supported the opening of the area out of self-interest and conviction that it would promote growth and unity of the United States. One supporter of the act maintained that the question rested with the supremacy of U.S. sovereignty over the Indians. H. H. Sibley, delegate from Minnesota Territory, observed that the United States had always promised that the Indians would enjoy permanent tenure on their new lands and that the federal government consistently had broken these pledges. He thus implied that no precedent existed for the government to start upholding its treaty obligations with the Indians. Intense debate over the opening of the area to settlers and the organization of two territories developed in 1853 and 1854. In the latter year, when Congress passed the Kansas-Nebraska bill, debate included the issue of slavery, which soon overshadowed the Indian rights issue.[30]

With the passage of the Kansas-Nebraska Act, extinguishment of title to Indian lands became important to the settlers and territorial officials. Commissioner of Indian Affairs George Manypenny had traveled among the Indians in northern Indian Territory earlier, in 1853, discussing new treaties for the cession of all or part of their lands to the U.S. government. After the establishment of Kansas and Nebraska territories, Manypenny renewed his efforts to obtain treaties. In 1854 the commissioner concluded treaties with the Wyandots, Omahas, Missouris, Otos, Sac and Fox of the Missouri, Iowas, Kickapoos, Delawares, Shawnees, Miamis, and the confederated tribes of the Peoria. Although each of the Manypenny Treaties varied somewhat they either led to a reduction in tribal domains or to the allotment of tribal lands in fee simple and sale of surplus lands to settlers and railroads. Some tribal bands or tribes temporarily retained tribal reserves because of their refusal to accept individual ownership of lands and to abolish their tribal government.[31]

The treaties failed to satisfy all the demands of settlers because the Indians still held some of the best agricultural land. As a result a few frontiersmen squatted on tribal lands and committed acts of violence against Indians. Settlers and railroad officials continued to agitate for complete Indian removal, and the federal government attempted to meet their demands. Treaties concluded during the 1850s and 1860s led to the steady diminution of tribal lands and extinguishment of Indian title. To help promote Indian removal from Kansas, territorial and later state officials in the early 1860s taxed the Indians' lands and confiscated them as a result of failure to pay taxes. This action violated the terms of the Kansas-Nebraska Act, which exempted the Indians' lands from taxation. Alien to Indians, taxation provided an effective means for the state to obtain their lands. Some of the treaties providing for the allotment of lands in severalty limited the alienation of the allotment to the federal government, but other treaties failed to provide such protection. Indians with unrestricted lands lost most of them in a relatively short time and became homeless and destitute.[32]

Settlers' hostility and intrusion on Indian lands and the state's illegal actions led most of the tribes in the 1860s and 1870s to move to new reservations in Indian Territory. The Omnibus Treaty of 1867 signed with the Ottawas and Wyandots, and the Miami and Peoria Confederacy, included provisions for selling their Kansas lands and purchasing new domains in Indian Territory. A number of other tribes residing in Kansas concluded similar treaties with the United States in 1867. The Shawnees, Delawares, and Munsees with two bands of Chippewas purchased land and citizenship rights in the Cherokee Nation and settled in the northern part of its territory. The Delawares in 1860 in a treaty with the United States had allotted their lands in severalty and sold surplus lands to the railroads. The Munsee and Chippewa bands had confederated in 1859 and received a Kansas reserve in that year. The Potawatomis had agreed to a treaty in 1861 that followed the usual pattern of allotment, and most sold their lands within a short period. The Prairie band refused to accept individual ownership of land. The Sac and Fox tribe accepted the allotment of lands in severalty and sold their surplus lands to settlers. By 1867 both tribes, weary of the treatment received from Kansas settlers, negotiated with the United States for cession of their lands in Kansas and the purchase of a new reservation in Indian Territory. The Sac and Fox and Potawatomis accepted new domains in east central Indian Territory.[33]

During the 1870s other tribes residing in Kansas and Nebraska ceded their lands and removed to Indian Territory. The Osages returned to a reservation in northern Indian Territory. The Kaws sold their Kansas lands and immigrated to a new reserve in the Cherokee Outlet. The Pawnees, who had successively ceded their lands in Nebraska, sold the last of their reservation and accepted a domain in the Cherokee Outlet during 1873. In 1865 the Poncas ceded one-third of their lands in South Dakota and Nebraska to the United States, and the federal government further reduced their territory in 1868. A congressional act in 1876 provided for the complete removal of the Poncas from their remaining lands in the north. After Ponca leaders saw the lands assigned them in Indian Territory, they refused to emigrate. Although the legislation contained a provision allowing the Poncas the privilege of approving a proposed reservation, the military forcibly removed them to the Cherokee Outlet reserve. The federal government later sanctioned the return of some Poncas to their lands in Nebraska.[34]

After 1871 Congress officially ceased making treaties with tribes and thereafter used legislation and executive orders to handle Indian affairs. Under this new policy, tribes moving to Indian Territory received their reservations by congressional act or executive order. In 1872 Congress provided a reserve for the Absentee Shawnees in east central Indian Territory and in the 1880s authorized the sale of the remainder of the Oto and Missouri lands in Kansas and Nebraska and the purchase of a new domain in the Cherokee Outlet. Another tribe, the Iowas, still retained land in Kansas but following an executive order in 1883, the tribe moved to east central Indian Territory. The Mexican Kickapoos also received a reserve in the same area by executive order in 1883. An act in 1885 authorized relocation of the Tonkawas, originally a Texas tribe, to a reserve vacated by the Nez Percés in the Cherokee Outlet.[35]

Indian Land Cessions in California and the Northwest

Settlers immigrating to California after the discovery of gold in 1848 devastated resident Indian tribes and tribelets. Pioneers swarmed over Indian hunting grounds, destroying villages and killing Indians. Between 1849 and 1859 approximately 70,000 Indians died from murder, disease, or starvation. The federal government, far removed from the scene, had little control over activities on the West Coast. In the early 1850s, federal officials signed treaties with some of the surviving tribes and tribelets in which the Indians ceded title to their lands and received reservations. Unfortunately, the designated reservations comprised lands desired by frontiersmen who did not want the treaties ratified and successfully pressured Congress to reject them.[36] The California Indians were later given smaller reservations.

Appropriation of Indian land in the Pacific Northwest followed a pattern consisting of military conflict followed by treaties in which the tribes ceded large amounts of their ancestral lands and received in turn reduced reserves. Conflicts between Indians and settlers developed soon after the United States acquired Oregon in 1846. Following the usual pattern American pioneers intruded on Indian lands and threatened the existence of the tribes, which resulted in Indian attempts to expel the squatters. The Rogue River Indians in southwest Oregon, for example, fought with the miners. Federal officials unsuccessfully tried to persuade the Oregon Indians to move east of the Cascades. The commissioners in 1851 negotiated six treaties that allowed the Indians to remain on a small portion of their ancestral lands. Congress never ratified any of these treaties. The increasing demand of settlers for rich agricultural land led federal officials to enter into new treaties. The tribes ceded much of their land and federal authorities placed them on limited reserves.[37]

Soon after Isaac Stevens became governor of Washington Territory in

1854, he sought to acquire Indian land for settlers and to assure the completion of a transcontinental railroad from Minnesota to Puget Sound. In 1854 and 1855 he forced the tribes in the Puget Sound area and the interior to cede large tracts of land and to accept greatly reduced reservations. Tribesmen resisted but were easily defeated. Military engagements with the interior tribes continued until 1858 when the Yakimas, Cayuses, Walla Wallas, Spokans, Palouses, and Coeur d'Alenes capitulated. Military tribunals executed the Indian resistance leaders. The federal government forced the tribes to settle on small reserves and opened their original territories to white settlement.[38]

The Nez Percés who resided on the Washington, Oregon, and Idaho border had always been at peace with the United States, but they too endured a reduction of their lands. In 1855 Nez Percé leaders negotiated a treaty with the United States that guaranteed the tribe perpetual tenure to its lands. In 1860 intruders on Nez Percé lands discovered gold and the subsequent extension of the mining frontier endangered Nez Percé claims to the area. In 1863 government commissioners used coercion and bribery with selected tribal leaders to gain the cession of Nez Percé territory. Although the chiefs of bands who had not approved the treaty argued that they were not bound by its terms and would not move to the reduced reserve, government agents declared that the entire tribe must adhere to the treaty provisions.[39]

Chief Joseph's band steadfastly refused to leave the Wallowa area of northeast Oregon, but in 1877 the military threatened to forcibly remove the Indians to the new reservation and reluctantly Chief Joseph agreed to relocate. Meanwhile his warriors killed intruders, and federal troops immediately attacked the band. After defeating the federal troops, Chief Joseph fled with his band of nearly four hundred men, women, and children. Other bands who had refused to migrate to the new reserve joined Chief Joseph. They fled from the pursuing troops in an effort to reach Canada. Just short of the border in the Bear Paw Mountains of Montana, the army overtook the Nez Percés and a battle raged for five days. Chief Joseph finally surrendered to save the freezing and starving women and children. The surrender terms agreed to on the field of battle allowed Chief Joseph and his people to return to a reservation in the Pacific Northwest. Government officials, however, countermanded this agreement and escorted the Nez Percés to a reserve in the Cherokee Outlet in Indian Territory. After sustained pleas from Chief Joseph, the Indian Rights Association, and Presbyterian church leaders that the federal government honor its pledges, the Nez Percés in 1885 were permitted to return to the Pacific Northwest. The federal government sent Chief Joseph and one group to the Colville reservation in Washington. Another group was settled on the reserve in Idaho where they joined their kinsmen.[40]

The U.S. government forced other tribes, including the Flatheads in western Montana, to cede large tracts of land and to accept smaller reservations. The Shoshones and Bannocks of southern Idaho resisted white intruders, but federal troops forced the insurgents to surrender and to settle on a reservation.[41]

The Modocs also were faced with the familiar format of military conquest and reduced reservations. This tribe, native to the Tule Lake area in northern California and the Klamath region in southern Oregon, endured for over twenty years the intrusion of settlers into their territory. Once entrenched the Americans agitated for all of the tribe's land. Thus in 1864, along with the Klamaths, the Modocs ceded their lands to the United States in return for a reservation to be shared by both tribes in southern Oregon. The Modocs, led by Captain Jack (Kenitpoos), resented not having received a reserve in their homeland area and complained that the Klamaths mistreated them. Captain Jack and fifty warriors left the Klamath reservation and returned to their homeland near Lost River. They petitioned the government for a reservation in that area, but federal officials refused the request. Finally the military's attempt to return them to the Klamath reservation led to the Modoc War of 1872–1873. Greatly outnumbered, the Modoc warriors fought five battles without a defeat. The army pushed them to the lava beds south of Tule Lake, where after six months of warfare, sixty-five Modocs surrendered in mid-1873. Ten days later the military, with the aid of some Modocs, captured Captain Jack and twenty-five warriors. Federal officials removed one hundred Modocs as prisoners of war to northeastern Indian Territory. In 1909 the government allowed them to return to the Klamath reservation, although some of the Modocs elected to remain in Oklahoma.[42]

The Southwest Tribes

Tribes in the American Southwest experienced the same pattern of military conquest, cession of tribal lands, and placement on reduced reservations. The Mescalero Apaches and Navajos were defeated by Union troops during the Civil War and concentrated at Bosque Redondo in eastern New Mexico, where they lived until 1868. The Mescaleros were then assigned a small reservation in southeastern New Mexico and the Navajos a larger one in northeastern Arizona. Conflict between the Mimbreno and Chiricahua Apaches and settlers in Arizona and New Mexico erupted in 1862, due largely to the expansion of the mining frontier onto Apache territory. Under the leadership of Mangas Coloradas and Cochise, Apache raiders depredated white settlements across the Southwest. By 1871, however, these Apaches agreed to surrender vast territories and to move to four reservations established for them by the federal government in New Mexico and Arizona territories. Most Apaches remained on the reservations, but some became incensed at the actions of corrupt agents and injustices perpetrated against them by local residents, and renewed attacks on southwestern settlements. From 1874 to 1883 Apache leaders including Victorio, Nana, and Geronimo conducted destructive raids. In 1883 Geronimo and his followers capitulated and returned to the reservation. Two years later, Geronimo left the reservation with a band of about fifty men and one hundred women and children. A federal army of nearly five thousand pursued Geronimo's band. Finally, in 1886 after receiving assurance that he could keep his people on the Arizona reservation, Geronimo surrendered. However, federal officials countermanded this agreement and shipped Geronimo and five hundred other Apaches to military prison in Florida and later to Alabama. At least one-fourth of the interned Apaches died from illness and diseases while in the South. In 1894 the government moved them to the Kiowa-Comanche Reservation in Indian Territory, and their status as prisoners of war continued until 1913. At that time most of the Apaches returned to New Mexico and joined the Mescalero Apaches, although some remained in Oklahoma and purchased land from the Kiowas and Comanches.[43]

During the Civil War, tribes in Colorado, Nevada, and Utah territories lost land following defeats by volunteer infantry and cavalry regiments. These tribes were assigned to reservations. In 1868 the Utes, after suffering a long period of warfare and loss of territory in Colorado, were assigned a reservation in the western third of Colorado. Soon miners demanded the Ute reserve, and in 1873 the tribe ceded a portion of it. Rebelling against the White River Indian agent's aggressive attempts to persuade the Utes to become agriculturalists, some of the tribesmen revolted in 1879. The Meeker Massacre led to increased pressure on Congress to remove the Utes from Colorado. The following year, tribal representatives accepted a compromise: the White River Utes were to relocate to the Uintah Reservation in Utah; the Southern Utes (Weeminuche, Mouache, Capote bands) were to accept allotments on unoccupied lands along the La Plata River in Colorado; and the Tabeguaches were to settle on lands near the Gunnison River. In 1895 Congress established the Ute Mountain Ute Reservation in Colorado for the Weeminuche band.[44]

The federal government compressed other tribes' territories in the West. The Havasupai, native to the Grand Canyon area, were required to accept reductions of their original land base several times during the nineteenth century. Like many western tribes, the Havasupais offered no military resistance to this reduction of their tribal lands.[45]

Land Cessions from the Plains Tribes

War between various Plains tribes and the U.S. Army in the second half of the nineteenth century led to the inevitable reduction of Indian land through treaties enforced by the military. Hostilities developed in eastern

Colorado during the Civil War because Southern Cheyenne territory lay in the path of miners moving into the Rocky Mountains. The federal government's effort to coerce the tribes to cede the territory guaranteed to them by the Fort Laramie Treaty of 1851 precipitated the conflict. After government agents attempted to appropriate Southern Cheyenne and Arapaho lands, intermittent conflict continued for three years. In 1864 the Indians sued for peace. Chief Black Kettle and White Antelope concluded an armistice and settled for the winter at Sand Creek. In a surprise attack Col. John M. Chivington and a force of Colorado militia ravaged the camp, killing many of its inhabitants. Black Kettle and a few warriors escaped the Sand Creek Massacre. This atrocity led to renewed warfare. The Cheyennes and Arapahoes scattered; most of them settled in western Kansas where bands of the Brulé and Oglala Sioux and Northern Cheyenne warriors joined them. They attacked settlements from the Platte in Nebraska to South Pass.[46]

In 1865 leaders of the Cheyenne, Arapaho, Kiowa, Comanche, and Kiowa-Apache tribes met with federal commissioners and concluded the Little Arkansas Treaties. The provisions included the cession of Indian lands north of the Arkansas River and acceptance of reduced reservations in Indian Territory, southwestern Kansas, and the Texas panhandle. Despite the treaties, conflict continued on the southern plains. The Senate failed to ratify the agreements and federal officials refused to protect the tribes from trespassers. Hunters crossed Indian lands, killing the buffalo that provided the tribes' subsistence. In an attempt to protect their rights, the Indians struck back at the intruders. By 1867 federal officials believed that the domains assigned to these tribes at the Little Arkansas Council needed to be reduced to satisfy the demands of settlers and railroad builders for additional lands. Despite protestations eloquently delivered at the grand council at Medicine Lodge Creek, the chiefs of the Kiowa, Comanche, Cheyenne, Arapaho, and Kiowa-Apache tribes submitted to the commissioners' demands for drastically compressed reserves in Indian Territory.[47]

The Northern Plains Indians experienced similar loss of tribal territories. Their lands lay in the path of the proposed transcontinental railroad and trails leading to Washington and Oregon territories. Federal officials thus determined to remove them from the path of expansion. Hostilities began in 1854 after a settler claimed the Indians had killed one of his cows. Federal troops attacked the Sioux and in 1855, Spotted Tail, the leader of the Brulé Sioux, surrendered and government officials summarily imprisoned him. This brought temporary peace to the northern plains. Peace in this region continued until 1862 when hostilities broke out in Minnesota between the Santee Sioux and intruding settlers. Eventually federal troops defeated the insurgent tribesmen, hanged thirty-nine of their leaders, and relocated the survivors on small reservations, taking most of the Santee Sioux's land as reparations. Some of the tribesmen fled to Canada or joined the Teton Sioux in the Dakotas.[48]

The Northern Cheyennes and Sioux stood as a barrier both to transcontinental railroad construction and the expansion of the mining frontier in Montana. Successive victories over federal troops led to the settler evacuation of the tribes' hunting grounds in the Powder River country of Montana. During April 1868, Sioux and Northern Cheyenne leaders met with government officials at Fort Laramie and negotiated a treaty. Its terms stated that the government would abandon military posts in the Sioux hunting grounds; the tribes would allow peaceful passage of the railroad through tribal territories; and the Sioux and Northern Cheyennes would accept smaller reserves in the Dakota, Montana, and Wyoming territories with a hunting area in the Big Horn–Powder River area.[49]

Settlers on the eastern boundary of the Indians' new reservations desired these lands, and government officials attempted to compress the tribesmen on even smaller reserves. They also encouraged slaughter of buffalo because they believed that once the buffalo were exterminated, the tribes would have to move to reservations and accept government rations for survival. After the Fort Laramie Treaty of 1868, skirmishes continued between the Indians and soldiers, railroad workers, and settlers. The Sioux alleged that the conflicts resulted from trespass on their lands and violation of rights guaranteed them by the treaty.[50]

In the mid-1870s hostilities reached a fateful climax. Gold discovered in the Black Hills in South Dakota attracted many miners to the region during 1875. The Sioux threatened retaliation if the military did not expel the trespassers, and the army initially attempted to do so. Then the government tried to purchase the Indian claim to the Black Hills, but the Sioux refused to sell. In an attempt to prevent clashes the military ordered the Sioux and Northern Cheyennes to settle near the agencies on the reservations, where they could be watched. Many of the Sioux complied with the government's demands, but a large group journeyed to the Big Horn Mountains for their annual summer camp and sun dance. The military attacked a band of Northern Cheyennes on their way to the agency, and a band of Oglala Sioux under Crazy Horse rescued them. The Northern Cheyennes then joined the Sioux at the Little Big Horn. Determined to bring these tribesmen back to the agencies, federal troops attacked the encampment with the resulting annihilation of Col. George A. Custer and a portion of the Seventh Cavalry. The military relentlessly pursued the Indians. Sitting Bull and a group of his followers, the Hunkpapa Sioux, fled to Canada where they remained until 1881. Other bands fought until forced to surrender. By the end of 1876 the Northern Plains Indians had been subdued. The same year the Sioux surrendered the Black Hills and accepted a reservation in central South Dakota; the Indian barrier to white expansion in the northern plains finally had been eliminated.[51]

Alaska Native Land Cession

Federal policy toward the Alaska Natives essentially followed the same pattern as that employed toward other Native Americans. When the United States purchased Alaska from Russia in 1867, Congress recognized the natives' right to use or occupancy of the lands in their possession. Article 3 of the Treaty of Cession pledged protection for the natives' enjoyment of their property. The act of 17 May 1884, which created a civil government for the territory of Alaska, guaranteed that the native inhabitants "shall not be disturbed in the possession of any lands actually in their use or occupation or now claimed by them but the terms under which such persons may acquire title to such lands is reserved for future legislation by Congress." Several acts passed by Congress subsequently reiterated this promise, and the judiciary also consistently recognized the right of the Alaskan Natives to use and occupancy. Congress, however, neglected to clarify aboriginal title until 1971. During this century of uncertain tenure, American settlers, the federal government, and the territorial and state government made substantial inroads into native lands. Most of the aboriginal lands have been alienated in the twentieth century. As will be shown later, the U.S. Bureau of Land Management granted title to lands used by Alaska Natives to various nonnative individuals.[52]

During the early twentieth century, the federal government established twelve reservations by executive order. A 1936 law that brought the Alaska Natives under the provisions of the Indian Reorganization Act authorized the Department of the Interior to establish reservations for them subject to the approval of the Alaska Natives. In the early 1940s the federal government established six reservations and submitted proposals for additional ones. The Alaska Natives, however, rejected them largely because of the activities of special interest groups. These nonnative individuals aroused native opposition by frightening them with exaggerated tales of their fate on reservations. The plight of the reservation Indians in the lower United States encouraged this belief. In the next decade, ninety native villages petitioned for reservation of their land. Caught up in termination, the federal government was not receptive.[53]

The 1958 Alaska Statehood Act reaffirmed native use and occupancy but authorized the state to choose 102,550,000 acres from the public domain, which included aboriginal lands. This led to conflict with native groups who frequently lived on the lands selected by the state. During the 1960s the Aleuts, Eskimos, and Indians of Alaska, encouraged by American Indian groups, formed a united opposition to alienation of their land rights. Special-interest groups, such as the oil companies and the state government, also promoted a settlement so they could surge ahead in their exploitation of the land and its resources.

In 1966 Secretary of the Interior Stewart Udall placed a freeze on further allocation of Alaskan lands until the natives' claims had been settled. In 1971 this culminated in the enactment of the Alaska Native Claims Settlement Act. The Alaska Natives received clear title to 40,000,000 acres and compensation for relinquishing claim to the remaining Alaskan lands.[54]

The Dawes Act and Allotment

After the abolition of treaty making in 1871 the federal government commenced a new policy for dealing with Indians, including the Alaska Natives, who are legally referred to as American Indians. This policy eventually led to additional appropriation of Indian lands by various unilateral actions of the federal government. The most important of these actions was the General Allotment Act, adopted in 1887, which broke up the reservations and assigned each Indian a homestead of 160 acres. The allotments in severalty were usually inalienable for twenty-five years. The surplus land on each reservation was first sold to the federal government, then was opened to settlement.[55]

Most Indians and some congressmen opposed allotment. In 1880 a minority group of congressmen in the House of Representatives expressed their dismay with the proposed legislation and emphasized the land hunger that brought allotment to fruition.

> The main purpose of this bill is not to help the Indians . . . it is a method of getting at the valuable Indian lands and opening them up to white settlement. . . . If this were done in the name of Greed, it would be bad enough; but to do it in the name of Humanity, and under the cloak of an ardent desire to promote the Indian's welfare . . . is infinitely worse.[56]

Over the next several decades the act failed to fulfill the expectations of the reform element, but its results met the desires of western expansionists.

The Dawes Act exempted the lands of the Osages, Miamis and Peorias, Sac and Fox, the Sioux in Nebraska, the Senecas of New York, and the Five Civilized Tribes. These tribes had exerted great pressure on Congress against allotment. Most of these tribes later came under the act's provisions, either through amendments to the Dawes Act or by separate allotment statutes. Survey and assignment of allotments eventually erased most tribally owned lands, except deserts and mountainous sections of the United States that government officials considered unsuitable for agricultural purposes. On many reservations the government started the allotment process soon after passage of the Dawes Act.[57]

An amendment to the Indian Appropriation Bill of 1889 authorized the formation of a federal tribunal, the Jerome Commission, to negotiate allotment agreements with the tribes of western Indian Territory. During the next five years the Jerome Commission concluded agreements with the Iowa, Sac and Fox, Potawatomi, Shawnee, Tonkawa, Pawnee, Cheyenne, Arapaho, Kickapoo, Kiowa, Comanche, Caddo, Apache, Ponca, Oto, Missouri, and Kaw tribes. In 1889 the federal government removed the last obstacle to homesteading in the unassigned lands in Indian Territory by purchasing the "residual interest" of the Seminoles and Creeks in those lands. The Cherokees sold the Cherokee Outlet in Indian Territory to the United States in 1893. During the early 1890s the federal government signed allotment agreements with the small tribes at the Quapaw Agency in northeastern Indian Territory, and Congress passed a law in 1906 allotting all Osage lands to tribal members.[58]

In 1893 Congress authorized a commission to negotiate with the Five Civilized Tribes to change their land system and to accept individual land ownership. After a period of resistance tribal leaders submitted to intense pressure from both the Dawes Commission and Congress and agreed to allotment. Between 1898 and 1906, leaders of the Five Civilized Tribes signed allotment agreements with the federal government, and by 1907 most of their lands had been divided among tribal members.[59]

Some Indians continued to oppose division of tribal lands into individual parcels. The Keetoowah Society among the Cherokees and the Snake group among the Creeks refused to take allotments and attempted to stop the partitioning of their communal lands. Finally federal authorities forced the recalcitrants to accept allotments by threatening to imprison them.[60]

The federal government also extended the General Allotment Act to other tribes, including the Sioux. In 1889 Congress enacted legislation that divided the Great Sioux reservation into three smaller ones and provided for their eventual allotment. Beginning in 1904 the Sioux on Pine Ridge, Rosebud, and Devils Lake divided their reservations among tribal members and the government purchased the surplus land. In 1907 and 1910 Congress approved the sale of the former Indian lands to settlers. The Sioux retained some of the lands as tribal property.[61]

Removal of Trust Restrictions

The disastrous leasing program approved by Congress in 1891 as an amendment to the General Allotment Act provided the means for non-Indians to obtain the use and in many cases de facto ownership of Indian lands. The policy of leasing ran counter to the goals of the General Allotment Act, which intended to speed assimilation by turning Indians into self-sufficient farmers and instilling in them a belief in individual ownership of land. In 1900 Indians leased about 13 percent of their allotted lands. Among some tribes the leasing agreements extended over most of the reserve. In 1898 the Omaha and Winnebago had leased 80 percent of their 140,000-acre reservation. By 1919 Cheyenne and Arapahoe allottees leased about 95 percent of their lands in Oklahoma to non-Indians. Real estate agents assisted members of the Five Civilized Tribes in selecting their allotments and then leased the lands from the Indians. The agents made their profit by subleasing the property at higher rates. These speculators often encouraged members to select timber acreages that could be profitably exploited by lessees.[62]

Some Indian agents advocated selling Indian lands. They believed that alienation of at least part of the allottees' land would force Indians to accept the white man's work ethic, adopt agriculture, and assimilate into Ango-American society. Another vocal force advocating sale of Indian lands included western farmers, ranchers, businessmen, lawyers, and bankers. Congress ultimately listened to these special-interest groups.[63]

Soon after 1900 Congress began enacting legislation permitting the removal of all trust provisions on allotted lands and granting fee simple titles. In 1902 a clause in the Indian Appropriation Act removed the restrictions on alienation of lands inherited from original allottees. Four years later the Burke Act amended the General Allotment Act and authorized the secretary of the interior to award at his discretion unrestricted title to "competent" Indians. In 1907 a new provision in the Indian Appropriation Act allowed "incompetent" Indians to sell or lease their allotments with the approval of the secretary of the interior. This clause made possible the alienation of all allotted lands.[64]

The continual erosion of restrictions on trust lands paved the way for the sale of a large amount of Indian property. After the Sisseton Sioux divided their reservation, they allotted 300,000 acres among tribal members and then sold 600,000 acres to the federal government as surplus lands. By 1909, after the restrictions on alienation had been removed, two-thirds of the Sisseton Sioux allottees had sold their land. In 1917 Commissioner of Indian Affairs Cato Sells instituted a more liberal policy of removing restrictions on the trust lands. The administration created numerous commissions to determine the competency of Indians with restricted allotments. Between 1917 and 1921 the government issued about 20,000 titles in fee simple. Many of these fee patents were issued without Indian consent. In 1921 the Board of Indian Commissioners investigated the Indian land situation and revealed that an extremely high percentage of Indians had alienated their lands. As a result, the government ended the Sells' policy and during the 1920s the secretary of the interior allowed fewer lands removed from their restricted status.[65]

Scandals, Fraud, and Corruption

Non-Indians took advantage of the removal of restrictions on Indian trust lands, using various methods to obtain land. Some simply exploited the Indians' inexperience with Anglo economic values and purchased land at prices far below the fair market value, while others resorted to more under-handed tactics. One technique involved kidnapping a minor to consum-mate the marriage of an Indian youth to a white person. Soon after the wedding the minor was pressed to sign over the allotment to the husband or wife, and the spouse would then disappear. Other non-Indians would persuade an Indian to write a will leaving all his property to his white friend; the Indian would then die of undetermined causes. A few docu-mented murder cases were discovered, one of which involved the bombing of two young children. Another practice used by speculators consisted of obtaining guardianship rights over minors or incompetent adults, at which point permissive state courts would allow the guardian to use the Indian's lands in his own self-interest. One notable case involved the unsuccessful attempt by a speculator to obtain guardianship of 161 Choctaw minors whose allotments covered valuable timberland.[66]

Some speculators acquired Indian lands through county or state taxation of allotments. In the early 1860s Kansas authorities taxed the allotments of resident Indians (which by treaty were tax-exempt), then seized the lands for delinquent taxes. Oklahomans in the early twentieth century used a similar method in acquiring Indian property. Although Congress exempt-ed the allotments from taxation, the lands sometimes appeared on the county tax rolls. A non-Indian cognizant of the incorrectly listed allotment paid the taxes and remained silent until the statute of limitations expired. He then took actual possession of the land.[67]

One of the more flagrant abuses of federal trust responsibility over allot-ted lands occurred at the White Earth Chippewa Reservation in northern Minnesota. At its formation in 1867 the reservation encompassed over 800,000 acres. By 1980 Indian landholdings had been sold, probated, or otherwise alienated and had dwindled to fewer than 55,000 acres. Although these numbers may not differ in terms of percentage from some other allotted reservations, White Earth stands out because of the large number of clouded land titles uncovered in a recent investigation. A Department of the Interior study revealed that about one-fourth of the private land titles within the reservation (about 100,000 acres) were unlaw-fully transferred from the original Indian allottees. The study was under-taken in light of a 1977 Minnesota Supreme Court decision that declared that the Clapp amendment, which applied only to the White Earth Reser-vation, had not, despite previous policy, terminated trust patents on cer-tain allotments belonging to mixed-blood Indians.[68]

The Clapp amendment, which facilitated alienation of land by mixed-bloods, led to a series of land scandals shortly after its enactment in 1907. The amendment, along with lenient court interpretations of the meaning of mixed-blood Indian, inspired a rush of speculators to the rich timber and farm lands of the White Earth Reservation. Allegations of fraudulent land dealings soon prompted the Department of Justice to initiate an investigation. The findings resulted in approximately 1,600 federal lawsuits against lumber interests, speculators, and others who apparently took advantage of unassimilated mixed-bloods. The lawsuits, first filed in 1910, attempted to recover land, to clear titles encumbered by mortgage or taxes, and to settle timber trespass violations. Over the next eight years the lawsuits covered approximately 142,000 acres of illegally transferred land. Some individuals and lumber interests faced federal charges of conspiracy to defraud the government, but no convictions were obtained.[69]

The more recent land scandal first surfaced in the 1977 Minnesota Supreme Court decision of *State of Minnesota v. Zay-Zah.* In 1927 Zay-Zah, a mixed-blood (also known as Charles Aubid), received a trust patent for forty acres. He apparently abandoned the land and never attempted to sell it. In 1961 Clearwater County turned the property over to the state for unpaid taxes. Later, a purchaser initiated a suit to quiet title to the land. The case eventually reached the state supreme court. The justices held that the state or county did not have the authority to tax trust land because the Clapp amendment never terminated the trust patent on the original allottee's land unless he applied for a fee patent or tried to sell the land.[70]

The implications of the decision were immense. Private landowners, both Indian and non-Indian, worried about the security of their land titles. The controversy prompted federal investigation, and in 1978 the Department of the Interior announced that titles to over 100,000 acres of land were not valid and might rightfully belong to the original Indian allottees or their heirs. The new interpretation of the Clapp amendment created title flaws that fell into three broad categories: trust lands forfeited improperly to the state for unpaid taxes, trust lands probated through state courts instead of through the Department of the Interior, and other miscellaneous transactions including those of underage (18–21 years) female allottees.[71]

The ensuing land-title controversy devastated local real estate prices and attracted much media attention. The press often gave sympathetic treatment to the white farmer who had "owned" his farm for years, could not collateralize it for crop loans, and stood a realistic chance of losing his property. Some members of the Indian community accused the media of bias for ignoring the impoverished Indian allottee who traded the last of his ancestral lands to a speculator for a "sack of groceries."[72]

Public clamor for a solution resulted in the enactment of Public Law 99-

264 in 1986. The White Earth Chippewas received 10,000 acres, which brought their total land holdings to approximately 65,000 acres, along with $10.4 million in federal compensation for lands lost and $6.6 million in economic aid. The bill extinguished Indian title to over 110,000 acres held privately and by the county and state governments.[73]

Some congressmen opposed the settlement because they thought it did not compensate the Chippewas enough. Minnesota's offer to give back only 10,000 acres paid too little respect for past injustices and for the Chippewas' court-backed claims to a much larger amount of land. Senator John Melcher, a Democrat from Montana, scolded Minnesota officials for asking Congress to "legislate that everything is honky-dory for Minnesota" by clearing title to the land. Melcher's amendment calling for the return of all lands unlawfully seized for taxes was defeated.[74]

Heirship Lands

Another problem for Indians after the government persuaded them to divide their reservations into allotments involved heirship lands. The death of an original allottee frequently left his lands shared by numerous heirs, and additional deaths of heirs increased the fractional interests in the allotment. By 1920 some allotments had over fifty heirs, and the number continued to proliferate over the following generations. In 1909 more than 80,000 acres of original allotted lands on the Sisseton Sioux Reservation had been divided by heirship procedures into smaller plots. By the 1970s over 6 million acres of Indian land in the United States possessed heirship status. The use or selling of these heirship lands required the consent of all heirs, and this has led over the years to de facto alienation of lands from Indians. In the 1970s and 1980s Congress passed legislation enabling tribes to more effectively consolidate tribal land holdings. The Indian Land Consolidation Act of 1982, as well as separate legislation applying to specific tribes, allowed tribes to purchase fractional heirship interests and exchange tribal lands for individually owned acreages.[75]

General Impact of Allotment

Allotment in severalty failed to accomplish assimilation and produced a further decline in the Indians' economic position. In choosing their allotments Indians often selected land without regard for its agricultural or pastoral potential. They instead picked land near their old homes or relatives. Thus, the most valuable land soon passed out of their possession. Forests, fertile farmland, and rich grassland went to non-Indians. As indicated earlier most Indians, with their spiritual valuation of land, failed to understand the Euro-American concept of private ownership, the economic value of land, and economic practices. Consequently many Indians quickly sold or leased their lands at low prices. Others became easy victims of swindlers and shady speculators. For the most part, allotment left them poverty-stricken, landless, and dependent on the small income generated from leasing their allotments.

In 1887 the tribes owned 138 million acres. Over the next forty years the Dawes Act and its amendments resulted in the loss of about 90 million acres. Most of what was left consisted of desert or semidesert lands. The government declared 50 million acres as surplus lands to be sold to settlers. The Indians who received title in fee simple alienated 27 million acres or two-thirds of their allotted lands between 1887 and 1934. In 1934 Congress passed the Indian Reorganization Act, which among other things ended allotment and extended the restrictions on alienation of trust lands. Certain provisions in the Indian Reorganization Act enabled the tribes to acquire additional lands and between 1934 and 1947 the Indian land base increased by 3.7 million acres.[76]

Federal Policy of Termination

The federal government's emphasis on rebuilding the tribal land base and on affirming tribal status had a short duration. Following World War II Congress began to consider returning to a policy of assimilation. In 1953 Congress officially announced, in House Concurrent Resolution 108, that termination of the federal trust relationship with tribes was the policy of the United States. In 1953 and 1954 Congress passed termination bills that ended the wardship status of some Indians, forced them to accept individual ownership of reservation lands, and provided for the disposal of all tribal assets. As some tribes fell under this policy they had to sell their reservation lands. Consequently the size of the Indian land base eroded.[77]

In 1954 the Menominee, one of the most prosperous tribes, was selected to be terminated. Seven years later federal trusteeship over the tribe ended. Under the termination plan, the Menominee reservation was organized as a county of Wisconsin and tribal assets were transferred to a tribal corporation, Menominee Enterprises, Incorporated. To pay taxes on the formerly tax-exempt property, MEI was forced to sell 9,500 acres of prime land.[78]

The federal government also selected the Klamaths as a model for termination. Tribal members were given a choice whether to accept a per capita payment for their interest in tribal property or to have their share transferred to a private trust. Approximately 77 percent of the Klamaths voted to accept their pro rata share and to withdraw from the tribe. To raise the money the Klamaths had to sell a large part of their 1-million-acre reservation, most of which went to the government to form the Winema

National Forest. For those members who elected to take their portion of tribal assets in land, the federal government placed 135,000 acres under the trusteeship of the U.S. National Bank of Oregon. In 1969 the Klamath shareholders in the trust lands voted to end the trust. Many tribal members took that stand because they believed they voted only to end improper management of their lands by the bank and would thereby regain control of their property. Instead the bank immediately put the lands on the market. After years of controversy, the federal government in 1973 purchased the 135,000 acres for $60 million and added the land to Winema National Forest. All of the Klamath shareholders accepted their per capita payment except for one man, Edison Chiloquin, who refused to accept his check for slightly over $100,000. Chiloquin remained steadfast and stated that to take the money would be like "selling my people, my dead people." He added that "to me, the land is sacred—the money can't replace it." In 1975 the U.S. Forest Service allowed Chiloquin to build a traditional village and for this purpose closed off 800 acres from public access.[79]

Many tribes lost their federal status, but some effectively resisted government attempts to terminate them or escaped implementation of the policy. Although the main thrust of termination existed during the 1950s, it lasted until 1970 when President Richard Nixon officially repudiated the policy.

Legislative Attempt at Repudiation of All Indian Treaties

In 1977 a new movement initiated by western congressmen, notably Jack Cunningham of Washington, unsuccessfully attempted to abrogate all Indian treaties. The bill would have ended protection of Indian rights guaranteed by treaty relating to land, water, fishing, and hunting. Cunningham introduced the legislation in support of western sportsmen, commercial fisheries, and other special-interest groups who opposed the Boldt decision acknowledging the Indians' right to fifty percent of the fish harvest in their traditional fishing places. Other support came from the backlash caused by those Indians asserting large eastern land claims and the exercise of increased tribal jurisdiction and sovereignty. Undoubtedly opposition also resulted from the adversaries of Indian reserved water rights. Organizations such as Protect America's Rights and Resources (PARR), which has opposed Indian treaty rights in the 1980s, reflect a continuing desire on the part of some non-Indians to end the Indians' relationship with the federal government and to erode further the Indian land estate and resource rights.

4

Appropriation of the Indian Landed Estate: Part II

DURING the twentieth century several federal agencies, allied with public and private special-interest groups, continued to erode the Indians' land base and land resources. The Department of Reclamation, the Bureau of Land Management, and the U.S. Army Corps of Engineers have been the primary government adversaries of the Indian. These agencies persistently have taken Indian land and water rights for dams, irrigation projects, forest reserves, and other economic or recreational programs.

A conflict of interest exists within the Department of the Interior, which includes the Bureau of Indian Affairs, the Bureau of Mines, the Bureau of Sport Fisheries and Wildlife, the Bureau of Land Management, the National Park Service, and the Bureau of Reclamation. Often the secretary of the interior, as the final decision maker within the department, must either choose between a course of action recommended by the Bureau of Indian Affairs and another Department of the Interior agency or accept a compromise. In either case, Indian interests are often not adequately served. When an Indian claims a violation of his land or resource rights, interior and justice department lawyers must represent Indians against adversary interests in government agencies defended by lawyers from the same offices. Bureau of Indian Affairs officials often acquiesce to attorneys in other departments and fail to fulfill their trust responsibilities. Frequently the Bureau of Indian Affairs must rely on expert opinions concerning land and resource issues that come from those departments that challenge Indian rights. As a result Indian interests are often ignored or eroded. Powerful special-interest groups such as lumbermen, oil and gas companies, state and city governments, ranchers, farmers, mining companies, hydroelectric corporations, and powerful western private spokesmen add to the conflict within the federal government over the use of Indian land and its resources.

EROSION OF INDIAN LAND RIGHTS

Alaska

Before federal enactment of the Alaska Native Claims Settlement Act in 1971, the Bureau of Land Management was one of the leading adversaries of the Alaskan Natives' land interests. The bureau approved grants to recreation groups, nonnative homesteaders, the federal government for forest reserves, and the state for selection of lands allowed under the Alaska Statehood Act. Such disposal of the public domain, which included lands used and occupied by Alaska Natives, required sufficient notice to all concerned so they would have the opportunity to protest the action. Frequently the bureau provided inadequate notice to native inhabitants, which prevented them from rendering necessary remonstrations. The only announcement given to Alaska Natives consisted of an advertisement in an Alaskan newspaper. For those living in remote villages with poor avenues of communication, this action provided little, if any, notification.[1]

The Bureau of Land Management continually failed to approve claims of residents of native villages for the land occupied and used by them. In the late 1960s almost fifty villages, mainly Eskimo, filed claims with the Bureau of Land Management for title to land they occupied and used. This action blocked the state selection of lands. Even though the Alaska Natives had the support of Bureau of Indian Affairs Area Director James Hawkins, the Bureau of Land Management refused to approve the applications. Other native villages, including Tanacross, persistently filed claims for the lands they used but the Bureau rejected them. In the early 1960s the Bureau granted title to the state for 63,533 acres of village lands. Even while the Tanacross were asserting their land rights the state attempted to sell town sites, and the Bureau of Land Management promoted the sale of "wilderness estates" at the New York World's Fair. Exposure of these plans and of the unclear title by the *Tundra Times,* a newspaper published in Fairbanks, Alaska, temporarily ended these efforts.[2]

Federal Power Project Legislation

The development of water-source projects by the Bureau of Reclamation, the Army Corps of Engineers, and licensees of the Federal Power Commission during the twentieth century has reduced the Indian land base. Constructed for flood control, irrigation, recreation, and hydroelectric-power production, these projects generally have provided few, if any, benefits to Indians. Instead they resulted in the loss of Indian land and water rights and the depletion of water resources for tribal use. In some cases entire reservations, tribal economies, and tribal life have been virtually destroyed. For the construction of hydroelectric projects, licensees of the Federal

Power Commission have acquired Indian land by condemnation, purchase, long-term leases, and perpetual easements. Authority for this acquisition was provided in the Federal Water Power Act of 1920 and in its successor, the Federal Power Act of 1935. Under section 4(e), the commission had to render a finding that the license would not "interfere or be inconsistent with the purpose for which such reservation was created or acquired" before reservation land could be included in a project. The secretary of the interior was also authorized to include provisions in the license for "the adequate protection and utilization" of the reservation.[3]

Lac Courte Oreilles and the Northern States Power Company

Before the enactment of the Federal Water Power Act, the Wisconsin-Minnesota Light and Power Company attempted to acquire land from the Lac Courte Oreilles band of Chippewa for a hydroelectric-power project. In 1916 Congress authorized the company to purchase or lease land from the northwestern Wisconsin tribe if the company could obtain tribal consent. The Lac Courte Oreilles rejected all of the company's proposals. In 1920 the right of consent was effectively taken away from the tribe when Congress passed the Federal Water Power Act.[4]

The following year the newly created Federal Power Commission granted a license to the Wisconsin-Minnesota Light and Power Company, later a part of Northern States Power Company, to build a dam and reservoir to regulate the flow of the Chippewa River for downstream hydroelectric plants. Ignoring tribal opposition the commission approved a fifty-year lease of 315 acres of tribal land that was later amended to 525.5 acres. Northern States also acquired through purchase or condemnation 5,500 acres of allotted fee lands and flowage easements to 1,745 acres. It purchased the Indian land for extremely small sums. According to the Chippewas, real estate agents sometimes used fraudulent methods to buy the land and later sold it to the power company. Northern States flooded the land, inundating Indian towns, graves, timber, and hunting grounds and ruining wild rice production.[5]

In 1970, a year before the license expired, Northern States applied for a new license. The tribe, the Department of the Interior, and the Department of Agriculture opposed the renewal, advocating instead federal takeover of the project. If the latter occurred, the 5,500 acres of formerly allotted lands acquired by Northern States would be returned to tribal ownership. The remaining project lands would be managed by the U.S. Forest Service. The Lac Courte Oreilles argued that the Federal Power Commission could not approve the license, since the commission would be unable to make the necessary section 4(e) finding. The tribe also maintained that tribal consent was required before the license could be granted. Unpersuaded by the tribe's arguments, the Federal Power Commission issued an annual license to Northern States. The Lac Courte Oreilles appealed to the U.S. Court of Appeals for the District of Columbia Circuit. The court, however, affirmed the commission's ruling.[6]

The commission deferred making a decision whether to reissue a long-term license, pending the outcome of its federal recapture proceedings. In 1977 the commission decided that continued operation of the project by Northern States Power would be more in the public interest than its operation under the proposed federal takeover plan. The commission also ruled that the license would not interfere or be inconsistent with the purpose of the reservation and that tribal consent to the license was not required. The Lac Courte Oreilles and the Interior and Agriculture departments took exception to the commission's decision to issue a thirty-year license to Northern States. Subsequently the commission referred the case to a settlement judge for a final resolution. After several years of negotiation, the parties reached an agreement in 1984. Northern States would pay the tribe $250,000 and return 4,500 acres of project lands to tribal ownership. For their part, the Lac Courte Oreilles would convey perpetual flowage easements to the 525.5 acres of tribal land included in the project. The settlement also exempted the project from future licensing requirements by the commission.[7]

The Tuscarora Case

In the 1950s the Tuscaroras in New York had a portion of their lands acquired by a licensee of the Federal Power Commission. The New York Power Authority attempted to purchase 1,300 acres of tribal fee land for the construction of a storage reservoir for a hydroelectric-power project. The tribe refused to sell its land and fought the inclusion of the land in the project by appealing to the Federal Power Commission and the federal courts. In 1960 the case reached the U.S. Supreme Court. The Tuscaroras argued that their land could not be alienated without the consent of Congress, nor could it be acquired under the provisions of the Federal Power Act. To issue a license authorizing the taking of tribal land embraced within a reservation, the Federal Power Commission had to make a finding "that the license will not interfere or be inconsistent with the purpose for which such reservation was created or acquired." The Supreme Court, however, declared that a reservation as defined by the Federal Power Act included only those tribal lands that the federal government held in trust or had a property interest in. Therefore the Court held that this provision, which protected most tribal land, did not apply to the Tuscaroras because they owned their land in fee simple. The Court ruled that a licensee of the

Federal Power Commission could exercise federal eminent domain powers and condemn tribal land owned in fee. The power authority eventually condemned 553 acres of Tuscarora land.[8]

Reclamation Projects

Many Indians and their white supporters consider the Bureau of Reclamation the Indians' worst enemy. Since the early twentieth century Congress has passed numerous laws providing for reclamation projects on reservations, causing much land to pass from native ownership. One of the earlier statutes in 1904 directed homestead entry on the Yuma and Colorado River Indian Reservation in California and Arizona. Each tribesman received an allotment of 5 irrigable acres, whereas each non-Indian settler could obtain 160 acres of former reservation land. In 1911 the government increased the Indian's allotment to 10 acres. Besides receiving insufficient land these Indians also lost most of their reservation. The Reclamation Act also effectively denied vital water rights to the tribes on these reservations. Both the Quechans on the Yuma Reservation and the Pyramid Lake Indians suffered economically from reclamation projects, and they have fought persistently to recover their territories. The federal government also opened the Flathead Indian Reservation of Montana to non-Indians through a reclamation project; the results proved devastating.[9]

The Seneca and Kinzua Dam

The Army Corps of Engineers and the Bureau of Reclamation have used federal powers of eminent domain to condemn Indian land for the construction of dozens of dams and reservoirs. In 1964 the corps finished building Kinzua Dam in Pennsylvania. The agency took 10,000 acres of the Seneca Indians' Allegany reservation in New York and the Cornplanter reserve in Pennsylvania. After the condemnation, only 2,300 acres of habitable land remained on the reservation, and over one-third of its population had to relocate. The tribe bitterly opposed the condemnation. A tribal member expressed the reason for the Indians' attachment to their homeland when he stated that land "is a spiritual as well as a sustaining resource." The Seneca proposed an alternative site that was less costly and more convenient yet left their land free from condemnation. The powerful Army Corps of Engineers refused to consider the Seneca plan.[10]

This action by a federal agency violated a 1794 treaty in which the United States promised that it would never take or claim Seneca land. Although Congress has the power to abrogate or modify a treaty, the issue often has been, as it was in the Seneca case, whether Congress had clearly expressed this intention. The U.S. Court of Appeals for the District of

Columbia, in denying the tribe's request for an injunction against construction of the Kinzua Dam, found congressional authorization in the legislation establishing the Ohio River project and in its legislative history. The documentation cited by the court seemed insubstantial to support such a far-reaching decision. However, most courts have found that Congress passed similar legislation knowing that Indian land would be condemned and that this action would violate a treaty.[11]

The Missouri River Basin Projects

More Indian land was appropriated for water-development projects in the Missouri River Basin than in any other region of the United States. The Pick-Sloan Plan, authorized by Congress in 1944, was designed to provide flood control, hydroelectric power, irrigation, recreation, and navigation. Jointly developed by the Army Corps of Engineers and the Bureau of Reclamation, this public-work project affected twenty-three reservations. In South Dakota and North Dakota alone, over 352,000 acres of Indian land were destroyed. The corps concentrated on the construction of main-stem dams on the Missouri River and flood-control projects on its tributaries; the bureau focused its attention on irrigation projects and smaller dams on tributaries. From 1946 to 1966 the Army Corps of Engineers built five major dams: Gavins Point, Garrison, Fort Randall, Oahe, and Big Bend.[12]

The latter four dams seriously affected the Three Affiliated Tribes of Fort Berthold Reservation and five Sioux tribes—the Crow Creek, Lower Brulé, Yankton, Standing Rock, and Cheyenne River. These Sioux tribes lost over 202,000 acres, or approximately 6 percent of their land base, and one-third of their population had to relocate. The Oahe Dam inundated more total Indian land than any other single project; it flooded 160,887 acres of the Cheyenne River and Standing Rock reservations. Because of poor long-range planning by the Army Corps of Engineers some of the Crow Creek Sioux were forced to move twice, first for Fort Randall Dam and the second time for the construction of Big Bend Dam. These statistics only suggest the destructive impact of the water-development projects on the Sioux tribes. The flooding of their rich bottomlands destroyed most of their valuable farm and grazing lands, most of the timberland, and 75 percent of the wild game and plants. The destruction of the environment they depended on for subsistence and the unavailability of comparable lands to move to forced the Sioux to transform their way of life.[13]

Although the Pick-Sloan projects adversely affected the five Sioux tribes, the single group most devastated was the Three Affiliated Tribes of Fort Berthold Reservation. In 1953 the Army Corps of Engineers completed its construction of Garrison Dam. After six years of protest and the presentation of several alternative plans by the Three Affiliated Tribes, approximately 80 percent of the reservation population had to relocate. Subsequently the corps flooded 152,360 acres, one-fourth of the reservation including the fertile bottomlands that comprised the basis of the tribes' economy. The inundation of 94 percent of their agricultural lands destroyed their long-successful farming and ranching operations. Other crucial effects resulted from the construction of Garrison Dam, which divided the reservation into five separate waterbound sections, thereby complicating the existing checkerboard pattern of tribal lands. The community and kinship groups were scattered, since the corps removed and relocated the Indian residents by alphabetical order. Garrison Dam almost caused the complete destruction of the Three Affiliated Tribes.[14]

The Bureau of Reclamation acquired tribal land in Wyoming, Montana, and North Dakota for its Pick-Sloan projects on tributaries of the Missouri River. Some of these tribes included the Shoshones and Arapahoes on Wind River Reservation, the Sioux and Assiniboines on Fort Peck Reservation, the Blackfeet, the Crow, and the Turtle Mountain Chippewa. The Reclamation bureau condemned 6,846 acres of Crow lands for the construction of Yellowtail Dam in Montana.[15]

Pacific Northwest

Tribes in Washington also lost some of their lands to dam construction. The Bureau of Reclamation took a portion of the Confederated Colville's lands for Grand Coulee Dam. The Wanapum Indians also had lands flooded by the construction of Priest Rapid Dam on the Columbia River. The inundation of other Indian lands along the Columbia River resulted when the Army Corps of Engineers built Dalles Dam.[16]

Dams Affecting the Tohono O'odham Nation

Federal agencies have also taken tribal land in the Southwest for water-development projects. Some tribes such as the Tohono O'odham, formerly known as the Papago, have lost land several times for the construction of dams. A portion of this tribe's land was acquired by the Army Corps of Engineers to build Painted Rock and Tat Momolikot dams. The former project resulted in the nearly complete economic destruction of the Gila Bend Reservation.

Established in 1882, Gila Bend reserve comprised the San Lucy political subdivision of the Tohono O'odham Nation and was one of the tribe's three reservations in Arizona. Originally consisting of 22,400 acres, Gila Bend's total land base was reduced in 1909 to less than one-half of its former land area.[17]

During the second half of the twentieth century, the Gila Bend Reserva-

tion again faced federal attempts to reduce its size. In 1949 the Army
Corps of Engineers recommended the construction of Painted Rock Dam
on the Gila River at a site ten miles downstream from the reservation. The
agency's report to Congress did not mention any impact on Papago lands.
The following year Congress authorized the corps to build the flood-control project. Throughout the 1950s the agency attempted to obtain reservation lands. First it tried to purchase 7,700 acres from the tribe; then it
offered to buy perpetual easements to the land; lastly it suggested an
exchange of the reservation for public lands of equal value. The Bureau of
Indian Affairs also offered to sell the reservation. The tribe rejected all of
the proposals. Nevertheless, the Army Corps of Engineers completed the
construction of the dam in 1960. The following year the agency filed an
eminent domain suit in federal district court to secure perpetual flowage
easements to over 7,700 acres that constituted 75 percent of the reservation and all of its arable lands. In 1964 the court granted the request and
the Army Corps of Engineers paid $130,000 in just compensation for the
taking. The easements gave the corps the right to occasionally flood, sub-
merge, and overflow that portion of the Gila Bend Reservation and to prohibit human habitation within the reservoir area. After a 40-acre tract was
purchased and new houses and a community building were built on it, the
people residing in the reservoir were relocated to the new village of Lucy
located one and one-half miles outside the southern boundary of the reservation.[18]

The Tohono O'odham were assured by Bureau of Indian Affairs and
Army Corps of Engineers officials that flooding would be infrequent and
would not unduly interfere with the tribe's agricultural use of the Gila
Bend Reservation. However, major flooding occurred in 1978–1979, and
again in 1981, 1983, and 1984. The consequences were devastating. The
successive floods deposited silt and saltcedar seeds throughout the reservoir, and the saltcedar seeds produced dense thickets covering a large portion of the reservation. The cumulative effect was the destruction of the
unpaved road system, thus restricting access to the reservation's grazing
lands. Also, the agricultural lands could not be farmed unless the thickets
were removed and the soil leveled. In 1983 the Bureau of Indian Affairs
estimated that rehabilitation would cost $5 million. Restoration expenses
were prohibitive and the expenditure questionable, especially given the
continued risk of flooding. The construction and operation of Painted
Rock Dam had destroyed the economic viability of the Gila Bend Reservation.[19]

Since 1981 the Tohono O'odham Nation and Congress have moved
toward replacing the Gila Bend Reservation with a new reservation. Acting
in response to tribal requests, Congress in 1982 authorized the secretary of
the interior to conduct a study to determine how much reservation land

had been made unsuitable for agriculture by the operation of Painted Rock Dam and to exchange those lands for an equivalent acreage of agricultural lands within the public domain. The study mandated by Congress was completed the following year and it revealed that the reservation had been rendered useless for agriculture and grazing purposes. The secretary then contracted with the tribe to examine the public domain lands for replacement agricultural lands. Unable to find any suitable lands within a 100-mile radius, the Tohono O'odham petitioned Congress for a new settlement.[20]

In 1986 Congress enacted the Gila Bend Indian Reservation Lands Replacement Act, which authorized the payment of $30 million in three equal annual payments to the tribe for its assignment to the United States of all its title, rights, and interests in 9,880 acres of the Gila Bend Reservation. The tribe retained 417 acres of reservation land near the village of Lucy. With the settlement funds, the tribe could purchase up to 9,880 acres of privately owned land, buy water rights, pay relocation expenses, or use the money for community and economic development. The acquired land would be held in trust for the tribe if the land consisted of no more than three adjacent tracts, one of which had to be contiguous to Lucy village. The land also had to be located in at least one of three specified counties, and it had to lie outside any town or city limits. The tribe was prohibited from ever asserting any reserved-water-rights claims to the acquired lands.[21]

The legislation also required a tribal waiver of all reserved-water-rights and land-injury claims "from time immemorial" with respect to the Gila Bend Reservation. The Tohono O'odham had suggested the $30 million settlement figure, basing it on the estimated value of the reservation's unquantified reserved water rights. The Department of the Interior opposed the legislation because it questioned the legitimacy of any water or land claims the tribe might have against the United States. Arguing against passage of the settlement, the Army Corps of Engineers maintained that the Tohono O'odham had already been compensated for any damages arising from the construction of Painted Rock Dam and for the flowage easements. The House of Representatives committee in its report on the bill noted that these agencies had been so concerned with the legal claims that they had neglected to consider "the broader responsibility of the United States as trustee, to take action to resolve the tribe's immediate problem of an utterly uneconomic land base."[22]

The construction of Tat Momolikot Dam on the Sells Papago Reservation by the Army Corps of Engineers further reduced the landholdings of the Tohono O'odham Nation. In 1962 the tribe agreed to provide appropriate rights to tribal land needed for the dam and reservoir on condition that the federal government provide certain benefits to the tribe, including the construction of the Vaiva Vo irrigation project. Three years later, Congress authorized the joint proposal of the Army Corps of Engineers and the Bureau of Indian Affairs to provide flood control, water conservation, irrigation, and other area redevelopment benefits. In 1974 the corps completed construction of the dam and reservoir, but the Bureau of Indian Affairs had built less than half of the irrigation project. The O'odham refused to agree to demands by the corps to donate 5,324 acres for the dam and reservoir until the Bureau of Indian Affairs completed the irrigation project and other promised redevelopment projects. However, the tribe offered to conclude the transaction for flowage easements to over 9,000 acres of tribal land and to accept compensation for property losses incurred by the relocated residents of the village of Tat Momoli. But the corps refused to pay for the flowage easements or the property losses until the O'odham conveyed their rights and interests to the other 5,324 acres. Neither the agency nor the tribe would compromise and the stalemate lasted until 1986.[23]

In the meantime the O'odham had to end their farming operation in the Vaiva Vo area, in large part due to a depletion of ground-water resources and a lack of irrigation water. The tribe sought a legislative solution that included the completion of the irrigation project and repair of the section already built. Opposed to the pending bill, the secretaries of the interior and army recommended that Congress legally scrap the irrigation project, purchase the tribal interest in the dam and reservoir lands, and pay for the flowage easements and property losses to the former residents of Tat Momoli village. The tribe agreed to accept a cash settlement if Congress added compensation for the loss of the irrigation project and other benefits. In 1986 Congress approved the tribal compromise. The $6-million settlement, however, was less than the amount the tribe had requested.[24]

The Orme Dam and the Fort McDowell Reservation

Another recent case involved the attempt to appropriate Indian land by the Bureau of Reclamation in the 1970s and 1980s. Construction of Orme Dam for the Central Arizona Project would have inundated most of Fort McDowell Indian Reservation, located near Phoenix. Federal and state wildlife agencies and several conservation and environmental groups joined the Yavapai tribe in opposing the dam project. An Arizona Bureau of Mines report revealed that several geological faults ran through the Orme Dam site. Refusing to succumb to the Bureau of Reclamation's threat to condemn the Yavapai lands, tribal members voted to reject the federal offer of over $31 million for the Verde River bottomlands. This left the Reclamation Bureau with only two alternatives—to force condemnation or to select another site. In 1977 President Jimmy Carter, as part of his plan to balance the federal budget, removed the immediate threat by eliminating economically and environmentally unsound water programs, including Orme Dam, from the list of federally funded water-resource projects. In the early 1980s the Arizona congressional delegation and Arizona water officials tried to reactivate the Orme Dam project.[25]

In July 1981 Arizona water officials submitted a water-control study favoring Orme Dam to the Interior Department, then headed by Secretary James Watt of the Reagan administration. This study, funded by the Arizona Public Service Company, suggested that previous federal surveys had incorrectly estimated construction costs by overestimating the maximum amount of runoff that could drain into the Salt and Verde rivers. The new calculations increased the feasibility of the proposed dam.[26]

Public opposition quickly arose from environmental groups and the Yavapai Indian community. Environmentalists maintained that the area to be inundated was a nesting site for bald eagles. The Yavapais, who earlier had suffered a loss of federal farm aid due to the possible inundation of their bottomlands, marched thirty miles to the state capital in their own version of the "Trail of Tears." A report released by the federally directed Arizona Water Control Study stated that relocation of the Yavapais would cause severe hardship and destroy their culture, despite monetary compensation and removal to land near the reservation. Responding to the public outcry, federal and state water authorities in late 1981 opted for a less controversial site. However, the possibilitiy of the Orme Dam project continued to threaten the Fort McDowell Reservation. As late as 1986, Arizona state legislators unsuccessfully tried to obtain approval of the dam by including it in state appropriations for the Central Arizona Project.[27]

THE EROSION OF INDIAN WATER RIGHTS

The limited quality of water in the western states poses the same problem as the diminishing land for Indians. The loss of water rights threatens many western tribes and endangers their water for fish production, irrigation, and household use, all of which are required for a viable level of tribal subsistence and well-being. Although these threats have existed throughout the twentieth century, the increased growth of western states' population and their needs for drinking water, irrigation, hydroelectric power, and other requirements for a growing industrial and corporate society have increased the conflict over the Indians' rights to water resources. Since water has increasingly assumed importance to both groups for economic exploitation and survival, the issue will continue to be volatile in the arid western states. In some cases the requirements and rights of reservation Indians already have been circumvented to the requirements of non-Indians. But the unified and nationalistic stance of many Indians in recent years may yet help protect the water and other resource rights of the tribes.

General Background

The U.S. Supreme Court first enunciated water-rights doctrine for Indian reservations in *Winters v. United States* in 1908. Since then the *Winters* doctrine has been accepted in the courts. Later the Court reaffirmed and elaborated on certain aspects of the reserved-water-rights doctrine in *Arizona v. California* and *United States v. Cappaert*. In *Winters v. United States* the federal government brought litigation on behalf of the Fort Belknap tribe of Montana against Winters and other settlers. The plaintiffs attempted to enjoin Winters from diverting water from the Milk River above Fort Belknap Reservation. In its opinion the Supreme Court presented the idea of implied reservation of water. The Court decided that when Congress established reservations, it intended to provide a homeland so the Indians could transform from a nomadic and uncivilized life to a civilized and pastoral one. Without water the Indians could not survive on arid and valueless lands, and the purpose of the reservation would be defeated. The Court therefore held that Congress in creating the reservation by treaty guaranteed the Indians a necessary amount of water.[28]

The *Arizona v. California* decision added that the volume of water rights retained by the tribes could be determined by the necessary quantum required to meet not only present needs but also future requirements. The quantity should be calculated by the practicably irrigable acreage of the reservation. The Court declared that reserved water rights pertained to executive-order reservations as well as reserves created by treaties. *Arizona v. California* also affirmed the doctrine that Congress intended to reserve water for the tribes. Indian water rights have a priority date effective at the creation of the reservation.[29]

Apparently reserved water rights include not only surface water but also groundwater. The Supreme Court in *Cappaert v. United States,* a case involving federal rights to water on federally owned land, determined that the implied reserved-water doctrine applied to both sources of water. Although there are some differences between federal and Indian reserved rights, it is logical that the *Cappaert* determination would apply in the latter case. Several lower federal courts have defined Indian water rights to include both ground and surface water.[30]

Historically the tribes have competed with non-Indians both on and off the reservation for water, especially when the tribal water rights have not been quantified. Compounding the uncertainty of the exact quantity of reserved water rights has been the question of how much water, if any, Indian allottees and their non-Indian successors in interest were entitled to appropriate. Although the U.S. Supreme Court in a 1939 decision, *United States v. Powers,* declared that they had some water rights, it did not determine the exact degree or nature. The Court has not subsequently resolved the issue.[31]

Some lower federal courts, however, have elaborated on the water rights possessed by Indian allottees and non-Indian successors. The Court of Appeals for the Ninth Circuit in *Colville Confederated Tribes v. Walton* specified the nature of those rights. An allottee had a pro rata share of the reservation's reserved water rights. This quantity set the upper limit on the amount of water that a non-Indian successor was entitled to appropriate. The non-Indian owner secured rights to the quantity of water used by the Indian allottee at the time of conveyance of the acreage plus the amount he subsequently appropriated with reasonable diligence. The original purchaser and his successors lost rights to water not continually put to a beneficial use. The priority date of the water rights for both allottees and non-Indian owners was that of the creation of the reservation.[32]

Eighty years after the Supreme Court first enunciated the reserved-water-rights doctrine, the scope still has not been clearly defined. A number of issues remain unresolved, including whether tribes are entitled to a certain quality of water, to a minimum stream level, to sell or lease their reserved water rights, and to have reserved rights for purposes other than agricultural development.

State Jurisdiction over Indian Water Rights

Since the mid-1970s the extension of state jurisdiction over the adjudication of Indian reserved water rights has been an important issue facing tribes. In 1976 the Supreme Court in *Colorado River Water Conservation District v. United States* reversed its traditional policy on Indian water rights by removing them from the exclusive jurisdiction of the federal courts.[33]

The Supreme Court based its opinion on the McCarren amendment and the necessity for judicial economy. The McCarren amendment, enacted by Congress in 1952, allowed the United States to be joined as a defendant in state court general-stream adjudications. Although neither the amendment nor its legislative history mentioned Indian water rights, the Court interpreted the McCarren amendment as giving state courts concurrent jurisdiction over not only federal reserved water rights but also over Indian water claims. The Court reasoned that Congress had intended to have all water claimants present in the state adjudication. The United States would represent its own claims as well as those of the tribes, acting as their trustee.[34]

To avoid what it considered piecemeal litigation, the Court approved the dismissal of water-rights cases filed in federal courts by the United States in deference to concurrent proceedings in state courts. The Court, however, did not rule that all federal cases had to be dismissed. It was left to the lower federal courts to determine on a case-by-case basis whether the facts warranted federal dismissal in favor of a state court adjudication. The Court declined to decide whether the same policy of deference should be applied to suits brought by tribes on their own behalf.[35]

The *Colorado River* decision caused intense apprehension for many Indians who considerd state courts as a forum consistently hostile to Indians. Believing that state judges as elected officials were responsive to the desires of their white constituency, Indians feared that their guaranteed rights would be jeopardized. Consequently several tribes filed suits in federal court to adjudicate their water rights.

In 1983 the Supreme Court in *Arizona v. San Carlos Apache Tribe* declared that the *Colorado River* doctrine applied to federal suits filed by tribes even when the suits involved only Indian claims to the use of water in a stream system. State courts were the preferred forum for all water-rights litigation. The Court also ruled that the McCarran amendment had removed any barriers to state jurisdiction contained in clauses in state enabling acts that disclaimed state jurisdiction over reservations.[36]

Subsequent to the decision, the lower federal courts have not dismissed all Indian water-rights litigation. Occasionally the courts have determined that a particular issue warranted federal court jurisdiction. In *United States v. Adair* the Court of Appeals for the Ninth Circuit held that the federal district court was the proper forum to determine whether Indian water rights survived the termination of the Klamath Reservation in Oregon. An important factor in the court's decision was that wise judicial administration required the district court to exercise its jurisdiction. The court reasoned that *San Carlos Apache* did not require federal courts to abstain from deciding all Indian water-rights cases and that the Supreme Court had recognized that occasionally prudent judicial administration would favor federal court adjudications.[37]

Although violations occurred throughout the twentieth century, the conflict over water rights reached new levels in the 1970s. More government preference to the needs of industry and municipalities led to an erosion of Indian water rights. The tribes have objected increasingly and demanded compliance with their reserved rights.

The Mission Tribes from Pala, Pauma, La Jolla, Rincon, and San Pasqual

In California several tribes once possessed fertile lands that yielded abundant crops, but the construction of a canal diverting the water supply from the Indian reservations to the cities and agribusinesses destroyed the tribes' prosperity. The Mission Bands from Pala, Pauma, La Jolla, Rincon, and

San Pasqual reservations in southern California had sufficient water sources until the Department of the Interior allowed two water companies to divert water from the San Luis Rey watershed to water the citrus and avocado groves and to provide water for Escondido and Vista. Between 1894 and 1924 the secretary of the interior, on behalf of the bands, entered into a series of contracts and permits with the private companies giving them rights-of-way for a canal across La Jolla, Rincon, and San Pasqual reservations; a hydroelectric plant on Rincon; and associated power-transmission lines and roads. The bands did not receive any compensation for these rights-of-way. In 1924 the Federal Power Commission granted a fifty-year license for the project, which included the Escondido canal, a storage reservoir, and two power plants. The secretary of the interior neglected to include in the license any provisions protecting the reservations. Since 1922 the project has diverted 90 percent of the water from the San Luis Rey River to non-Indian communities.[38]

The five bands have been engaged in litigation for almost two decades to regain their water rights. In 1969 they filed suit against the U.S. government, Escondido Mutual Water Company, and Vista Irrigation District, petitioning the federal district court to void all the contracts and permits, to adjudicate their *Winters* rights, and to recover monetary damages from Escondido and Vista. Later the Department of the Interior joined the lawsuit on behalf of the Indians. In the mid-1980s the court case was postponed indefinitely while the bands, the project licensees, and federal officials negotiated a settlement.[39]

In 1985 the three groups agreed to a settlement that required congressional approval. The bands would give up their *Winters* water rights but would receive 50 percent of the water from the San Luis Rey system and 22,700 acre-feet of water imported annually from the Bureau of Reclamation's Central Valley Project (CVP). Any water not used by the bands would be sold to the local water-use agencies. The agreement also provided for a division of costs associated with the production, delivery, and storage of the water. The proposed legislation has encountered opposition from CVP water-use agencies and California congressmen from the districts using CVP water. Supporters of the plan argued that the delivery of CVP water to the bands would fulfill for the first time one of the project's original purposes. Although Congress in its 1937 authorization stated that the purpose of the CVP was to assist the reclamation of lands including Indian reservations, CVP water has never been distributed to Indian reservations. Several bills incorporating the settlement plan have been introduced in Congress but have not been approved by both the House and Senate.[40]

The legal battle also took place before the Federal Power Commission and the Federal Energy Regulatory Commission. After the city of Escondido and the Escondido Mutual Water Company applied for a new license in 1971, the secretary of the interior requested that the commission recommend federal recapture of the project. Subsequently the bands applied for a nonpower license under the supervision of the Interior Department, effective on the expiration of the original license. In 1979 the commission declined to act upon these requests and instead issued a new thirty-year license to Escondido, Mutual, and the Vista Irrigation District. It also refused to include in the license the conditions that the secretary of the interior considered necessary for the adequate protection of the reservations and their water resources. The commission further ruled that the secretary's protective authority only extended to those reservations on which project facilities physically existed, and not to other reservations that were impacted by them. The bands' and secretary's arguments that tribal consent for the project was required by certain statutes, including the 1891 act establishing the reservations, were also rejected. Subsequently the U.S. Supreme Court affirmed the commission's rulings on the latter two issues. The Court, however, held that the commission did not have the authority to exclude or modify the conditions imposed on the license by the secretary of the interior and only the federal courts had jurisdiction to determine their validity. The case was remanded to the commission for further proceedings.[41]

The Soboba Tribe

The Soboba Indians in California also lost their water source to the residents of southern California. In the 1930s the Metropolitan Water District of Southern California constructed a tunnel through the San Jacinto Mountains to obtain water from the Bureau of Reclamation dams on the Colorado River. As a result the large underground water supply that fed the springs on Soboba lands flowed into the tunnel to southern California and cut off the water source for the Soboba Indians. The Bureau of Indian Affairs and the Department of the Interior continually failed to protect the water rights of this tribe. In 1976 the Indian Claims Commission decided in favor of the Soboba Indians and charged the federal government with neglecting its trustee responsibilities by not safeguarding the Indians' water rights.[42]

The Chemehuevi, Cocopah, Quechan, Colorado River, and Fort Mojave Tribes

In 1963 and 1964 the Supreme Court adjudicated the reserved water rights of five Indian reservations in California, Arizona, and Nevada. In *Arizona v. California* the Chemehuevi, Cocopah, Quechan (Fort Yuma), Colorado River, and Fort Mojave Indian tribes were allocated an annual diversion of

905,496 acre-feet of water from the Colorado River. The quantified water rights were based on the practicably irrigable acreage of the reservations. Included in the decree was a provision allowing the Court to modify the allocations upon a final determination of the boundaries of the Colorado River and Fort Mojave reservations. The adjudication resulted from Arizona's initiation of a lawsuit to determine the quantity of water each of the states of California, Arizona, Nevada, Utah, and New Mexico had legal right to use from the Colorado River. The United States, as trustee, represented the five tribes in the litigation.[43]

In the late 1970s these tribes petitioned to intervene in the ongoing case and to receive additional allocations. Initially the Department of the Interior opposed tribal intervention but later supported the tribes' intervention and request for a supplemental determination of their water rights. The Indians based their claims on the United States' failure to include all irrigable acres in the inventory presented to the Court for its 1964 decree. In addition to these omitted lands, the tribes argued that they were entitled to increased allocations for irrigable land subsequently determined to be within the reservations' boundaries. In 1983 the Supreme Court ruled that the tribes could intervene but refused to modify its earlier decree to include additional water rights for the omitted lands. Even though the tribes had not been parties to the original litigation, they were bound by the Court's determinations in the 1964 decree because their interests had been adequately represented by the United States. The Court agreed to allocate additional water for lands included within the reservations' boundaries by judicial action in the 1970s. It refused, however, to approve increased allocations for those lands that the secretary of the interior in the 1970s had unilaterally determined to be within the original boundaries of the reservations. The Supreme Court left the settlement of the boundary disputes to the lower federal courts, at least initially.[44]

Subsequently, the federal district court for Southern California in a lawsuit brought by the Metropolitan Water District of Southern California held that the secretary of the interior's *ex parte* determination of the Fort Mojave Reservation boundaries exceeded his authority and violated due process. The district court ruled that it would hold a *de novo* trial to decide the legal boundary. After the tribes appealed the decision, the Court of Appeals for the Ninth Circuit ordered the lower court to dismiss the case for lack of jurisdiction.[45]

The Rio Grande Basin and the San Juan–Chama Water Project

The Pueblos in New Mexico have suffered at the hands of state, local, and federal officials who ignore Indian water rights by planning diversion projects to supply urban and industrial needs. The Pueblos have attempted to protect their water rights in the Rio Grande Basin. Middle Rio Grande Conservancy District officials commented that ultimately the municipalities and industries will obtain the limited water supply, and irrigation will end. One water district official also noted that water will become so scarce that only the highest bidder will receive it. The Northern Pueblos of Tesuque, San Ildefonso, and Jemez already have experienced water shortages.[46]

The state brought suit against the Northern Pueblos of Nambe, Pojoaque, San Ildefonso, and Tesuque and other water users on the Tesuque and Nambe/Pojoaque stream system (a tributary of the Upper Rio Grande) to ascertain their water rights. A state official remarked that New Mexico took this action to limit Indian water rights rather than to protect them. The reason for the litigation rested with federal and state desire to determine the water distribution from the San Juan–Chama Project, which transported water across the Continental Divide from the Upper Colorado River Basin to the Rio Grande.[47]

Not content with their water rights being solely represented by the United States, the Pueblos sought to intervene in the stream adjudication. They also argued that the district court should apply federal law, rather than state law, in determining their water rights. The court ruled against the Pueblos on both issues. In 1976 the Tenth Circuit Court of Appeals reversed the lower court's opinion. The appeals court ruled that the Pueblos could intervene and that New Mexico's water laws of prior appropriation did not limit the Pueblos' water rights, since the federal government had never relinquished jurisdiction to the state. It further declared that the *Winters* doctrine did not technically apply to the Pueblos because they held fee simple title and had never received reservations. The Tenth Circuit court in *State of New Mexico v. Aamodt* remanded the quantification of the Pueblos' water rights to the district court and directed it to follow the standards of *Arizona v. California* and, if necessary, consider the effects of the laws of Spain and Mexico on the Indians and water use.[48]

Nine years later the district court determined the extent of the Nambe, Pojoaque, San Ildefonso, and Tesuque Pueblos' water rights. The court declared that the Pueblos had aboriginal water rights, modified by the laws of the United States, Spain, and Mexico. The Pueblos have a prior right to all of the surface water and groundwater of the stream system necessary for domestic and irrigation purposes. The priority applies only to those lands the Pueblos irrigated between 1846 and 1924, except for the acreage removed from Pueblo ownership by the 1924 Pueblo Lands Act. That legislation provided the cutoff date for measuring Pueblo water rights. *Winters* water rights exist only for the few Pueblo lands set aside by executive order or congressional action. The irrigable acreage standard of *California v. Arizona* applies to those reservations. Prior appropriation water law determines the priority rights of non-Indians.[49]

The San Juan–Chama Project limited water supplied to the Indian reservations located south of the San Juan River in northwestern New Mexico and endangered the water rights of the Jicarilla Apaches, Ute Mountain Utes, and Navajos. During the 1970s the three tribes were forced to have their water rights to the San Juan watershed adjudicated in the state courts of New Mexico. All water users of the river's stream system, including the United States as representative of its own interests and those of the three tribes, were joined as defendants. The United States and the Jicarilla Apaches were unsuccessful in their efforts to remove the proceeding to the federal courts. The Jicarilla Apaches also sought an injunction in federal district court against the secretary of the interior to prevent him from diverting water from the San Juan watershed to the San Juan–Chama project. The tribe charged that the diversion violated its water rights.[50]

The San Juan–Chama Project was planned in conjunction with a scheme to build an irrigation system on the eastern part of the Navajo reservation. To obtain the irrigation system the Navajos waived their *Winters* rights (estimated to be over 787,000 acre-feet annually) to water in the San Juan watershed, accepted a guaranteed annual delivery of 508,000 acre-feet, and agreed to share the water equally with other water users during years of water shortage. In 1962 the agreement was incorporated in the congressional legislation jointly authorizing the two projects. Eleven years later the Department of the Interior unilaterally decided that it would deliver only 370,000 acre-feet of water, since that amount would irrigate the same acreage planned for under the enabling legislation. The loss of Navajo water rights demonstrates the hazards of negotiating away reserved *Winters* rights and the Interior Department's lack of concern with preserving and protecting Indian water rights.[51]

Indian irrigation projects also have lower priority than do projects developed to serve non-Indian water users. This inequality is illustrated by the different rates of speed at which the two projects moved toward completion. The San Juan–Chama Project became operational in 1971, although water flowed at less than full capacity. Federal officials neglected the Navajo project and consequently the completion date drastically fell behind schedule. In 1976 the irrigation system commenced the first stage of operation.[52]

The Central Arizona Project

The Central Arizona Project, a massive plan for the development of water from the drainage system of the Lower Colorado River Basin, has affected the water rights of tribes in the basin. Although Arizona had attempted to obtain congressional authorization for the project since 1948, Congress refused to authorize it until 1968. The *Arizona v. California* decision in 1963 removed a major obstacle that had prevented Congress from approving the project. The U.S. Supreme Court allocated the water of the Lower Colorado River among Arizona, California, and Nevada. Finally Arizona had a legal right to sufficient water to develop its plan.

One component of the Central Arizona Project affected the Navajo tribe. The Bureau of Reclamation along with a group of electric utility companies constructed a generating station near Page, Arizona, next to Lake Powell. The Black Mesa coalfields on the Navajo reservation supply the coal for the plant, and the necessary water comes from the Colorado River watershed. The project required agreement by the Navajo tribe to limit its water rights under the *Winters* doctrine. The details of the negotiations revealed that officials from the Department of the Interior and the Bureau of Indian Affairs failed to stress the extent of the Navajos' historic water rights and instead emphasized the economic benefits the tribe would obtain from jobs and increased revenue. The latter seemed of utmost importance to tribal leaders. The water-resource information given them was derived from adversary interests such as the Bureau of Reclamation and the Colorado River Commission. Bureau of Reclamation agents had too much at stake both in this project and future plans for the Southwest for the secretary of the interior to fulfill his duties as trustee.[53]

The Central Arizona Project affected other tribes within Arizona, including the Gila River Pima-Maricopas, the Salt River Pima-Maricopas, the Papago, the Fort McDowell Yavapai, and the Ak-Chin Papagos-Pimas. These tribes argued that the secretary of the Interior's 1976 allocation of 257,000 acre-feet of Arizona project water was insufficient to meet their irrigation needs. Claiming a historic right to most of the water, they sought to enjoin further allocations of project water until the resolution of their water right claims.[54]

Water projects in central Arizona, including the Salt River Reclamation Project and Coolidge Dam and Reservoir, as well as groundwater pumping endangered the required water supply of tribes. The *Winters* doctrine, which stated that reservations had prior claim to water to meet their present and future needs, was basically ignored. When the Bureau of Reclamation constructed Coolidge Dam and Reservoir, the federal government promised that the Pima-Maricopas would receive additional water; instead the project diverted water from the Gila River and dried up the stream along the Pima reservation. For centuries the tribe had relied on the water from the Gila to irrigate its farm lands.[55] Since the mid-1970s central Arizona tribes have been engaged in litigation concerning their water rights in the Salt, Gila, Verde, and San Pedro rivers. Legal proceedings, first filed in 1979 in the state courts by Arizona officials to adjudicate the rights of water users in these four watersheds, have been adamantly opposed by the tribes and the United States. They preferred the federal courts to quantify their water rights; the case reached the U.S. Supreme Court in 1983. In

Arizona v. San Carlos Apache the Court declared that the state court was the proper forum. United States and tribal resistance to state jurisdiction over federal and Indian water rights continued after *San Carlos Apache;* however, the courts have ruled against them. The White Mountain Apaches have been particularly opposed to state adjudication of their water rights in the Gila River watershed and to United States representation of their interests. The tribe alleged that the United States, because of conflict of interests, will not present an accurate claim of its water rights. The White Mountain Apaches also attempted through tribal court action to prevent removal of legal documents from the reservation by Department of the Interior officials for use in the ongoing state adjudication.[56]

The Ak-Chin Reservation

Off-reservation pumping by non-Indians has depleted groundwater and surface-water supplies for the Ak-Chin and San Xavier Papago reservations and the Schuk Toak and Chuichu districts of the Sells Papago Reservation. Between 1942 and 1984 the water table beneath the Ak-Chin Reservation fell from 40 or 50 feet to 400 feet below the surface. By 1986 the Santa Cruz River no longer flowed through the Chuichu district except during severe flooding. The loss of water supplies forced the Ak-Chin and Papago communities, which were traditionally agricultural, to stop farming completely in the affected areas or to severely curtail farming. The drying up of domestic wells in the Chuichu district threatened the abandonment of three villages in 1986. Over the years the Department of the Interior quietly watched or even encouraged non-Indian irrigation, mining, municipal, and industrial water usage. At the same time, the agency neglected the requirements of Indian reservations and their reserved water rights. The severity of water-supply problems led the Papago and Ak-Chin communities to negotiate a settlement. Congress approved the Ak-Chin water-rights settlement in 1978 and its revision six years later. The negotiated settlement of the San Xavier and Schuk Toak Papagos' claims was enacted in 1982. The water-rights claims of the Chuichu district have not been resolved.[57]

The settlements shared several features. The tribes waived their claims to reserved water rights and for injuries to their water rights. In return they received promises for delivery of a permanent and guaranteed water supply to their reservations from the Central Arizona Project. Also, the tribes' use of the water was not limited to irrigation. The Papago settlement required the city of Tucson to provide an additional supply of reclaimed water to the San Xavier Reservation and the Schuk Toak district of the Sells Reservation and permitted the tribe to sell or lease excess water on a temporary basis.[58]

The Missouri River Basin Tribes

The Missouri River Basin presents another area where the combination of industrial interests, state desires for economic development, private interests, the Bureau of Reclamation, and the Army Corps of Engineers threatens the water rights of Indians residing on reservations in Wyoming, Montana, North and South Dakota, and Nebraska. The desire to use the water source from the Missouri River Basin by industries interested in exploiting the coal, taconite, and other mineral resources within these states and reservations for energy development affected twenty-six tribes including the Sioux, Cheyenne, and Crow. Starting in 1967 the Department of Reclamation sold water from the Yellowstone River Basin, a part of the Upper Missouri River watershed, to various industries. In Montana the federal agency issued industrial permits for water from the Tongue, Powder, and Big Horn rivers in excess of the actual water present in those streams. Selling water to the energy corporations endangered the Crow and Northern Cheyenne tribes in Montana and the Arapaho and Shoshone tribes of the Wind River Reservation in Wyoming. The marketing program did not take into account Indian reserved water rights and left little water available for future tribal development. The policy was extended to the mainstems of the Missouri River during the 1970s. Spurred on by the national energy crisis, the Bureau of Reclamation and the U.S. Army Corps of Engineers agreed to an interagency plan to market "surplus" water to energy corporations. Again tribal water rights were not protected.[59]

Comments made in the Bureau of Reclamation's environmental impact study on energy development within the Missouri River Basin revealed the attitude held toward the social impact on the tribes, especially those on the Fort Peck, Fort Berthold, Lower Brulé, and Crow Creek reservations. The report stated that energy development would materially affect the prosperity of the Indian communities, although it could also destroy Indian culture. The statement added that the effects would promote the assimilation of Indians into the greater American society. Officials in the Bureau of Reclamation advocated a policy and applied rhetoric similar to the promoters of the General Allotment Act and termination.[60]

The Department of the Interior, although divided on the tribes' water rights, persisted in its policy. Officials within the Bureau of Reclamation maintained that Indian water rights were limited to agricultural purposes, thereby freeing water for the use of the bureau's allies, the industrial corporations. Judicial decisions differ with this interpretation and uphold the superior rights of Indians to use the water for any beneficial use, including industrial as well as agricultural purposes. The stance of the Department of the Interior seemingly reflected its reluctance to fulfill trustee obligations in protecting Indian water rights. Some tribes asserted their right of tribal sovereignty and established tribal water codes. This action has caused some concern among officials of the Bureau of Reclamation, the Department of the Interior, and the coal industry. The Interior Department placed a moratorium on tribal water codes. Many tribal leaders believe that their rights will be protected only through their own efforts. Twenty-six tribes formed the Missouri River Basin Indian Tribal Rights Coalition with the objective of protecting and preserving their reserved water rights.[61]

Since the 1970s seven tribes in Montana have been involved in litigation to adjudicate their water rights. In 1975 the Northern Cheyenne initiated the extensive legal battle by filing a suit in federal district court to safeguard their rights to Tongue River and Rosebud Creek. Within the next four years the United States, acting in its trustee capacity, brought suit on behalf of the Northern Cheyenne and six other Montana tribes to determine their water rights in certain streams. The Crow tribe petitioned to intervene so that its own attorneys could represent its interests.[62]

After the initiation of legal proceedings by the Northern Cheyenne and the United States in 1975, the state of Montana filed for a general stream adjudication in its state courts. Intent on extending state jurisdiction over the settlement of all water claims including Indian water rights, the Montana legislature in 1979 passed Senate Bill 76, which established a comprehensive water-adjudication plan. Representative Jack Ramirez of Montana, a leading opponent of Indian reserved water rights, maintained that the "vague" *Winters* doctrine provided a "vehicle which could allow the Indians to take over every drop of water that flows through Montana Indian reservations." He advocated adjudication of Indian water rights by the state courts.[63]

Until 1985 the tribes and the United States fought to have the tribes' water rights determined by the federal courts. In that year they suffered a crucial defeat when the Montana Supreme Court ruled that the clause in the state constitution disclaiming jurisdiction over Indian lands did not disqualify it from adjudicating Indian water rights and that the Montana Water Use Act could adequately determine them. This decision resolved two issues left open by the U.S. Supreme Court in its 1983 consolidated opinion in *Arizona v. San Carlos Apache*. State courts could be foreclosed from adjudicating Indian water rights claims if state law prohibited it and if the state adjudication plan was inadequate. Even after the U.S. and Montana supreme courts had issued these decisive rulings, the Blackfeet tribe persisted in its opposition to state jurisdiction over Indian water rights. The Court of Appeals for the Ninth Circuit firmly reminded the tribe, as it had told the White Mountain Apaches, that the state had jurisdiction.[64]

Determination of the Montana tribes' water rights, except those of the Sioux and Assiniboine tribes of the Fort Peck Reservation, is still pending in the state court. The Fort Peck–Montana Compact of 1985, a negotiated agreement, settled the water claims for that reservation. The state legislature directed the state's Reserved Water Rights Compact Commission to make negotiation of Indian water rights a high priority.[65]

The Pacific Northwest Tribes

Non-Indian agricultural development in Washington has persistently eroded the Indians' reserved water rights. In 1908 non-Indian farmers obtained an agreement from the Bureau of Indian Affairs that authorized the diversion of Ahtanum Creek. The Yakima tribe lost 75 percent of the creek's natural flow, leaving only 25 percent for its use. After years of protest, the Supreme Court in 1964 ruled in the Indians' favor, but it allowed the 75-percent quota to stand with some limitations on the seasons it could be applied. Although the court upheld the *Winters* doctrine, state officials continued to issue water permits to non-Indians. This practice has led to the overappropriation of water on Indian reservations in the state. Washington officials often neglected to inform involved Indians that the state issued such licenses.[66]

During the 1970s and 1980s the Colville, Yakima, and Spokane tribes in Washington challenged state regulation of nonreserved water used by non-Indian owners of fee lands within the reservation. Nonreserved or excess water consisted of water not appropriated to the tribe based on its reserved water rights. The Colville Confederated Indians argued that Washington did not have jurisdiction to grant water permits in the No Name Creek hydrological system on the Colville Reservation. The Circuit Court of Appeals for the Ninth Circuit in *Colville Confederated Tribes v. Walton* agreed that the state could not regulate nonreserved water.[67]

The court held differently in *United States v. Anderson* when it considered the validity of state jurisdiction over use of excess water by non-Indians in the Chamokane Basin on the Spokane Reservation. A basic difference in the geography and hydrology of the two basins accounted for the contrary rulings. The Chamokane Creek, which originated north of the reservation, flowed south along the eastern boundary and past the southern reservation boundary into the Spokane River, whereas No Name Creek was a small, nonnavigable stream, located entirely within reservation boundaries. Non-Indian water users in the latter basin could destroy agricultural development on downstream Indian allotments and the tribal fishery. State regulation was therefore impermissible because it would endanger the existence of the tribe, whereas in *Anderson* the court decided that the tribe's political and economic integrity was not threatened by state control and that the state had greater interests at stake than the tribe did in regulating the surplus water. The court declared that the state could issue permits to excess water. It noted, however, that "if those permits represent rights that may be empty, so be it."[68]

In 1977 The Yakima Nation adopted a comprehensive tribal water code that regulated all water on or flowing through the reservation, including excess water used on fee land owned by non-Indians within the limits of the reservation. Nine years later a federal district court declared that the tribe did not have the inherent power to regulate the surplus waters. The court reasoned that the political and economic welfare of the tribe was not endangered by non-Indian conduct. Also critical to the decision was the absence of any agreement by the non-Indians to place themselves under the civil jurisdiction of the tribe. The court declined to decide whether the state or the federal government had regulatory authority. Future court decisions will probably make findings similar to those of the Yakima and Spokane cases.[69]

Both the *Walton* and *Anderson* cases determined that the Colville and Spokane tribes had reserved water rights to maintain tribal fisheries. The two decisions reflect a developing area of the *Winters* doctrine. The U.S. Supreme Court, however, has not determined whether reservations have *Winters* water rights for the purpose of maintaining tribal fisheries.[70]

The Pyramid Lake Paiutes

Until the 1970s the federal government did not claim reserved water rights; nor did it protect tribal fisheries from the often devastating effects of non-Indian development in the West. One notable instance where the Department of the Interior failed to fulfill its duty of federal supervision occurred among the Pyramid Lake Paiutes of western Nevada. The Newlands Project, a water diversion project carried out by the Bureau of Reclamation, diverted water from the Truckee River, the main water source for the Paiutes. As a result of the water diversion program Pyramid Lake, which provides the major economic resource for the tribe, decreased to one-third of its former size. This destroyed the ecological balance of the lake, and led to the death of most of its fish.[71]

In 1970 the Paiutes initiated litigation in the federal courts seeking to protect Pyramid Lake. They opposed regulations issued by the secretary of the interior that allowed the Truckee-Carson Irrigation District (TCID) to divert Truckee water in excess of the amount allocated by earlier court decrees. In 1972 the federal district court for Nevada, finding that the sec-retary had breached his fiduciary duty, ordered him to submit regulations that would protect the tribe's water rights in the Truckee River. Dissatis-fied with the secretary's proposed regulations, the court adopted modified versions of those submitted by the Pyramid Lake Paiute tribe. After the regulations were issued, the irrigation district refused to comply with them and diverted water in excess of its allocation. Subsequently the secretary of the interior terminated TCID's contract with the Department of Reclama-tion. In 1974 the irrigation district filed suit challenging the regulations, which now supported the Paiutes, and requesting reinstatement of the contract. Ten years later the U.S. Court of Appeals for the Ninth Circuit upheld the district court's ruling in favor of the secretary of the interior.[72]

Although the Paiutes won this phase of their battle to obtain more water for Pyramid Lake, they lost in their effort to secure *Winters* water rights for the Pyramid Lake fishery. In 1973 the Department of Justice finally filed suit on behalf of the tribe to establish its right to sufficient water from Truckee River to preserve the fishery. The Paiutes intervened in the litigation. The United States and the tribe argued that the 1944 *Orr Ditch* decree establishing the tribes' water rights to Truckee River should be invalidated because of strong conflict of interest with the federal government representing both the Paiutes and the Truckee-Carson Irrigation District. Federal officials, concerned with obtaining water rights for the reclamation project, had not claimed reserved water rights for the fishery. The U.S. Supreme Court in *Nevada v. United States* determined that the tribe's water rights had been adjudicated in *Orr Ditch* and could not be relitigated. Although the tribe had not participated in the *Orr Ditch* proceedings, it had been represented by the United States and was therefore bound to the government's decision not to claim fishery water rights. The 1944 decree prohibited any later claims by the litigating parties to water rights concerning the Truckee River and its tributaries.[73]

Significantly, the Court did not accept the conflict of interest argument asserted by the tribe and the United States. The Supreme Court stated that since Congress had given the secretary of the interior the responsibility to represent both the reclamation project and the Pyramid Lake Paiutes, he could not be held to the high standards of a private fiduciary in protecting tribal water rights. In *Nevada v. United States* and *Arizona v. California* in 1983, the tribes argued that their water allocations should be increased because the federal government's conflict of interest resulted in inadequate representation of their water rights. A strong desire on the part of the Court to have finality of judgment in cases affecting property rights in the West led the Court to rule against the tribes. Since 1983 several tribes have asserted a conflict of interest argument, but the lower federal courts have rejected it on the basis of *Nevada v. United States*.[74]

Since 1978 the federal government has encouraged a policy of negotiation among the Department of the Interior, tribes, states, and private interests in settling water claims. Both the Carter and Reagan administrations have supported negotiation, contending that it provides a less expensive, divisive, and time-consuming approach and would offer a more satisfactory settlement. Many Indians believe that a policy of negotiation will result in the surrender of their water rights, and they place it on the same disastrous level as the General Allotment Act. Some tribes have turned to negotiation either as a result of their fear of state court adjudications or because of pressing water needs that cannot await the lengthy judicial process. Many tribes, however, have continued to pursue litigation. In 1986 more than thirty-six Indian water-rights cases were pending in the courts.[75]

BUREAU OF INDIAN AFFAIRS LEASING POLICY AND EROSION OF INDIAN LAND RIGHTS

The secretary of the interior and the Bureau of Indian Affairs continually failed to uphold the federal government's trustee duties in the leasing and protection of Indian lands during the twentieth century. The Bureau of Indian Affairs frequently did not obtain the highest rates possible, ineffectually regulated leasing, and sometimes leased Indian land without permission. Lands were leased to oil and gas companies on the Shoshone and Arapaho portion of the Wind River Reservation in Wyoming and on Turtle Mountain Reservation in North Dakota without the Indians' permission. Some Osages in Oklahoma reported that bureau agents leased allotments without the owners' knowledge and that they received no money from the transactions. Among the Navajos the Bureau of Indian Affairs often failed to obtain fair market value on leases. At Fort Hall, Idaho, non-Indian lessees received a 90-percent reduction on their rates if they installed a well or irrigation system (these improvements usually proved to be of inferior quality). Some leases on the reservation lands provided Indians with less than 1 percent of the profit made by the lessees in their exploitation of the property. Some Indians charged the Bureau of Indian Affairs with not adequately supervising leasing, as in the case of a Comanche woman in Oklahoma. The agency leased her allotment to an unemployed high school student who had no collateral. Earlier his grandfather, an individual with a poor record for lease payments, unsuccessfully applied for a lease on the allotment. The youth did not make the payments on time, but the bureau extended the lease.[76]

A well-known example of private exploitation of Indian land promoted by a lack of sufficient supervision by the Bureau of Indian Affairs involved the Agua Caliente Indians of California. This tribe owned valuable lands in Palm Springs until the federal government allotted the lands among tribal members in 1959 (the lands retained their trust status). The Bureau of Indian Affairs transferred its trusteeship to the state courts, who then appointed guardians. Under a 1957 California law, the state courts possessed broad powers to assign conservators to landowners considered incapable of handling their affairs. Edmund Peter Silva, an Indian conservator, maintained that by 1961 "everybody was grabbing himself an Indian." The guardians and their attorneys pocketed large amounts of lease money, kickbacks, and high fees while the Indians received only small portions of their income. After years of allegations and protests by Indians, Department of the Interior agents investigated and revealed the validity of the charges. In 1968 Congress ended conservator management of Agua Caliente property. As indicated, opportunists used similar tactics to obtain powers of guardianship over incompetent Indian adults or minors during the early part of the twentieth century in Oklahoma. They, as well, exploited the leasing of the ward's land for their own economic benefit.[77]

Critics of the Bureau of Indian Affairs have disapproved of several leasing methods. They objected to Blank-Check leases in which the Indians signed leases without the particulars being specified. The lessee then filled in the details and Bureau of Indian Affairs agents enforced these leases. Opponents also criticized the "90-day authority," a process that involved leasing land without the owner's permission; after a lapse of 90 days the Bureau of Indian Affairs confirmed the lease. The Oto in Oklahoma claimed they had to honor leases approved by this method.[78]

The secretary of the interior must approve the early termination of a lease—unilateral action by a tribe is insufficient to cancel it. Critics have disapproved of the Bureau of Indian Affairs procedures for appeals concerning leases because they frequently worked to the Indian lessor's disadvantage. The lengthy appeal process often allowed a recalcitrant lessee free use of the land or additional time to exploit it. If the Bureau of Indian Affairs finally determined the lessee had failed to fulfill his part of the contract, it could abrogate the lease. The Indian lessor, however, generally lost income on the transaction.[79]

During the 1970s the Northern Cheyenne in Montana attempted to cancel all coal leases and permits on their reservation. Realizing the potential devastating impact of massive strip mining on tribal culture and the environment, the tribal council in 1973 passed a resolution to terminate the leases and permits and requested the secretary of the interior to act accordingly. Tribal officials argued that the agreements covering 56 percent of their land had been illegally approved by Bureau of Indian Affairs officials from 1966 to 1971. To support their claim, they presented a lengthy list of violations. These charges included extremely low royalty rates, excessively large acreages, and absence of environmental impact statements.[80]

Refusing to cancel the leases and permits outright, the secretary stated that the acreages in each lease must conform to the 2,560-acre limitation established by federal regulations unless the energy companies and the tribe jointly demonstrated that the limitation should be waived. Interior Secretary Rogers C. B. Morton also required conformance with the National Environmental Protection Act. In effect, Morton's action left matters at an impasse from 1974 to 1980. The Northern Cheyennes refused to agree to a waiver of the acreage limitation, and the energy company lessees and permit holders would not accept cancellation unless they received compensation. Hoping to avoid costly and time-consuming litigation, the Northern Cheyennes turned to Congress for a legislative solution. In 1980 Congress, recognizing that the secretary had probably failed to fulfill his trustee responsibilities, terminated the leases and permits. The legislation satisfied the energy companies by giving them certain economic rights to federal coal deposits and leases.[81]

The federal government's management of oil and gas resources on Indian and federal lands has resulted in a loss of millions of dollars in royalties. Energy companies underreported royalties due, failed to make payments, or made late payments without penalties being assessed. Theft of oil was reported on the Blackfeet, Wind River, and Navajo reservations, among others. Until the 1980s the conservation division of the U.S. Geological Survey supervised royalty accounts for oil and gas leases and relied almost exclusively on data supplied by oil and gas companies. The division's failure to conduct adequate on-site inspection of wells, to make frequent audits of lease accounts, to reconcile production and sale reports on the leases, and to maintain an adequate accounting system resulted in lost revenue to the lessors. Although critics had long pointed out the existence of these problems, several federal government studies in 1979 and 1982 documented the seriousness of the allegations.[82]

These investigations, coinciding with the increased assertiveness of tribes and the rising value of energy resources, persuaded Congress and the Department of the Interior to make certain changes in the management of oil and gas leases. In 1982 Congress passed the Federal Oil and Gas Royalty Management Act. One of its purposes was to fulfill the government's trust responsibility to tribes. The legislation included provisions for new reporting procedures, inspection, investigation, enforcement, and penalties. Tribes and states were authorized to participate in the supervision of oil and gas leases. The secretary of the interior abolished the conservation division in the U.S. Geological Survey and turned over responsibility for royalty management to the newly created Minerals Management Service. These reform measures did not bring a final solution, however, since theft of oil from Indian lands has been reported as recently as 1987.[83]

Some tribes have charged that the Department of the Interior has illegally delegated its trust reponsibility over Indian oil and gas resources to states. Since the early 1980s the Sioux and Assiniboine of Fort Peck Reservation have been involved in litigation opposing certain Interior Department policies in Montana. In 1982 the tribes won a federal court case in which the court ruled that the Department of the Interior, not the Montana Board of Oil and Gas Conservation, had jurisdiction over the placement and spacing of oil and gas wells on Indian trust lands. The Bureau of Land Management, who along with the Bureau of Indian Affairs oversees the actual leasing of oil and gas lands, entered into an agreement with the state board for the latter to review applications for drilling permits and exemption requests for wells on trust lands. The tribes charged that the Bureau of Land Management did not conduct independent reviews of the state board's decisions, merely rubber-stamping their decisions in mass. The Ninth Circuit Court of Appeals stated that if the tribes' allegations were true the secretary of the interior's delegation of his fiduciary responsibility would be unlawful. The court remanded the case to the district court to determine the validity of the tribes' charges.[84]

In the past decade tribes have played an increasingly active role in the management and exploitation of their mineral resources. Until 1982 tribes were usually restricted to lease agreements with an initial ten-year term that could be extended if there was production in paying quantities. Typically the Bureau of Indian Affairs and the mineral lessee established the terms, and the tribe passively approved the lease. The Indian Mineral Development Act of 1982 enabled tribes to use other economic approaches, such as joint ventures and production-sharing agreements, with no limitations on the type of agreement or on its terms. The initiative for the enterprise rested with the tribe and the mineral developer. The tribe could request assistance and advice from the secretary of the interior during the negotiation process,[85] but approval or disapproval of the agreement by the secretary had to be in accordance with procedures set out in the Indian Mineral Development Act. The legislation also listed several factors that the secretary should consider when making the decision: the best interests of the tribe or individual Indian who had mineral resources included in a tribal agreement; potential economic return to the tribe; potential environmental, social, and cultural effects on the tribe; and dispute-resolution provisions. Disapproval actions could be reviewed by the federal district courts. The legislation did not affect the federal government's trust obligations to tribes and individual Indians.[86]

Beginning in the late 1950s Congress permitted certain tribes, subject to approval by the secretary of the interior, to enter into ninety-nine-year leases. By 1986 thirty tribes had authorization for these long-term surface leases for "public, religious, educational, recreational, residential, or business purposes." Fifty percent of these tribes received congressional authorization between 1966 and 1970. Although ninety-nine-year leases can be beneficial to a reservation's economic development, leases should be evaluated carefully for potential cultural, social, environmental, and jurisdictional disruptions in the reservation community.[87]

Some tribes have complained about the Bureau of Indian Affairs' policy of approving the ninety-nine-year leases. They claimed that prior to the implementation of this type of lease few land developers came to the reservations but that under the new policy many real estate investors invaded the reservations, particularly in the Southwest. Some tribal members accused the Bureau of Indian Affairs of supporting these businessmen, often to the disadvantage of the Indians. Such a situation occurred on the Cochiti Reservation near Santa Fe, New Mexico. Tribal members contended that originally the U.S. Army Corps of Engineers insisted that a dam be constructed on reservation lands and, after the tribe refused to negotiate, corps spokesmen told the Indians to accept the proposal or face condemnation of their lands. After completion of the dam, Bureau of Indian Affairs officials stated that since the Cochiti Reservation possessed recreational potential, the tribe should invite land companies to submit plans for development. Tribal governor Celestino Quintana asserted that "We were faced with no choice" but to cooperate with the Bureau of Indian Affairs and the development companies. As a result one-third of the reservation became a subdivision called Cochiti Lake, which covers 7,500 acres. The lease agreement provided that the tribe receive 5 percent of the revenue from the sale of lots and a larger percentage on other properties within the development.[88]

A ninety-nine-year lease for residential development at Tesuque Pueblo in New Mexico was also approved by the secretary of the interior. Seven years later, in 1977, the secretary cancelled the lease. He justified his decision on the basis of tribal opposition and adverse jurisdictional and environmental impacts from the development project. The Pueblo had requested termination of the lease for several years.[89]

TRESPASSING

Other Indians have observed the Bureau of Indian Affairs' failure to enforce trespass restrictions on Indian lands. In Minnesota a resort owner constructed a canal across the property of the Consolidated Chippewas at Leech Lake. On Fort Berthold Reservation in North Dakota, white ranchers grazed their cattle on the tribal reserve without obtaining lease permits. Tribes increasingly assume responsibility for enforcing trespass laws on their reservations. Many tribal councils have enacted licensing and other regulatory laws for both tribesmen and non-Indians. Non-Indians have challenged a number of these actions of tribal sovereignty in the courts.[90]

OTHER FEDERAL POLICIES THAT ENCOURAGE INDIAN LAND ALIENATION

Some Indians charged the Bureau of Indian Affairs with promoting the alienation of Indian lands when exercising their authority to approve and regulate the selling of Indian trust lands. When an Indian desired to sell his land to the tribe or another Indian, the bureau either sold the land at public auction to the highest bidder or restricted the sale to a particular individual selected by the bureau's realty agent. Another method approved by the Bureau of Indian Affairs that sometimes led to alienation of Indian land emerged from the power of bureau realty officers to decide when land can be efficiently divided. A non-Indian obtained a share in property owned by several Indians and then sought to purchase the remaining interest from the Indian owners. If unable to persuade them to sell the land the individual sometimes convinced the Bureau of Indian Affairs to declare that the land could not be partitioned, and the realty officers allowed him to purchase the shares from the Indians at forced sale. The Bureau of Indian Affairs also often questioned wills that left land to an Indian's heirs by declaring that the documents failed to provide "adequate provision" for the heirs. In 1970 the U.S. Supreme Court held that the secretary of the interior could not set aside a will on the basis of his "subjective feeling" that the will was not "just and equitable."[91]

Another system used to alienate Indian lands arose when a destitute Indian tried to obtain welfare but could not because he owned land. The Bureau of Indian Affairs then assisted the Indian in selling his property, but the money from the land transaction made him ineligible for welfare benefits. The bureau then held the funds in trust and the Indian received the money in gradual payments.[92]

By the 1980s many Indians still failed to exploit their land resources because many adversities faced them. Over six million acres of land possessed heirship status, thus making use of the property difficult. The checkerboard separation of Indian and non-Indian land created another obstacle. Much of the Indians' real estate, as well, consisted of submarginal lands. Many Indians also lacked sufficient capital to effectively develop their land, the inclination to adopt alien patterns of farming or ranching, or the requisite business skills. These latter reasons result in leasing to non-Indians. Many tribes increasingly move in the direction of developing their land resources either in agribusiness, industrial development, or recreational facilities. Tribes such as the Navajo, Northern Cheyenne, and Crow represent only a few examples of the Indian people playing a more active role in the exploitation of their lands, either through business or in obtaining better leases for their remaining resources.[93]

5

Appropriation of the Hawaiian
Landed Estate: Part I

JAMES COOK's discovery of the Sandwich islands in 1778 brought an era of change to Native Hawaiians. Increasing contact with traders and missionaries from Europe and the United States transformed native culture and drastically diminished the Hawaiian population. The publication of Cook's Pacific travels announced the presence of the Hawaiian islands and revealed the rich Chinese market for furs collected in the Pacific Northwest. Consequently a prosperous trade dominated by Americans developed between the northwest coast and China. After the American Revolution, Great Britain closed many trading centers to American ships. Seeking new markets, New England traders developed the triangular China trade. Traveling from Boston, the traders based themselves in Hawai'i. From there they traded for furs among the Pacific Northwest tribes, then proceeded to China to trade them for tea, silk, and other goods, which they carried to New England. The Hawaiian islands were excellent for obtaining water, wood, and fresh provisions and for wintering.[1]

Trading ships began to frequent the islands after 1785. Early traders bartered nails, pieces of iron, and trinkets for Hawaiian vegetables, meat, water, and firewood. After the Hawaiians became more adept in commercial transactions, they demanded a more equitable exchange and additional items including guns, ammunition, and cloth. After 1810 sandalwood became an important Hawaiian exchange item.[2]

Within a decade after Cook's visits, Britishers, Spaniards, Russians, and Americans realized the rich trade potential of the Hawaiian islands and recommended that their governments establish some form of control over the archipelago. In 1789 a Spanish naval officer, Ens. E. J. Martinez, suggested to the viceroy of New Spain that Spain colonize the Hawaiian islands and prohibit trade with other nations. Although the viceroy remained uncertain about the proposed endeavor, in 1791 he sent Lt. Manuel Quimper to explore the islands. Spain, however, was declining as a maritime power and thus was unable to carry out Martinez's recommendations.[3]

In 1790 John Meares, a British subject who had visited the Hawaiian islands in 1787 and 1788, stated that the islands possessed great commercial potential for Great Britain and observed that Providence, by allowing a Britisher to discover the islands, intended them to become a part of her empire. George Vancouver, a British navigator, visited Hawai'i in 1792, 1793, and 1794 and attempted to extend British sovereignty over the islands. In 1794 the Hawaiian ali'i, the island chiefs, agreed to cede Hawai'i to Great Britain. Although Vancouver believed the ali'i formally ceded the Hawaiian islands, the chiefs conceived of the transaction on a different level. They believed that they had arranged a defensive alliance that assured British protection from their enemies. Unfamiliar with Western practices and terminology, the Hawaiian chiefs did not understand the role of a colony. Vancouver agreed that the chiefs retained their power and authority. At any rate the British government did not ratify the agreement, although many foreign nations apparently assumed that Great Britain had obtained sovereignty over the islands. In 1816 a British naval officer proposed that Great Britain establish jurisdiction because a colony in the islands would benefit British commerce and perhaps check Russian expansion in the Pacific. This recommendation was ignored.[4]

Between 1815 and 1817 Russia threatened Hawaiian sovereignty. A German, Georg Anton Scheffer, received a commission from Alexander Baranov, director of the Russian American Company, to recover the cargo of a wrecked vessel at Kaua'i, to arrange for trade between the Hawaiian islands and the Russian American Company, and possibly to secure "a footing" in the islands. Baranov promised to provide Scheffer with three vessels to carry out the mission. Posing as a naturalist, Scheffer gained the favor of Kamehameha I, king of the islands, who granted him the use of land to raise food. Scheffer then told Kamehameha I of his mission to recover the cargo of the wrecked Russian vessel.[5]

Scheffer went to Kaua'i and eventually established a close relationship with Kaumuali'i, the island's chief, by demonstrating his skills as a physician and promising to help free the Kaua'i chief from Kamehameha I's rule. Scheffer became the virtual ruler of Kaua'i until 1817 and placed the island under Russian dominion. Kaumuali'i agreed to grant the Russian American Company a monopoly over Kaua'i's sandalwood, the right to establish plantations on the island, the possession of one-half of the island of O'ahu, and absolute control over four harbors on O'ahu. Since Kaumuali'i did not control O'ahu, Scheffer arranged to provide him with 500 Russians and a vessel to enable Kaumuali'i to conquer O'ahu. Kaumuali'i agreed to pay for the vessel with sandalwood and other supplies. Scheffer then returned to O'ahu to institute the terms of the agreement made with Kaumuali'i.

The German also built a blockhouse at Honolulu and flew the Russian flag over it. The Russians entered a *heiau,* a Hawaiian sanctuary, as well.[6]

Aroused by these activities, Kamehameha I ordered the Russians to leave the islands. Scheffer left Oʻahu but returned to Kauaʻi, erected a fort, and exchanged a ship with Kaumualiʻi for valuable tracts of land. Protests lodged by foreign traders, mainly American, against Scheffer's ventures, Kamehameha's order for Kaumualiʻi to oust the Russians, and perhaps Kaumualiʻi's distaste for Scheffer's domination, combined to persuade Kaumualiʻi to expel the Russians. After a show of resistance by the Russians, Kaumualiʻi forcibly drove them off Kauaʻi.[7]

Scheffer journeyed to St. Petersburg hoping to persuade Czar Alexander I to conquer the Hawaiian islands. The directors of the Russian American Company wanted the czar to consider colonization there. The Russian government's refusal evidently rested with the belief that Great Britain would protect the islands, and the czar hesitated to antagonize the British. According to some reports, Baranov repudiated Scheffer's activities. Otto von Kotzebue, a Russian naval officer who visited the Hawaiian islands in 1816 and 1817, assured Kamehameha I that the Russian emperor did not sanction Scheffer's aggression. This information evidently strengthened Kamehameha I's resolve to expel Scheffer and his men.[8]

Commercial intercourse with foreign traders had far-reaching repercussions in the internal affairs of the Hawaiian islands. The Hawaiian chiefs, impressed with guns, eagerly demanded and received arms and ammunition from many of the traders. Possession of Western military war materials and training by foreign residents in Western techniques of warfare caused an increase in interisland wars. Many Hawaiians died in these contests, crops were neglected, and much land was left idle. More important for the future of the archipelago, the use of guns enabled Kamehameha I to unify the islands. By 1795, Kamehameha controlled all of the Hawaiian islands except Kauaʻi and in 1810 its ruler, Kaumualiʻi, agreed to accept Kamehameha I as sovereign although Kaumualiʻi retained actual control of Kauaʻi until his death in 1824.[9]

Foreign contact slightly altered the land tenure system during the early period of the trading era and set the stage for substantive modifications in later years. After commencing commercial activities with Westerners, the Hawaiians, especially the chiefs, developed a desire for the products of Western technology and an awe for the skills and knowledge of the foreigners. As a result, the chiefs and Kamehameha I eagerly requested foreign seamen to work in the islands as carpenters, shipbuilders, masons, interpreters, blacksmiths, physicians, gunnery instructors, and advisors. In return the chiefs gave the foreigners land. To Hawaiians this meant free use rather than title to land. Early residents accepted Hawaiian customs, including the land tenure system. Their property rights paralleled those of Hawai-

LOCATION OF HAWAIIAN HOMELANDS

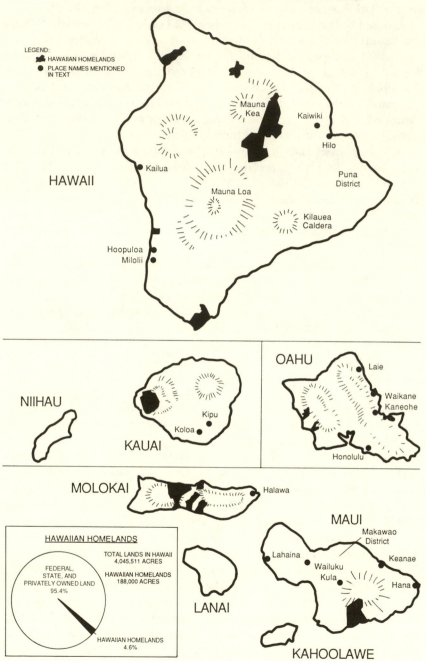

LEGEND:
■ HAWAIIAN HOMELANDS
● PLACE NAMES MENTIONED
  IN TEXT

HAWAII

Mauna
Kea

Kaiwiki

Hilo

Kailua

Puna
District

Mauna Loa

Kilauea
Caldera

Hoopuloa
Milolii

NIIHAU

KAUAI

Kipu

Koloa

OAHU

Laie

Waikane
Kaneohe

Honolulu

MOLOKAI

Halawa

MAUI

Makawao
District

Lahaina

Keanae

Wailuku

Kula

Hana

LANAI

HAWAIIAN HOMELANDS

TOTAL LANDS IN HAWAII
4,045,511 ACRES

HAWAIIAN HOMELANDS
188,000 ACRES

FEDERAL,
STATE, AND
PRIVATELY OWNED LAND
95.4%

HAWAIIAN HOMELANDS
4.6%

KAHOOLAWE

ians, with their tenure being revocable at the will of the higher chiefs or the king. If the foreigners conducted themselves properly, their tenure remained fairly stable. Many of the settlers received the status of chiefs. They paid tribute to the higher chiefs and king and in turn received tribute from the commoners residing on their lands.[10]

Some of the early residents, including Englishmen Isaac Davis and John Young and the American Oliver Holmes, closely associated with Kamehameha I and became his trusted advisors. The aliʻi accepted them as chiefs and Kamehameha I appointed Young governor of Hawaiʻi and later Oʻahu. Holmes occasionally assumed the same position on Oʻahu. In 1795 Kamehameha I left Davis in charge of Hawaiʻi while he waged war on some of the other islands.[11]

Many of the early Western residents encouraged Hawaiian dependence on Western skills. Archibald Campbell residing in the islands in 1808 observed that foreigners in the king's service refused to instruct Hawaiians in Western arts. Boyd, the king's carpenter, believed, as did many other whites, that he should not teach the Native Hawaiians since their acquisition of Western knowledge or skills would lessen his status. Isaac Davis noted that the chiefs would cease to encourage trade with foreigners if the Hawaiians acquired abilities to make and utilize foreign materials. John Adams, a Hawaiian chief, requested Campbell to teach him to read but Davis refused to give permission, explaining, "They will soon know more . . . than ourselves."[12]

Only five whites resided in the Hawaiian islands in 1790 but by 1817 nearly two hundred lived there. The size of the foreign community varied greatly because many foreigners were transient seamen who remained in the islands for a short time. Some sailors deserted their ships, or their captains released them while in the harbors. Frequently maritime traders preferred to recruit Native Hawaiians to replace the white sailors, since Kanakas were considered superior mariners. Vancouver recommended that Kamehameha expel sailors and prohibit most foreigners from residing in the islands because of their propensity for drinking and carousing. Kamehameha I desired only industrious whites, but he refused to deport sailors because he valued their knowledge of firearms. In late 1814 and early 1815, however, he ordered all whites without land assignments to leave the islands. In 1820 Liholiho (Kamehameha II) attempted to banish undesirable white residents.[13]

While Kamehameha I ruled the islands, the land tenure system retained its basic structure. He subdivided the lands according to ancient custom, although he gave the largest districts to the highest aliʻi. The heirs of deceased chiefs were frequently allowed to retain possession of the ahupuaʻa and ʻili kūpono. Kamehameha's policy of requiring the higher chiefs to remain with him continuously somewhat altered the land system. Landlords often were absent, and the actual management of the aliʻi's lands fell to subordinate chiefs or konohiki. In the precontact period, the higher chiefs actually resided within their ahupuaʻa or ʻili kūpono.[14]

The organization of the royal government closely paralleled that of the land system. Kamehameha I added one important feature to the government structure by installing a governor over each island except Kauaʻi, where Kaumualiʻi, the former king of that island, remained the ruler until his death. On the other islands Kamehameha changed governors frequently to prevent rebellion and break the close ties of the higher chiefs to their home regions and resident commoners. By having the higher aliʻi continually in his royal court, Kamehameha required agents to oversee the affairs of the islands. The duties of the governor largely centered on ensuring the efficient collection of taxes by the konohiki.[15]

With the onset of a relatively peaceful era the king no longer required warrior chiefs to defend his lands, thereby bringing an end to the need for redivision of lands. This factor, along with the increasing power of the higher aliʻi, resulted in minimal reallocation of lands in 1819 when Kamehameha II ascended to the throne. In 1825 the hereditary holding of lands became a legal part of the land tenure system when the council of chiefs who appointed Kamehameha III as sovereign sanctioned this principle.[16]

Trade with foreigners brought a change from a subsistence economy with land valued for its use and resources to a commercial economy with the land and its products assuming commercial value in which the commodities could be exchanged for foreign goods. The chiefs' desire for trade and foreign goods led them to exact increasingly excessive demands from the makaʻāinana, which had the effect of worsening the commoners' material welfare and producing greater insecurity in their land tenure. At the same time the aliʻi's wealth and stability in property rights increased. The high demand for foodstuffs required for trade with the increasing number of traders caused the chiefs to require larger amounts of produce and to increase the work load of the commoners in their production of yams, hogs, and vegetables.

During the 1790s Hawaiian chiefs began trading sandalwood, although it did not become a major item of trade until after 1810. The mountainous areas where sandalwood was grown assumed a high value, whereas formerly they possessed only a nominal value. Kamehameha I placed a royal monopoly on sandalwood until 1819 when the chiefs forced his successor, Kamehameha II, to share the trade with them.[17] The flourishing sandalwood trade undermined the native land tenure system and the chiefs, especially the konohiki, became capricious in their treatment of the makaʻāinana and made oppressive demands of the commoners. Frequently the makaʻāinana remained in the mountains for months at a time felling trees and dragging the logs on their backs for long distances over rough terrain to store the sandalwood in the chiefs' warehouses. Farming consequently suffered and at times, cultivation and fishing virtually ceased. The makaʻāinana often produced only slightly more than the amount required by the chiefs and konohiki. Enforcement of *kapu*s (religious prohibitions) on fishing grounds during the spawning season ended, which resulted in the depletion of breeding grounds for fish. Deep-sea fishing, a cooperative effort, also came to a standstill. The inattention to fishing and farming organization materially affected the food supply of the commoners and the efficient utilization of the land and sea.[18]

The growth of the whaling industry after 1820, the subsequent use of the Hawaiian islands as a refreshment place, and the influx of commercialists associated with whaling augmented the economic oppression of the commoners. If the makaʻāinana failed to meet the excessive labor and tax requirements, the konohiki often removed the commoners from their lands and reassigned the fields. The chiefs, who often maintained a paternal attitude toward the makaʻāinana on their lands before the development of a trading economy, became concerned primarily with their own private needs. The commercial emphasis within the Hawaiian economy caused many commoners to move to the towns springing up on the coasts. Urbanization undoubtedly resulted from the oppressive demands of the aliʻi and the lure of town life.[19]

After 1820, Hawaiʻi developed as a frontier for American commercial and religious expansion. Many New England missionaries, traders, and merchants turned toward the islands, and the influence of these new immigrants and of European settlers led to intensive alterations within Hawaiian society, ultimately transforming the native land tenure system into one based on Western concepts of property. By obtaining extensive influence with the chiefs and king as trusted advisors, infiltrating the Hawaiian government in important positions, and acquiring possession of land within the kingdom, these immigrants overturned the native land tenure system and government through internal subversion.

In contrast to their treatment of most American Indians, foreign invaders secured control of the Hawaiian government and undermined the native land system in a comparatively short time. The ancient Hawaiian property, social, and governmental system largely provided the requisite factors enabling the whites to quickly subvert the native order. The Hawaiians' high respect for individuals with military power, knowledge, and skills led the aliʻi to accept Westerners as equals or chiefs. The aliʻi also allowed the foreigners to use land and accept the customary tribute. Since many Westerners possessed knowledge of technology and Western civil and diplomatic law, the chiefs relied heavily on the settlers' abilities in dealing with the imperialistic nations whose citizens frequently visited Hawaiian shores. Hawaiians followed certain Western patterns of international relations to retain their independence as a nation. Another important reason for the foreigners' ascendancy to positions of power lay with the Hawaiians' awe of Western military superiority. Hawaiian leaders realized the need for compromise with the imperialistic nations when they appeared with their warships to require the Hawaiians to guarantee security of foreign property. The settlers' acquisition of land and native dependence on Westerners set the stage for alienation of Hawaiian land and sovereignty.

Although dispossession occurred with less military action than that engaged in by Indians, the Hawaiians did not alter their government or land tenure system without resistance. The opposition to change surfaced in their slowness to compromise, with the chiefs gradually succumbing to foreign pressure. Finally when foreign advisors had assumed effective control of the government and Hawaiians could no longer forestall the pressure of the settlers and gunboats, the old order collapsed.

Although numerous visitors commented on the insecurity of land tenure and the need for change, agitation for revision of the property system developed among foreign residents and representatives only after 1820. The later immigrants brought with them close ties to their culture and its concepts of a highly developed sense of individual ownership of property. They opposed the Hawaiian land tenure system in which the inhabitants possessed usufruct with revocable tenure. These later colonists differed remarkably from the earlier residents, who had accepted the Hawaiian customs.

Normally the first settlers retained only a loose relationship with their country and families, thus enabling them to have more flexibility in their attitudes toward the native order. The Hawaiians, by treating these early residents as chiefs, bestowed a status and subsequent wealth upon them superior to that which they possessed among their own countrymen. Their high positions and prosperity rested with the maintenance of the traditional land system and the superior property rights of the king and chiefs. Evidently few of these men had commercial or entrepreneurial ambitions of promoting a personal empire, which would have necessitated the acquisition of land in fee simple. The later settlers, however, were concerned with increasing their material welfare and promoting the economic prosperity of the Hawaiian nation. They saw the indigenous land system as an impediment to such economic advancement.

After 1820 commercialists settling in the islands requested land for the erection of their houses, stores, and warehouses. The king and chiefs granted usage of plots of land but retained "ownership." Foreigners in service of the ali'i also continued to receive the use of land. Some settlers obtained lands by marrying Hawaiian women or by becoming naturalized citizens. The foreigners' tenure paralleled that of the chiefs and was revocable. However, once *haoles* (whites) secured land they tended to consider it

in terms of Western property rights. They proceeded to lease, buy, or sell
the land to fellow foreigners. This attitude often brought them into conflict with the chiefs, who held to the traditional concepts of property.
After 1830 numerous cases arose of violation of the Hawaiian property system by foreigners.[20]

The chiefs frequently bestowed the use of fertile lands on the New England missionaries who began arriving after 1820. The missionaries accepted these lands to provide subsistence for their families and to instruct the
commoners in Western techniques of land utilization and husbandry. They
also encouraged the commoners to construct stone walls around the farm-
lands to protect the fields from cattle and horses that freely roamed the
countryside and often destroyed crops. These animals, descended from
livestock left by Vancouver and early traders, had proliferated. The missionaries opposed the Hawaiian land tenure system because they viewed it
as a detriment to the commoners' prosperity. They urged alleviation of the
oppressive system of taxation and the enactment of laws promoting Hawaiian industry. Both missionaries and commercialists advocated the transformation of the property system to one conforming to Western concepts of
private ownership.[21]

The haole rationale for changing Hawaiian land tenure resembled that
applied to Indians. Western morality and philosophy as well as desire for
land constituted the major factors motivating appropriation of land. Most
missionaries sincerely believed that owning land in fee simple would save
Hawaiians from extinction. They maintained that the traditional Hawaiian
system of land tenure exploited the commoners and encouraged them to
be "lazy and unproductive." Haoles asserted that insecurity of land tenure
and excessive taxation of the products of the soil comprised a major obstacle to industry. Economic progress and prosperity would not come until
Hawaiians tilled the soil with industry. Both missionaries and commercialists contended that private ownership of land and secure rights to its
produce would promote sedulity and motivate the commoners to increase
production. Inspired by self-interest the Hawaiians would augment their
productivity. Each commoner would become attached to his land and
would have "his home, his house, his cattle, the products of his own
industry to love, to defend." The commoners would become small, independent farmers with flourishing and productive farms. Furthermore,
prosperous Hawaiians would be inclined to propagate more children, thus
arresting the decline in native population. The haoles also believed that to
become civilized a people must accept the concept of private property and
become cultivators of the soil. Some of the missionaries wanted the Hawaiians to own land but opposed white ownership.[22]

After 1820 hostile feelings developed between the missionaries and
many of the commercialists. The former condemned the commercialists

for encouraging un-Christian behavior, and the latter denounced the missionaries for inducing the Hawaiians to adhere to Puritan practices that hindered activities of the foreigners. Businessmen charged missionaries with promoting idleness and lack of industry among the commoners by keeping them from the fields to instruct them on religion and educational pursuits. Missionaries defended their activities by arguing that religious and educational enlightenment encouraged the Hawaiians to become industrious. They also maintained that since the climate enabled the commoners to labor for only short periods to meet their needs, time remained for instruction in religion, morality, and learning.[23]

A majority of the foreigners, excluding many missionaries, wanted land for agricultural, commercial, and private use. Demand for private ownership of land increased in the 1830s and 1840s when the foreign community realized the profitability of agriculture in the Hawaiian islands. American expansion into California and the Pacific Northwest in the 1840s opened new markets for Hawaiian produce. Most haoles were reluctant to invest heavily in land that they could not sell and that could be taken from them at any time. Whites also argued that possession of individual property by foreigners would increase the prosperity of the Hawaiian islands and the commoners, and that their industry would provide models for the Hawaiian people and motivate them.[24]

The haoles believed that land should be used to its utmost potential. They contended that under the traditional land tenure system Hawaiians failed to exploit the land to its maximum utility and wasted the fertile soil. With individual ownership haoles could develop the land, and they believed they should have that right. The whites, however, failed to consider the conflict between native concepts of land utilization and Western ideals of land usage. Traditionally the commoners normally worked the soil to the degree required to satisfy their families and the ali'i's immediate needs. Westerners viewed agricultural pursuits along commercial lines. Extensive production above that required for their own subsistence was needed to promote commercial enterprises and increase the prosperity of the Hawaiian islands.[25]

Adding to the haoles' desire for land for commercial and agricultural pursuits was the prevailing belief that the Hawaiians were quickly becoming extinct. The native population had decreased dramatically since the first contact with whites because of the introduction of venereal disease, measles, and other diseases, and the acceleration of warfare. Exploitation in the sandalwood industry and other economic enterprises also contributed to the high death rate. The haoles sought to ensure that the land would be theirs when the indigenous population expired.

Proponents of allodial land tenure advocated several plans that ensured both Hawaiians and foreigners would receive sufficient land for production. One advocate suggested that the government award to each commoner five times the amount of land he cultivated. If the maka'āinana did not till their fields the lands would revert to the government, which would place the lands on the market at a price conducive to foreign investment. After the commoners obtained their allotments, sufficient land would remain for foreign purchase.[26]

Foreign residents frequently requested the aid of representatives of their home governments to persuade the Hawaiian government to grant more secure property rights and individual ownership of land. American and European diplomats in the Hawaiian islands frequently brought foreign property claims to the attention of the Hawaiian government, and the foreign representatives often attempted to intimidate the king and chiefs into approving the claims through the use of abusive language and threats of force by foreign warships. Many naval officers visiting Hawaiian shores urged Hawaiian leaders to institute changes in the land system. This sustained pressure reinforced the inward forces working to destroy the ancient land tenure system.[27]

In 1825 Lord Byron arrived at the Hawaiian islands on the British warship *Blonde,* which carried the bodies of King Kamehameha II and the queen, who had died while visiting Great Britain. Lord Byron attended the meeting of the council of chiefs that conferred the kingship on the deceased king's younger brother, Kauikeaouli, and he delivered a speech on civil and political affairs. Byron and Kalanimoku, the young king's appointed guardian and regent, recommended that the Hawaiian chiefs adopt the principle of inheritance of lands. The council of chiefs approved the proposal. Sustained pressure to adopt this change before Byron's arrival had softened resistance. The chiefs were ready for the change, and Byron's recommendation simply represented a climax to an extended campaign.[28]

During the 1820s and 1830s John C. Jones, Jr., the U.S. Agent for Commerce and Seamen, frequently requested the American secretary of state to send warships to the islands on a semiannual basis. Jones believed the presence of American vessels in Hawaiian anchorages would ensure security of property for American residents and provide protection for their growing commercial activities. In 1826 at the request of Jones and American traders, the United States sent two warships to the Hawaiian islands to assist them in collecting money owed to Jones and the traders by the chiefs and kings. The commander of the U.S.S. *Peacock* was the most successful in his mission. Capt. Thomas Jones secured an agreement from the Hawaiian rulers to pay all outstanding debts that had accumulated over a period of years to American traders.[29]

Captain Jones also persuaded the Hawaiian government to agree to a commerce treaty with the United States. Provisions included the admission of American ships into Hawaiian ports, protection of Americans in lawful pursuits in the Hawaiian islands, and extension of rights enjoyed by the most-favored nation concerning import tariffs and trade privileges. Although the treaty was favorable to the United States, the Senate never approved the treaty. The Hawaiian government, however, acted on the assumption that it had been ratified. In fact, on several occasions during the 1830s U.S. naval officers and government representatives appealed to the treaty as guaranteeing certain privileges to Americans. It was the first treaty the Hawaiian government had entered into and was the nation's only formal agreement with a foreign power for a decade.[30]

By the mid-1830s British, American, and French naval officers regularly tried to persuade or compel Hawaiian officials to conclude treaties that provided certain guarantees for foreign property. These representatives believed it was their duty to enforce property rights of their countrymen residing in the islands. The presence of warships and consultations by naval officers with the chiefs led to a reconsideration of the property system and encouraged the changes urged by the commercial residents and missionaries.

In September 1836, Commodore E. P. Kennedy of the U.S.S. *Peacock* arrived at Oʻahu and attempted to settle complaints from the foreign community, especially those of Americans. Kennedy discussed with Kamehameha III and the major chiefs such issues as foreign tenure, property rights, the privilege of transferring property, and the right to lease agricultural land. Kīnaʻu, governor of Oʻahu and kuhina nui, maintained that when the king allowed foreigners to use lots for houses and buildings he never alienated his right to the land. When the possessor of the lot left the islands or died, the land reverted to the king. Kīnaʻu further stated that the king would agree to the sale or transfer of such property if the transferee met the king's approval. Kamehameha III contended that he would lose his right to the land if he allowed the free transfer of property and that he would soon alienate the entire country from his sovereignty. Although the king approved the leasing of agricultural lands on a selective basis, he refused to sanction the principle of leasing because he had not given the matter sufficient thought.[31]

Commodore Kennedy failed to reach an agreement with the king but left a letter stating his views on foreign property rights. Kennedy hoped that the talks would lead the chiefs to guarantee the right of transfer of property and the leasing of agricultural lands. Kennedy, in agreement with many foreign residents, asserted that the Jones treaty of 1826 implied the existence of these rights and privileges for American residents. He further argued that such property rights would increase the prosperity of the Hawaiian nation.[32]

C. K. Stribling, the acting commander of the U.S.S. *Peacock*, recommended that the Hawaiian government change its land tenure system to ensure the prosperity and continued existence of the Hawaiians. He urged the chiefs to place a fixed rent on a tenant's land with the remainder of the produce assured to the cultivator. Stribling also suggested that the chiefs institute a policy providing for security of property for both Hawaiians and foreigners, equal and moderate taxation, cessation of compulsory labor, and the leasing of agricultural lands to foreigners for cotton, coffee, and sugar production. A crew member of the U.S.S. *Peacock* in a letter to the editor of the *Sandwich Island Gazette* stressed the need for security of land tenure, since this would lead to an increase in land cultivation and halt the decrease in the Native Hawaiian population.[33]

In contrast to the American naval officers, who were relatively diplomatic in their discourses with Hawaiian officials, the U.S. commercial agent, John C. Jones, Jr., was generally abusive and belligerent. Jones frequently became embroiled with Hawaiian officials over the nation's internal policies, and in 1837 he accused the Hawaiian government of seizing an American chartered vessel by forcibly placing two expelled Catholic priests on board. He lodged vehement protests, demanded reparations for the alleged seizure, and threatened reprisal by the United States.[34]

The efforts of Lord Russell, British commander of the warship *Acteon,* and the British consul, Richard Charlton, in late 1836 led to a treaty between the two nations that contained a Hawaiian guarantee of certain property rights for foreign residents. The treaty came at the height of foreign agitation for allodial ownership of land. One of the major issues that Charlton brought forward was the security of ownership of buildings. Before Russell's arrival, Hawaiian officials had seized the house of an Englishman, George Chapman. Charlton and Russell pressed for the restoration of the house in the same condition as when taken, and finally the king agreed to the demands. Lord Russell also intended to obtain a treaty guaranteeing security of property for foreigners. He presented to the king a treaty written by a British resident, but Kamehameha III refused to agree to some of its terms. The chiefs produced their own treaty, which the British officials considered unsatisfactory. British officials threatened to end friendly relations between England and the Hawaiian islands unless the Hawaiians agreed to more liberal terms. Under the threat of force and after much debate the chiefs and Kamehameha III concluded a treaty that acknowledged foreign ownership and protection of buildings and the right for haoles to transfer property with the prior knowledge of the king. The treaty also enabled the heirs of a deceased resident or the British consul to settle the debts and estate without interference by Hawaiian authorities. The British representatives, however, did not gain the right for foreigners to own land. Lorenzo Lyons, a missionary, stated that Lord Russell's activities frightened the Hawaiians into "selling" land to the foreign residents. In 1837 Henry A. Pierce, a resident American businessman, remarked that the visits of the American, English, and French warships during the preceding sixteen months had "established inviolability of property and persons, and the natives taught and made to fear the 'Laws of Nations'."[35]

Another instance of foreign naval officers impairing the king's control of land occurred when the French frigate *L'Artemise* arrived in Honolulu. Capt. C. P. T. Laplace primarily was concerned with the religious freedom of French Catholic priests and their Hawaiian converts. On the day of his arrival, 9 July 1839, Laplace delivered an ultimatum to the king stating that unless he agreed immediately to five listed demands, the frigate would attack Honolulu. One demand ordered Kamehameha III to grant a plot of land to the Catholic priests for the construction of a church in Honolulu. Laplace offered his ship as a place of safety for all foreigners except Protestant missionaries, whom he considered responsible for the Hawaiian policy of persecution of French priests and Catholics. In the absence of the king from Honolulu, the kuhina nui (prime minister of Hawai'i) Kekāuluohi and the governor of O'ahu agreed to the terms. Before leaving the Hawaiian islands, Laplace signed a treaty with Kamehameha III that guaranteed the protection of French residents in their "persons and property."[36]

The visits of the American, British, and French warships between 1836 and 1839 secured the protection of certain property rights for foreign residents in the Hawaiian islands. The British and French treaties specifically guaranteed these privileges for their subjects, whereas the American position remained uncertain. In 1839 P. A. Brinsmade, the American commercial agent, sought to ascertain the status of American residents. The previous year William Richards, an American political advisor to the Hawaiian government, had sent a proposed treaty to officials of the U.S. government in which the chiefs and king reiterated their views on the traditional land tenure system and American property rights in the islands. The proposed treaty declared that Americans could "hire and occupy" houses and warehouses "in accordance with the laws and customs of the country." It reaffirmed the king's ownership of all lands in the islands and stated that any house lots taken within ten years would be reimbursed by the governor. State Department officials placed the document in their files without attempting to gain Senate approval for it.[37]

The next major foreign interference in internal land matters occurred in 1842 when Lord George Paulet arrived on the *Carysfort* at Honolulu. Paulet specifically visited the Hawaiian islands at the request of former British consul Richard Charlton, who had brought a list of charges against the Hawaiian government for unfair treatment of British subjects. Lord Paulet immediately demanded a personal interview with the king but the Hawaiian government denied his request and instead suggested that Paulet speak with Gerrit P. Judd, the king's representative. Lord Paulet then issued an ultimatum consisting of six demands to be met by the following afternoon or the *Carysfort* would attack Honolulu. Paulet offered asylum to English residents on board a British ship, and Commodore John C. Long provided his vessel as a place of safety for American residents. The foreign residents, fearful of a British attack, began moving their possessions on board the ships until they learned that the king acquiesced under protest.[38]

One of the major demands, which would involve the Hawaiian government in a lengthy period of litigation and difficulties with the British government, concerned a land claim of Richard Charlton. Charlton had brought a claim for certain lands in the center of Honolulu in 1840, and the Hawaiian government had refused to acknowledge title to most of the land claimed by the British consul. Paulet ordered the immediate removal of the attachment the Hawaiian government had placed on the property, surrender of all land claimed by Charlton, and reparation for losses incurred by him and his representatives as a result of the government's proceedings. Not content with the king's agreement to the demands, Alexander Simpson, the acting British consul, and Paulet required the king to sign a confirmation of the 299-year lease allegedly given Charlton in 1826. Charlton had appointed Simpson as his replacement when he returned to England to report his difficulties with the Hawaiian government. The Hawaiian government refused to acknowledge Simpson's appointment until Paulet forced acceptance as one of the six demands.[39]

Paulet and Simpson also interfered in the internal affairs of the Hawaiian nation by ordering the king to reverse certain court decisions and pay large indemnities to foreigners. Kamehameha III refused to agree to these demands and after many conferences with the British officials, Judd and Kamehameha III decided that Paulet and Simpson were seeking to take possession of the islands. The Hawaiian officials decided to cede the islands provisionally to Great Britain under protest and with the understanding that the Hawaiians would rely on the British government's sense of justice to restore the islands to the king once it learned of Paulet's activities. The provisional cession was decreed on 25 February 1843 and included provision for the operation of a provisional government. The king and chiefs retained authority to rule on native affairs, and a commission composed of Kamehameha III or his deputy, Lord Paulet, and two other British officers would deal with affairs concerning the foreign residents. No sales, leases, or transfers of land by the commission or by Hawaiians to foreigners would occur until the Hawaiian representatives had returned from England. Paulet dispatched a ship to London with the details of the proceedings in the Hawaiian islands. Without Paulet's knowledge the Hawaiian government also sent a report to the British government via an American merchant, James F. B. Marshall, who traveled on the British ship as business agent for Ladd and Company.[40]

When Hawaiian officials in London learned that the British government had appointed William Miller as the new British consul and delegated to him the authority to settle the affair in the Hawaiian islands, they wrote to Lord Aberdeen, British foreign minister, requesting that he adjudicate the matter in England. The Hawaiian government distrusted Miller and believed that Aberdeen, who agreed to accept jurisdiction, would render a just decision. The king's representatives in London, William Richards and Timothy Haalilio, possessed the necessary authority to accept the British ruling. Charlton fully documented his charges, whereas the report given to the British lord by the Hawaiian officials contained only partial substantiation. The Hawaiian government was hampered in preparing its case because it did not have access to the Hawaiian archives and had no knowledge of the exact nature of the charges brought by Charlton. The Hawaiian government did not dispute Charlton's holding of a tract of land granted to him by Kalanimoku that he had occupied since 1826 but did refuse to acknowledge Charlton's right to an area of land surrounding this plot that in 1840 Charlton claimed as being part of the original grant. The Hawaiian government argued that Kalanimoku never awarded Charlton the land and that his retainers and heirs had lived there since 1826. Hawaiian officials further maintained that the grant was invalid since Ka'ahumanu was regent in 1826 and the land was hers, not Kalanimoku's, and that the latter could not give away land without Ka'ahumanu's consent.[41]

Lord Aberdeen rendered a judgment in favor of the Hawaiian government on all issues except the Charlton land claim. Lord Aberdeen's verdict stated that the final decision rested with the genuineness of the grant and the power of the person executing it. The power of the person hinged on who was regent in 1826, and Aberdeen stated that the evidence submitted indicated that Kalanimoku occupied the office of regent at that time and therefore possessed the authority to give the land to Charlton. The decision also indicated that the entire area claimed by Charlton lay in the original grant. Aberdeen declared that the final decision of the authenticity of the grant must be decided in Hawai'i upon an examination of the deed to clarify whether the signatures were genuine. If the deed proved to be authentic, then the Hawaiian government must immediately restore all the land in question to Charlton or his representatives.[42]

Upon learning of Aberdeen's decision, Haalilio and Richards rejoiced at the favorable settlement of most of the claims but objected to the verdict on Charlton's land claim. They submitted new evidence that well substantiated their arguments, but Aberdeen refused to alter his decision. Haalilio and Richards accepted the verdict but attempted to obtain indemnities for losses and damages inflicted in the Hawaiian islands by Paulet and Simpson. Aberdeen refused to award these and justified his position by stating that Kamehameha III did not have to cede the islands. If Paulet had carried

out his threat of a siege, then the Hawaiian government would have possessed a basis for seeking compensation.[43]

British Consul Miller decided that the signatures on the title were genuine, but Hawaiian government officials nonetheless believed the grant was
invalid. They interpreted Aberdeen's orders broadly by substantiating that
certain chiefs, commoners, and white residents held the land outside of the
enclosed area occupied by Charlton and that the former British consul
never had indicated otherwise until he submitted his claim in 1840. Miller
considered the actions of the Hawaiian officials as an attempt to evade
Aberdeen's decision and consulted with the British government, who then
ordered the Hawaiian government to give the contested lands to Charlton.
Miller delivered these demands to the Hawaiian officials and the king
acquiesced in August 1845. Hawaiian attempts to have the British government review the decision continued, and in 1847 the British government
reaffirmed its previous ruling. Conflict over the Charlton land case continued for several more years.[44]

Paulet's seizure of the Hawaiian islands caused Americans much concern
for the security of their lands because they realized that the manner in
which they had acquired and held their lands would not secure a title
under British law. American subjects, including the missionaries, opposed
British rule and desired Hawaiian independence. Even President John
Tyler on 30 December 1842 stated that the extent of American interests in
the Hawaiian islands gave the United States a special interest in the continuation of Hawaiian independence. American commissioner William
Hooper objected to Paulet's activities, thought the Hawaiian islands
should be independent, and believed the United States should exert influence to gain foreign recognition of Hawaiian independence. Hooper also
pointed out the unjustness of Paulet's demands and that the Hawaiian
government had ceded the islands under protest. The American commissioner suggested to the U.S. secretary of state, Daniel Webster, that the
American government should persuade Great Britain to restore sovereignty
to the king. Hooper also questioned whether the United States should
allow a foreign naval officer to usurp the powers of the Hawaiian government.[45]

British admiral Richard Thomas arrived at Honolulu in July 1843 and
restored sovereignty to Kamehameha III. Thomas declared that the
Hawaiian government had ceded the islands unwillingly and maintained
that Great Britain did not authorize Paulet's actions. Thomas concluded a
treaty with the Hawaiian government that contained ten articles, including
one that restored Charlton's land to his possession. The treaty also guaranteed the protection of and respect for the rights of British subjects.[46]

Restoration of the islands to Hawaiian rule relieved American residents.
Hooper believed that the Americans were better off as a result of Paulet's

proceedings—the Hawaiian government had settled all American claims. France and Great Britain also clearly desired Hawaiian independence. Before Paulet's arrival, a general fear existed that France would seize the archipelago. All three nations desired the neutrality of the islands because of their strategic position in the Pacific trade.[47]

The frequent urging of foreign naval officers to change the land tenure system, interference by foreign diplomatic representatives in internal land affairs, forced recognition of property rights for foreign subjects, increasing influence and control of the Hawaiian government by haoles, and intensified remonstrations on the part of foreign residents combined to influence the king and chiefs to alter the land tenure system. They resisted as long as prudence allowed but finally the forces demanding change prevailed. Even so, the transformation to a property system based on Western concepts of individual ownership of land occurred over a period of years and with much difficulty.

6

Appropriation of the Hawaiian Landed Estate: Part II

THE DEVELOPMENT OF FEE SIMPLE LAND TENURE

UNTIL the 1840s Kamehameha III persisted in claiming ownership of the land, although the representatives of foreign nations forced him to grant some guarantees for the security of property to foreigners. As of 1836 Kamehameha III reasserted that foreigners and natives alike held their plots of land at the will of the king and reaffirmed his power to dispossess them.[1]

In 1839 Kamehameha III granted major concessions in the Declaration of the Bill of Rights. This document as well as the constitution of 1840 revealed foreign influence in both concepts and phraseology. Kamehameha III surrendered his right of arbitrary dispossession of foreigners and Native Hawaiians from their lands or building lots. The Bill of Rights also strengthened the practice of hereditary inheritance of land and property. Kamehameha III limited this principle by stating that if an individual held three or more divisions of land, one-third of the land reverted to the king. The laws of 1839 with some modifications became part of the constitution of 1840. One article allowed landless Hawaiians to acquire uncultivated land provided they farmed it and received the landlords' cooperation. This provision also placed restraints on the dispossession of tenants by landlords. It did, however, reaffirm the ancient idea that a landlord could remove a commoner who failed to till his farm. Penalties were included for those chiefs and landlords who continued to oppress tenants. The constitution provided that there would be only one landlord, with the exception of the king, over each makaʻāinana. Sections clearly established a uniform system of poll taxes, labor taxes, and land taxes to relieve people from excessive exactions by chiefs and konohiki. Other articles enunciated new fishing rights and use of water for irrigation. The Bill of Rights and the constitution did not completely alleviate the abuses of the land system because the concepts embodied within them went against the ancient usage system.[2]

The Constitution of 1840 and Subsequent Developments

The constitution of 1840 established a constitutional monarchy. While reaffirming the king's control of the land, the constitution acknowledged that the chiefs and commoners had an ownership interest in the lands, that they held the land in common. The following section from the constitution revealed this concession:

> Kamehameha I was the founder of the kingdom, and to him belonged all the land from one end of the islands to the other, though it was not his own private property. It belonged to the chiefs and people in common of whom Kamehameha I was the head and had the management of the landed property. Wherefore there was not formerly, and is not now, any person who could or can convey away the smallest portion of land without consent of the one who had or has direction of the kingdom.[3]

The Hawaiian government issued a proclamation in 1841 that attempted to persuade foreign landholders to sign written leases for land in their possession unless they already had formal leases. A fifty-year limit was placed on the leases. For long-term leases the rent would be high; low rents would prevail for short-term leases. The government's attempt failed because many haoles opposed leases; they wanted title in fee simple and they believed the government's action was an attempt to deprive them of their rights. The foreign landholders applied Western concepts of allodial tenure once they received possession of land and persisted in the belief that the lands belonged to them. The government did not press the leasing issue, realizing that it possessed insufficient military power to prevent foreign intervention, which it feared especially since Hawai'i had not gained international recognition of independence. A letter to the American consul explained the government's position:

> We renounce the right of dispossessing them [the foreigners] at pleasure. We lay no claims whatever to any property of theirs, either growing, or erected on the soil. That is theirs, exclusively. We simply claim the soil itself, but do not claim that even that should be restored, though from of old we have never had the smallest idea of alienating any portion of our land. But if the soil be not restored then we claim a reasonable rent. We prefer not to make a direct assessment, but rather negotiate. . . .[4]

Kamehameha III and the chiefs had earlier refrained from granting leases. The first significant departure from this policy occurred in 1835 when they signed a fifty-year lease with the American-owned mercantile firm of Ladd and Company. The agreement stipulated that the firm could employ commoners without any interference from the chiefs. The contract reflected the strength of American influence with the Hawaiian rulers. The missionaries supported the efforts of P. A. Brinsmade and the other company officials in securing a lease to establish a sugar plantation at Kōloa on Kaua'i. The missionaries thought highly of Brinsmade, a former theology student, and some believed his agricultural project would promote development of industry among the Hawaiians. In 1841 Hawaiian rulers signed another agreement with Ladd and Company for additional lands, contingent on formal recognition of Hawaiian independence by the United States, Great Britain, and France. The Hawaiian government concluded only a small number of formal leases and usually avoided the practice.[5]

The Hawaiian government, attempting to prevent future alienation of land, issued a proclamation in 1842 that prohibited the sale of land and fixed property, the transfer of such property, and its seizure for debts. An exception was allowed for individuals leaving no personal estate. In this case the land and fixed property upon it could be sold at an auction, but only to Hawaiians whose rights of possession would parallel those of other commoners. The government reaffirmed its ownership of land and the requirement of the king and premier's approval of leases.[6]

During this period numerous foreigners became naturalized citizens to gain security for their lands or to satisfy the government requirement that its officials be Hawaiian citizens. Agitation for land reform for both Hawaiians and foreigners continued to grow during the early 1840s. Most foreign subjects wanted allodial tenure, although some missionaries and naturalized government officials advocated individual ownership for Hawaiian citizens while opposing alien possession of titles in fee simple and even leases for large acreages for commercial and agricultural activities. Gerrit P. Judd, a former medical missionary; Levi Chamberlain, a missionary; and other government officials maintained this view. Sincerely concerned with the welfare of the Hawaiian nation, these individuals believed that individual ownership by commoners would alleviate their distressed economic and social state.[7]

Hawaiian newspapers and reports of conferences between government officials and foreign consuls revealed that Hawaiian rulers were on the verge of major land reform. In August 1844, Hawaiian Minister of Foreign Affairs Judd wrote to British proconsul Robert C. Wyllie that the Hawaiian envoys in Europe were obtaining necessary information for settling all land claims. Judd declared that the next legislature would adopt an "equal, just, and uniform system" for the adjudication of land titles. Later that year *The Polynesian* postulated that the government would soon reform the land tenure system.[8]

The Second Organic Act

On 21 May 1845, Judd delivered a report to the legislature that recommended establishing a committee to investigate the validity of land titles, to award new written titles for authentic claims, to review the land tenure system, to grant security of tenure to landholders, and to sell government lands in fee simple to Hawaiian subjects. Attorney General John Ricord drafted the provisions agreed to in the legislative council and the legislature enacted the terms with some amendments as the Second Organic Act on 27 April 1846. The article establishing the Board of Commissioners to Quiet Land Titles had been separately passed on 10 December 1845; it became effective on 7 February 1846. The land commission received the authority to determine the validity of both native and foreign claims to land possessed prior to the enactment of the above act. The law required the board to give public notice of the provisions of the act, and for ninety days its decisions could be challenged in the Supreme Court. Claimants had two years to file claims, although the legislature later extended this limitation until 31 March 1855. If the Board of Commissioners determined that the claim was authentic, it awarded title to the landholder. To receive a royal patent, the awardee presented the award to the minister of the interior and paid a commutation to receive relinquishment by the government of its interest in the land. Normally the commutation consisted of one-third of the unimproved value of the land, although the Privy Council on 8 June 1847 reduced the rate of commutation to one-fourth for house and building plots. During the first two years of operation the board of commissioners mainly determined the validity of foreign claims to house and building lots and leased land. Few natives presented claims during this period.[9]

The Second Organic Act also established a land office with the authority to regulate Hawaiian land matters. The legislation allowed the government to sell land in fee simple to Hawaiian citizens but not to foreigners. Hawaiians and aliens could lease government lands although foreigners were restricted to a fifty-year limit on their leases. The land commission wrote "The Principles adopted by the Board of Commissioners to Quiet Land Titles, in their adjudication of claims presented to them," which enunciated the history of land tenure in the Hawaiian Islands and the rules the commissioners would follow in settling claims. The document declared that the tenants, landlords, and king or government shared rights in the lands of the kingdom. It distinguished between the king's private lands as a landlord and the public lands he held as head of the government.[10]

The Great Mahele

Transition to a land tenure system based on fee simple ownership depended on devising a judicious manner for dividing the lands among the king, government, chiefs, and tenants. Until the undivided rights to the land were settled, clear title often could not be granted; this state of affairs hindered the landholders, including the government, from selling land. The board of commissioners commenced an investigation of the problem, and debate ensued for two years among the chiefs, king, members of the Privy Council, and legislature. Judge William Lee suggested a plan that allowed the king to retain his lands as private property; the remaining lands would be divided equally among the government, chiefs, and tenants. The adoption of these rules by the Privy Council provided the basis for the division of the lands of the kingdom, although the rules were not adhered to strictly. A committee was appointed to oversee the division of lands among the king and the chiefs. The government would retain a share interest in the land until both groups commutated that interest.[11]

The Great Mahele or land division began on 27 January 1848 and continued until March 7. Individually 245 chiefs or konohiki divided their lands with the king. To receive title to the lands, the chiefs presented their claims to the land commission. To abrogate the government's share, the chiefs had to relinquish a portion of their lands to the government for commutation of the interest or pay one-third of the value of the unimproved lands. Kamehameha III and the Privy Council waived the commutation fee for some chiefs. By the summer of 1850 many of the konohiki had received titles in fee simple. Some of the chiefs failed to apply for the awards and sporadically until 1892 the legislature enacted laws allowing the konohiki or their heirs to acquire titles. The king divided his lands into two parts: the larger section became government lands, and the smaller part remained private lands or Crown lands.[12]

Kuleana Grants

The land division among the king, government, and chiefs cleared the way for the makaʻāinana, who retained an interest in the lands, to acquire ownership of their *kuleana*s or farms. To complete the transition from the ancient Hawaiian land tenure system to a Western pattern of fee simple ownership the tenants' claims, which were restrictions on the land titles of the chiefs, king, and government, had to be extinguished. This meant providing a means by which the makaʻāinana could own the land they used. After the Mahele, members of the Privy Council discussed the best methods for protecting the tenants' interest in the land. The need for establishing a single system of land tenure throughout the Hawaiian islands was accompanied by the haoles' belief that individual ownership would transform the makaʻāinana from what they described as lazy, indolent people to industrious farmers. In 1847 Robert C. Wyllie, minister of foreign relations, recommended that the government give fee simple title to the tenants. He contended that allodial ownership would cause the commoners to increase both agricultural production and their population. Wyllie also promoted the immigration of "good people" to the islands and argued that it would stimulate native cultivation and would "show them how to make money—how to use it, and how to keep it—that would give your people examples of industry, thrift, sobriety and virtue. . . ." A widespread fear that the French or Californian filibustering activities would lead to a foreign takeover of the Hawaiian kingdom also encouraged the government to grant fee simple titles to tenants. If either increased immigration or a foreign takeover occurred, the only method of assuring commoners security in their land tenure was to give them individual ownership in accordance with Western concepts of property rights.[13]

Judge William Lee, at the request of the cabinet, prepared a plan for native ownership of land that the Privy Council passed on 21 December 1849 and the legislature subsequently enacted on 6 August 1850. The legislation allowed every tenant to receive title to the land he occupied and cultivated, with the exception of town lots in Honolulu, Hilo, and Lahaina. The commoners had to present their claims to the land commission and upon verification of the claims' authenticity, the tenants received titles in fee simple to their kuleanas. The agency recommended that each commoner combine his separate tracts into one continual tract by negotiating with other tenants before the surveyor's arrival. Each tenant had to pay for the survey of his kuleana. Those house lots that existed apart from the cultivated land were limited to one-fourth of an acre. According to the terms of the legislation the tenants retained the right to use firewood, house timber, aho cord, thatch, or ti leaves for their personal requirements from the landlord's lands, but they had to obtain the konohiki's consent. The tenants also retained the right-of-way as well as the right to use water sources on the landlord's land. Any commoner unable to establish claims or who received insufficient lands could purchase plots ranging from one to fifty acres from government lands set aside on each island. The maka'āinana would pay a minimum of fifty cents per acre.[14]

The kuleana grant was not the first opportunity offered some Native Hawaiians to own their lands. After 1845 the Hawaiian government experimented by granting fee simple titles to commoners in the Makawao district on Maui and in Mānoa valley on O'ahu. The missionaries aided in surveying the land, explaining the government's plan to the tenants and persuading the commoners to buy the land. Altogether they purchased approximately 130 parcels of land, each ranging from one to ten acres.[15]

Some of the maka'āinana took advantage of the kuleana grant, and 13,514 claims were presented by 1855. The land commission approved only 9,337 kuleana grants. The reasons for the board's failure to award all the original petitions included overlapping claims, the death of the claimant, or a tenant's failure to appear before the commissioners to support his claim. A few tenants relinquished claims for the kuleanas to the chief of the ahupua'a or 'ili kūpono in which their lands existed. The size of the award varied, with the surveyor largely determining the dimensions of the grant. Some surveyors, using surveying methods that were often crude and inaccurate, included only the fields cultivated at the time of the survey; others took into account the Hawaiian system of letting a field lie fallow for several years and therefore included those fields in the kuleana grant. Most of the kuleanas awarded consisted of less than ten acres. Commoners from Kaiwiki signed a petition questioning one surveyor's capabilities. In response to their complaint, A. G. Thurston, land clerk in the Department of the Interior, remarked that "ignorant natives cannot be judges of the correctness of what they know nothing about."[16]

Many Hawaiians unfamiliar and afraid of the alien system of allodial tenure failed to make claims for their kuleanas. Some did not understand the procedures to follow in filing for title or lacked the necessary funds to hire the services of a surveyor. A haole purchased the entire island of Ni'ihau because the native tenants did not file their claims. The missionaries persuaded some of the commoners to obtain titles in fee simple. Undoubtedly many of the maka'āinana did not desire individual ownership and would have preferred to maintain a system with which they were familiar. Some tenants arranged with their former landlords to continue certain features of the ancient land system. The commoners agreed to labor for three days each month on the konohiki's land in exchange for the right to continue using the landlord's land for grazing purposes. Many Native Hawaiians failed to understand the Western concept of individual ownership of land and could not comprehend a property system in which everyone did not have the right to use the land and its products.[17]

The land commission proceeded slowly in settling the claims, partly due to the number of counterclaims. At the end of the distribution in 1855, the Crown's lands consisted of about 1,000,000 acres; the chiefs' lands, about 1,500,000 acres; the government's lands, about 1,500,000 acres. In contrast the common people received a little less than 30,000 acres. Only 20 percent of the adult Hawaiian population received land. Before the kuleana grant, many Native Hawaiians had moved to the cities. The only way these commoners could acquire land was to purchase the government lands set aside for that purpose on each of the islands.[18]

Attempts at Land Alienation Restrictions for Native Hawaiians

Concerned that the commoners would sell their lands to foreigners, some haoles suggested that the government institute safeguards against alienation. During a Privy Council meeting, Wyllie recommended that each title granted to tenants should bear advice from the king stating that they should not sell their lands "for an inadequate consideration." The government neglected to carry out this suggestion or to provide any protections.[19]

The Reverend Richard Armstrong and Judge William Lee, members of the Privy Council, revealed their concern about the possible repercussions of granting individual ownership to the maka'āinana in statements addressed to the commoners in the native newspaper, the *Elele*. These government officials explained the nature of the kuleana grant legislation and cautioned the commoners against alienating their lands. Judge Lee stated, "Two courses . . . are open for you. Either to secure your lands, work on them and be happy, or to sit still, sell them and then die. Which do you choose?" Armstrong advised the maka'āinana to cultivate their lands, be industrious, and teach their children productive activities and Western learning. He maintained that the Hawaiians' prosperity and continued existence as a race depended only on themselves since they could own land; and they could either sell the land, fail to cultivate it, or farm it. Other haoles expressed a similar sentiment and believed that foreigners should encourage the commoners to develop habits of industry and a sense of the value of land. Some members of the foreign community believed that individual ownership of land would transform Native Hawaiians into industrious farmers.[20]

Agitation for Haole Land Rights

When the Hawaiian government granted aliens the right to buy or sell land in fee simple in 1850, the transformation of the native land tenure system was completed. In the previous decade foreigners had increased their remonstrations about the abundance of idle lands throughout the islands and agitated for alien ownership of land. They contended it would lead to general prosperity in the Hawaiian kingdom and to immigration and settlement of respectable foreigners. Although after 1845 residents with valid titles to lands could secure allodial titles on the same basis as Hawaiians by applying to the land commission, most foreigners remained dissatisfied with the government's property system. Those aliens entitled to fee simple titles resented the commutation fee of one-third or one-fourth of the unimproved value of the land that the government required of all Hawaiian subjects receiving royal patents because they evidently believed they were paying for land they already owned.[21]

American and British consuls supported the foreign residents in their belief that aliens should receive fee simple title for lands possessed for as long as five years. Foreign representatives actively interfered in internal land matters by trying to convince the Hawaiian government to alter its land policy toward aliens. American consul William Hooper believed his government should intervene and force the Hawaiian government to guarantee additional property rights to American citizens. In 1845 Hooper objected to the Hawaiian government's auctioning of the estate of Joseph Bedford, an American citizen. He argued that the American consul should have the responsibility of settling the estate since the lands belonged to Bedford. Hawaiian officials contended that the lands belonged to Bedford's Hawaiian wife, therefore giving the government jurisdiction over the estate. Hooper opposed the public auction of lands, which the government supposedly restricted to Hawaiian subjects.[22]

Even more than the other foreign consuls, U.S. commissioner Anthony Ten Eyck, who arrived in the Hawaiian islands soon after the passage of the land act in 1846, gave adamant support to the foreigners in their protests. He became the spokesman for the interests of the foreign community and soon earned the enmity of Hawaiian officials, who withdrew their recognition of Ten Eyck as American commissioner in 1848.[23]

Widespread discussion of the rights of long-term settlers to the lands they held led the Hawaiian legislature to enact a law in June 1847 that allowed aliens to receive royal patents in fee simple for lands in their possession at that date. The government required the foreign claimants to pay the regular rate of commutation. The legislation restricted the aliens' rights of private ownership, since the act stipulated that foreigners could sell their lands only to Hawaiian subjects.[24]

Even after passage of this act, Ten Eyck continued his effort to obtain a treaty that would allow foreigners to secure allodial title to the land in their possession without a commutation fee and that would permit them to purchase land in fee simple. Ten Eyck suggested that Hawaiian denial of such rights justified foreign intervention. American secretary of state James Buchanan refused to support Ten Eyck. Buchanan advised Ten Eyck to refrain from trying to dictate land policy to the Hawaiian government and suggested that he restrict his activities to upholding valid claims of American citizens. Buchanan noted that American recognition of Hawaiian independence precluded interfering in the internal affairs of the Hawaiian kingdom. The secretary of state also informed Ten Eyck that most nations refused to grant fee simple title to aliens.[25]

Foreigners remained dissatisfied with their limited property rights, and agitation continued for the establishment of a land system comparable to the one existing in the United States. Numerous editorials and letters to the editor of the government newspaper, *The Polynesian*, advocated the selling of lands to aliens and Hawaiian citizens on an open market. Westerners complained of the lands lying idle because of what they termed "native laziness," and they argued that the continued prosperity of the nation depended on alien ownership of land. Haoles decried the slowness of land-commission procedures and suggested that the government survey the land, grant fee simple titles to all commoners, then sell the remaining lands at a public auction for a nominal price. Some haoles believed that a landholder who failed to cultivate his land should lose possession of it, whereas others recommended that the government levy a tax on all uncultivated property to force the chiefs to sell some of their lands. The idea of taxing uncultivated lands persisted even after the aliens obtained the right to purchase and convey lands, since the haoles still desired to acquire additional land. Aliens supported their demands for unrestricted rights of buying and selling land by arguing that such a policy would promote Hawaiian prosperity, encourage native acquisition of the habits of industry by foreign example, ensure foreign residents' allegiance to the Hawaiian government, and curtail requests for foreign intervention in Hawaiian land matters.[26]

Foreign-born officials in the Hawaiian government differed in their views on giving aliens the privilege of buying and selling land. Judd opposed granting that right but believed that older settlers should have fee simple title to land already in their possession. Wyllie held the opinion that haoles should have the right to purchase and convey land without any restrictions and urged the chiefs to sell land to foreigners. He contended that such transactions would get the chiefs out of debt and increase the value of their remaining land. He denounced the Hawaiians' traditional belief that "mere possession of land constitutes wealth" and enunciated the Western concept that "land is of no value unless there are men to buy it or lease it, and to cultivate it." William Lee, a member of the board of commissioners and chief justice of the Supreme Court of Law and Equity, commented on Wyllie's views. Lee objected to Wyllie's suggestion that the king had deprived foreign residents of their rights. Lee stated that he favored a liberal policy toward foreigners and that

> no one has a stronger desire to see the lands of this Kingdom thrown open to the permanent possession and enjoyment of the natives and those who will cultivate them. But to unlock these lands, and promote the great cause we have at heart, agriculture, and the good of the Hawaiian nation, we must avoid anything, like harshness, and move the King by persuasion.[27]

Foreigners Gain Access to Fee Simple Land Titles

On 10 July 1850 the Hawaiian government acquiesced to the internal forces advocating alien ownership of lands and unrestricted rights of alienation. The law included the provision that any landholder who requested intervention by foreign governments or their representatives would forfeit his lands to the Hawaiian government. It further stipulated that this clause must be contained in every deed for the title to be valid.[28]

After 1850 when aliens gained the right to purchase and sell lands without restriction, alienation of Hawaiian lands proceeded at an even greater rate. Both the chiefs and commoners readily sold their lands to foreign capitalists. Unfamiliar with the concept of private ownership of land, the commoners did not realize that they surrendered all rights to the use of the land when they sold their kuleanas. The Hawaiians parted with lands, often for small sums of money. Frequently commoners and chiefs acquired debts or mortgages to haoles and consequently lost their lands. Others lost their lands by neglecting to pay taxes levied on their property. When native landowners died without heirs or intestate, their lands reverted to the chief or owner of the ahupua'a in which the kuleana was located, which further promoted the process of haoles obtaining title to Hawaiian land. The increase in plantations also tended to separate the maka'āinana from the soil.[29]

EROSION OF NATIVE HAWAIIAN LAND RIGHTS

Adverse Possession

Owners of plantations, ranches, large corporations, big estates, and churches have used adverse possession in the nineteenth and twentieth centuries to obtain ownership of kuleanas. Adverse possession is a legal method of acquiring title by possessing land for a statutory period under certain conditions. Under the adverse possession statute enacted in 1870, the true owner has to recover possession before the statute of limitations runs out by either filing a lawsuit or repossessing the land for a year. Failure to take the appropriate action cuts off the true owner's remedy for recovery and possibly his rights to the land. To perfect his title, an adverse possessor must file a quiet-action suit in circuit court. The Torrens land registration system of the Land Court, which was established in 1903, has also been an arena for many quiet-action proceedings brought by landowners with extensive holdings.[30]

The adverse claimant has to fulfill certain court-determined prerequisites to obtain ownership. His possession must be exclusive, actual, continuous, hostile, and open and notorious for the entire statutory period. The adverse possessor has to show hostile intent by claiming an interest adverse to that of the true owner. He must claim the land as the sole owner. Such hostile action marks the time the statute of limitations begins to run against the true owner; it establishes the time his cause of action for recovery of the property accrues. Any number of methods can be used to satisfy the element of actual possession. The intruder can build a house or other structure, graze cattle, raise crops, construct a drainage ditch, irrigate the acreage, erect fences, and lease the land to another party. He does not have to live on the land. Any tenant or lessee must acknowledge the claimant's ownership. Exclusive possession satisfies another prerequisite. No party other than a tenant or lessee may use the land during the statutory period. Use of the property must be clearly evident and sufficiently open and notorious to alert the true owner that someone has adversely possessed his land. The construction of a house or fence or other visible sign such as an irrigation ditch would satisfy this criterion. A claimant does not have to pay taxes on the land, although doing so can strengthen his case. Even if the true owner pays the property tax, his action does not prevent a claim of adverse possession.[31]

During the past thirty years the Hawaii state courts have established several rules of conduct that must be followed by a tenant in common who claims adversely to the interests of his cotenants. In 1960 the court ruled that there was a fiduciary relationship between cotenants and that this relationship might require the cotenant claiming adversely to give actual notice to other cotenants. Eleven years later the court held that a tenant in common claiming by adverse possession must give actual notice to blood-related relatives unless they had actual knowledge of the adverse claim.[32]

In 1976 the court in *City and County of Honolulu v. Bennett* laid down a stricter rule when it declared that the adverse claimant must prove that he acted in good faith toward his cotenants. This requirement of good faith usually required him to give his cotenants actual notice of an adverse claim. The court stated that the good faith requirement could "be satisfied by constructive notice and 'open and notorious possession' " only in certain exceptional circumstances:

> Where the tenant in possession has no reason to suspect that a cotenancy exists; or where the tenant in possession makes a good faith, reasonable effort to notify the cotenants but is unable to locate them; or where the tenants out of possession already have actual knowledge that the tenant in possession is claiming adversely to their interests.

Noting that a claimant's alleged ignorance of the existence of a cotenancy did not prove good faith, the court stated that the good faith standard "includes an objective requirement of reasonableness, in addition to a subjective requirement that the claimant believe himself to be the sole owner." The statute of limitations for the tenant's recovery does not begin to run until he is given proper notice of the adverse claim. This good faith test has made it more difficult for adverse possessors to acquire Native Hawaiian land.[33]

If the adverse possessor took possession of the land after 1973, he must have continuous or unbroken possession for at least twenty years. An adverse claimant who entered onto the land before that year only needs such possession for ten years. "Tacking" can satisfy the requirement in the following situation. An adverse possessor dies and leaves the real property to an heir in a will. The inheritor occupies the land for a period of time and then sells the acreage to a third party, who proceeds to claim the land adversely to the true owner. The total years of possession by the three owners counts toward the statutory period because there was privity among the three individuals. When there are no legal agreements between the parties, tacking does not satisfy the criterion of continuous possession.[34]

Native Hawaiians and their supporters persuaded the 1978 Hawaii Constitution Convention and the citizens of Hawaii to approve an amendment abolishing adverse possession of acreages greater than five acres. A claimant asserting title by adverse possession to five acres or less can make such a claim only once every twenty years, and it must be made in good faith. The purpose of the amendment was to prevent large landowners from continuing to acquire numerous kuleanas and small, family owned acreages by adverse possession and at the same time to allow small landowners to clear title to their land. The Hawaii legislature subsequently passed legislation to implement the amendment, which apparently had only prospective application. The statutory provisions allowed adverse possession for acreages greater than five acres when the claim had matured prior to the effective date of the amendment, 7 November 1978. The legislature amended the quiet-action statute in 1983 to define good faith. Essentially it established an objective standard of reasonableness that the adverse possessor would have to satisfy. His claim must be based on inheritance, a written instrument of conveyance, or a court judgment. His belief that his interest in title to the lands derived from one of these sources cannot be subjective; it must be objective—one that a reasonable person under all the facts and circumstances would hold.[35]

A review of the statistics of past cases involving adverse possession provides some idea of the extent of its use. In 1968 the Land Court awarded title to Molokai Ranch, formerly American Sugar Company, for 8,471 acres. The state title examiner determined that the ranch had no claim for all of the land because some of it lay outside the boundaries set forth in the application and some parcels were never claimed. Nevertheless the court issued title for the entire acreage. In 1955 the court had awarded 50,761 acres to Molokai Ranch; thirty years earlier its predecessor had acquired 5,221 acres. Although the ranch did not receive all of the land through adverse possession, it did obtain large amounts of it by this method. The Molokai Ranch owns one-third of the entire island of Moloka'i. The Castle estate acquired kuleanas in Kailua and Kāne'ohe through adverse possession in both the Land Court and circuit court. They based their applications on a deed that excluded kuleanas and other small holdings situated within each of the ahupua'a. Although the circuit court found the paper title defective, it awarded title to 1,500 acres or almost all of the Waikāne Valley to the McCandless family because its members had fulfilled all the requirements for adverse possession. The Mormon church, through its business extension, Zions Securities Corporation, obtained ownership of large areas in Lāʻie, Oʻahu, through adverse possession. In 1978 the circuit court index listed over ten pages of individuals, mainly Hawaiians, who had lost land to the corporation.[36]

Although adverse possession was used to obtain property of small, individual landowners in general, Native Hawaiians lost title most frequently. Adverse possessors often won their cases through default. Native Hawaiians often failed to file lawsuits to recover possession or to appear in court to contest adverse claims. Several reasons accounted for this failure. Testimony delivered to a committee of the 1978 Hawaii Constitutional Convention revealed that many Native Hawaiians did not know about or understand the law. They also feared the judicial process.[37]

Another explanation rested with the method of notifying those with any claim to the property. The applicant had to make personal service on known parties holding an adverse interest, post a notice at the site of the property subject to the pending court action, and publish a legal notice in a newspaper addressed to all potential owners. The publication notice told them to appear in court on a certain date if they wanted to protest the proceedings. However, these methods of notification had their deficiencies. Many people did not read the notices, understand legal language, or receive the newspaper. Consequently many Hawaiians affected by the proceedings remained unaware of the hearings and did not appear in court to contest them. Adverse claimants often were able to avoid making personal service by claiming they did not know the identity of the heirs of a known interest holder.[38]

A recent court decision, *Hustace v. Kapuni,* should have an important impact on preventing adverse claimants from so easily resorting to giving only publication notice. The court held that claimants must show due diligence in trying to identify and locate the heirs. A mere statement of due diligence is insufficient. The claimant must include in an affidavit a listing of sources consulted and specific actions taken before the court would authorize a notice solely by publication. The ruling set aside a default judgment because the plaintiff's affidavit was devoid of such a showing. The court noted that the claimant could have located the heirs without much effort, since a genealogist hired by a defendant had found them after a few weeks of research.[39]

Another difficulty that sometimes prevented Native Hawaiians from contesting adverse claims or successfully opposing them was the lack of genealogical documentation to prove they were descendants of a kuleana

grant owner. Increasing numbers of Hawaiians have used available resources at the state archives to trace their family lines back to original
kuleana owners. A lack of financial resources also limited the number of
Native Hawaiians who protested adverse possession. They lacked sufficient
money to hire an attorney, much less to engage in expensive litigation.[40]

Another factor enabling claimants to easily obtain parcels of land
involved the inability of Hawaiians to transmit the location of their property to their heirs. The basis of the problem rested with the ancient land
tenure system and the lack of surveys at the time of the Great Mahele. The
kuleanas were contained within the ahupua'a and boundaries were natural
features such as a rock or tree. Since haole ranchers and plantation owners
frequently obtained leases for many contiguous kuleanas, the tracts became
one undivided field or pasture and the natural boundaries disappeared. A
returning commoner could not distinguish his fields from the other
kuleanas. Consequently the descendants of kuleana owners often did not
know the site of the land or that they held part interest in a particular
acreage.[41]

Hawaiians are still threatened with the loss of their lands through
adverse possession. Testimony presented to the Hawaii Constitutional
Convention in 1978 revealed that approximately thirty cases were pending
in the Land Court and circuit court. Many of these cases involved lands
owned by Native Hawaiians. Large landholders claimed land by adverse
possession in Kīpū Kai on Kaua'i; Hāna, Ke'anae, and Kula on Maui; Puna
and Miloli'i-Ho'ōpūloa on Hawai'i, and Hālawa Valley on Moloka'i. An
examination of reported cases since 1979 indicated that adverse possessors
are still obtaining title to land owned by Native Hawaiians.[42]

Other Problems Resulting in Land Alienation

The problem of heirship that plagues American Indian land titles has
created favorable situations for adverse possessors in Hawaii. The fact that
many individuals hold a share interest in a small parcel of land often prevents all of the owners from using the property. With multiple owners the
title remains clouded, and without a clear title none of the shareholders can
get a mortgage or loan on the property. This creates vacant land that
potential adverse possessors take advantage of. An outsider can also purchase part interest from one of the owners and subsequently enter into
possession adversely to his cotenants.[43]

Haoles sometimes used unscrupulous methods to deprive the Hawaiians
of their lands. As in the case of American Indians, some Native Hawaiians
signed a document with a cross mark without knowing what they were
signing. They later discovered they had conveyed away their land. In the
1920s and 1930s the MacBride Sugar Company on Kaua'i induced kuleana

owners to exchange their fertile lands and water rights for other property located on the beach. Since the native owners were fishermen most of them agreed to the exchange. After these Hawaiians died, company officials evicted the heirs from their new lands. The original agreement included a clause, unknown to the Hawaiians, that gave Native Hawaiians who initially signed the papers only tenure to occupancy for life.[44]

The Claus Spreckels affair of the 1880s augmented the alienation of land from the Hawaiians. In 1880 Claus Spreckels, a major sugar plantation owner, purchased Princess Ruth Keʻelikōlani's rights to one-half of the Crown lands for $10,000. Although Keʻelikōlani did not have a clear title, the legislature wanted to settle the claims being asserted by Spreckels. It therefore granted Spreckels fee simple title to 24,000 acres, an entire ahupuaʻa, of good sugar land on Maui in exchange for his claim to one-half interest in the Crown lands.[45]

Foreigner Pressure for More Land

Numerous factors generated a greater demand for land by haoles. In the 1850s the discovery of gold in California and the subsequent settlement of the state, as well as expansion in the Pacific Northwest, precipitated a large trade with the Hawaiian islands. Ranchers, plantation owners, and land speculators obtained large acreage either in the form of leaseholds or freeholds from Hawaiians. The haoles' desire to attract permanent American settlement in the islands also motivated them to acquire additional land and to remonstrate for the sale of government lands.

Foreign agitation for placing Hawaiian lands on the market did not end when aliens acquired the right to purchase and sell lands in fee simple. Editorials and letters to the editors of the Hawaiian haole newspapers clearly reflected this continued desire for land. Some foreigners attacked the Hawaiian government's policy of land division and complained that the land commission operated in a slow, tedious, complicated way that hindered island prosperity. A segment of the foreign community suggested that the king initially should have asserted his ownership of all the lands, awarded titles to the occupants of the lands, and then sold the remaining lands on the open market at nominal prices. Other foreigners recommended that the government alter its policy to stimulate settlement and agriculture in the islands. They advocated that the government conduct an inventory of government and Crown lands, survey them, and lease or sell the lands on the open market. The king's private lands had diminished in size by 1865 due to continued sale, and as a result the legislature in that year made the Crown lands inalienable. Some haoles wanted the Hawaiian government to remove this restriction.[46]

Sanford Dole advocated selling government and Crown lands to promote settlement of the islands by small landholders. Dole proposed that the government purchase most of the Crown lands, sell the unoccupied government and Crown lands in plots consisting of 40 to 160 acres, and sell the acreages held by leases as they expired. An English resident proposed another method that would place additional lands on the market. He suggested that the government seize a Native Hawaiian's kuleana if he did not cultivate it efficiently and add the farm to the government lands.[47]

Land Acts of 1884 and 1895

Several land acts were passed in 1884 and 1895 to promote homesteading. This legislation attracted few settlers, however, and enabled speculators and large landholders to acquire additional lands. Speculators took advantage of the 1884 land act that permitted the acquisition of small plots of less than 20 acres; much of this land ended up in the control of the plantations. The land act of 1895 had the same effect. This law provided for leasing of lands for not more than 21 years and was limited to 1,200 acres per applicant. A 1,000-acre limitation was placed on the auctioning of public lands, which were formerly Crown and government lands, but individuals or plantation owners usually devised a way to evade the limitation. The act provided for the homesteading of smaller plots of land in three ways: a right-of-purchase lease for 21 years with the option of buying the land after 3 years; a cash freehold that allowed a purchaser to pay one-fourth of the value of the land immediately and then pay the remaining amount with interest in small installments and receive a fee in patent when all payments had been made; and homestead leases for 8- to 60-acre tracts, tailored largely for Native Hawaiians. These latter leases were inalienable and after 6 years of occupying the land and improving it according to preset conditions, the holder could obtain a 999-year lease. Only a small percentage of Hawaiians made use of the homestead lease. Haoles usually opted for the right-of-purchase leased land. Overall, the land acts of 1884 and 1895 augmented the alienation of lands from Hawaiians.[48]

Loss of Crown and Government Lands

When haoles overthrew the native government in 1893, the provisional government claimed title to both Crown and government lands, which became the public lands of the new Republic of Hawaii. With the loss of independence as a sovereign Hawaiian nation, the natives also lost their public domain to a haole-dominated government. Although the natives could acquire lands by the provisions of the land act of 1895, few possessed the financial resources to obtain farms. According to the Annexation Treaty of 1898 with the United States and the Hawaiian Organic Act of

1900, which created the U.S. Territory of Hawaii, the Republic of Hawaii transferred title to its public lands to the United States, although the actual management of the lands remained with the territorial government, whose land laws remained in force.[49]

Concentrated Land Ownership

During the second half of the nineteenth century the plantation system dominated the Hawaiian economy and by the end of the century land control was concentrated in the hands of a few owners. This concentration of lands continued through the twentieth century. By 1967 seventy-four owners held title to 96 percent of the lands in the state of Hawaii: the state owned almost 39 percent, the U.S. government almost 10 percent, and seventy-two private owners held 47 percent with seven owning nearly 30 percent.[50]

In 1967 the Hawaii legislature passed a land reform act to change the pattern of land ownership. Since World War II, large landowners had leased residential lots to private parties rather than selling the land in fee. Many individuals wanting residential housing had to buy their houses and off-site improvements and pay property taxes and levies for special improvements, but they could only rent the lots. The Hawaii legislature believed that this practice increased land prices to unreasonable levels, reduced the availability of fee simple residential property, elevated inflation, and endangered the economic prosperity of the state. Through use of a condemnation scheme, the state intended to attack the land oligopoly and thus promote the public welfare.[51]

The Hawaii Land Reform Act provided that the state, acting through the Hawaii Housing Authority, could condemn residential tracts of five acres or more. Upon receipt of a petition signed by either twenty-five or one-half of the lessees in a residential development, the housing authority would hold a hearing to determine whether the condemnation satisfied a public purpose. If it did, the housing authority would condemn some or all of the lots. Then the fee would be sold to the resident lessees. Although enacted in 1967, the land reform act was not implemented until eight years later.[52]

The land redistribution plan will have a significant impact on land ownership patterns, particularly on Oʻahu, where twenty-two owners held almost 75 percent of the land. The Bishop Estate, along with other Native Hawaiian trusts and organizations, opposed the Hawaii Land Reform Act. The Bishop Estate, established by Princess Bernice Pauahi Bishop, held title to 8 percent of the land in the state and 15 percent in Oʻahu. Under the terms of her will, the revenue from the lands owned by the estate was to be used to establish a school for Native Hawaiians. One-fourth of its income came from residential leases. The Bishop Estate argued that the loss of its residential property and lease income would endanger the future of Kamehameha Schools. One of its trustees, a Hawaiian, stated, "I've seen us get ripped off for too long. It's the survival of a race that's the issue. Right now, we need Kamehameha Schools and all the assets it has to help a group of people become more productive."[53]

The Bishop Estate filed suit, alleging that the land conversion law was an unconstitutional taking of private land. It maintained that the taking violated the "public use" clause of the Fifth Amendment to the U.S. Constitution and a comparable provision in the state constitution. The estate further argued that the Hawaii Land Reform Act exceeded the state's power of eminent domain by condemning land for a private purpose. In 1984 the U.S. Supreme Court held that transfer of the fee interest to private parties did not necessarily constitute a taking for a private purpose; the crucial question was whether it was condemned for a public use. The court ruled that the state's exercise of eminent domain was rationally related to a public purpose—to reduce "certain perceived evils of concentrated property ownership." On similar grounds the Hawaii Supreme Court upheld the constitutionality of the redistribution act.[54]

Native Hawaiian Fishing Rights

Native Hawaiian rights in the sea fisheries have changed since European-American contact. Today Native Hawaiians have public fishing rights, in common with other citizens of the state. In addition some individuals retain rights in certain private fisheries adjoining the ahupua'a they live in or own. This right is not restricted to Native Hawaiians, but extends to all tenants or residents in the ahupua'a and to the owner of vested konohiki fishing rights.[55]

The legal foundation of these rights originated in laws promulgated in 1839. Kamehameha III declared that the fishing grounds beyond the coral reefs belonged to the people, whereas those from the reefs to the beach were for the exclusive use of the konohiki and tenants of the ahupua'a. The laws of 1840, which incorporated the law issued a year earlier, set out the respective fishing rights of the landlord and tenants. The act of 1846 stated that the konohiki held the fisheries as private property, subject to the rights of the tenants. In 1851 the government declared that the fisheries adjoining government land were open to the public. When government land was sold or leased, owners or lessors did not acquire any exclusive fishing rights. Eight years later the legislature codified the fishery laws.[56]

In 1900 Congress intended to destroy exclusive fishing rights and open the private fisheries to all U.S. citizens. Provisions in the organic act repealed the Hawaiian laws on konohiki fishing rights except as they applied to persons with vested rights. Another section authorized the condemnation of exclusive fishing rights upon payment of just compensation.

To establish vested rights, claimants had to register their claims in circuit court within two years of the effective date of the organic act. If the judicial determination validated the private fishing right, the territorial government could acquire it for public use by means of condemnation. Approximately 100 of more than 300 private fisheries were registered and judicially established. Only some have been condemned. Nonregistration of claims resulted in the loss of the konohiki and tenants' exclusive fishing rights and of their entitlement to compensation. These fisheries became public fishing grounds.[57]

Both konohiki and tenants have statutorily defined fishing rights in the remaining private fisheries. These rights have been essentially the same since the 1850s. The fishing ground extends from the beach to the reefs, or where there are no reefs one "mile seaward of the beach at low watermark." Although it is "the private fishery of the konohiki," he holds it for the "equal use" of the tenants and himself. Tenants can take the aquatic life of the fishery for domestic or commercial uses. Each year the konohiki is entitled, upon notice to the tenants, to reserve for his exclusive use one "species or variety of aquatic life" for a "specified period." Or the konohiki may ban all fishing within the private fishery for part of the year and during the remaining months take up to one-third of the tenant fishermen's harvest of aquatic life. Violators of the konohiki's statutory rights are subject to civil and criminal penalties.[58]

NATIVE HAWAIIAN RESISTANCE

Alienation of the Native Hawaiians from most of their lands and ultimately the loss of their sovereignty as an independent nation did not occur within a vacuum. Hawaiian resistance assumed a more subtle form than that frequently displayed by American Indians in their contest against white control of their sovereignty and lands. They did share certain stances in their opposition to white expansion, however, such as passive resistance, occasional legal maneuverings, and compromise.

Hawaiians frequently revealed their fear of foreign control of their land and nation. During his tour of Hawai'i in 1822, William Ellis remarked that the commoners believed they would become an extinct people and foreigners would obtain their lands if the chiefs allowed the missionaries to reside in the Hawaiian islands. Native Hawaiians also believed that if their lands were alienated they would lose control of their government. This view originated with the ancient land tenure system in which government and control over the lands were inseparable. The commoners feared that a rapid increase of the foreign population and wealth would eventually place haoles in control of the government. These attitudes led the chiefs to oppose foreign ownership of land and increased immigration. Numerous foreigners complained of the chiefs' reluctance to sell land to whites and to grant them security of property. The haoles' power and influence proved too strong for the Hawaiian government to withstand; its officials gradually compromised. The chiefs and king played a game of tactical delay. Kamehameha III continued to reassert his sovereignty and his ownership of the land while granting piecemeal concessions to haoles. The Hawaiian government tried to preserve the quasi-feudal land tenure system by slowly reforming it along Western lines. Even after the overthrow of the old feudal land system, some chiefs refused to sell their lands to haoles.[59]

Strong opposition to haole ascendancy in the Hawaiian government, to naturalization of haoles as Hawaiian citizens, and to their accompanying right to hold land occurred in 1845. The antiforeign agitation among Native Hawaiians revealed their fear of foreign domination in land matters and governmental affairs. Commoners from Lahaina and Wailuku on Maui petitioned the king and chiefs for the removal of all foreigners from government positions and to end naturalization of aliens. Natives from Kailua, Hawai'i, presented a petition to the Hawaiian rulers protesting sale of land and granting of citizenship to foreigners. The Hawaiian government responded to the demands by explaining the need for foreigners in government service because only haoles had the requisite knowledge and skills to conduct relations with foreign nations and maintain Hawaiian independence. Hawaiian officials argued that naturalized subjects had to be loyal to the king and protect his sovereignty from foreign infringement. The response also enunciated that it was only fair to grant naturalized citizens the same land rights held by Native Hawaiians. The chiefs reaffirmed the government's position that aliens could not own land. The king reiterated this view during a tour of Maui in December 1845 and January 1846. Apparently these explanations eased the fear of the Hawaiian people because antiforeign agitation subsided. In 1855 opposition to foreign ownership of land resurfaced. Natives from Lana'i presented a petition enunciating their belief that foreigners should not be allowed to purchase land.[60]

Some Hawaiians revealed their reluctance to accept a land system based on individual ownership by establishing *hui*s, which provided a transition between the old land tenure system and the new order of allodial ownership. A group of Native Hawaiians obtained communal title to a tract of land, then allotted specific plots to individual families to farm while retaining common rights to pasture and gathering areas. Some of these huis continued to exist into the twentieth century, but they have been plagued with heirship problems and other difficulties.[61]

Native Hawaiian Opposition to U.S. Reciprocity Treaties

A major native resistance to haole attempts to obtain control of Hawaiian soil and sovereignty occurred during discussions of a reciprocity treaty with the United States in the 1860s and early 1870s. To persuade a reluctant U.S. Congress to agree to a reciprocity treaty, American haoles wanted to arrange for the cession of Pearl Harbor and a ten- to twelve-mile area surrounding it to the American nation for a coaling and repair station. They believed that such a treaty was vital to the growth and prosperity of the Hawaiian nation, since it would allow the sugar plantations to export their crop to the United States duty free. American advisers urged King Lunalilo to support the treaty and its provision of the cession of Pearl Harbor. Most haoles, with the exception of British subjects and Catholic priests, endorsed the proposed treaty. Extensive debate developed over the issue among both haoles and Native Hawaiians. Opponents of the reciprocity treaty argued that such concessions would eventually lead to U.S. control of the Hawaiian islands. Advocates maintained that future Hawaiian prosperity depended on acceptance of the treaty. They contended that other nations had ceded lands willingly to other foreign powers, that the cession would not endanger the sovereignty of the Hawaiian kingdom, and that it was right to cede land when the good of the country demanded it. Protreaty forces charged those haoles opposing the treaty with stirring up native prejudices by presenting unfounded arguments that the treaty provided the first step toward annexation and the subsequent alienation of lands and sovereignty, and that Native Hawaiians would share a fate similar to that of the American Indian. Those favoring the treaty asserted that it would stop haole demands for annexation to the United States because reciprocity would bring the same benefits desired by the annexationists while strengthening the Hawaiian government.[62]

Many of the haoles supporting the treaty believed that annexation to the United States would come eventually but that it should be postponed until Native Hawaiians either desired it or became extinct. Although Henry A. Peirce, the American minister to Hawai'i, preferred annexation, he recommended to the American secretary of state that the United States should agree to the proposed treaty because it would tie the two nations together "with hooks of steel." The *Pacific Commercial Advertiser,* a haole newspaper in Honolulu, supported the treaty and observed that reciprocity was necessary for the prosperity of the Hawaiian nation. The editor also stated that the treaty would maintain U.S. influence until annexation occurred at the time of native depopulation. Peirce accused the proannexationists of stirring up the Native Hawaiians' feelings against the reciprocity treaty in hopes of causing a native revolution that would bring American intervention and ultimately American possession of the Hawaiian islands.[63]

The haoles were aware of widespread native opposition to cession of Pearl Harbor but dismissed it by rationalizing that whites knew what was best for Hawaiians. Haoles believed that the Hawaiians were motivated by irrational, ignorant, and prejudicial fears. On several occasions large numbers of Hawaiians met to listen to white and native opponents of the treaty and cession. At one meeting in June 1873 the Native Hawaiians passed resolutions opposing the cession of Pearl Harbor. Most of the Hawaiian opponents did not oppose reciprocity per se, but rather ceding Hawaiian land and abdicating sovereignty over it. Some of them objected because they feared that reciprocity would lead to alienation of Hawaiian sovereignty. Lunalilo and his cabinet finally acquiesced to massive native protest and withdrew their offer of the reciprocity treaty. The commercialists verbally attacked the ministers for their changed position and demanded their resignation, but Lunalilo requested that the ministers retain their government positions.[64]

In 1875 the United States and the Hawaiian kingdom agreed to a reciprocity treaty that did not include the cession of Pearl Harbor. One of the provisions of the treaty limited Hawaiian sovereignty by forbidding the Hawaiian government to lease or cede a harbor or any territory to any foreign nation. After 1875, Native Hawaiians increasingly opposed reciprocity. The influx of foreigners and the increase of American economic activity in the islands that resulted from the reciprocity agreement, along with the treaty's limitation of Hawaiian sovereignty, led to the opposition. Hawaiian legislators protested that reciprocity would culminate in annexation. The agitation caused the formation of a new ministry in 1878 that had more native representation. A strong nationalistic movement developed by 1880, resulting in Native Hawaiian control of the legislature. The Hawaiians' nationalistic sentiment, economic depression, and political, moral, and financial excesses in government policy led to the Revolution of 1887.[65]

The 1887 Constitution and the Alienation of Pearl Harbor

Native opposition failed to prevent the cession of Pearl Harbor in 1887. In that year the U.S. Congress reviewed the reciprocity treaty and added an amendment that gave the United States the "exclusive right to enter the harbor . . . and to establish and to maintain there a coaling and repair station for the use of vessels of the United States." The Hawaiian government at first refused to agree to the revised treaty but finally acquiesced. The king reluctantly approved the Pearl Harbor cession, although he realized that Native Hawaiians opposed it. King David Kalākaua and his reform cabinet based their decision on the American secretary of state's assurance that the concession of Pearl Harbor was coterminous with the existence of the treaty, and that no loss of Hawaiian sovereignty occurred with the transaction. The United States failed to improve the harbor during the remaining years of the Hawaiian kingdom.[66]

In 1887 the haoles forced a constitution on Kalākaua that greatly restricted his authority as sovereign and limited the rights of Native Hawaiians. Many Hawaiians were upset with the "bayonet" constitution and wanted the king to regain his former prerogatives. Robert Wilcox, a part-Hawaiian, led an insurrection in 1889, but the reform government quickly brought it to an end. Other Hawaiians formed a party called the Hui Kalaiaina to restore the constitution of 1864 and native control of the government. Native leaders attempted and sometimes secured limited control of the Hawaiian government until the Revolution of 1893. The clashing of two nationalities for supremacy culminated in the overthrow of the monarchy.[67]

Resistance to U.S. Annexation

Native Hawaiians opposed not only the Pearl Harbor cession but also haole attempts at annexation to the United States, which occurred regularly during the second half of the nineteenth century. Many chiefs, Prince Alexander Liholiho, native newspapers, and mass meetings held by native leaders expressed the opposition of Hawaiians to annexation. Opponents raised racial arguments in support of their views. They suggested that Hawaiians would become enslaved and would lose their lands, as had the American Indians. In 1851 when a French takeover appeared imminent, Kamehameha III secretly agreed to cede the Hawaiian islands to the United States in the event of a French seizure, but the feared usurpation failed to materialize. During 1852 and 1853 a large number of haoles actively favored annexation to the United States. In 1854 some of the king's ministers persuaded Kamehameha III that internal threats of revolution by haoles and proposed Californian filibustering endangered the continued existence of the Hawaiian kingdom. In February of that year, the king authorized Robert C. Wyllie to commence negotiations with the United States for annexation. The Hawaiian government agreed to an annexation agreement that American commissioner David L. Gregg submitted to the U.S. secretary of state for his consideration. The king became reluctant to continue negotiations after the threat of the overthrow subsided. His death in December 1854 and the ascendancy of the nationalist Alexander Liholiho to the throne as Kamehameha IV brought an end to annexation discussions. Liholiho withdrew the annexation offer.[68]

A haole minority continued to lobby for immediate annexation to the United States. During the discussion of the reciprocity treaty from 1868 to 1873, annexation became a subject of debate. American supporters of annexation presented it as a preferable alternative to reciprocity and the only means that would ensure lasting prosperity and stability of government and property. Many haoles failed to support annexation because they believed the time was not right for it, although many of them contended that manifest destiny made annexation inevitable at a future date. A number of newspapers in the United States also expressed the sentiment that the Hawaiian islands would "sooner or later become American property."[69]

During the 1860s and 1870s, some U.S. officials desired annexation. Secretary of State William Seward favored annexation but believed that American concern with economic entrenchment due to Reconstruction would prevent extension of American sovereignty over the islands. In 1873 President Ulysses S. Grant instructed Secretary of State Hamilton Fish to approach the Hawaiian government about its views on annexation. For several years the American minister to Hawai'i, Henry A. Peirce, had ardently argued for annexation. Peirce stressed that the geographic location of the Hawaiian islands made them strategic to the north Pacific trade, valuable for a naval depot and coaling station, and vital for military protection of Pacific trade in wartime. He also expressed his fear that if the United States did not annex the islands, or at least agree to reciprocity, another world power would take possession of the islands.[70]

The expansionist secretary of state, James Blaine, in 1881 summarized American policy toward the Hawaiian islands and the importance of Hawai'i to the United States:

> The situation of the Hawaiian Islands, giving them the strategic control of the North Pacific, brings their possession within the range of questions of purely American policy. . . . Hence the necessity, as recognized in our existing treaty relations, of drawing the ties of intimate relationship between us and the Hawaiian Islands so as to make them practically a part of the American system without derogation of their absolute independence. . . . The position of the Hawaiian Islands as the key to the dominion of the American Pacific demands their neutrality. . . .

Blaine went on to say that if the Hawaiian government could not maintain its neutrality, then the United States would "unhesitatingly meet the altered situation by seeking an avowedly American solution for the grave issues presented."[71]

In 1889 Secretary of State James Blaine appointed John Stevens as U.S. minister to Hawai'i. Both Stevens and Blaine were avowed expansionists, and their imperialistic views extended to Hawai'i. From the time of Stevens' arrival in Hawai'i, he ardently supported the foreign residents who favored annexation to the United States. In March 1892 he requested instructions from the secretary of state on what his role and that of the American naval commander should be if the anticipated overthrow of the Hawaiian government occurred. Evidently the secretary of state never admonished him to refrain from involving himself and the United States in local politics.[72]

In January 1893 a small group of proannexation revolutionists overthrew the Hawaiian government with the assistance of American officials. At the request of the revolutionists, on 16 January Stevens and Capt. G. Wiltse of the U.S.S. *Boston* landed American marines and placed them at a strategic location between the palace and the government building. Stevens ordered the American forces ashore on the pretext of protecting American property and safety. On 17 January the revolutionists proclaimed the establishment of a provisional government, and Stevens almost immediately recognized its legitimacy, even though the revolutionists were not in complete control of the government. After Stevens recognized the provisional government Queen Lili'uokalani, provisionally and under protest, surrendered her authority to the United States because of the active involvement and presence of U.S. troops. She believed the U.S. government would restore her sovereignty once it learned of Stevens' illegal activities and the use of the American military in the overthrow of the legitimate Hawaiian government, and she requested that the U.S. government restore Hawaiian sovereignty (most Native Hawaiians opposed the overthrow of their government and queen). Since the Harrison administration had previously indicated its support of annexation, the provisional government immediately sent representatives to Washington to negotiate an annexation treaty. The Senate was considering such a treaty within thirty days after the establishment of the provisional government.[73]

On 1 February 1893 Stevens declared an American protectorate over the Hawaiian islands. Although Secretary of State John Foster reprimanded him for this action and disavowed the protectorate, the American flag remained raised over the government building and the marines stayed on guard until early April. On the same day that he declared an American protectorate over Hawai'i, Stevens wrote to the secretary of state that "the Hawaiian pear is now fully ripe, and this is the golden hour for the United States to pluck it."[74]

Congress delayed action on the annexation treaty until President-elect Grover Cleveland took office. Cleveland questioned the proceedings in the Hawaiian islands and appointed James H. Blount to conduct an investigation of the American role in the revolution. Blount's report indicted the actions of the American minister, the American naval forces, and some haole residents. Based on Blount's findings, President Cleveland concluded that "the Provisional Government owes its existence to an armed invasion by the United States" and that the overthrow of the monarchy was "dependent for its success upon the agency of the United States acting through its diplomatic and naval representatives."[75] Cleveland refused to restore the monarchy by using military force against the revolutionists; instead he tried to persuade the provisional government to restore Queen Lili'uokalani to the throne. The revolutionists refused. Cleveland did not resubmit the annexation treaty to the Senate.

The next president, William McKinley, supported annexation. He was initially unable to garner enough support in the Senate to approve the treaty. In 1898 the annexation efforts successfully culminated in annexation. The U.S. government recognized the importance of the Hawaiian islands to America's position in the Pacific. Even so, supporters lacked the necessary two-thirds majority to approve the annexation treaty, so they resorted to a joint resolution that only required a simple majority. In a departure from previous federal policy, Congress did not require the people of Hawai'i, including Native Hawaiians, to vote on the issue of annexation. Hawai'i became an incorporated territory of the United States in 1900 with enactment of the Hawaii Organic Act. This ended any Native Hawaiian hopes of restoring the sovereignty of their nation.[76]

Several motives impelled haoles to overthrow the royal Hawaiian government, establish a provisional republic, and seek and eventually gain absorption by the United States. Certainly a principal reason was to guard their tenure in the rich agricultural lands that they had methodically stripped from the Native Hawaiians during the nineteenth century.

7

Restitution Attempts

DURING the 1970s and 1980s both Native Hawaiians and American Indians became increasingly active in asserting claims for land. Native Americans channeled most of their efforts through legal means; however, some of their actions were extralegal. Hawaiians and Indians focused their activities on four main areas. These included obtaining actual restoration of land; obtaining monetary compensation for lands taken from them; preventing additional alienation and misuse of land or natural resources; and recovering or affirming historic fishing, hunting, gathering, access, and water rights. The three land issues are discussed herein; recovery of traditional rights is discussed in chapter 8. Most of the gains made by Native Americans resulted from their assertive actions and a favorable judicial and legislative climate.

MONETARY COMPENSATION FOR EXPROPRIATED LANDS

Compensation for American Indians

Hawaiians and Indians have sought monetary compensation for lands taken illegally or unfairly. Indians pursued this course of action because they believed it offered the only alternative. Most Indians would have preferred that the federal government pay restitution in the form of land, but that seemed like an impossible dream. Some have steadfastly refused to accept payment, maintaining that their land could not be sold.

Before congressional enactment of the Indian Claims Commission Act of 1946, Indians requesting restitution first had to obtain congressional approval for a suit against the federal government. Sovereign immunity protected the federal government unless it authorized litigation in the U.S. Court of Claims. Congress narrowly conceived the basis for tribal claims and consequently approved few petitions. On those it sanctioned, the legislative process sometimes lasted for forty years.

After a decade and a half of congressional attempts to formulate a system to adjudicate Indian claims, Congress established the Indian Claims Commission in 1946. Essentially a jurisdictional act, the legislation allowed the tribes five years to register claims with the commission. Only those claims arising before passage of the act could be heard by the commission. The act required the commission to adjudicate the claims by 1957. Congress later extended the life of the commission five times. The commission finally dissolved on 30 September 1978.[1]

The act permitted suits for claims arising in regard to the constitution, treaties, and executive orders; claims sounding in tort or involving fraud, duress, or mutual or unilateral mistake; and claims "based on fair and honorable dealings not recognized by any existing rule or equity." Indians based most of their cases on the first argument. The majority of suits involved uncompensated taking of land or payments below the fair market value of the land. Claimants had to prove exclusive occupancy of a definable territory. The commission recognized claims showing aboriginal title to exclusive use and occupancy, even if only seasonal or ritualistic. They refused compensation for claims of areas shared by more than one tribe or band, except when the federal government had moved several tribes into an area and then removed them.[2]

The litigation involved a lengthy process, and the commission completed its work slowly. Originally tribes presented 370 claims, but the commission separated some into individual dockets resulting in a total of 614. By the end of 1967, the Indian Claims Commission had dismissed 132 dockets and approved 100 for awards for about $226 million; during the next eleven years it approved an additional 242 dockets for awards and denied 72 petitions. By September 1978 the commission had decided 546 dockets for $818,172,606.64, less attorneys' fees. The Indian Claims Commission transferred the remaining 68 dockets to the U.S. Court of Claims for settlement.[3]

Before deciding the amount of compensation, the commission determined the fair market value of the land at time of taking and then deducted offsets that included the original sum paid the tribe plus additional costs of supporting the tribe. The commission never formulated an exact method of determining what items comprised offsets. Congress justified the deduction of offsets by claiming that the tribes would not have needed gratuities if they originally had received sufficient compensation for their lands. It failed to consider that the tribes would not have needed gratuities if they had not been forced to cede their lands and also would not have wanted or bought certain things considered as offsets. Without the offset provision, Congress probably would not have passed the act of 1946, since it believed the total amount of restitution awards would have been too high.

Before the commission settled a claim, it conducted three hearings. The first decided the validity of the claim. If it was justified, a second hearing determined the fair market value of the land. The third hearing set the total amount of the offsets. Both the tribe and federal government could appeal the commission's finding to the court of claims. After the commission awarded monetary compensation, Congress had to approve the tribe's plan for using the money. Generally Indian tribes opted for a per capita settlement. In 1973 Congress passed legislation authorizing the secretary of the interior to approve a method of distribution, contingent on congressional approval. The same act required each tribe to allocate for tribal use a minimum of 20 percent of its award.[4]

The Indian Claims Commission became closely associated with the termination policy. Some congressmen believed that payment for past wrongs would remove all moral and legal claims for a continuing federal trust responsibility. The national honor would be cleared. Others believed that the monetary payments would make Indians economically self-sufficient and promote their assimiliation into mainstream society.

Some Indians viewed termination as a possible outcome of a claims award. As justification for their attitude they pointed to the fate of the Menominee tribe. The Menominee, along with other tribes who appeared economically prosperous, was among the first to be terminated from federal trust status. In 1951 the Menominees received a settlement of $7,600,000 after a seventeen-year court case. The Menominees decided to award $1,500 per tribal member and invest the remaining funds in their thriving lumber operation, their hospital, and other community enterprises. Congress refused to approve the distribution plan unless the Menominees agreed to accept termination. By the time of their final termination in 1961, they had spent most of their money attempting to defeat termination. Almost bankrupt, they reluctantly sold 9,500 acres of land before Congress restored their tribal status in 1973.[5]

Some tribes such as the Oglala Sioux have refused claims awards. They have maintained that the land cannot be sold at any price and that the imposition of Western legal techniques (e.g., treaties, conquest, and claims awards) has not extinguished their title. They want recognition that the land is still held by the tribe.

The native population of Alaska received monetary compensation for the extinguishment of their aboriginal title as part of the Alaska Native Claims Settlement Act of 1971. Congress awarded them $462.5 million with 2 percent royalty on mineral development on state and federal lands in Alaska, up to $500 million.

Attempts at Compensation for Native Hawaiians

Encouraged by congressional passage of the Alaska Native Claims Settlement Act in 1971, Native Hawaiians actively campaigned for comparable legislation for their benefit. Aboriginal Lands of Hawaiian Ancestry (ALOHA) led the movement for reparations for lands taken in the 1890s. Numerous other Native Hawaiian organizations that originated in the 1970s joined with older native organizations to support a claims settlement. Many Hawaiians disagreed on the method of restitution. Some nationalists have demanded the establishment of an independent Hawaiian kingdom or a tribal government possessing sovereignty much like the reconstituted Indian tribes, and coexisting within certain states.[6]

The movement for restitution has based its claims on the illegal actions of the U.S. minister to Hawaiʻi, John Stevens, in 1893 when he ordered the U.S. naval forces to land in Hawaiʻi. Use of the American military to support the revolutionary white settlers led Queen Liliʻuokalani to surrender her kingdom to the United States to avoid bloodshed. The provisional government and later the Republic of Hawaii ruled the islands without the consent of the Native Hawaiians and designated the Crown and government lands as its public lands. When the United States annexed the Republic of Hawaii in 1898, the revolutionary government ceded these public lands to the federal government without the consent of the Hawaiian people. According to Hawaiian leaders the federal government assumed illegal ownership through an act of conquest as a result of the activities of American representatives in 1893 and 1898; this argument formed the basis for the Native Hawaiian claim for compensation. Native Hawaiians maintained that they lost both dominion and domain over their nation and land.[7]

In 1974 representatives Spark Matsunaga and Patsy Mink from Hawaii introduced the first Native Hawaiian claims bill, but the House Interior Committee failed to report it out of committee. Matsunaga and Mink reintroduced the measure during the next session; it met the same fate. In February 1975, however, the Subcommittee on Indian Affairs of the Committee on Interior and Insular Affairs held hearings in Hawaii on the native claims bill. Under the provisions of the bill, the secretary of the interior would establish a roll of all living Native Hawaiians. The roll would be maintained by adding the names of newborn Hawaiians. To qualify as a Native Hawaiian, an individual had to be the descendant of the aboriginal race inhabiting the Hawaiian islands before 1778. A person lacking sufficient genealogical documentation of his ancestry could still be enrolled if other Native Hawaiians considered him a native. The claims bill called for the creation of a Hawaiian Native Corporation to manage the one hundred million dollars to be paid annually by the federal government for a period of ten years; the total settlement amounted to one billion dollars. The members of the corporation would consist of the Native Hawaiians listed on the proposed rolls. Another provision gave the Hawaiian Native Corporation first right to claim any federal land in Hawaii that the government classified as surplus lands.[8]

Undaunted by the apparent lack of congressional support, leaders of ALOHA, congressmen from Hawaii, and other Hawaiian organizations continued their drive for recompense. In 1975 Representative Matsunaga and Senator Daniel Inouye introduced a measure providing for the establishment of a Hawaiian Native Claims Settlement Study Commission to investigate the claims. The bill directed the commission to determine the validity of the claims; if justified, then the commission would decide how to rectify them and report their recommendations to Congress. Congress would not be bound by the suggestions. ALOHA preferred its newly formulated bill, which closely resembled the original bill but contained an additional provision calling for the return of approximately 2.5 million acres of land, which represented the size of the Crown and government estate in 1893. ALOHA reluctantly supported the alternative legislation that would establish the Hawaiian Native Claims Settlement Study Commission, because the congressmen assured ALOHA leaders that their bill would not pass Congress.[9]

For the next four years congressmen from Hawaii reintroduced the study commission bill, with some modifications. During 1976 and 1977 congressional committees conducted hearings in Hawaii on the measure, causing members to alter the original bill. They incorporated certain requests expressed by members of the Hawaiian community who desired more Native Hawaiians on the proposed study commission and more representation for all the main islands in the Hawaiian archipelago. Finally in October 1977 the Senate passed the bill without opposition, but in May 1978 the House failed to approve the measure. Motivated by a belief in the need for quick enactment, Senator Inouye reintroduced the bill during the same session but Congress did not vote on the proposal again that year. Finally in 1980 Congress passed legislation establishing the Native Hawaiian Study Commission.[10]

The legislation provided for a nine-member commission, six members from the mainland and three from Hawaii. On his last day in office President Jimmy Carter appointed the commissioners. President Ronald Reagan subsequently dismissed and replaced them with his own appointees. The mainland commissioners were all members of the executive branch of the federal government.[11]

The commission was unable to produce a report unanimously supported by its members. Consequently, the mainland commissioners prepared a report (referred to as the majority report), and the Hawaii members wrote a supplemental minority report. The major area of disagreement was over the mainland commissioners' conclusions on U.S. responsibility and liability for the overthrow of the Hawaiian monarchy in 1893 and loss of sovereignty and domain. The majority report concluded that the United States was not legally or morally responsible for the overthrow. It also declared that even if such responsibility existed, Native Hawaiians had no "compensable interest." The Hawaii commissioners argued that the majority report's conclusions resulted from flawed methodology, interpretation, and legal analysis. The selective use of facts distorted the interpretation of American participation in the overthrow. The minority members also objected to the majority's conclusion that the United States' failure to act in accordance with international standards and with its own prior policy in annexing new territories did not justify a claims settlement. Also, the inappropriate application of American Indian law precedents to the Hawaiian claims ignored the important point that even Indian claims settlements had occurred only when Congress authorized or approved legal or moral claims against the federal government. The Hawaii commissioners maintained that there was a moral basis, if not a legal one, for compensable claims. They also criticized the majority report for its failure to examine adequately the federal government's trust responsibility to Native Hawaiians and their "cultural and social needs." The minority members produced their own study "to correct these errors."[12]

Hawaii congressmen have not introduced any restitution bills in Congress since these reports were presented in 1983. They are undoubtedly waiting for a favorable political climate and administration. When that time arrives, Native Hawaiians will remind Congress of President Cleveland's statement that the United States "can not allow itself to refuse to redress an injury inflicted through an abuse of power by officers clothed with its authority and wearing its uniform. . . . [T]he United States can not fail to vindicate its honor and its sense of justice by an earnest effort to make all possible reparation." Passage of restitution legislation would affect possibly fifteen percent of the population of Hawaii who claim descent from the indigenous race of the Hawaiian islands.[13]

Many Native Hawaiians encouraged the 1978 constitutional convention to incorporate an amendment to Hawaii's constitution. The voters of the state supported an amendment that provided for the establishment of an Office of Hawaiian Affairs. Along with other responsibilities relating to Native Hawaiian concerns, the new government agency would receive and manage any funds or property designated for Native Hawaiians. Its promoters advocated the creation of such an office partially in anticipation of receiving a settlement from the federal government. During the 1979 session the state legislature passed a bill creating an Office of Hawaiian Affairs.[14]

RESTORATION OF LAND BASE

Both Native Hawaiians and American Indians have endeavored to rebuild their land base during the twentieth century. They began making such attempts earlier in the century but achieved only limited success. American Indians accomplished more in this sphere than Native Hawaiians; the former have made significant progress in the 1970s and the 1980s in regaining former lands.

Restoration of the Indian Land Base

Under provisions of the Indian Reorganization Act, unallotted surplus lands have been restored to tribal trust status. Some tribes purchased land with loan funds authorized by the act for that purpose. However, Congress failed to appropriate sufficient funds to adequately support the program. Some Indians deeded their allotments to their tribe. Tribes acquired four million acres by 1950. In the 1970s and 1980s the secretary of the interior approved the addition of land to existing reservations or established new reservations under the authority of the Indian Reorganization Act. Tribes also purchased land in fee simple with their own funds, later transferring the land to trust status.[15]

In 1977, under provisions of the Indian Reorganization Act, the Bureau of Indian Affairs transferred lands to trust status for the Puyallup tribe and Sault Ste. Marie Chippewa Indians. Previously the Puyallup tribe or tribal members had fee simple title to lands within the boundaries of Puyallup Reservation and the city of Tacoma, Washington. The Sault Ste. Marie Chippewa Indians purchased a seventy-six-acre tract in the city limits of Sault Ste. Marie, Michigan, and requested the Bureau of Indian Affairs to transfer the land to trust status. The cities of Tacoma and Sault Ste. Marie challenged the action. Until the courts resolved the issues, the secretary of the interior stayed additional taking of lands in the city limits for these tribes. In separate decisions reached in 1978 and 1980, the U.S. District Court for the District of Columbia determined that the secretary of the interior had the authority to place lands in trust for the Puyallup tribe and the Sault Ste. Marie Chippewa Indians. The court held that the secretary could take land in trust for tribes who were not officially recognized as tribes in 1934 but subsequently were determined to have that status. It also declared that the secretary could acquire land and hold it in trust for tribes who were not completely "landless."[16]

During the 1970s and 1980s Congress returned land to the holdings of numerous tribes. In 1975 the Submarginal Lands Act conveyed over 370,000 acres of submarginal lands to trust status for seventeen Indian tribes. During the 1930s, the federal government had purchased these former reservation lands from homesteaders to return the land to the original tribal owners. Much of this submarginal land had remained in the public domain until Congress passed the Submarginal Lands Act in 1975.[17]

In 1975 Congress authorized the administrator of general services to transfer federal surplus lands located on former tribal trust lands in Oklahoma or on existing reservations in other states to the secretary of the interior to be held in trust for tribes. Subsequently excess lands have been returned to numerous tribes. The acreages ranged in size from one-half-acre plots to over 1,600 acres. Land restoration occurred by administrative action when the land was returned to the original tribal owner; otherwise congressional action was required. For example, in 1986 Congress authorized the partitioning of 5,824 acres, formerly Chilocco Indian School lands, among the Otoe-Missouri, Pawnee, Ponca, Tonkawa, Kaw, and Cherokee tribes in Oklahoma. This action required congressional approval since only the Cherokee formerly owned the land. Separate legislation was also necessary to return over 2,800 acres of federal surplus land to the Washoe in Nevada and California. Although the former Stewart Indian Boarding School lands were Washoe aboriginal lands, they were not located within an existing reservation. Consequently the land could not be restored through administrative action authorized by the surplus property act.[18]

Other congressional land returns involved land for which the aboriginal or legal title had not been legally extinguished or that had been improperly placed in the public domain or within another tribe's reservation. Some of these lands were sacred and vital to the continuation of traditional tribal religions. Most of the land restorations transferred the title to the United States in trust for the tribe. Congress returned the lands without a requirement of compensation by the tribes. This was done even during President Reagan's administration. From 1982 until the end of his presidency, his official policy was to require tribes to pay fair market value for formerly held lands that are now part of the public domain. The Bureau of Indian Affairs has often opposed land restitution bills because they did not require monetary payment by the tribes.[19]

Taos Blue Lake and Other Sacred Lands

Legislation returning the Taos Blue Lake and its watershed area to the Pueblo Indians in 1970 represented one of the most celebrated cases of land restitution. Taos Pueblo leaders had continually attempted to regain ownership of these sacred areas since 1906. At that time President Theodore Roosevelt placed Blue Lake and its environs in Taos National Forest, which later became Carson National Forest. The Taos Pueblo received no compensation for these lands. Before 1906 and until 1918 the U.S. government "recognized and protected the special and exclusive interests" of the Taos Indians in this area. In 1924 Congress enacted the Pueblo Land Board Act to settle land disputes between the Pueblos and non-Indians. The Board offered $458,520.61 to the Taos Pueblo for lands that had been taken by non-Indians. The government paid part of the settlement, but the Taos Pueblo requested the return of Blue Lake and its watershed area in exchange for the remaining cash payment. The Indians continued to insist on receiving title to the land, and Commissioner of Indian Affairs John Collier agreed to help them attain their goal. In 1933 Congress passed legislation providing for a fifty-year permit with right of renewal for 31,000 acres of the Blue Lake area. Because of difficulties in concluding a satisfactory agreement, the Indians did not sign the permit until 1940. It granted the Taos Pueblo exclusive use to the area for their annual ceremonial period and free use of wood, forage, and water for personal and tribal needs.[20]

The Taos Pueblo continued their efforts to regain title to Blue Lake and the Rio Pueblo de Taos watershed. In 1965 the Indian Claims Commission affirmed the Taos Indians' exclusive aboriginal use and occupancy of 113,000 acres. The commission awarded a claims settlement but the tribe refused to accept monetary compensation and held out for the land. The commission supported the Taos Pueblo's efforts for return of the land, but it did not possess the authority to return it. Tribal efforts garnered widespread national support from representatives of the Roman Catholic Church, National Organization of Churches, Indian Rights Association, National Organization of American Indians, and former secretary of the interior Stewart Udall. A group of prominent Americans formed the National Committee for Restoration of Blue Lake Lands to the Taos Indians. Other individuals, including President Richard Nixon and New Mexico governor David Cargo, also joined the large number of supporters.[21]

The Taos Indians maintained that Blue Lake and its watershed area possessed spiritual significance and absolute sanctity. Blue Lake, their principal shrine, had been the site of the Indians' annual pilgrimage for seven hundred years, and individual Indians used the lake for religious worship daily. The Taos Pueblo argued that the existence of their traditional religion and cultural survival depended upon protection of the area. The tribe desired to prohibit all commercial exploitation. The Taos Indians maintained that timber, grazing, and recreational use had desecrated Blue Lake and its watershed.[22]

White supporters argued that the Taos Indians should have the land returned to their possession because of its sacred importance to the Pueblo religion. They maintained that the tribe's situation differed from other Indian efforts to regain land because of its spiritual significance, and the Taos wanted the land for religious rather than economic reasons. They also cited the Taos Indians' long history of endeavors to regain ownership of Blue Lake and its environs.[23]

A small group of vocal congressmen, lumbermen, sportsmen, and U.S. Forest Service officials opposed the return of Blue Lake. They claimed that the Taos Indians possessed every right to religious freedom under the supervision of the U.S. Department of Agriculture as they would with the land held in trust by the Bureau of Indian Affairs. Some opponents argued that conservation practices would best be served with jurisdiction of the land under the forest service. Most of the adversaries argued that return of Blue Lake would establish a precedent that would enable other tribes to regain claimed lands in place of traditional monetary compensation.[24]

In December 1970, Congress restored 48,000 acres to the Taos Indians. The U.S. government held the land in trust for the tribe. The legislation stipulated that Blue Lake and the surrounding land remain a wilderness area and that the tribe only use it for traditional purposes, such as conducting religious ceremonies, hunting and fishing, accessing water sources, providing forage for domestic livestock, and harvesting timber, and for personal uses.[25]

Although the return of Taos Blue Lake to the Taos Pueblo has been the most publicized restitution of sacred lands, several other tribes have also regained such lands. The Pueblos in New Mexico have been the most successful. Since 1978, Congress has restored sacred lands to the Zuñi, Zia, and Cochiti Pueblos. Within the areas returned are religious shrines, which still play a prominent role in the Pueblo religion and culture. The Pueblos wanted the lands to be held in trust for their use so they could perform their rituals in private and prevent outsiders from desecrating the sacred places. The aboriginal Zuñi lands that Congress returned to tribal ownership in 1984 could be used only for religious purposes. The Cochiti return was unusual in that the Pueblo's claim was based not only on aboriginal use, but also on a paper title dating to 1744. Furthermore the United States had purchased the land in the 1930s for tribal use but instead of returning the land to the Pueblo, the federal government had allowed non-Indians to use the submarginal lands. A few other tribes such as the Makah and the Yakima in Washington also had sacred lands returned to their ownership.[26]

Several tribes unsuccessfully attempted to protect sacred sites, located in the public domain, from desecration by commercial development or tourism. They filed lawsuits basing their religious freedom claims on the First Amendment and on the American Indian Religious Freedom Act of 1979. The courts, to date, have ruled against the tribes, denying them constitutional protection. The Hopis sought to enjoin the construction of a ski resort in the San Francisco Peaks, the home of their Kachinas. The Yurok,

Karok, and Tolowa tribes in Northern California fought to prevent the completion of a logging road through their most sacred lands in the Six Rivers National Forest. Its construction would destroy the religious sanctity of the area. The Navajo and the Sioux also have tried to prevent further desecration of sacred sites.[27]

Congress has restored land to a few other tribes during the 1970s and 1980s. In most cases the tribes had a valid claim to the land. The Bureau of Land Management had placed lands belonging to the Santa Ana Pueblo in grazing districts during the 1930s. The property was returned to tribal ownership in 1978. Several land restorations involved tribal land that had been excluded from the reservation and included in U.S. forests as a result of erroneous boundary surveys in the late 1800s. This occurred on the Warm Springs, Yakima, and Tule River reservations. Federal surveys of the Ute Mountain Ute Reservation and the Navajo Reservation had included the same 15,000 acres of land within the boundaries of both reservations. After the Supreme Court ruled that title belonged to the Navajo, Congress passed legislation conveying title in fee simple to 3,000 acres of federal lands to the Utes and awarding them $4 million as compensation for lost oil and gas royalties. The tribe had previously leased the grazing land from the Bureau of Land Management.[28]

Havasupai Land Return

Congressional approval of the return of 185,000 acres in the Grand Canyon to the Havasupais in 1975 marked another significant settlement of Indian land claims. Havasupai attempts to regain some of their ancestral lands dated to the early twentieth century. For six centuries, the Havasupais migrated from the plateau lands on the rim of the canyon to the canyon floor in the summer. Use of both areas provided subsistence for the tribe. In 1882 the Havasupais were allotted a 518-acre reservation on the floor of the Grand Canyon. In 1919 Congress established Grand Canyon National Park but allowed the tribe to continue using the plateau. National Park Service officials restricted Indian free use of the area, however, compressing the Havasupais on 518 acres of which only 200 acres were arable. The tribe maintained that their survival depended on the return of the plateau lands. In January 1975, President Gerald Ford signed the legislation designating 185,000 acres as trust lands for the Havasupais. Restrictions limit tribal use of the land to religious rituals and grazing.[29]

Alaska Native Claims Settlement Act

The year after the Taos Blue Lake restoration, Congress enacted the Alaska Native Claims Settlement Act. It awarded title in fee simple to the largest amount of land ever received by American Indians for the extinguishment of aboriginal title. The Alaskan tribes claimed ownership to most of the

375 million acres contained in the state's land mass. According to the provisions of the settlement act, Alaska Natives received clear title to 40 million acres, $462.5 million, and 2-percent royalty on mineral development on state and federal lands in Alaska up to $500 million. The act authorized the land distribution among twelve native profit-making district corporations. They would allocate acreages to eligible villages, who would receive fee simple title to the surface estate while the regional corporation retained subsurface rights. Some Alaska Natives chose to select fee simple ownership of land instead of coming under the provisions of the act.[30]

In 1972 Secretary of the Interior Rogers C. B. Morton reserved 99 million acres from which the Alaska Natives could select their 40-million-acre allocation. Four years later, the secretary of the interior made the first land conveyance to a regional corporation.

Much litigation has resulted from passage of the Alaska Native Claims Settlement Act. Some of the lawsuits have contested the secretary of the interior's rulings that declared certain native villages ineligible for receiving land. Other legal disputes have developed over the pattern of selection by native corporations, the state of Alaska, and the federal government.[31]

The adjudication of Indian land claims culminated a century of unsettled title to 90 percent of the land in Alaska and several decades of native efforts to obtain title. A number of native organizations originated in the mid-1960s as a result of the land-rights issue. In 1966 Alaska Natives created a statewide association, the Alaska Federation of Natives. The discovery of oil in Alaska promoted the swift settlement of native claims. Desire for immediate exploitation of this valuable resource prompted the oil companies to join forces with Alaska Natives to clear land titles. A receptive administration in Washington also contributed to an early settlement. The Nixon administration wanted to settle the land-claims issue before it approved the Alaskan pipeline project.[32]

From the time the United States purchased Alaska in 1867 from Russia, Congress had neglected to clarify aboriginal land rights. The purchase agreement, the organic act, and the statehood act recognized native rights of use and occupancy. The latter two documents left the settlement of such rights to Congress.[33]

Some Alaska Natives withheld approval of the Alaska Native Claims Settlement Act. William Willoya, an Eskimo, believed the legislation would be detrimental to the continuation of the aboriginal subsistence lifestyle and entailed a sellout to the corporations. He maintained that Congress excluded traditional hunting, fishing, and wood and berry gathering areas used seasonally by nomadic Alaska Natives from the land allotted to the native corporations. He claimed that more than twenty thousand tribesmen would be forced off the land in the next twenty years. Willoya also expressed a concern shared by other Alaska Natives that the legislation would force them to accept a business economy. Congress established the profit-making corporations and thus forced an alien concept on Alaskan tribes. To become self-sustaining organizations, the corporations would be expected to join with multinational corporations to exploit the mineral resources. Several Native American leaders declared that the organizations would be more concerned with profits than with protecting the traditional subsistence methods and culture of Alaskan Natives. Willoya also feared that the native corporations would have to sell some of their land to pay taxes after 1991. Until that time shareholders could not alienate their non-taxable shares in the corporation. After the twenty-year nonalienation period the corporations could sell the land and native shareholders could market their shares, although nonnatives could not receive voting rights in the operation of the corporations. Opponents of the legislation also lamented the loss of traditional hunting, fishing, gathering, and water rights. The laws of Alaska became applicable to Alaska Natives with the passage of the Alaska Native Claims Settlement Act (ANCSA). Even some of the Alaska Native supporters of the claims settlement voiced displeasure with the act but were convinced that it was the best agreement they would obtain.[34]

Since enactment of the ANCSA some observers have feared the loss of native access to federal and state lands for subsistence hunting and fishing. Under the ANCSA, the state could restrict subsistence activities to benefit sport hunting and fishing interests. It could also encourage certain kinds of commercial and mining development that would destroy wildlife resources. Congress allayed some of these concerns, however, when it amended the Alaska National Interest Lands Conservation Act (ANILCA) in 1980. The act stated that the United States would take over game management on federal lands if the state of Alaska failed to protect native subsistence uses. The legislation also mandated that companies wanting to exploit mineral resources on federal lands must provide a "subsistence impact" evaluation to protect Alaska Natives.[35]

Provisions of the ANILCA (in section 810) protecting Alaska Native subsistence rights were tested in *Kunaknana v. Clark*. Two Inupiat Eskimos sued to block Bureau of Land Management oil and gas lease sales within the Alaska National Petroleum Reserve. The area encompassed 23 million acres on the North Slope of Alaska. The Eskimos argued that a major objective of the ANILCA was to "provide rural residents engaged in a subsistence way of life the [opportunity] to do so." The district court at first issued a preliminary injunction preventing exploration but six months later ruled in favor of the bureau after the agency produced a favorable "subsistence impact statement." The Eskimos disputed the statement and contended, among other things, that the court unreasonably refused to consider the natives' own expert testimony. An appeal to the Ninth Circuit

Court of Appeals failed when that court affirmed the lower court's decision and ruled the evidence to be inadmissible.[36]

This legislation was tested again in *Village of Gambell v. Hodel*. In the early 1980s several Alaska Native villages brought suit to prevent the sale of oil and gas leases on federally owned lands in the outer continental shelf (OCS) area. They sought a court injunction preventing exploration of the OCS, claiming that it fell under the Alaska National Interest Lands Conservation Act provision requiring "subsistence impact" evaluations. The Alaska Natives maintained that oil drilling activity would adversely affect their fishing and marine hunting subsistence in the area.

Because of conflicting rulings the case was tossed between the federal district court and the Ninth Circuit Court of Appeals for several years before it eventually made its way to the U.S. Supreme Court. In a complete victory for the energy interests, the high court ruled that the geographic boundary of Alaska defined by the ANILCA extended only three miles from shore. Thus the OCS lay outside of the state and did not fall under the provisions of the act. The Supreme Court also agreed with a lower court finding that oil and gas exploration would not significantly restrict native subsistence uses. The justices stated that an injunction would result in a greater harm. It would be detrimental to the national interest of maintaining adequate petroleum reserves and to the oil companies who had already invested approximately $70 million in exploration.[37]

One disturbing dispute between traditional Alaska Natives and a native corporation resulted in the court case of *City of Angoon v. Hodel*. Shee Atika, Inc., a native corporation that claimed 23,000 acres on Admiralty Island, wanted to establish a logging facility there. Angoon, the only permanent settlement on the island, objected because it feared that the timber harvesting would disrupt the traditional subsistence culture of its five hundred Tlinget inhabitants. Environmentalists, led by the Sierra Club, also opposed the logging facility because they wanted to protect the wilderness ecology of Admiralty Island. Congress had earlier recognized the island's natural beauty by designating three-fourths of it as a national monument. Over the past twelve years the controversy has included several court decisions and two land swaps involving congressional action. In the most recent ruling the U.S. Court of Appeals in 1986 held in favor of Shee Atika, noting that the defendant's environmental impact statement was adequate and that the defendant did not have to make "subsistence evaluations," as described in the Alaska National Interest Lands Conservation Act. The village of Angoon is currently attempting to get congressional backing to buy out Shee Atika's lumbering interest in Admiralty Island.[38]

The passage of the ANILCA in 1980 implied that Congress intended to continue its special relationship with Alaska Natives despite section 2(b) of the ANCSA, which referred to a congressional mandate implementing a settlement "without creating a reservation system of lengthy wardship or trusteeship." Although some courts have interpreted the language in the section to imply the complete termination of trust status for Alaska Natives, the provision seems to run contrary to the general intent of the act. ANILCA provides native corporations with special protections to ensure their survival, and it implied trust status by not repealing any previous legislation regarding native welfare or sovereignty. Section 2(b) will most likely be ignored in the future as a misplaced carryover from a much harsher settlement bill sponsored by Senator Jackson two years before the enactment of the Alaska Native Claims Settlement Act.[39]

The special federal relationship with Alaska Natives was further implied with the implementation of the Alaska Native Claims Settlement Act Amendments of 1987. By adding more special protections, the new legislation reduced Alaska Native fears of a reenactment of the Dawes Act. The provision mandating that native corporations issue salable stock in 1991 was repealed, among other reasons, to prevent takeover by nonnatives. The native shareholders were given the option to decide as a group if and when they want to sell their shares. The amendments also protected Alaska Natives from the rigors of economic cycles by making undeveloped lands of the native corporations immune from adverse judgments originating from unpaid taxes, corporate debt, or bankruptcy. Some Alaska Natives opposed the legislation because it did not grant similar recognition of tribal sovereignty enjoyed by Indians in the lower forty eight states.[40]

Final assessment of the overall benefits of the legislation cannot be made for some time. But thirty years from now the settlement act may be seen, despite added protections, in the same light as the General Allotment Act with its resulting loss of native landownership, dislocation, and loss of native culture. Much will depend on the success of the native corporations in retaining title to the land and maintaining traditional lifestyle and culture. The white ideological basis of the Alaska Native Claims Settlement Act rested with the hope of assimilating the Alaskan Eskimos, Indians, and Aleuts into the Western business economy. Profit-making organizations with a competitive corporate structure comprised a concept alien to most Alaska Natives' cooperative subsistence culture. The impact of mineral exploitation, speculation, and a money economy threaten their traditional way of life.

Lands Returned through Executive Authority

In addition to regaining land by congressional legislation, Indians have also secured possession of former lands through presidential executive orders. On 20 May 1972, President Richard Nixon issued an executive order directing the return of part of Mt. Adams and 21,000 acres to the Yakima tribe, culminating over four decades of tribal efforts at recovery. After discovering a map delineating the proper boundaries set by the 1855 Treaty of Walla Walla, the Yakimas presented their claims to the federal government. The map showed that errors made by the surveyors resulted in a reduction of 421,465 acres of their reservation. In 1904 the federal government restored 300,000 acres to the tribe. Finally the Indian Claims Commission in 1968 ruled that the Yakimas were entitled to an additional 121,465 acres. Since 98,000 acres comprised rich farmland owned by whites, the commission awarded the tribe fifty cents an acre for them. The remaining lands were located in the Gifford Pinchot National Forest. The commission determined that the federal government did not have to return the land and left the ultimate decision to the discretion of the president. Since the government's acquisition of the land had not constituted a legal taking, it could be restored to the tribe by executive action. This led to Nixon's executive order returning some of the land. Although the Yakima considered Mt. Adams to have special religious significance, they did not urge its restoration on the basis of its sacred nature.[41]

Land Returns and Attempted Returns through Judicial Action

Indians also used the judicial system to regain lands. During the 1970s the Pomo Indians on Robinson Rancheria in California obtained the return of their reservation to trust status. The U.S. Supreme Court in 1970 determined that the Cherokee, Choctaw, and Chickasaw tribes owned the riverbed of the Arkansas River in Oklahoma. A U.S. Circuit Court of Appeals decision in 1978 declared that the Western Shoshones might possess aboriginal title to twenty-two million acres in Nevada. The appellate court remanded the case to U.S. district court to determine whether the Western Shoshones had beneficial title to the disputed lands.[42]

The issue centered around the Shoshones' refusal to accept a $26-million Indian Claims Commission judgment for the extinguishment of their aboriginal title. On remand, the district court held that payment had been made and the Shoshones possessed no aboriginal claims. The U.S. Court of Appeals again reversed the district court and the case ended up in the Supreme Court. The Western Shoshones lost the case in 1985 when the Court ruled that payment of the claims award to the United States as the tribe's trustee and its placement of the funds in a tribal account maintained by the U.S. Treasury Department had extinguished aboriginal title to the twenty-two million acres. Tribal approval of the award was not necessary when the tribe's trustee had accepted it as a settlement for outstanding claims.[43]

The Pit River Indians of northern California tried to get their land-claims case before the courts throughout the 1970s. They claimed title to 3.5 million acres of land taken by the federal government in the 1850s. The Indian Claims Commission acknowledged their aboriginal use and occupancy of the area in question and awarded a cash settlement of $29 million as part of a joint judgment with a loosely named group, the California Indians. Other state tribes readily accepted the restitution. The Pit River Indians, however, rejected the money settlement and requested return of their former lands. The Bureau of Indian Affairs invalidated the results of the Pit River election and conducted a subsequent election through the mails that overturned the earlier tribal decision. Tribal leaders alleged that the Department of the Interior improperly conducted the election and deemed the later results invalid. The tribe later voted to reject the monetary compensation and demanded the return of their lands. The Pit River Indians appealed to the Indian Claims Commission to review the 1963 judgment but the commission refused the petition. Some of the Pit River Indians resorted to the tactic of occupying tracts of claimed land as well as bringing suit against the Hearst corporation, Pacific Gas and Electric, other giant corporations, and the federal government. In the mid-1970s a federal court decision declared that the Pit River Indians did not have title to the disputed lands. Some of the Pit River Indians declared their intention to continue their recovery efforts.[44]

Land Returns Resulting from Violation of the 1790 Trade and Intercourse Act

A significant number of Indian land claims have been based on state violations of the 1790 Trade and Intercourse Act. This federal statute prohibited states from obtaining Indian lands or treatying with tribes without federal approval. In most of these cases tribal leaders combined judicial efforts with negotiation and legislative action.

The Narragansett tribe of Rhode Island asserted claims against that state for making transactions in violation of the 1790 law. The Narragansetts based their claim for 3,500 acres of land on a series of state statutes enacted by the legislature before 1890. Tribal leaders initiated court action against the state of Rhode Island, and in 1978 the parties negotiated a settlement. Subsequently the U.S. Congress approved the agreement that provided for the return of 1,800 acres to the Narragansetts. In August 1979 the Rhode Island legislature approved it.[45]

The settlement authorized the appropriation of $315 million of federal funds to purchase 900 acres from private landowners and 900 acres of state public lands. A state-chartered corporation controlled by eight persons— five Indians and three state officials—would acquire and hold the land in trust for the tribe. Nine-tenths of the land was restricted to permanent conservation, and about 225 acres could be developed subject to the approval of the corporation. Terms of the settlement included tribal agreement to congressional extinguishment of any claim to land in Rhode Island.

During the 1970s the Penobscot and Passamaquoddy tribes asserted aboriginal ownership of a large part of Maine. Proceeding from the position that transactions between the state of Massachusetts and these tribes beginning in 1794, and later actions by the state of Maine, violated the Trade and Intercourse Act of 1790, Penobscot and Passamaquoddy leaders requested that the federal government assist them in bringing suit against these states. The Interior and Justice departments refused because the tribes lacked federal recognition. Then the Penobscot and Passamaquoddy tribes took their claim case to court and the resulting judicial decrees stated that the tribes possessed tribal status under the Trade and Intercourse Act and that the government must act as trustee on their behalf. Following the 1975 decision, Justice and Interior department officials assisted the Maine tribes in their land claims.[46]

Because of the cloud placed on the validity of land titles in Maine, President Jimmy Carter intervened in an attempt to settle the land controversy. In 1977 Carter assigned William Gunter as a special representative to investigate the land claims of the Maine Indians and to recommend a settlement plan. Gunter recommended that the federal government pay the tribes $25 million and that Maine provide 100,000 acres of its public lands situated in the claims areas to the Penobscot and Passamaquoddy tribes. In return the Indians would agree to relinquishment of all aboriginal claims to land in Maine. Tribal leaders refused to accept the plan. Not only had Gunter recommended a small land return, but also that Congress extinguish aboriginal title to the land claimed by the tribes, except state public lands, in the event the tribes refused to consent to the proposed settlement.[47]

At the request of the governor and attorney general of Maine, the state congressional delegation introduced legislation during the spring of 1977 that retroactively ratified the illegal treaties consummated with the Penobscot and Passamaquoddy tribes since 1790.[48]

In February 1978 leaders of the two tribes and a White House work group announced they had reached a "memorandum of understanding." However, the proposed agreement was not accepted by the disputing parties. The following year tribal leaders and state officials continued negotiations for settlement of the Penobscot and Passamaquoddy tribes' 12.5-million-acre land claim. The next compromise, the Hathaway Plan, was favored by the landowners and state officials, but did not satisfy the tribes. It would have awarded the Indians $37 million, plus options to purchase 100,000 acres of land from several major timber companies.[49]

Finally the parties reached an agreement and after Congress approved it in 1980, President Carter signed into law the Maine Indian Land Claims Settlement Act. It extinguished the aboriginal land claims of the Passamaquoddy tribe, the Penobscot Nation, and the Houlton Band of Maliseet Indians in the state of Maine. Monetary compensation totaled $81.5 million. A $27-million trust fund for general tribal purposes was established, $13.5 million for the Passamaquoddy tribe and $13.5 million for the Penobscot Nation. The legislation authorized $54.5 million for the purchase of 150,000 acres of land for the Passamaquoddy tribe, 150,000 acres for the Penobscot Nation, and 5,000 acres for the Houlton Band of Maliseet Indians. These lands were to be held in trust by the secretary of the interior for the benefit of the tribes. The Penobscot Nation and Passamaquoddy tribe would have generally the status of state municipalities with persons and property within these two nations subject to state law. Payments would be made in lieu of taxes on real and personal property within the Indian territories.[50]

Although the Maine Indian Land Claims Settlement Act was hailed by the *Christian Science Monitor* as the "biggest Indian victory since Little Big Horn," the act drew criticism from within the Indian community. Although the approximately 300,000 acres of newly purchased land would be held in trust by the federal government, the Indian nations would be subject to payments "in lieu of taxes" on these properties. This arrangement also applied to their reservations, which until the settlement had been tax-exempt. If the Indian nations failed to meet these obligations, the payments could come from the $27 million trust fund originally meant to create jobs. To pay the taxes the Department of the Interior could also open the lands to the kinds of economic development that violate the Indian nations' cultural values.[51]

Since the 1970s the Oneida tribe of New York has been involved in litigation against that state and Oneida County. The tribe filed suit for approximately six million acres they alleged was illegally obtained by the state. The Oneidas contended that their nation's land-cession treaties of 1785 and 1788 negotiated with the state of New York were void because federal approval, which was required according to the Articles of Confederation and other documents, was not given. Even if the treaties were ruled legal, the tribe maintained that the "rental agreements" stipulated in the treaties, not to mention fraudulent dealings by the state of New York, left it with some remaining interest in the lands. The Oneidas argued that the 1839 Act of New York, which capitalized all the remaining rent payments in one lump sum, was illegal because it also violated the 1790 Trade and Intercourse Act.

Federal courts ruled against some of these arguments in 1982 and dismissed the rest in 1986. They decided that the wording of the 1785 and 1788 cession treaties specified a sale of land with no reversionary interests to the Oneidas, regardless of rent payments. Thus, there was no interest to the land lost in the Act of New York and subsequently no violation of the 1790 Trade and Intercourse Act. The courts also ruled that the federal approval required for land transactions under the Articles of Confederation, Fort Stanwix Treaty and Proclamation of 1783 was not needed within state boundaries. Thus the state of New York had the right to purchase the Oneidas' land, which was located within its borders.[52]

The Oneidas had better luck in a parallel lawsuit, *Oneida County v. Oneida Indian Nation*. They sued for two years' rent from 900 acres currently owned by Oneida and Madison counties. This land was part of 100,000 acres the Indians conveyed to New York in a 1795 treaty. Since the state did not get federal approval, it was a direct violation of the 1790 Trade and Intercourse Act. The defense did not question the illegality of the land sale, but generally whether the Indians had the right to sue 175 years after the fact. In a five-to-four decision the U.S. Supreme Court ruled in favor of the Oneidas, stating that "the Indian's common law right to sue is firmly established."[53]

Although the amount of damages won was only two years' rent on 900 acres (about $20,000 plus interest), the implications of the suit are considerable. Oneida and Madison counties and the state of New York may be liable for the entire 100,000 acres, much of which is held privately. Local property values have suffered. Concern about land titles and predictions of evictions have led to uncertainty in the real estate market. To remedy the problem the Oneidas have supported a quick, negotiated settlement involving cash and land, and the Supreme Court has urged Congress to act on the claims in a manner similar to the Rhode Island and Maine settlements.[54]

The Catawbas in South Carolina also based their land claim on state violation of the 1790 act. The tribe sought to regain 140,000 acres. After the Fourth Circuit Court of Appeals ruled in favor of the Catawba claims, the Supreme Court in 1986 reversed and remanded the earlier decision. The adverse ruling was largely a result of the tribe's acquiescence to the termination policy of the 1950s. The Supreme Court held that the Catawba Tribal Division of Assets Act signed by the tribe in 1959 negated special federal protection to the tribe and subjected the Catawba land claim to the state statute of limitations. This, in effect, rendered the previous violation of the 1790 Trade and Intercourse Act null and void.[55]

Wampanoag Indians in Mashpee, Massachusetts, also attempted to regain land they claimed was alienated in violation of the 1790 act. In February 1979, the U.S. Court of Appeals for the First Circuit upheld the lower court decision that the act did not protect the Mashpees since they were not a tribe in 1790 nor in 1976. This ruling was reaffirmed in 1987 by the same court. In the second round of litigation the Mashpees submitted essentially the same nineteenth-century documents that supported their claim to tribal status. They argued that the documents showed tribal status through a principle akin to estoppel. The court found the documentation insufficient.[56]

A more successful land return based upon a violation of the Trade and Intercourse Act of 1790 involved the Wampanoag Tribe of Gay Head, Massachusetts. In 1746 the state legislature appointed trustees or guardians for the tribe and gave them authority to lease and allot land in the Gay Head area. This trustee arrangement continued until an act passed in 1869 gave citizenship to the Indians and guaranteed title to lands they owned individually. Another act, in 1870, incorporated the area into the town of Gay Head. All common lands, common funds, and fishing rights were transferred to the newly incorporated town. This arrangement did not seem to disturb the Gay Head Wampanoags in managing their financial and cultural affairs, since they owned and controlled most of the town at the time. But over the years many Indians sold their allotments to non-Indians, thus reducing the Wampanoags' local economic and political base.[57]

In 1974 a newly formed Wampanoag Tribal Council filed a lawsuit against the town of Gay Head. It alleged that the act of 1870 deeding the Indians' common lands to the town violated the 1790 Trade and Intercourse Act. Soon after the suit was initiated the litigants entered into negotiations. By fall 1983 an agreement had been ratified by the Gay Head Tribal Council, the town, and the state.

Congress approved the plan in 1987. The settlement provided the Wampanoags with 178 acres of land for tribal housing and an additional 250 acres to be held in trust in exchange for extinguishing all land claims within the town of Gay Head. The $4.5-million cost would be shared equally by the state of Massachusetts and the federal government.[58]

Native Americans have attempted to recover former lands throughout the twentieth century despite mixed results. Victories during the 1970s increased Indian nationalistic efforts to regain land. To obtain their goal, tribes have resorted to judicial and legislative action as well as negotiation.

Hawaiian Land Recovery

Hawaiian Homes Commission Act

Hawaiians also have attempted to regain possession of portions of their lands. The first major success occurred in the 1920s and has remained a consistent part of Native Hawaiian endeavors until the present time. In 1921 the nationalistic Kūhiō Kalanianaʻole, the part-Hawaiian congressional delegate from the territory of Hawaiʻi, succeeded in his attempts to have the U.S. government return some land for the use of Native Hawaiians. Congress enacted the Hawaiian Homes Commission Act, which created the Hawaiian Homes Commission with control over approximately 194,000 acres set aside for Native Hawaiians. Kalanianaʻole sincerely believed that the only hope for the continuation of the indigenous Hawaiians as a distinct race was to return them to the land. In 1920 he stated that "The Hawaiian race is passing. And if conditions continue to exist as they do today, this splendid race of people, my people, will pass from the face of the earth." Kalaniana'ole pointed out that Hawaiians possessed a metaphysical relationship with the land. He believed that if they could live on the land and return to their ancient relationship with it, the process of decimation and demoralization would come to an end.[59]

The death rate of the Hawaiians was higher than that of any other American minority. The population has been estimated at 300,000 at the time of Cook's visit to the Hawaiian islands. Full-blood Hawaiians numbered only 40,000 at the time of annexation, and by 1920 the figure had declined to 23,723. In addition the native birth rate fell below the national level and infant mortality was eight times as high as the national average. Western diseases were primarily responsible for the dramatic decimation rate. Thousands of Native Hawaiians died from measles, cholera, smallpox, and venereal disease introduced by traders, sailors, and missionaries. Hawaiians developed some immunity to these pestilences only in the latter part of the nineteenth century. Demoralization caused by alienation of the Hawaiians from their land and nation and disorientation prompted by the influx of foreign settlers and their growing influence in the economic, religious, and governmental structure of Hawaiian society also contributed to their decline.[60]

The rhetoric of American supporters of the Hawaiian homes legislation contained a philosophy similar to that espoused by promoters of removal of the Five Civilized Tribes from the South in the 1830s and the General Allotment Act of 1887. Advocates claimed the proposal would save the dying Hawaiian race and rehabilitate it by restoring the Native Hawaiians to the land. No one considered placing them on reservations although some Americans regarded Hawaiians as "blanket" Indians. Advocates of the Hawaiian Homes Commission Act hoped to Americanize the Native Hawaiians and then assimilate them. They wanted to create a class of small independent New England–type farmers. Then, they believed, the race would once again thrive, prosper, and become self-reliant.[61]

Besides saving the Hawaiian race from extinction, supporters of the act also wanted to return land that had been taken from them in the nineteenth century. When assessed in terms of benefiting the Hawaiians, earlier attempts at land distribution had been ineffective. Supporters of Hawaiian rehabilitation claimed that the native people had not obtained their equal share of the lands in the mid-nineteenth-century land revolution. Speculators also had taken advantage of Native Hawaiians, stripping them of their tiny parcels. In addition, advocates of native rehabilitation maintained that the United States had gained possession of Hawai'i's public lands after the revolutionaries seized control of the government with the aid of the United States minister to Hawai'i. [62]

Other supporters perhaps were motivated by a twinge of guilt. They believed that native deterioration had resulted from contact with Western civilization. American-European intrusion had overwhelmed the native race with an alien society and left it disoriented. The Hawaiians never recovered. Representative James Strong of New York stated that "we went there with our Christianity and civilization and 'demoralized' a thriving race." Chairman of the House Committee on Territories Charles Curry, referring to the Blackfeet, compared the rehabilitation proposal to that of the U.S. policy of rehabilitating Indians. "They were warriors, hunters and not agriculturalists and now they grow crops for private consumption and grains for cattle. They were a dying race but now are a prosperous and multiplying race."[63]

Sincere concern and compassion for Native Hawaiians were not the only motives directing the passage of the rehabilitation bill. The elite in Hawaii, primarily the Big Five—Brewer and Company, Ltd.; Castle and Cooke, Ltd.; Alexander and Baldwin, Ltd.; American Factors; Theo. Davies & Co.—who dominated Hawaiian economic and political life, supported the legislation. The Big Five promoted the program largely because the bill exempted sugar-producing lands from homesteading. Leases on 200,000 acres of government lands were to expire between 1919 and 1921, including more than 26,000 acres of cultivated sugarcane. Federal and some local forces advocated opening these lands to homesteading. The American belief that homesteading produced a stabilizing influence on individual and family life and that public lands should be used by small farmers motivated this position. Congress in the Hawaiian Organic Act of 1900 permitted withdrawal of certain public lands for homesteading upon the petition of twenty-five qualified citizens. The Wilson administration declared that sugar lands would become available for homesteading. With the expiration of the leases on sugar lands, the Big Five feared that they would lose prime crop lands to homesteaders. The Hawaiian Homes Commission Act removed this threat.[64]

An opponent of the Hawaiian Homes Commission Act testified before the Senate Committee on Territories that "The only object of this rehabilitation bill—the real reason for this rehabilitation bill—is in order that the present leases of highly cultivated lands may be renewed. . . ." By removing the sugar-producing lands from use as homelands, the bill left only the poorer agricultural and pastoral lands. Much of the available land was marginal because of a lack of water or soil unsuited for farming. Most attempts to farm these lands failed. By the late 1920s many Hawaiian homesteaders had signed contracts with the pineapple-producing firm of Libby, McNeill, and Libby.[65]

Congressmen studying the bill realized that, without the provision exempting the sugarcane lands, it would be difficult, if not impossible, to win approval of the legislation. They, however, neglected to analyze the effects this provision would have on the success of restoring land for native use.

Congress approved the rehabilitation scheme on an experimental basis for five years. The program appeared successful at the end of the probationary period, so Congress extended the program. During the experimental stage Congress limited homesteading to designated lands on Molokaʻi and to small tracts on Hawaiʻi. To qualify as a homesteader, the applicant had to be at least 50 percent Hawaiian. Congress required this percentage of native blood, since these individuals needed the most help. The commission leased the lands to qualified Hawaiians at one dollar a year for ninety-nine years. They could lease from 20 to 80 acres of agricultural lands, 100 to 500 acres of first-class pastoral lands, and 250 to 1,000 acres of second-class pastoral lands. The title remained with the U.S. government.[66]

To prevent alienation of the lands from Native Hawaiians congressional leaders excluded from the act a provision granting the land in fee simple. Recipients could not mortgage, sell, or lease land issued to them—each tract had to remain within the grantee family. The federal government's paternalistic stance was calculated to protect Hawaiians from their "own thriftlessness and against the predatory nature" of individuals wanting to obtain property. Previous experience in Hawaiʻi revealed the Native Hawaiians' tendency to alienate their lands. A 1919 report revealed that Hawaiians owned only 6.23 percent of the land and approximately one thousand wealthy Hawaiians held title to this property. During the second half of the nineteenth century native people lost or sold most of their land to enterprising white men. This occurred largely because Hawaiians lacked a clear understanding of the Western concept of property, the value of land, or the procedures necessary to retain possession of their kuleanas. Many lost their lands through an inability to finance farming. Some congressmen familiar with the Indians' tendency to alienate land received in fee simple through the implementation of the General Allotment Act realized that the same problems existed among Hawaiians. Undoubtedly they recognized the similarities and wished to avoid the difficulties experienced by Indians in the alienation of their property.[67]

Other provisions of the Hawaiian Homes Commission Act designated that rent from leases on sugar lands and water licenses serve as revenue for the one-million-dollar revolving home loan fund. It furnished the capital

to construct buildings and make improvements on the tracts, to purchase
livestock and equipment, and to aid in developing land. The act also
required that three of the five commission members be at least 50 percent
Hawaiian.[68]

Subsequent Changes in the Hawaiian Homes Commission

During the next fifty-five years, the Hawaiian Homes Commission under-
went numerous organizational and procedural changes. One of the most
significant modifications in the home program came in 1923: an amendment that enabled homesteaders to lease one-half-acre lots for residential
purposes. Subsequently, the commission established residential additions
around Hilo, Honolulu, and other cities. By 1977 these small house lots
composed almost 90 percent of the land leased to native homesteaders.
Most Native Hawaiians currently request house lots.[69]

The success of the rehabilitation scheme has been limited, since it
accommodates only a small segment of the Hawaiian population. Prince
Kuhio's designs have been circumvented, and most of the lessees live on
house lots rather than on kuleanas as he had envisioned. After fifty-eight
years of operation, the Hawaiian Homes Commission and the Department
of Hawaiian Home Lands had granted only 2,997 leases for approximately
25,032 acres or 12.5 percent of the homelands. The commission set aside
over 45,000 acres of marginal homelands for conservation purposes.[70]

A combination of factors has obstructed the successful culmination of
Kalanianaole's goal of returning his people to the land. Some of these
impediments existed from the beginning of the program, whereas others
have developed recently. Unsuitability of a large portion of the Hawaiian
homelands for farming, ranching, or house lots hindered the use of these
lands for homesteading. The lands often lacked water, good soil, or easy
accessibility. The sugar interests secured the removal of prime agricultural
public lands from homesteading as a condition of their support for passage
of the Hawaiian Homes Commission Act. This left, for the most part, only
marginal lands for the rehabilitation program.

During the early years of the Hawaiian homes project, the commission
instituted regulations guiding the development of the homelands that
tended to restrict the acreage available for homesteading. Before a qualified
Native Hawaiian could receive land, the area had to have roads, water, and
utilities. The requirement that the homesteaded acreage must have a house
and other improvements financed by the Hawaiian Homes Commission
also restricted the granting of leases. Often when lessees attempted to fund
the development of their land with their own resources, the Department
of Hawaiian Home Lands refused to allow it. During the 1970s the department also demanded that all fixed improvements must have the department's prior approval. One Hawaiian claimed that department officials

told him that he must return the plot on which he had constructed a barn without approval or the department would revoke the ninety-nine year lease on his entire homestead.[71]

In 1970 the Department of Hawaiian Home Lands also placed a $10,000 ceiling on the amount of improvements the lessee could institute on his acreage. These rules hampered leasing and development of homestead lands. Many of the homes constructed on the residential tracts consequently took on the appearance of slums.[72]

Because of requirements made by the Department of Hawaiian Home Lands and insufficient funds, widespread leasing had not occurred. Many Native Hawaiians had to wait long periods before receiving lands. The average waiting period was fifteen years. The waiting list contained the names of over 6,000 applicants, and it would have included many more if qualified Hawaiians believed they could receive a lease. Native people discovered that Department of Hawaiian Home Lands officials had been careless with their applications, losing or destroying vital papers. A number of Hawaiians waited eighteen years for a homestead only to discover that the Department of Hawaiian Home Lands considered them ineligible because it gave priority to those with children. By this time the children of these applicants were grown and had left home.[73]

Both critics and supporters of the Department of Hawaiian Home Lands argued that a lack of money restricted the successful leasing of homelands to Native Hawaiians. From the institution of the program, it has depended on revenue obtained from the leasing of sugar lands and water leases; Congress has not appropriated funds for its operation. The state of Hawaii occasionally has allotted funds for the program, but always insufficient amounts.

The Hawaii legislature in 1965 amended the Hawaiian Homes Commission Act in an apparent attempt to generate funds for the department and undoubtedly to enable non-Hawaiians to lease desired lands. This statute sanctioned the leasing of homelands to non-Hawaiians. The Department of Hawaiian Home Lands leased large acreages on long-term leases for relatively small sums of money. The cosponsor of the legislation, Elmer Cravalho, former mayor of Maui and former speaker of the Hawaii House of Representatives, leased 15,000 acres at about $1.60 an acre. In 1971 state representative Diana Hansen tried to obtain a list of industrial and other leases to non-Hawaiians, the lease rental price, and the length of lease from the Department of Hawaiian Home Lands, but she claimed that employees told her that they did not have such a list and they would not compile one for her information. Hansen argued that this amendment violated the original legislation because it specifically stated that the Hawaiian Homes Commission must lease lands only to qualified Hawaiians, and for the amendment to be valid it required congressional approval. The

Hawaii attorney general maintained that the amendment did not require congressional approval. By 1976 non-Hawaiians had leased 112,000 acres of homelands. Sometimes indigenous Hawaiians unsuccessfully tried to lease lands already leased to non-Hawaiians. These long-term leases effectively removed potential homesteading lands from Native Hawaiian use.[74]

Subletting homestead lands to pineapple companies on Moloka'i also subverted Prince Kūhiō's goal of returning native people to the land. Although the Hawaiian Homes Commission Act specifically prohibited subleasing, since the 1920s state officials have sanctioned subleases. On Moloka'i 153 families had leases for 6,000 acres divided in farm plots. Many of the lessees originally received their leases based on an oral agreement that they would lease 35 of the 40 acres to pineapple companies. Dole, Libby-McNeill, Del Monte, and California packers refused to allot the homesteaders water for the development of their remaining 5-acre plots. Since they could not farm the tract, and since few jobs existed on Moloka'i, the homesteaders relied on the lease money received from the pineapple companies. Their dependence resembled the American Indians' reliance on lease money. Originally the homesteaders received $23 a ton for all pineapples harvested. This netted each lessee a total of $8,000 to $10,000 a year. When the pineapple companies rewrote the leases in 1927, they paid only $840 a year, and the companies raised the annual sum to $1,080 fifty years later in new leases. In 1957 some Hawaiians wanted to farm the 40-acre plots but representatives of the pineapple companies harassed them into signing new leases. Seven farmers refused to renew the leases and attempted co-op farming with other agricultural products. The Hawaiian Homes Commission hampered this action by refusing to loan them money and not approving improvements on their homesteads. The commission also awarded residential lots to native lessees contingent on receiving farm tracts that they would lease to the pineapple companies. These homesteaders did not even know the location of their farm plots. When one Hawaiian lessee tried to obtain the location of his farm plot, he claimed that the company told him that he would not receive his monthly rental check if he continued his inquiries.[75]

Critics of the Department of Hawaiian Home Lands claimed that mismanagement by the department has undermined the stated purposes of the act. The commissioners allegedly awarded lots to friends on a first-priority basis and skipped over Hawaiians first in line for lands in preference of more "suitable" applicants. Through the use of executive orders the Department of Hawaiian Home Lands and the governor occasionally traded valuable Hawaiian home lands for other acreages. The state then leased these lands to private parties for large sums of money. Some critics claimed that proper management by the department would entail retaining these lands and leasing them to generate needed revenue for increased distribution of homelands to Native Hawaiians.[76]

A rule established by the Department of Hawaiian Home Lands in 1970 required that only lessees with residential lots could receive farm and pastoral lands. This regulation effectively hindered the 9 percent of Hawaiians who requested the latter type of acreages from obtaining lands. The governor of Hawaii often appointed friends as commissioners, and this made them politically susceptible to the desires of the governor. Hawaiians frequently complained of the administrators' condescending attitude toward them. In 1970 a commissioner allegedly asked some native people why they wanted land since "all you Hawaiians want to do is sit around and play your ukulele and be tour drivers."[77]

Even though the rehabilitation program accomplished few of its initial publicly stated objectives of returning Native Hawaiians to the land and uplifting their social, economic, and health status, Hawaiians favored the Department of Hawaiian Home Lands' continued existence. Territorial, state, and congressional officials correctly assessed this attitude.

Congress recognized the federal government's special responsibility to Native Hawaiians by including certain provisions in the Hawaii Statehood Act of 1959. The admission act required the inclusion in the state constitution of the Hawaiian Homes Commission Act and a compact clause establishing a trust relationship over the program. The statehood act vested administrative control of the Hawaiian homes program in the state and transferred title of the homelands to the state. The Hawaiian Homes Commission Act could not be amended, except for administrative purposes, or repealed without the consent of Congress. Any land exchanges had to be approved by the secretary of the interior. To ensure that Hawaii faithfully fulfilled the provisions of the Hawaiian Homes Commission Act, the admission act included a clause reserving the right of the United States to sue the state of Hawaii should a breach of the trust occur.[78]

In 1967 two bills introduced into Congress attempted to amend the enabling acts of New Mexico, Arizona, and Hawaii in respect to the enforcement of trust provisions. This proposed act, originating within the Department of Justice, was based on the view that the states were capable of enforcing their own laws. The bills called for repeal of section 5(f), which provided that the "proceeds and income" from the homelands that the United States held in trust

> shall be managed and disposed of . . . in such manner as the constitution and laws of said state may provide, and their use for any other object shall constitute a breach of trust for which suit may be brought by the United States.

This proposed legislation aroused the concern of Native Hawaiians, and many of the homesteaders of the Hawaiian homelands circulated petitions advocating the defeat of the bills. The native peoples' opposition hinged on their fear that the removal of federal enforcement of the trust provisions would allow the state to subvert the "assets" of the Department of Hawaiian Home Lands "to the detriment of the homestead program." Congress relieved their anxiety by not approving the proposed legislation.[79]

Native Hawaiians realized the shortcomings of the homelands program. They believed, however, that reform of its administration would lead to the successful fulfillment of Kalaniana'ole's goals. Efforts to initiate reform of the Hawaiian homes program began in the 1950s. In 1957 the Hawaiian congressional delegate, John Burns, introduced a bill that would have partially remedied the difficulties of the commission. In a speech made in the House of Representatives, Burns appealed for federal contributions to the home loan fund so that the commission could award additional tracts. The delegate also proposed a mandatory requirement that the Hawaiian Homes Commission lease at least 20,000 acres within a five-year period. This amendment intended to extend the program to include more qualified Hawaiians. Congress refused to act; Burns reintroduced the bill during the following session of Congress but the measure again died in the House Territories Committee.[80]

In 1971 Hawaii state representative Diana Hansen prepared an investigative report revealing mismanagement of the Department of Hawaiian Home Lands and requested Congress to sue the state of Hawaii for breach of the trust compact. Her efforts failed to bring an investigation of the program or a federal suit against Hawaii. Some Department of Hawaiian Home Lands officials recommended reforming the department by placing its operation under the supervision of the Hawaiian court system and eventually allotting homelands on a fee simple basis. Native Hawaiians did not support this proposal.[81]

During the 1970s native homesteaders began a drive for reform of the commission on a state and federal level. Native supporters proposed numerous reform proposals for the commission and the Department of Hawaiian Home Lands in the 1978 Hawaii Constitutional Convention. Several of the more significant proposals included giving preference to Hawaiians in the leasing of homelands; establishing lessee election of the commissioners; permitting lessees to approve any rules adopted, amended, or repealed by the Department of Hawaiian Home Lands; authorizing homesteaders to present petitions that have 10 percent of the lessees' approval to the commissioners for review of a department rule; and allowing lessees' children of one-fourth Hawaiian blood quantum to inherit the homestead. The delegates failed to adopt most of these amendments but did make various changes in the administration of the Department of Hawaiian Home Lands. The state legislature subsequently passed legislation implementing some of the proposals. In 1986 Congress approved the amendments, one of which allowed homeland lessees to leave their homesteads to heirs who had one-fourth Native Hawaiian blood quantum.

Another amendment provided that the Department of Hawaiian Home Lands would give preference to Native Hawaiians when leasing homelands to the public.[82]

In the mid-1970s a group of Hawaiian homesteaders filed suit to enjoin the construction of a county flood-control project on homelands in the Waiākea-Uka area on the Big Island. The lessees opposed the project for several reasons. They had tried unsuccessfully for years to have these lands leased to Hawaiians. Instead the Native Hawaiian Commission had agreed to the county's request to exchange the twelve acres for equivalent state lands. The trade had not occurred. The situation characterized a serious problem with the administration of the homelands. Thousands of acres had been transferred by executive order to the use of local, state, and federal agencies. Often the homelands program received no compensation for these lands and a land exchange seldom took place. The homesteaders maintained that this policy violated the trust established by the admissions act.[83]

In the late 1970s the courts and the Department of the Interior interpreted differently the legal obligations of the federal government. The Department of the Interior concluded that its role was that of a trustee. However, the United States has never taken legal action to enforce the trust. The courts have not broadly construed the legal obligations of the federal government. In 1978 the Court of Appeals for the Ninth Circuit stated that the admission act transferred exclusive administrative and enforcement responsibility of the Hawaiian homes program to the state of Hawaii and that the "United States has only a somewhat tangential supervisory role under the Admission Act, rather than the role of trustee." The court also ruled that Native Hawaiians could not file a lawsuit to enforce the trust. Six years later the same court agreed that Native Hawaiians did not have a private cause of action to sue. The court, however, ruled that the federal government did have a trust responsibility to Native Hawaiians. It also held that they did have federal rights under the statehood act that were enforceable under title 42, section 1983 of the U.S. code. Still the beneficiaries did not have a private right to sue to enforce the trusts. In 1988, individual Hawaiians and Hawaiian organizations pushed through the state legislature a right-to-sue bill. Their efforts sparked a heated controversy. Opponents feared that such authorization would result in the state paying large sums in compensation for its failure to fulfill its trust responsibilities. Supporters of the right-to-sue bill assured legislators that this would not occur.[84]

In conformity with the Department of the Interior's view of its trustee role, it took two actions in response to widespread allegations, made by Native Hawaiians, of mismanagement and trust violations of the Hawaiian homes program. In early 1982 the inspector general of the U.S. Department of the Interior began an eight-month audit of the homelands program. In July 1982 Secretary of the Interior Cecil Andrus and Governor of Hawaii George R. Ariyoshi established a federal-state task force to investigate the allegations. A year later the task force completed a report containing its findings and 134 recommendations. Subsequently, the Department of Hawaiian Home Lands and the Hawaiian Homes Commission developed a plan to comply with the recommendations.[85]

Individual Native Hawaiians and Native Hawaiian organizations petitioned Congress to implement the recommendations and to initiate appropriate legal action for breach of trust involving the management of the Hawaiian homes program. Supported by the findings of the federal-state task force, these Hawaiians stated that over 80 percent of the homelands were leased to non-Hawaiian beneficiaries in violation of the Hawaiian Homes Commission Act. They also maintained that over 30,000 acres had been illegally transferred to federal and state departments or agencies and individuals, without fair compensation or exchange of lands. They further stated that less than 15 percent, or less than 30,000 acres, of the homelands were leased to Native Hawaiians. Less than 3,500 awards had been made and almost 8,000 Native Hawaiians were on the waiting list. Some of the applicants had waited for over thirty years to receive land. The task force investigation came after more than a decade of allegations by Native Hawaiians and other concerned individuals that the Hawaiian homelands trust was being mismanaged to the detriment of its intended beneficiaries.[86]

The Department of the Interior audit recommending "accelerated distribution" of homelands to Native Hawaiians resulted in a significant change in the Department of Hawaiian Home Lands policy. The more liberal policy was further bolstered by the 1983 federal-state task force report recommending immediate distribution of raw land to Native Hawaiians. Such a policy drew immediate criticism from Governor Ariyoshi, who called it "irresponsible and detrimental" to Native Hawaiians. Previously the department had held lands until enough money could be appropriated or raised privately to bring whatever lands were distributed to county zoning and building standards. The "proper" improvements would make mortgage money more available to Native Hawaiian lessees. Advocates of an accelerated distribution policy stated that the chronic lack of money for land development could prevent the majority of the homelands from ever being distributed.[87]

The Department of Hawaiian Home Lands, following the task force's recommendations, further liberalized its policy to include distributing unimproved land. Since 1983 it has granted over 2,500 homesteads; a large figure considering that only 3,300 homesteads were granted in the previous sixty-three years. However, the amount of money recommended by the task force to develop the lands has not been appropriated. To raise more money, the Department of Hawaiian Home Lands has considered commercial development of some of its land, including a resort that would replace a popular public beach park on Oʻahu.[88]

The Hawaiian homes program has provided a beginning for rebuilding the native peoples' land base. The program established a potential resource for a land base, especially if the management and operation of the department changes to a degree that it can lease the remaining homelands to Hawaiians, enable them to freely develop their land, offer guidance upon request for efficient economic development of their property, and extend capital for improvements. The potential land base, though small, exists and every effort should be made to enable Hawaiians to use it in whatever method they choose. Many Native Hawaiians desire land either for house lots, ranches, or farms. Some aspiring farmers want to return to their ancestral subsistence method of food production, whereas others want to farm using Western techniques.

In the Hawaii Admission Act, Congress transferred ownership of the public lands in Hawaii to the state in the form of a public trust. The public lands consisted of the government and Crown lands that the Republic of Hawaii had designated as its public lands and ceded to the United States at the time of annexation. The statehood act required that the public land and its revenue be used for the "betterment of the conditions of Native Hawaiians" of at least 50 percent Hawaiian ancestry and for four other stated purposes. Congress reserved to the United States the right to sue the state for breach of the public land trust.[89]

Until 1978 the state evidently considered that the Hawaiian homelands program satisfied its public land trust obligation to Native Hawaiians. All the income and proceeds from the public lands were consequently allocated to public education. In 1978 the state reaffirmed that all revenue from the public lands would be used for two classes of beneficiaries—the general public and Native Hawaiians—and that a pro rata share would be used for the betterment of conditions of Native Hawaiians. The Office of Hawaiian Affairs was created to carry out this objective.[90]

In the 1980s several lawsuits were filed by Hawaiians or Hawaiian organizations. The Office of Hawaiian Affairs brought legal action seeking a declaratory judgment that it was entitled to 20 percent of the income derived from certain public trust lands. In 1987 the Hawaii Supreme Court declined to make such a determination. The court declared that the issue was a political question that the legislature, not the judiciary, must resolve. If the court ruled on the issue, "it would be encroaching on legislative turf because the seemingly clear language of HRS 10-13.5 actually provides 'no judicially discoverable and manageable standards' for resolving the disputes and they cannot be decided without 'initial policy determination[s] of a

kind clearly for nonjudicial discretion.' " An action filed by the Hou
'Ohana, an association of Hawaiians, to enforce the trusts also was unsuccessful.[91]

In 1984 Native Hawaiian organizations petitioned Congress to establish
a federal-state commission to review the status of the public land still controlled by the federal government. By 1984, the United States had
returned to the state only 600 acres of the approximately 400,000 acres it
had withdrawn for its own use, primarily for military purposes, while
Hawaii was an American territory. Under the terms of the statehood act,
the federal government had five years to determine the future status of the
appropriated public lands. In 1963 Congress enacted a statute that provided that the lands would be returned to the state as part of the public
land trust whenever the General Services Administration designated them
as surplus lands. Native Hawaiians also requested that Congress grant the
federal-state commission the authority to declare federally controlled public lands surplus and available for return to the state. These petitions are
part of a continuing effort by Native Hawaiians to persuade the federal
government to fulfill its trust responsibility to them.[92]

Possible Land Restitution for Native Hawaiians
In addition to attempts to make additional lands available to Hawaiian
homesteaders through the Hawaiian homelands program, indigenous
Hawaiians since the 1970s have attempted to add new lands to their holdings. The first bill, formulated by ALOHA calling for reparations for former lands, contained a section providing for the return of surplus federal
lands to Native Hawaiians. In 1976 ALOHA presented a bill to their congressmen; while closely resembling the first Native Hawaiian claims bill
presented in 1974, the ALOHA proposal included a provision calling for
the return of approximately 2.5 million acres. This acreage equaled the
amount of Crown and government lands acquired by the provisional government in the 1890s. Congressmen Spark Matsunaga and Senator Daniel
Inouye persuaded the organization's officials that the Native Hawaiian bill
would fail to pass Congress and urged them to support a measure establishing a commission to study the validity of the land claims.[93]

Although desiring monetary compensation, many Hawaiians want land
more than money. They consistently expressed this sentiment throughout
the congressional hearings conducted in Hawaii from 1975 to 1977. While
some Hawaiians would settle for monetary restitution, others demanded
both land and financial compensation. Peter Hauano, speaking for the
Puna Hui Ohana organization, presented some of the opportunities monetary reparations would open for native people. One included funds for
defense of Hawaiians in quieting title to land inherited through the generations. Natives in Puna possessed much of their lands through tenancy-in-

common or undivided interest. Such uncertainty of title leaves the door open for others to step in and claim the land through adverse possession. Hauano suggested that reparations could provide needed revenue for costly legal procedures required to obtain clear title to the lands.[94]

Some haoles believed that any land reparations should be given in the form of kuleanas held in fee simple. They wanted to end, rather than perpetuate, the perceived paternalism manifested through holding lands in trust. During the 1977 hearings, a haole married to a half-Hawaiian expressed this idea:

> The Hawaiians are quite capable of paddling their own canoes individually when they are given enough education and some land of their own that is usable and that is the kind that they know how to take care of.[95]

Many Native Hawaiians and haoles promoted the idea of continuing to have land held in trust. One of the constitutional amendments adopted by the citizens of Hawaii in 1978 provided for the establishment of an Office of Hawaiian Affairs. This department would manage any lands received for the sole benefit of native people, including lands awarded as reparations.[96]

Naval Exercises at Kahoʻolawe

Some Native Hawaiians have demanded the return of the federally owned island of Kahoʻolawe to the state of Hawaii. The U.S. military has used this island for bombing practice since World War II. The military and some Native Hawaiians consider the continuation of the site in its current status as vital for national security and to a lesser extent for the economic welfare of the state of Hawaii. Those seeking restoration of the island cite the religious, cultural, and historic value of Kahoʻolawe. In 1977 a group of Hawaiians occupied Kahoʻolawe but authorities removed them. Since the mid-1970s, congressmen from Hawaii have introduced legislation authorizing the return of Kahoʻolawe to Hawaii.[97]

Under pressure from a court order issued by Federal Judge William Schwartzer, the U.S. Navy agreed in 1979 to allow access to the island for several days each month. Negotiation continued between the navy and the Protect Kahoʻolawe ʻOhana, a group representing the Native Hawaiians. In 1980 the parties reached a settlement in which the navy, among other provisions, agreed to (1) allow access to the island at least four days per month, ten months per year; (2) clear one-third of the island of military ordnance, the areas to be designated by the ʻOhana; (3) protect archaeological sites around the island. Shortly afterward the National Register of Historic Places surveyed Kahoʻolawe. The abundance of ancient sites prompted the agency to list the island as an archaeological district.[98]

Native groups continue to work for a complete cessation of the bombing. The Hawaii legislature, along with some members of the Hawaii congressional delegation, has openly opposed the use of Kahoʻolawe for military exercises. Although the United States invites its allies to participate in the exercises, in recent years only Canada has joined the U.S. Navy in the bombings.[99]

Those wanting the protection of Kahoʻolawe from destruction by the military also extend their efforts to protection of other land in Hawaii. Becoming more vocal and assertive, Hawaiian activists articulate the restoration and protection of their ancient rights and land. Many native people oppose the construction of additional expressways and condominiums that despoil the land. The following statement by a Native Hawaiian made during congressional debate on the Hawaiian Homes Commission still represents the attitude of many Hawaiians in 1988:

> This is our land. It belongs to us. Strangers have come here from the other side and have fattened on the land. Everybody gets rich through the Hawaiians, and we are thrown out.[100]

Attempted Preservation of Sacred Lands

Native Hawaiians recently attempted to preserve sacred land associated with the goddess Pele on the island of Hawaiʻi. They sued to prevent development of geothermal resources in the Kīlauea Middle East Rift Zone (KMERZ), which is located in the vicinity of the Kīlauea volcano. In 1983 the Hawaii legislature passed the Geothermal Energy Act giving the Board of Land and Natural Resources (BLNR) the authority to designate geothermal resource zones and to issue development permits. The BLNR, amid controversy, approved an application to develop geothermally generated electricity in the Kahaualeʻa area near the Kīlauea volcano. In 1984 a volcanic eruption in the area created concerns for safety. The development site was subsequently moved approximately six miles further away from the eruption to the KMERZ area. The BLNR eventually approved 9,000 acres as a geothermal resource subzone in the new area and issued a development permit.

Some Native Hawaiians opposed the project because they believed it would infringe on their religion as "Pele practitioners." Both the Kahaualeʻa and KMERZ areas were part of a volcanic region they identified with the goddess Pele. According to oral traditions, she came from Tahiti and migrated down the archipelago until she reached the island of Hawaiʻi, where she lives today. They feared that digging into the ground would desecrate her body and geothermal exploitation would destroy her by robbing her of vital heat. The destruction of Pele would cause spiritual, sociological, and cultural damage to the people who worship and respect her.[101]

The Pele practitioners sued the BLNR, contesting the constitutionality of the geothermal zone designation and the granting of a development permit. The Native Hawaiians argued that their right to practice their religion was jeopardized by the impending destruction of Pele. In July 1987 the Hawaii Supreme Court ruled otherwise. The decision noted that the Pele worshipers did not use the land in the past to practice their religion. Thus a generating plant would not physically prevent them from performing sacred rituals. To restrict development because of alleged injury to Pele would imply that the state endorsed the religion. This also violated the First Amendment.[102]

Restrictions on Adverse Possession

In an attempt to prevent additional alienation of land from Native Hawaiians, sympathetic supporters persuaded the 1978 constitutional convention to accept an amendment to the state constitution. The voters of Hawaii approved the measure that ended adverse possession on property over five acres. For decades large landholders had used this method to obtain tracts of land in Hawaii, and much of the property belonged to Native Hawaiians. As originally written, the proposal completely ended the practice. The constitutional convention initially passed the unaltered proposal but a few days later the delegates approved an amendment that excluded acreages under five acres. Both opponents of the movement to end adverse possession, such as the sugar interests and those Native Hawaiians who wanted to end the practice, voted against the revised amendment. Those delegates approving the proposal agreed to the amendment because they believed that it would aid Native Hawaiian landowners. The Sugar Planters' Association and others argued that the measure as originally written would hurt Native Hawaiians who owned small acreages without a clear title. The kuleanas originally had comprised about five acres. By including the five-acre provision, Native Hawaiians could still clear title to their land through adverse possession.[103]

In 1987 the Hawaii legislature passed legislation providing for the disposition of kuleana lands when an owner dies without making a will. When this occurs, his interest in the property will be transferred to the department of land and natural resources and held in trust until the Office of Hawaiian Affairs develops a land management program. This escheat provision will provide an additional land base for Native Hawaiian use. It also prevents surrounding landowners from acquiring the kuleana when its owner dies intestate.[104]

8

The Struggle for Use
and Access Rights

IN THE precontact period Native Americans possessed user rights in the resources of land. During the twentieth century and especially within the last decade, Native Americans have asserted these traditional rights and attempted, with some success, to secure judicial and legislative acknowledgment and use of them.

NATIVE HAWAIIANS

Although controversy over fishing, hunting, water, access, and gathering rights focused mainly on Indians, Hawaiians also vocalized their demand for recognition of these historic rights. In earlier times the tenant could use the resources of the entire ahupua'a for subsistence or cultural purposes. When the Hawaiian government converted its land tenure system to one based on fee simple ownership, it reserved certain traditional and customary rights for the tenants of the ahupua'a. One provision in the Kuleana Act of 1850, later codified as section 7-1 of the Hawaii Revised Statutes, permitted the tenants to retain gathering rights to some products of the land, rights of access or rights-of-way, and water rights. Kamehameha III reportedly wanted these resource rights reserved for the Hawaiian people so they could make their lands productive. He realized that a "little bit of land even with allodial title, if they [the people] be cut off from all other privileges would be of very little value." Later some judicial decisions and the statutory law recognized that tenants retained some ancient use rights that were not specifically included in the Kuleana Act. Section 1-1 of the Hawaii Revised Statutes provided that Hawaii common law included rights established by "Hawaiian usuage."[1]

In practice, fee simple landowners often prevented Hawaiians from exercising traditional use rights. Private property owners opposed the continuation of such rights because they believed these practices interfered with their exclusive rights as fee simple owners.

Since the late 1960s Hawaiians and their supporters have sought judicial and legislative affirmation of access, hunting, fishing, gathering, and water rights that they believe they inherited from their ancestors. The 1978 constitutional convention and later the voters of the state of Hawaii approved an amendment, which became section 7 of article 12 of the state constitution, guaranteeing Native Hawaiians their traditional and customary rights for religious, cultural, and subsistence purposes. Under this provision Hawaiian tenants in an ahupua'a could freely exercise these rights within the boundaries of this land division. The state legislature, however, could establish the means of regulation to prevent abuse of private property. Determination of the scope of these rights has rested with the judicial system.[2]

In 1982 the Hawaii Supreme Court declared that the constitutional amendment obligated the court to enforce those traditional rights retained by Native Hawaiians. The court held that Native Hawaiians who lived in an ahupua'a retained rights to gather certain natural products on its undeveloped lands for the purpose of practicing Native Hawaiian customs and traditions. This included an access right to enter or cross privately owned land for gathering purposes. The court determined that section 7-1 of the Hawaii Revised Statutes guaranteed gathering rights only to those items specifically enumerated in the statute. Rights to collect additional products as well as to practice other traditional customs were possible under the Hawaiian usage provision in section 1-1. The existence of a customary right depended on a case-by-case determination. To qualify, the custom must have been an ancient cultural practice "which continued to be practiced and which worked no actual harm upon the recognized interests of others." The court attempted to conform customary and traditional rights with a system of fee simple land tenure.[3]

In 1987 the state legislature recognized that Native Hawaiian tenants retained traditional and customary rights to ahupua'a resources. Such rights included gathering rights to certain natural products other than those enumerated in section 7-1. The recognition, however, does not bestow any affirmative rights on Native Hawaiian tenants except that the state's new water code cannot be applied to abridge or deny these rights.[4]

The doctrine of Hawaiian custom or usuage, as well as the statutory tenants rights of section 7-1, can also authorize access to beaches. The ancient trail system consisted of interconnecting paths allowing passage to the mountains, sea, and valleys. Maps clearly marked the various access paths even when they traversed private property. For decades Hawaiians used the ancient trails, but in recent times large landholders including corporations, estates, ranches, and hotels have closed off their usage. By the 1970s the growth of tourism and construction of resorts and beachfront properties increasingly threatened access to beaches.

Beach access for fishing purposes has been an important issue for Native Hawaiians. During the 1970s political activists demonstrated for recognition of Hawaiian access rights. On Moloka'i dissidents marched across Molokai Ranch protesting its blockage of public access to beaches on the west end of the island. The activists argued that as Native Hawaiians they had traditional rights of access based on the existence of ancient trails to the beaches. On the Big Island, other activists camped on beachfront property and demanded that the developer provide beach access to a traditional fishing area. They maintained that they were camping on public property, since the state supreme court had ruled that the boundary of state-owned beaches extended inland to the "upper reaches of the wash of waves." The court based its decision on the prevailing belief or ancient custom at the time of the Great Mahele.[5]

Beach access concerned not only Native Hawaiians but also the general public. During the 1970s the Hawaii legislature passed legislation to promote public access to the beaches by authorizing counties to acquire public rights-of-way by means of condemnation. Lacking sufficient funds, the state has not pursued all cases of beach-access blockage. For this reason it supported the filing of an access lawsuit by private parties on behalf of the public and residents of two ahupua'a. In 1982 the state supreme court approved of a lower court's certification of the class action suit. The court noted that the legislation did not preclude a private action for public access.[6]

Another concern of Hawaiians has been obtaining access or rights-of-way to their kuleanas. These small plots in the ahupua'a, surrounded by privately owned land, have often been landlocked. This prevented effective use of the kuleanas. Aggrieved owners had to resort to the courts for a determination of access rights. During the last two decades, state courts have provided legal remedies for some kuleana owners. In 1968 the Hawaii Supreme Court ruled that an ancient Hawaiian right-of-way across privately owned lands allowed ingress and egress to the kuleana. Testimony revealed that the trail had been used by the kuleana owner's predecessor in title. Section 7-1 of the revised statutes and the concept of reasonable necessity provided the legal basis for the court's decision. In 1982 a lower state court declared that section 7-1 established an easement by necessity to a landlocked kuleana. This provision reserved rights-of-way to landlocked parcels that were kuleanas at the time of the Great Mahele. The judicial decisions have not limited these rights-of-way to only Native Hawaiians. The right of access attached to the land or the kuleana.[7]

Water Rights

Both American Indians and Native Hawaiians have been concerned with affirming and preserving their water rights. The scope of their water rights and the laws determining them differ substantially. As discussed earlier, the water rights of most Indian tribes date back to the establishment of their reservations and to the *Winters* case. Since the Great Mahele, Native Hawaiians' right to water has been the same as that of all landowners in Hawaii. Although the water law was supposed to protect the rights of all users, plantation owners and other water users sometimes diverted water from kuleanas.

With the development of the plantation system after 1850, non-Hawaiians viewed water as a commodity that could be owned, sold, and transferred from one location to another. Under the judicially established doctrine of appurtenant water rights, which was based on a judicial perception of the ancient konohiki system, landowners were entitled to the amount of water that had been used on their lands for the production of taro at the time of the Great Mahele or when the lands were converted to fee simple ownership. Landowners could use water they had a right to for any purpose and could divert the water outside of the watershed as long as the rights of others were not injured. The konohiki of the ahupua'a owned as private property the surplus water—water in excess of all the other landowners' water requirements.[8]

In 1973 the Hawaii Supreme Court ruled that landowners did not own water as personal property, but had only appurtenant or riparian use rights. The state held the surface waters for the benefit of the public. Since landowners had riparian rights adjoining natural watercourses, the court determined that surplus waters were nonexistent. Neither appurtenant or riparian rights could be transferred to other lands. Riparian rights were traced to the Kuleana Act, which preserved the landowners' rights to flowing and running water in the ahupua'a. The court in a subsequent case compared riparian rights to *Winters* rights; both were reserved by the government to make the lands productive.[9] In 1987 the Hawaii legislature passed a water code to regulate the waters of the state. The code provided for the continuation of reasonable, beneficial uses of water. It also authorized the establishment of water management areas in localities threatened by the withdrawal or diversion of water. Landowners, at least those in water management areas, were permitted to divert water to nonriparian lands or outside the watershed. Under certain conditions, water permits could be transferred to other users.[10]

The water code also included a section on Native Hawaiian water rights. It preserved and protected the traditional and customary rights of Native Hawaiian ahupua'a tenants. These rights included, but were not restricted to, taro cultivation and gathering rights of certain products of the land for subsistence and for religious, and cultural purposes. Native Hawaiians were defined as "descendants of native Hawaiians who inhabited the Hawaiian Islands prior to 1778." The appurtenant water rights belonging to kuleanas and taro fields, as well as the other traditional and customary rights, were also protected from an adverse impact of the water code.[11]

AMERICAN INDIAN FISHING, HUNTING, AND GATHERING RIGHTS

Indian fishing and hunting rights have been subjected to much debate throughout the twentieth century. Indians had to wage legal battles to obtain judicial recognition of the retention of these rights. The courts generally reaffirmed the existence of treaty rights, although their scope and degree of control by the states have remained open to interpretation. Certain aspects of these rights, such as the Indians' freedom to fish and hunt on the reservation without state restriction, have not been questioned successfully. Other issues, including off-reservation treaty rights and the extent of state conservation regulations at "familiar and accustomed places," existed in an arena of controversy. The latter issues, along with tribal control over non-Indians fishing and hunting on the reservation, have been at the heart of the hunting and fishing controversy since the 1960s. These questions resulted in considerable animosity between Native Americans and their opponents, especially in the Pacific Northwest and the Great Lakes region. Indian efforts to exercise historic rights led to numerous confrontations and resistance among non-Indian fishing interests and state governments, who deny or disregard special treaty rights.

Off-Reservation Fishing and Hunting Rights

One of the first significant judicial opinions enunciating the retention of off-reservation fishing and hunting rights occurred in 1905. In *United States v. Winans,* the Supreme Court determined that Yakima Indians could enter private property adjoining the Columbia River to fish in the river. The decision stated that by treaty the Indians possessed the right to fish at "familiar and accustomed places" on former lands owned by the tribe. The opinion declared that the Yakimas retained those rights not explicitly given away in the treaty. Since the *Winans* case, the courts repeatedly have affirmed Native Americans' reserved fishing and hunting rights, although judicial opinions acknowledged that states usually had some degree of control over these rights in the name of conservation. Since the 1960s, courts have defined more concisely the degree of state regulation and in some cases have awarded complete jurisdiction to tribal fish and game codes.[12]

Many of the judicial opinions involved tribes from the Pacific Northwest. After 1965 the fishing dispute reached new heights and resulted in numerous confrontations between Indians asserting their fishing rights and state conservation officials enforcing state game laws. The Indians appealed their convictions for various offenses.

The major issue revolved around the Indians' right to fish in off-reservation waters without regard to state conservation laws. Indians argued that specific treaties guaranteed them the unrestricted right to fish or hunt on lands ceded to the United States. Historically Indians in the Pacific Northwest and the Great Lakes region depended upon fishing for subsistence and trade. Many contemporary Indians still follow this lifestyle and fish for food or for their livelihood.

Adversaries to the Indians' position maintained that Indians must obey conservation laws, and many argued that Indians possessed only the same rights as other fishermen. State conservation agencies—the political voice of commercial and sport fishermen—and fishermen opposed the Indians' right to fish without restrictions in off-reservation waters. These game laws often worked in a discriminatory manner against Indians. An expert state witness in one fishing case admitted that state officials employed conservation as a subterfuge, that game regulations promoted the non-Indian fishermen's interest. Another case pointed out that state officials can prevent Indians from harvesting any fish. Since the state regulates the licensing of sport and commercial fishermen, its officials can allocate so many fish to these non-Indians that all harvestable fish have been caught before they reach the Indian fishing locations.[13]

The courts usually have upheld Indian rights to fish and hunt on lands ceded to the United States, particularly on those classified as "open and unclaimed lands." In *Confederated Tribes of the Umatilla Indian Reservation v. Maison,* the U.S. District Court for Oregon determined that these rights included national forest land. The decree in *Kimball v. Callahan* extended the exercise of these rights on privately owned land where hunting, fishing, and trapping is permitted. However, in *Oregon Department of Fish and Wildlife v. Klamath Indian Tribe,* the U.S. Supreme Court ruled that the land cession agreement involved in the case did not reserve fishing and hunting rights free of state regulation in the ceded area.[14]

A number of off-reservation cases have centered on the Pacific Northwest tribes. One of these has included the lengthy litigation of the Puyallup tribe. After state game officers arrested some Puyallup Indians for violating conservation laws, the defendants took the issue to court. The suit finally rested before the Supreme Court. In *Puyallup Tribe v. Department of Game (Puyallup I),* the Court determined that the Medicine Creek Treaty of 1854 provided that the Nisqually and Puyallup tribes retained fishing and hunting rights "at all usual and accustomed places" on the lands they ceded to the United States. The opinion also declared that the state of Washington could regulate the time and means for fishing but that conservation must be necessary and reasonable and could not discriminate against Indians. The Court remanded the case to the state court to determine whether a total ban on net fishing was justified for purposes of conservation.[15]

In *Puyallup II, Department of Game v. Puyallup Tribe,* the U.S. Supreme Court prohibited the state's action of completely banning net fishing for steelhead trout, since this obstructed a treaty right by discriminating against Indians. All Indian fishers used nets, whereas non-Indians largely used hook and line, which the state allowed. The Court remanded the suit to the state court for determination of the number of catchable fish for Indian net fishing. The Supreme Court declared that regulations for Indian fishery conservation must be derived and supported by data concerning each species of fish in the Puyallup watershed. It further stated that should an Indian challenge a regulation, the Department of Game would be responsible for showing the necessity of the regulation for conservation. The Supreme Court in *Antoine v. Washington* added that the state must show that a regulation's application to Indians was necessary in the interests of conservation.[16]

After *Puyallup II,* but before the state court had carried out the Supreme Court's mandate, the Court of Appeals for the Ninth Circuit declared that the Puyallup Reservation still existed. This changed the litigation to an on-reservation case. The court supported the tribe's contention that it could fish free of state regulation on that part of the river within the reservation. This included most of the area covered in *Puyallup I* and *Puyallup II,* as well as much of Tacoma. The Superior Court of Washington for Pierce County persisted in its assertion of state authority to regulate fishing by the tribe on and off the reservation; this position was subsequently affirmed by the state supreme court. The state courts limited the number of steelhead trout that tribal members could catch with nets during the year and required the tribe to file a list of members authorized to exercise treaty rights. It also ordered the Puyallup tribe to report the weekly number of steelhead caught to the Washington Department of Game.[17]

The tribe appealed the regulations ordered by the state courts to the U.S. Supreme Court. In *Puyallup III, Puyallup Tribe v. Department of Game,* the Supreme Court upheld the 45-percent allocation of natural run of steelhead to Indians and the prohibition of catching harvestable hatchery breed steelhead. The decision allowed the Puyallup Indians to fish freely up to the limit without any restrictions as to time, place, or method. The decree supported the tribe's contention that the extensive regulations violated its sovereign immunity but maintained that the state could regulate Indian fishing rights. It, however, treated lightly the previous decision by the Ninth Circuit Court of Appeals that the reservation still existed and that the tribe held unrestricted rights within its boundaries. The Supreme

Court applied the principles previously applied to off-reservation rights, since most of the land had been alienated to non-Indians and the tribe did not have exclusive use of the Puyallup River. The Court applied article 3 of the 1854 Treaty of Medicine Creek, which provided for the retention of rights "in common with all citizens of the territory," rather than article 2, which gave the tribe exclusive rights on its reservation. The dissenting justices would have applied article 2 of the treaty. They asserted that the majority opinion denigrated the holding of the circuit court. They recommended that the case should be remanded to the state courts for determination of the state's right, if any, to regulate on-reservation fishing for purposes of conservation. They suggested that the Supreme Court's opinion might have been different if the Puyallup controversy had not been before the court for over ten years.[18]

Soon after the *Puyallup I* decision fourteen Yakima Indians brought suit against the Oregon Fish Department, contesting regulations that allowed non-Indian fishermen to catch most of the harvestable fish, thereby preventing the Yakimas from fishing at their "usual and accustomed" fishing sites guaranteed by an 1855 treaty. The plaintiffs charged that Washington also had failed to recognize the Indian fishery. On the latter complaint the U.S. District Court for the District of Oregon ordered the state of Washington to recognize officially the Indian fishery. *Sohappy v. Smith* also defined the treaty fishing rights of the Yakimas, Confederated Tribes of the Umatilla Reservation, and Warm Springs tribe. The decision declared that state fish regulations must accord the Indians a "fair share" of the harvestable fish on the Columbia River. Any regulation that did not allow a sufficient number of fish to pass through the lower river to the upriver Indian fishing sites would violate the Indians' treaty rights. The Indian fishermen's "fair share" catch must meet their economic needs, because fishing at the traditional sites provided the basis of those needs. The court determined that the state could regulate Indians to the extent required for conservation but that the rules must be reasonable and nondiscriminatory toward Indians. As a result of the decision, generally considered a victory for Indian fishermen, Oregon revised its regulations but did not conform to the court's rulings.[19]

In 1974 the district court altered its 1969 decree in response to a controversy over the 1974 run of Spring Chinook Salmon on the Columbia River. The court stipulated that the Indian treaty fishermen were entitled to 50 percent of the fish harvest. The states of Washington and Oregon objected to the allocation and appealed to the Court of Appeals for the Ninth Circuit. The court in *Sohappy v. Smith* upheld the lower court's ruling. It also stipulated that future allocations could be altered, if the states proved that a 50-percent allocation was "inequitable or impractical" and could present an alternate proposal that would equally protect the Indians' treaty rights.

The disputing parties reached an agreement concerning the Columbia River fishery and the district court incorporated it into the final decree in 1977. After this five-year conservation and management plan expired, the parties agreed to several one-year plans while continuing to negotiate for a comprehensive agreement.[20]

In 1974 the U.S. Court of Appeals for the Ninth Circuit in *Settler v. Lameer* ruled that the Yakima tribe possessed the jurisdiction to enforce its tribal fishing codes at all off-reservation traditional fishing sites. The court cited the *Winans* opinion that the 1855 treaty "was not a grant of rights to the Indians, but a grant of rights from them—a reservation of those not granted." This opinion differed substantially from earlier case law that allowed state regulation at off-reservation sites. Over ten years later the Oregon Appellate Court ruled that the state could not enforce its fishing and hunting laws on ceded lands subject to tribal control unless it proved the regulation was necessary for conservation purposes. However, the federal government under the Lacy Act can prosecute an Indian treaty fisher for violating state or tribal law. In 1985 the Ninth Circuit Court of Appeals affirmed the convictions of thirteen Indians for violating the Lacy Act by catching and selling fish during a closed commercial season under state law.[21]

The decisions made in favor of the northwestern Indians only seemed to intensify the hostility of non-Indian fishing interests. This animosity increased with the landmark court decision rendered in 1974. After years of litigation and numerous confrontations between Native Americans and state conservation officers or vigilante non-Indian fishermen that frequently culminated in violence and destruction of Indian property, federal district judge George Boldt issued a monumental decree concerning the coastal tribes of Washington. Previously the federal courts had moved in the direction of defining the limits of Indian fishing rights but had not dealt directly with the problem. Judge Boldt based his ruling on eleven treaties concluded in the 1850s between fourteen tribes and Territorial Governor Isaac Stevens, who represented the United States. The decision maintained that the tribes held historic rights to 50 percent of the state's commercial salmon catch, exclusive of fish landed on the reservation. The tribes retained fishing rights at all "usual and accustomed" fishing sites on off-reservation waters and held rights to self-regulation, thereby being exempt from state control. The state could exercise conservation measures in emergency situations.[22]

Massive reaction greeted this judicial decision. The state, commercial and sport fishermen, and their organizations took legal and extralegal action. Violence against the Indian fishermen and their property continued. Legally the non-Indian adversaries have taken a two-pronged approach. They appealed the Boldt decision first to the U.S. Court of

Appeals and then to the Supreme Court. In early 1976 the Supreme Court refused to review the court of appeals' affirmation of the Boldt decision. The non-Indian fishing interests and the state of Washington then started on a new series of court cases, beginning on the state level and proceeding to the U.S. Supreme Court. The federal courts upheld the treaty rights and Boldt's decision, whereas the state courts provided obstacles to enforcement of the district court's ruling on the Indians' fishing rights. In hearing *Puget Sound Gillnetters Association v. United States,* the Court of Appeals for the Ninth Circuit remarked that Judge Boldt had endured "the most concerted official and private efforts to frustrate a decree of a federal court witnessed in this century" while trying to enforce the decree in *United States v. Washington.*[23]

Before 1977 state officials only made stabs at enforcing the district court's opinion. Indian fishermen charged the state with openly violating the orders by abusing the emergency power provision. The Indians claimed state officials closed waters to Indian fishers. Neither the state, its courts, nor non-Indian fishermen accepted the validity of treaty rights by a minority with little political power. This attitude made enforcement of the district court's orders virtually impossible. After 1977 enforcement broke down completely. The state Department of Fisheries reluctantly published new regulations that met the court's guidelines. State officials issued citations to a few violators, but state courts dismissed the charges or prosecutors refused to prosecute the offenders.[24]

The Washington Supreme Court rendered a series of decisions stating that the state Department of Fisheries lacked jurisdiction under state law to enforce certain regulations devised to meet the district court's decree and that the department only had authority to pass regulations regarding conservation. The court declared that the decrees of *United States v. Washington* had been erroneous and that Indians held only the right to have the opportunity to fish in common with non-Indians. After the state supreme court's decisions, the Department of Fisheries issued new regulations that made no attempt to safeguard Indian fishing rights as enunciated by the federal district court.[25]

The combined efforts of the state government and courts had at best placed Indians' fishing rights on the same level as, or below, non-Indian fishermen. State regulations typically discriminated against Indian fishers. Opponents argued that Indian exemption from state conservation laws depleted the fish supply, particularly that of salmon. Tribal commercial fishermen, however, caught only a small portion of the total fish crop. The state's obstruction of Indian fishing treaty rights forced the federal district court to manage directly the enforcement of Indian fishing rights.[26]

Various non-Indian fishermen organizations brought suit challenging the district court decisions. In *Puget Sound Gillnetters Association v. United*

States, non-Indian fishermen in a consolidated appeal attempted to have various opinions of federal district courts in Washington and Oregon overruled. The Court of Appeals for the Ninth Circuit declared that both Washington and Oregon fishermen must abide by the lower court's decree. The plaintiffs appealed this decision, along with two other cases, to the Supreme Court. They challenged the constitutionality of the district court's decisions regarding allocation and enforcement. The continued obstruction and litigation reflected the unwillingness of state officials and non-Indian fishermen to accept the validity of the Boldt decision and Indian reserved fishing rights. The U.S. Justice Department took an unprecedented step when it encouraged the Supreme Court to review the *United States v. Washington* case. A successful litigant seldom wants a higher court to review the decision.[27]

In the aftermath of the Boldt opinion, congressmen, especially from the Pacific Northwest and the Great Lakes region, introduced bills calling for the abrogation of Indian treaties or of hunting and fishing rights. Congress refused to approve such legislation despite widespread support for such action from all areas of the nation. A backlash against Indian treaty rights occurred not only because of the landmark decision on Northwest Pacific tribes' fishing rights, but also because of Native Americans' nationwide assertions regarding land claims and tribal sovereignty, land, and resources.[28]

In late 1978 a group of national Indian leaders wrote to Attorney General Griffin Bell expressing their concern regarding his public opinions on Indian treaty rights. The attorney general had stated that he believed a conflict of interest existed in the Department of Justice between Indian rights and those of the American public. Bell suggested that the department should no longer defend Indians in cases against the general public. Indian leaders maintained that no such conflict existed.[29]

Indian leaders also expressed deep concern over Bell's response to a letter from Washington congressmen in regard to Indian fishing and hunting treaty rights in the Pacific Northwest. Bell implied that he sympathized with the congressmen and non-Indian fishing interests in their disdain for the Boldt decision. The Indian leaders feared that such a remark would only encourage additional obstructions to the fulfillment of Indian treaty rights. They added that the attorney general did not mention that non-Indian fishermen violated federal law. Indian leaders remarked that such an attitude held by the nation's supreme law enforcement officer could foreshadow the fate of Indian treaty rights.[30]

In 1979 the Supreme Court essentially upheld *United States v. Washington* and Judge Boldt's subsequent orders. The Court made a few modifications in the lower court's rulings. It held that the Puget Sound tribes' reservation and ceremonial catch must be included in their share of the fish harvest. The Court also declared that the 50-percent allocation to the tribes was a maximum amount, not a minimum share, that could be reduced by the district court if changing tribal needs required a lesser amount. The Supreme Court stated that "Indian treaty rights to a natural resource . . . secures so much as, but no more than, is necessary to provide the Indians with a livelihood—that is to say, a moderate living." Left unexplained was a definition of moderate living. What standards would be applied to make this determination? The Court chastised the state for its refusal to follow the district court's rulings. The supremacy clause of the U.S. Constitution prohibited such actions. The Court noted that the federal district court had the power to regulate the Puget Sound fishery and if the state persisted in its "recalcitrance," the lower court could have federal law enforcement agents enforce its orders.[31]

Following the Supreme Court decision, the tribes and the state continued to have conflicts over treaty fishing rights. State officials did begin to regulate the fishery in accordance with the ruling. However, in 1983 the state of Washington was held in contempt of court. Subsequent federal court decisions resolved some of the outstanding issues. They determined, for example, that salmon caught in state-regulated waters by nonresidents were part of the non-Indian share and that hatchery-bred fish were included in the fish crop apportioned by treaty. By 1985 the state and tribes were resolving their problems and cooperating in the management and conservation of the fishery. They participated in negotiations for the 1984 Pacific Salmon Treaty and under its terms and those of the implementing federal legislation, the tribes have a say in the management of the resource. These documents also recognized Indian treaty rights. In 1985 the federal district court approved a management plan agreed to by the Puget Sound tribes, the state, and the United States.[32]

Fishing, hunting, and gathering rights also have been a major area of controversy in the Great Lakes region. There, in common with the Pacific Northwest, most of the conflict has centered on off-reservation lands ceded to the United States. Indians, particularly the Chippewa, have exercised and demanded their rights to unrestricted fishing, hunting, and gathering of wild rice. These Indian peoples argued that they retained these rights on the land they ceded to the United States in treaties during the nineteenth century.

State and federal courts in Michigan and Minnesota usually have upheld these reserved rights, although certain decisions declared that some restrictions existed. The Michigan Supreme Court in April 1971 maintained that the treaty of 1855 with the Chippewas entitled the L'Anse and Vieux Desert bands of Chippewa to fish on all unsold lands in certain specified areas of Keweenaw Bay of Lake Superior. State game laws did not extend to these particular Indians in the specified areas. In 1971 a Chippewa from the Bay Mills Indian Community intentionally violated state fishing regulations so he would be arrested. State officials charged him with fishing without a commercial fishing license. He claimed immunity under the 1836 Treaty of Washington, which had ceded the land adjoining Pendills Bay of Lake Superior. After various decisions in the lower courts, the state supreme court rendered an opinion in December 1976. In *People v. LeBlanc* the court declared that the Treaty of 1836 reserved the Indians' fishing rights but that Michigan had limited authority to regulate off-reservation fishing rights of the Chippewas. Regulations promulgated had to meet a number of criteria. The rules must be necessary for the preservation of specified species of fish, application to Indians had to be necessary to preserve fisheries from irreparable harm, and the rules could not discriminate against treaty Indians. The state supreme court remanded the case to the district court to determine whether the ban on large gill nets satisfied the above requirements. The higher court declared that the treaty fishermen did not have to obtain a state commercial license to fish in the area covered by the 1836 treaty, which included much of Lake Superior and a portion of lakes Huron and Michigan.[33]

Indian endeavors to secure judicial confirmation of their reserved rights led to extensive conflict with non-Indian fishing interests, property owners, and the state's department of natural resources commission. Its agents arrested Indians exercising their rights in violation of state game laws and confiscated their fishing materials. In 1973 U.S. Department of Justice lawyers initiated a suit, *United States v. Michigan,* on behalf of the Bay Mills Indian Community and Sault Ste. Marie Chippewas, to determine their fishing rights. Both tribes intervened in the court action. In May 1979 the federal district court held that the Chippewas and Ottawas had aboriginal fishing rights in the Great Lakes that had survived the treaties of 1836 and 1855. Moreover, the Chippewas and Ottawas could fish free of state regulation. The state appealed the decision and in May 1980 the Court of Appeals for the Sixth Circuit delivered its opinion. Although the court agreed with the lower court's decision that the Indians had treaty fishing rights, it stated that in the absence of federal regulation Michigan could regulate the Indian fishery in accordance with the criteria enunciated in *People v. LeBlanc.* The sixth circuit court, however, remanded the case to the district court to determine if the comprehensive regulations issued six months earlier by the secretary of the interior on Indian fishing in the Great Lakes preempted the state's limited right of regulation. In July 1980 the circuit court issued an order allowing treaty fishing under the secretary of the interior's regulations on an interim basis.[34]

It was expected that the temporary regulations would be replaced by permanent ones before they expired on 1 January 1981. Instead President Jimmy Carter, under political pressure in an election year, only extended the expiration date to 11 May 1981. Bowing to intense political pressure,

President Ronald Reagan and Secretary of the Interior James Watt allowed the regulations to lapse, appparently on the basis that the federal government should permit state regulation of the Indian fishery in the Great Lakes.[35]

The state of Michigan then adopted emergency regulations governing gill-net fishing that were more restrictive than the federal regulations. The state requested the sixth circuit court to approve the emergency regulations and to vacate its remand order to the district court. The court ruled against the state's motions.[36]

Referring to Secretary of the Interior Watt's decision not to renew the federal regulations, the court commented that the federal government has a "solemn obligation" to protect the Indians' "treaty-guaranteed fishing rights" and that "no principle of federalism requires the federal government to defer to the states in connection with the protection of those rights. The responsibility of the federal government to protect Indian treaty rights from encroachment by state and local governments is an ancient and well-established responsibility of the national government."[37]

Realizing that federal preemption was no longer at issue, the court ordered the district court to reconsider the fishing rights case in light of *People v. LeBlanc*. The state of Michigan could restrict Indian fishing rights, including gill-net fishing, only if it could show that Indian fishing would cause irreparable harm to fisheries within its territorial jurisdiction, that regulation would be necessary to protect the resources, and that tribal self-regulation would be ineffective. As an interim measure, the tribes could regulate their fishing. Previously, the Bay Mills Indian Community and the Sault Ste. Marie Chippewas had adopted the secretary of the interior's regulations as part of their tribal code. On remand, the district court revealed that the state of Michigan had "no present intention" to satisfy the criteria necessary for state regulation. The court retained jurisdiction to determine the legality of any future attempts by the state to regulate treaty fishing. A year later, the district court authorized the adoption of new regulations that had been presented to the court by the Bay Mills Indian Community, the Sault Ste. Marie Tribe of Chippewa Indians, and the Grand Traverse Band of Ottawa and Chippewa Indians.[38]

The intensity of the fishing rights controversy in Michigan was evidenced by diverse efforts on both national and state levels. During January 1978, the U.S. House of Representatives conducted hearings on the Great Lakes fishing controversy and the Michigan disputes received most of the attention of the house committee. On several occasions Michigan congressmen introduced bills in Congress that would abrogate unilaterally treaty-guaranteed fishing and hunting rights. As indicated above, political pressure was also applied on presidents Carter and Reagan to withdraw the federal regulations on Indian fisheries in the Great Lakes. On the state level, state courts interfered with and obstructed the adjudication of the fishing rights issues by issuing orders inconsistent with those of the federal courts. State officials prosecuted Indian fishermen who were fishing in compliance with the circuit court's interim rules on treaty fishing, and in at least one case a state court convicted the Indian defendant for criminal contempt. They also threatened to prosecute other Indian fishermen.[39]

The district court did not want to "become a perpetual fish master" but believed it "must continue its role" in the controversy, if necessary. The district judge appointed a special master to resolve the issues and in 1985 representatives of all parties in the case reached an agreement. The state and federal governments, several non-Indian commercial and sport fishing groups, and two of the tribes subsequently ratified the agreement. The court made the agreement binding on all parties by including its terms in a court order. It accommodated all interests by allocating the fisheries in the Great Lakes among the tribes and commercial and sport fishers, by closing certain areas to tribal and commercial fishers, and by prohibiting the use of gill nets by Indian fishers in most areas. The tribal share of the allowable whitefish harvest will increase annually until 1990, when the tribes will be entitled to 73 percent from Lake Superior, 68 percent from Lake Huron, and 65 percent from Lake Michigan.[40]

Several courts have implied that tribes retained aboriginal hunting and fishing rights if their Indian title to use and occupancy had not been extinguished by the federal government. A member of the Idaho Kootenai tribe was arrested for hunting on lands traditionally occupied by the tribe. In 1976 the Idaho Supreme Court declared that the Idaho Kootenai tribe had its aboriginal rights, including those of hunting and fishing in the area, extinguished by Senate ratification of the Treaty of Hellgate, which ceded land to the federal government and reserved to Indians only a right to hunt on open and unclaimed lands. Judge J. Donaldson, in a dissenting opinion, argued that since the Kootenais had not signed the treaty, it did not affect their rights. He disagreed with the court's decision that Senate ratification of the treaty nevertheless took away their rights. Donaldson maintained that the Kootenai tribe's rights had not been extinguished by the Senate or by the Indian Claims Commission, which had compensated them for loss of possessory rights but not for those of hunting and fishing. In 1981 the California Supreme Court declared that when Congress extinguished the Pit River Indians' aboriginal title by paying them the Indian Claims Commission award, it simultaneously extinguished their aboriginal right to fish and hunt in their former territory. The Pit River Indians were therefore subject to state game laws.[41]

On-Reservation Fishing, Hunting, and Gathering Rights

Case law concerning on-reservation fishing and hunting rights for tribal members normally has included recognition of exclusive rights of tribal sovereignty over regulation of these rights unless Congress specifically abrogated them. In 1968 the U.S. Supreme Court determined that the Menominees retained the right to control hunting and fishing on their former reservation without state regulation, even though the Wolf River Treaty of 1854 had not specifically mentioned these rights. The court based its interpretation on the reserved-rights doctrine enunciated in the *Winans* decree in 1905. Indians retained those rights unless Congress clearly extinguished them by treaty or agreement. The Court stated that abrogation of treaty rights will not be lightly implied. Since the termination legislation of 1953 and 1954 specifically excluded fishing and hunting rights, the treaty survived the termination acts and the Menominee termination of 1954. The Court therefore declared that the Menominees had reserved treaty rights on their terminated reservation and the right of self-regulation.[42]

The Klamaths also have been involved in litigation concerning their hunting and trapping rights. The Klamath Termination Act reserved the tribe's fishing rights but did not mention hunting and trapping rights. In 1956 the Klamath tribe brought suit against the state of Oregon concerning these rights. The federal court decision declared that the act had not extinguished the Klamaths' historic right to hunt and trap. After the Klamath termination became effective in 1961, tribal members again had to take legal action to gain affirmation. The 1964 federal court decision ruled that the Klamath Termination Act abrogated the Indians' hunting and trapping rights.[43]

Ten years later in *Kimball v. Callahan (Kimball I)*, the Court of Appeals for the Ninth Circuit determined that termination legislation had not abrogated the withdrawn Klamath Indians' treaty rights to fish, trap, and hunt without state regulation on former reservation lands consisting of national forest lands and privately owned lands open to hunting, fishing, and trapping. The court held that before termination the tribe had those rights within the reservation and individual members had user rights. Termination had not affected those rights, and a withdrawn member under termination had not changed his relationship to the tribe in those matters unaffected by the act; that is, fishing, hunting, and trapping rights. The court overruled the 1964 decision. On remand from the higher court, the district court stated that these rights extended to the descendants of Indians listed on the 1954 final roll and that the court had no jurisdiction to permit state regulation of treaty rights.[44]

After an appeal to the Ninth Circuit Court of Appeals, the court in *Kimball v. Callahan (Kimball II)* upheld the district court's opinion and that of *Kimball I*. The court in *Kimball II* stated that tribal members did not contest the right of state regulation for purposes of conservation, nor did they claim exclusive rights since most of the former reservation had been transferred to other parties, but they did question the degree of state control.

The Klamaths wanted joint regulation by the tribe and state. The court ruled that the state of Oregon could limit the Klamaths' rights under appropriate regulations necessary for conservation. The opinion declared that the tribe and state officials should reach an agreement on appropriate standards. If they could not, then the district court should determine the extent of Oregon's authority and base its decision on the guidelines provided in *Puyallup I, II,* and *III, Antoine v. Washington, United States v. Washington, Sohappy v. Smith,* and *Settler v. Lameer.*[45]

Although termination did not destroy Klamath fishing and hunting rights on former reservation lands, a 1901 cession agreement did extinguish the tribe's rights on those lands ceded to the federal government. In 1985 the U.S. Supreme Court in *Oregon Department of Fish and Wildlife v. Klamath Indian Tribe* declared that Congress had clearly limited the tribe's fishing and hunting rights to remaining reservation lands.[46] The Eighth Circuit Court of Appeals rendered a similar opinion in *Sac and Fox Tribe of the Mississippi in Iowa v. Kicklider.* Sac and Fox tribal members residing on a reservation in Iowa objected to the extension of state game and fish laws on the reservation. In an attempt to stop state actions the Indians brought suit in federal court. The court determined that the Sac and Fox had extinguished their reserved rights in the treaty of 1842 and that the federal government had recognized state jurisdiction over the "de facto" reservation. The state of Iowa therefore could regulate fishing and hunting by tribesmen on the reservation.[47]

Several judicial opinions delivered in the 1970s and 1980s involved the question of the continued existence of a reservation and the Indians' reserved rights on lands within its boundaries. In 1969 the Leech Lake band of Chippewa Indians brought suit in federal court for affirmation of exclusive treaty rights on its reservation free of state control. The U.S. District Court of Minnesota in *Leech Lake Band of Chippewa Indians v. Herbst* declared that the Leech Lake band retained their reserved rights. The Nelson Act of 1889, which approved allotment and sale of surplus lands, did not abrogate the treaty of 1855, even though the statute contained a provision extinguishing "all our right, title, and interest" in the reservation lands. The reservation remained legally a distinct entity. The court determined that the Leech Lake Chippewas retained their historic fishing, hunting, and rice-gathering rights on all ceded public lands on the reservation. The disputants appealed and cross-appealed the band's alleged exclusive right to regulate fishing without state control on the reservation. Non-Indian fishermen and property owners in Leech Lake area tried to enjoin the case. While the suit pended before the Court of Appeals for the Eighth Circuit, the parties reached an agreement and the court remanded the case to district court. The agreement provided that members of the band would be excluded from state regulation of fishing, hunting, trapping, and rice-gathering on the reservation. The band agreed to prohibit commercial fishing and hunting, to conserve the resources for the tourist industry, and to regulate members with a tribal conservation code. The state assented to collect a supplementary licensing fee for the benefit of the Leech Lake Chippewas from non-Indians fishing, hunting, or trapping on the reservation. The district court incorporated this agreement into its final decree of 1973.[48]

The state legislature subsequently ratified the Leech Lake agreement and enacted implementing legislation. The tribe has the option to receive payment for all special licenses sold to nontribal members for fishing, hunting, and trapping on the reservation or to receive 5 percent of all fees collected for state licenses sold for these purposes. The state also will distribute 2.5 percent of all revenue from state fish and game licenses to the White Earth Chippewas, who were successful in their litigation against state enforcement of its fishing and hunting laws.[49]

A similar issue involved the former Cheyenne and Arapaho reservation in Oklahoma. The Cheyennes and Arapahoes asserted their right to fish and hunt on tribal trust lands and allotments free of state regulation. The state argued that it had regulatory authority under the Assimilative Crimes Act. The Tenth Circuit Court of Appeals held that the land in question was Indian country and that the act did not permit the extension of state fish and game laws over these lands. Whether the tribe had dual jurisdiction with the state to regulate fishing and hunting on non-Indian lands within the boundaries of the original reservation was not at issue. The court noted, without deciding, that shared jurisdiction had been recognized by other judicial decisions, such as *Puyallup I*.[50] As earlier indicated, the Court of Appeals for the Ninth Circuit in 1974 determined that the Puyallup Indian Reservation still existed, even though the lands had been allotted and sold to non-Indians. In *Puyallup III,* the Supreme Court applied those principles usually applicable to off-reservation rights; that is, that treaty Indians did not hold exclusive rights and that state regulations for purposes of conservation extended to include the Puyallups.

Another principle of case law concerning on-reservation fishing and hunting rights of Indians involved the extent of state jurisdiction given to some states by Public Law 280 over reservations within their boundaries. In 1976 the District Court for the Eastern District of Washington stated that Public Law 280, which specifically extended Washington jurisdiction over the Colville Reservation, had not included the Colville's reserved fishing and hunting rights. The confederated Colville tribes had complete jurisdiction over fishing and hunting on their reservation. A later opinion overturned the lower court's ruling that the tribes had control over non-Indians' fishing and hunting practices. A similar decree resulted in *Arnett v. Five Gill Nets.* The California state court determined that Public Law 280 did not extend state jurisdiction over the exercise of fishing rights by Indians on the Klamath Indian Reservation. The state had no authority under its police powers to restrict Indian subsistence fishing on the reservation by prohibiting the use of gill nets for purposes of conservation.[51]

In some instances the federal government has assumed authority to control Indian fishing on a reservation. In 1979 the Department of the Interior promulgated regulations for the Hoopa Valley Indian Reservation in California. The Yurok and Hoopa tribes claimed they should be allowed to regulate tribal fishing on the part of the Klamath River that runs through their reservation. Interior officials contended that the tribes had not completed the necessary organization for effective regulation and conservation. The codes prohibited commercial fishing and only approved Indian subsistence and ceremonial fishing. While tribal members were divided on the issue of commercial-versus-subsistence fishing, they agreed that extensive commercial fishing by non-Indian fishermen endangered the salmon resource and that construction of dams also depleted the fish supply.[52]

In 1985 Klamath fishers won a short-lived victory when a federal district court declared that the Department of the Interior's moratorium against commercial fishing substantially infringed on their reserved fishing rights. The following year the Ninth Circuit Court of Appeals upheld the validity of the regulations. It overturned the lower court's decision by holding that the Interior Department's regulatory control did not exceed its statutory authority. In 1987 a California state court complicated the situation when it ruled that the state had concurrent jurisdiction over the salmon fishery on the Hoopa Reservation. The judges based their decision on an analysis of *New Mexico v. Mescalero Apache,* a 1983 U.S. Supreme Court case that recognized the Apache tribe's exclusive jurisdiction over fishing and hunting by nonmembers. Undoubtedly the question of whether the state of California shares regulatory control with the federal government will be considered by the courts again in the future.[53]

Tribes have also asserted jurisdiction over hunting and fishing rights of nonmembers while they are on Indian reservations. Judicial opinions have varied in their interpretations, with some upholding the tribes' right to regulate nonmembers. Enactment of comprehensive tribal game codes sometimes has been a decisive factor in a court's ruling, but not always.

In the 1980s the Supreme Court delivered several opinions on the issue of tribal-versus-state jurisdiction over nonmembers fishing and hunting on reservations. *Montana v. United States* involved tribal regulation of duck hunting and trout fishing by nonmembers on the Crow Reservation. The Court stated that the tribe had the power on tribally owned or trust lands either to prohibit nonmembers from fishing and hunting or to regulate these activities. The central issue was whether the Crow could regulate non-Indian fishing and hunting on lands owned in fee by nonmembers.

The Court determined that neither the Crow treaties, a federal trespass statute, nor the tribe's inherent sovereignty provided a source for such tribal power. Since the tribal regulation of nonmembers on the fee lands did not have a direct effect on tribal self-government or relations among its members, the Crow did not have the inherent sovereignty to regulate non-members on lands no longer owned by the tribe.[54]

The Supreme Court in *New Mexico v. Mescalero Apache Tribe* held that the tribe and the federal government had exclusive jurisdiction over fishing and hunting by nonmembers on the reservation. The Court declared that the state did not have concurrent jurisdiction to regulate these activities. The comprehensive tribal management plan and the importance of tribal regulation to the tribe's economic welfare were considered crucial factors in the court's determination. The Court applied the interests test enunciated in its prior decision of *White Mountain Apache Tribe v. Bracker* to conclude that the interests of the tribe and the United States requiring tribal regulation outweighed those of the state.[55]

Case law concerning the exercise of reserved fishing and hunting rights continually changes. Opinions, especially in the federal courts, are affirming these rights and are moving in the direction of confirming increased tribal jurisdiction over non-Indians on the reservation and tribal members on off-reservation waters.

9

Conclusion

THE IMPACT of imperialistic nations, especially the United States, upon Indians and Hawaiians caused fundamental modifications in aboriginal land tenure systems and use of resources. Contact between the United States, with a superior technology, and the nativistic cultures ultimately destroyed the latter's absolute sovereignty, which had guarded aboriginal access to these lands and resources for centuries.

The time involved and the degree to which Native Americans lost sovereignty and their original form of land tenure differed substantially. The time span for Hawaiians was shorter than for most Indians. The relatively small land mass of the islands, especially those lands suitable for agricultural or pastoral purposes, intensified the contest for property. On the surface it appears that the land tenure system of each group completely changed. An argument can be made for this point of view, but some aspects of the old systems have survived to provide the foundation for a hybrid form of land tenure. This applies especially to the Indians. Some tribes such as the Hopi continue to apply historic land use systems. Other tribes allocate their communally owned trust lands among members for personal use. Most Indian nations still hold land in common and enjoy a degree of sovereignty over the use of the land and its resources, although the exact status has changed. The U.S. government holds most of these lands in trust for the tribes. Many of the reservations have a checkerboard character with both non-Indians and Indians owning land in fee simple along with tribally held land.

Contact between Westerners and Hawaiians essentially led to a rather rapid destruction of the native land tenure system. A few traces remain and the altered tenure shares some common elements with the Indian system. Some huis, a transitional form between the old system and Western individual ownership, survive. The members of the hui own the land in common and share part of the land, while maintaining individual plots for personal use. Unlike Indians, Hawaiians have no reservations. The state government holds the Hawaiian homelands in a form of trust for Hawaiians as a racial group. Furthermore the homelands have been slowly divided into acreages for use by individual families, although they remain a part of the homelands. Native homesteaders cannot own this land but rather lease it for ninety-nine years. Hawaiian lessees possess the status of tenants; like their ancestors who had to pay tribute to use the soil, they pay a small annual lease fee. Many Indians who received homesteads through allotment still have restrictions on the alienation of their property. Both Hawaiians and Indians were forced for a time to accept individual ownership of land. Both groups still view land in a metaphysical sense.

Traditional rights to the use of land for hunting, fishing, and gathering represent one area in which Native Americans have retained some control. Indians still have historic water rights and the Hawaiians hold access rights. These rights are distinct from those of other American citizens and derive from the aboriginal land system. Judicial opinions, particularly recent federal court decisions, have upheld these rights for Indians. Hawaiians usually exercised their historical rights, but in recent times large landholders have blocked access to gathering grounds. The 1978 Hawaiian constitutional convention and electorate adopted an amendment affirming these traditional rights.

Native Americans' economy and subsistence methods have changed. Alaska Natives, who have been the least affected, have survived contact with Western patterns of civilization, and many follow traditional lifestyles. Few Indian tribes have a self-sufficient economy, but many retain elements of their precontact systems. Some Indians continue to gather and fish according to the mode of their ancestors, although they apply more sophisticated techniques and equipment. Some have adopted Western business methods. Tribal economies frequently have a commercial overtone but with profits used for the benefit of the tribe. Many Indian tribes increasingly have moved in this direction. For the most part, the economy of Hawaiians exists as an indistinguishable part of the larger economy in the islands. A few traditional fishing and farming villages survive, as well as the native community on Ni'ihau.

At the time of first contact with Westerners, the land tenure systems of these two Native American groups were similar in several aspects. Neither followed the Western practice of individual land ownership. Title in fee simple constituted an alien concept to both. Most Indians held their lands in common with title vested in the group. Property rights varied with each tribe or kinship group, as well as with the particular use of the land. On the other hand, Hawaiians maintained a quasi-feudal land system. Numerous chiefs, each claiming title to all land under his dominion, ruled the Hawaiian islands. They subdivided their territories among lesser chiefs who controlled Native Hawaiian commoners and the use of the land. After unifying the Hawaiian islands in 1795, Kamehameha I, as supreme monarch, claimed some ownership of all land in the Hawaiian archipelago. Both Indians and Hawaiians based their land tenure system upon use rather than on consumerism; the Western practice of selling and buying land was alien to them.

Hawaiians and Indians suffered the common experience of loss of their lands to imperial nations. Hawaiians and Indians first met foreigners with friendliness and allowed them free use of their lands, which eventually led to conflict because of differing concepts of land tenure. Europeans and Anglos thought in terms of private property with title in fee simple and exclusive use. The initial confrontation of Hawaiians and Indians with Westerners over conflicts in land tenure differed, although the result was the same. Both native peoples lost most of their lands to intruders. Although Native Americans attempted to retain their systems of land tenure, Europeans and later Americans forced the Western concept of ownership and marketability of land upon them. During the early period of white contact with Hawaiians, the Polynesian concept of land tenure and use prevailed.

Americans applied similar methods to dispossess Hawaiians and Indians. Both groups lost their lands largely through peremptory appropriations by settlers. Pioneers constantly encroached on Indian lands, forcing the federal government periodically to legalize this occupation through token purchase from the Indian nations. The U.S. government also used military force to gain tribal land for its citizens. Indian tribes retained control over their diminished territories, but continuing settler pressure for more land threatened tribal sovereignty. In the Hawaiian islands the frequent objections of foreign nations to the native land system reinforced the inward forces working to destroy it. Displacement of the common people resulted from internal subversion. The Hawaiian government allowed haoles to use, then lease, and finally own land. Although the king allowed haoles property rights, he still retained sovereignty over the land in their possession. Haoles serving the king in his government and trusted missionary friends influenced Kamehameha III to change the land tenure system.

The rationale of the haoles for changing the Hawaiian land tenure system resembled that used by whites for expropriating Indian land. Western morality provided the rhetoric for dispossessing the native. Most missionaries and haoles believed that owning land in fee simple would save the Hawaiian race and that land should be used to its utmost potential. They argued that the "indolent native" did not fully utilize the land. The foreigners, mainly New Englanders, believed that Native Hawaiians must accept the Western concept of private property and become cultivators of the soil to become civilized. A majority of the haoles, excluding many of the missionaries, wanted land for agricultural, commercial, or private use. Similar attitudes existed in the United States toward the Indian. American pioneers hungered for Indian land; it seemed that their appetite for territory could not be satiated. Americans believed that Indians should not possess all of the land under the tribes' dominion because, it was claimed, they used only a portion of it. Missionaries, reformers, and national leaders, including Thomas Jefferson, thought that Indians should become farmers and live on small plots of land. These humanitarians viewed private property as a sign of civilization. The Western morality they used to justify dispossessing Indians of their land resulted in allotment in severalty of tribal land, which, it was claimed, would bring civilization to Indians and assure subsequent assimilation into American society.

Motives similar to those fostering the General Allotment Act prompted congressional passage of the Native Hawaiian Homes Commission Act in 1921. This legislation instituted a program to increase the land held by Hawaiians. Advocates of the Hawaiian Homes Commission Act hoped to civilize Native Hawaiians and assimilate them into American society. The proponents wanted to place the Native Hawaiians on the land and mold them into a class of self-sufficient farmers. The sugar interests supported the legislation because it set aside prime Hawaiian agricultural lands for their use. Officially, the federal government intended to prevent alienation of lands from Hawaiians. In common with its paternalistic attitude toward Indians, the federal government believed it had to protect Hawaiians from their "own thriftlessness and against the predatory nature" of individuals who wanted to obtain the Hawaiians' property. Nevertheless, the act allowed American pineapple corporations to sublease some of the Hawaiian homelands.

Native American attempts to rebuild their land base have increased in magnitude in the last decade. Some tribes purchase land or endeavor to enlarge their holdings by recovering former tribal lands. During the twentieth century, the American nation has attempted to compensate Native Americans for the deprivation of their lands and to restore some of them. With the enactment of the Indian Reorganization Act of 1934, the U.S. government reversed its policy of allotment and began to enlarge the tribal land base by purchasing land and restoring it to tribes. Throughout the twentieth century Indians have sought monetary compensation for former lands and often have been successful, especially since Congress established the Indian Claims Commission in 1946. In 1921 Native Hawaiian leaders and their supporters persuaded Congress to set aside about 190,000 acres for the exclusive use of Native Hawaiians. Since the mid-1970s Native Hawaiians have tried to obtain federal compensation for former lands, the right to claim any federal land in Hawaii that the government would classify as surplus, and the restoration of 2.5 million acres.

With one hand the government gives, but with the other it takes away. During the twentieth century federal agencies have also appropriated

Native American lands, but in a more subtle form than in the nineteenth century. In place of the U.S. Army, tribes have had to ward off government lawyers and adverse court rulings. Federal agencies have confiscated Indian land for dams, national parks, irrigation projects, and various other uses. The U.S. Navy impounded the Hawaiian island of Kahoʻolawe for bombing practice. The federal policy of termination during the 1950s also diminished the size of Indian land holdings.

Neither Hawaiians nor Indians accepted the alienation of their lands without resistance, but their opposition assumed different forms. Until the end of the nineteenth century, Indians often resisted with military force. Other methods tribal leaders used in the nineteenth and twentieth centuries consisted of encouraging their people to adopt some aspects of Western civilization, submitting to relocation if the Anglos wanted Indian lands, and resorting to legal proceedings when all else failed.

Although Hawaiians showed less armed resistance, their efforts were probably as effective as political and military conditions would allow. Withstanding great foreign pressure, Kamehameha II and Kamehameha III retained the essentials of the land system until the late 1840s. In 1845 Hawaiians held mass meetings to object to the number of naturalized aliens and to granting of land to foreigners. The threat of annexation to the United States and the leasing of Pearl Harbor to the American nation raised extensive objections from Native Hawaiians in the 1870s and 1880s. During the early part of the twentieth century, Territorial Representative Kūhiō Kalanianaʻole tried to revise the land laws to enable Hawaiians to homestead more government land. In the 1970s and 1980s Hawaiians endeavored to stop alienation of land through legislative and judicial means. They successfully promoted the adoption of an amendment to the Hawaiian constitution abolishing adverse possession except for plots with less than five acres.

Native Americans in recent decades, particularly in the last twenty years, have shown a resurgence of nationalistic sentiment and demand for their traditional rights in the exploitation of land and its resources. Hawaiians and Indians increasingly have sought to restore and affirm historic water, fishing, hunting, gathering, and access rights. Judicially and legislatively Native Americans have been moderately successful. Complete implementation of these rights awaits Hawaiians, whereas legal victory for Indians encounters increasingly strong opposition from special interest groups. The threat to water and fishing rights has assumed a position similar to that of the diminishing land for Indians in the nineteenth century. As land and its resources becomes more valuable, Native Americans will place even more emphasis on the restoration and affirmation of those rights. Their opponents correspondingly will increase their objections to special rights for American Indians and Native Hawaiians.

ABBREVIATIONS

AH	Archives of Hawaii
AKN	*Akwesasne Notes*
CCJ	*Journals of the Continental Congress*
CD	*Register of Debates in Congress*
CG	*The Congressional Globe*
CIAA Report	Commissioner of Indian Affairs, *Annual Report*
CR	*Congressional Record*
F.2d	*Federal Reporter, Second Series*
F.Supp.	*Federal Supplement*
F.O.EX.	Foreign Office and Executive File, Archives of Hawaii
HED	House of Representatives Executive Documents
HH	House of Representatives Hearings
HH-SH	Joint House and Senate Hearings
HR	House of Representatives Reports
MH	*Missionary Herald*
N.W.2d	*Northwest Reporter, Second Series*
P.2d	*Pacific Reporter, Second Series*
SED	Senate Executive Documents
S.Ct.	*Supreme Court Reporter*
SH	Senate Hearings
SR	Senate Reports
Stat.	*United States Statutes at Large*
UCPAAE	*University of California Publications in American Archaeology and Ethnology*
USC	*United States Code*
USCA	*United States Code Annotated*
US Reports	*United States Reports*

NOTES

Chapter 1

1. See Wilcomb E. Washburn, *Red Man's Land/White Man's Law: A Study of the Past and Present Status of the American Indian* (New York, 1971), 3–23; and Lewis Hanke, *All Mankind Is One: A Study of the Disputation Between Bartolomé de Las Casas and Juan Ginés de Sepúlveda on the Religious and Intellectual Capacity of the American Indians* (Dekalb, Illinois, 1974).

2. For a detailed examination of European-American relations with Indians in New England during the colonial period, see Francis Jennings, *The Invasion of America: Indians, Colonialism and the Cant of Conquest* (New York, 1975). See also Gary Nash, *Red, White and Black: The Peoples of Early America* (Englewood Cliffs, N.J., 1974); and Wilbur Jacobs, *Dispossessing the American Indian: Indians and Whites on the Colonial Frontier* (New York, 1972).

Chapter 2

1. See generally Patrick Vinton Kirch, *Feathered Gods and Fishhooks: An Introduction to Hawaiian Archaeology and Prehistory* (Honolulu, 1985). On pages 233–236, Kirch discussed the interrelationship of complex sociopolitical organizations, intensive agriculture, and population growth. See also Kirch, *The Evolution of the Polynesian Chiefdoms* (Cambridge, 1984), 204–211.

2. Marion Kelly, "Some Problems with Early Descriptions of Hawaiian Culture," in *Polynesian Culture History: Essays in Honor of Kenneth P. Emory*, ed. Genevieve A. Highland, et al., Bernice P. Bishop Museum Special Publication 56 (Honolulu, 1967), 399.

3. Kirch, *Feathered Gods and Fishhooks*, 204–211.

4. The Makahiki festival began in October or November and lasted for four months. David Malo, *Hawaiian Antiquities,* trans. Nathaniel Emerson (Honolulu, 1903; 2d ed., Honolulu, 1951; Honolulu, 1971), 81–95, 121, 124–125, 141–159; Edward S. C. Handy and Mary Kawena Pukui, *The Polynesian Family System in Ka'u, Hawaii* (Wellington, New Zealand, 1958), 28–29; Samuel M. Kamakau, *Ka*

Po'e Kahiko; The People of Old, trans. Mary Kawena Pukui, ed. Dorothy Barrère, Bernice P. Bishop Museum Special Publication 51 (Honolulu, 1964), 19, 27–28, 64–91, 128; Edward S. C. Handy, Elizabeth Green Handy, and Mary Kawena Pukui, *Native Planters in Old Hawaii: Their Life, Lore and Environment,* Bernice P. Bishop Museum Bulletin 233 (Honolulu, 1972), 42–43.

5. Although the Yuma did allow this practice, it seldom occurred. See C. Darryl Forde, "Ethnography of the Yuma Indians," *UCPAAE,* vol. 28, no. 4 (1931), 114; Harold Driver, *The Indians of North America,* 2d ed., rev. (Chicago, 1969), 281.

6. James Jarves, *History of the Hawaiian Islands. . . . , 4th ed.* (Honolulu, 1872), 17; Handy, Handy, and Pukui, *Native Planters,* 58–60, 63.

7. During the middle period of Hawaiian history the position of mō'ī frequently became hereditary, although this was tempered by the wars of conquest. Occasionally, powerful ali'i held title to land without regard to the mō'ī's supremacy. Abraham Fornander, *An Account of the Polynesian Race: Its Origin and Migrations and the Ancient History of the Hawaiian People to the Times of Kamehameha I,* 3 vols. (London, 1878–1885; Rutland, Vermont, 1969), 65–78, 91, 94–95, 205–215, 269–281, 290–294, 300; C. J. Lyons, "Land Matters in Hawaii," *The Islander* 1 (1875): 103, 104, 111, 118, 126, 135, 143, 150, 159, 168, 174, 182, 190; Handy, Handy, and Pukui, *Native Planters,* 41, 288.

8. Malo, *Hawaiian Antiquities,* 53, 61; Handy, Handy, and Pukui, *Native Planters,* 288; W. D. Alexander, "A Brief History of Land Titles in the Hawaiian Kingdom," *Hawaiian Annual* (1891), 108; Territory of Hawaii, *Indices of Awards Made by the Board of Commissioners to Quiet Land Titles in the Hawaiian Lands* (Honolulu, 1929), 1.

9. Malo, *Hawaiian Antiquities,* 16, 18, 58, 195.

10. Ibid., 53, 58, 61, 193, 195; Handy and Pukui, *Polynesian Family System,* 4; Archibald Campbell, *A Voyage Round the World, From 1806 to 1812 . . . ,* 4th Am. ed. (Rosbury, Mass., 1825), 130; Jon Chinen, *The Great Mahele: Hawaii's Land Division of 1848* (Honolulu, 1958), 6.

11. Malo, *Hawaiian Antiquities,* 53, 58, 60–61, 195, 202–203; Fornander, *Polynesian Race,* 290.

12. Malo, *Hawaiian Antiquities,* 141–159; Kamakau, *Ka Po'e Kahiko,* 19–21.

13. Valerio Valeri, *Kingship and Sacrifice: Ritual and Society in Ancient Hawaii* (Chicago, 1985), 154–156; Malo, *Hawaiian Antiquities,* 16. For discussion of the rise of mō'īs over one island, see Fornander, *Polynesian Race,* 300; Handy, Handy, and Pukui, *Native Planters,* 278–279.

14. John Papa Ii, *Fragments of Hawaiian History,* trans. Mary K. Pukui, ed. Dorothy B. Barrère (Honolulu, 1959), 13–15; Fornander, *Polynesian Race,* 67–78, 91, 94–95, 106, 145–146, 149, 205–215, 269–278, 292–294, 300, 302, 307–308; William Ellis, *Narrative of a Tour Through Hawaii . . .* (London, 1827; Honolulu, 1963), 106; Jarves, *History of the Hawaiian Islands,* 20; Malo, *Hawaiian Antiquities,* 194; Chinen, *Great Mahele,* 5.

15. Quoted in Martha W. Beckwith, "The Hawaiian Romance of Laieikawai," *Thirty-Third Annual Report of the Bureau of American Ethnology* (Washington, D.C., 1919), 310; Malo, *Hawaiian Antiquities,* 192; Chinen, *Great Mahele,* 5.

16. Lyons, "Land Matters in Hawaii," 103–104, 111; Alexander, "Brief History of Land Titles," 106; Chinen, *Great Mahele,* 3.

17. Lyons, "Land Matters in Hawaii," 104, 111.

18. Malo, *Hawaiian Antiquities*, 146; Alexander, "Brief History of Land Titles," 106; Ellis, *Narrative of a Tour Through Hawaii*, 250; James Cook and James King, *A Voyage to the Pacific Ocean . . . ,* 2d ed., 3 vols. (London, 1785), 3:158; Valeri, *Kingship and Sacrifice*, 154–156.

19. Malo, *Hawaiian Antiquities*, 16; Alexander, "Brief History of Land Titles," 106–107; Lyons, "Land Matters in Hawaii," 119; Jean Hobbs, *Hawaii: A Pageant of the Soil* (London, 1935), 14; Chinen, *Great Mahele*, 3–4.

20. Handy and Pukui, *Polynesian Family System*, 2–3, 5–6; Handy, Handy, and Pukui, *Native Planters*, 315–316; Chinen, *Great Mahele*, 5; Kirch, *Evolution of the Polynesian Chiefdoms*, 258; Malo, *Hawaiian Antiquities*, 146; Campbell, *Voyage Round the World*, 126, 130; Territory of Hawaii, *Indices of Land Commission Awards*, x, 134.

21. Kirch, *Feathered Gods and Fishhooks*, 218–223.

22. Ibid., 224–225.

23. Ibid., 211–214.

24. Julian Steward, "Linguistic Distributions and Political Groups of the Great Basin Shoshoneans," *American Anthropologist*, n.s. 39 (1937): 629–634; Julian Steward, "Ethnography of the Owens Valley Paiute," *UCPAAE*, vol. 33, no. 3 (1933): 241, 247–252, 305; Julian Steward, *Basin-Plateau Aboriginal Groups*, Bureau of American Ethnology Bulletin no. 120 (Washington, D.C., 1938), 252–258; Willard Park, et al., "Tribal Distribution in the Great Basin," *American Anthropologist*, n.s. 40 (1938): 623–633; Isabel Kelly, "Ethnography of the Surprise Valley Paiute," *UCPAAE*, vol. 31, no. 3 (1932): 75–78, 185; Isabel Kelly, "Southern Paiute Bands," *American Anthropologist*, n.s. 36 (1934): 549, 557, 560.

25. Herbert Spinden, "The Nez Perce Indians," *American Anthropology Association Memoirs*, vol. 2, pt. 3 (1908), 242, 245–246.

26. James Teit, "The Salishan Tribes of the Western Plateaus," ed. Franz Boas, in *Forty-Fifth Annual Report of the Bureau of American Ethnology* (Washington, D.C., 1930), 37–38, 88, 162–163.

27. Ibid., 198, 237, 277.

28. Jerald Jay Johnson, "Yana," in *California*, vol. 8 of *Handbook of North American Indians*, ed. Robert Heizer (Washington, D.C., 1978), 364; Francis A. Riddell, "Maidu and Konkow," in ibid., 373, 379; Isabel Kelly, "Coast Miwok," in ibid., 418; Michael Silverstein, "Yokuts: Introduction," in ibid., 454; Alfred Kroeber, "The Nature of Landholding Groups in Aboriginal California," *University of California Archeology Survey Reports*, no. 56 (1956), 109; Edward Gifford, "Miwok Lineages and the Political Unit in Aboriginal California," in *The California Indians*, ed. R. Heizer and M. A. Whipple (Berkeley and Los Angeles, 1951), 328; Edward Spicer, ed., *Perspectives in American Indian Culture Change* (Chicago, 1961), 14–15.

29. Sally McLendon and Robert L. Oswalt, "Pomo: Introduction," in Heizer, *California*, 275–276; Lowell John Bean and Dorothea Theodoratus, "Western Pomo and Northeastern Pomo," in ibid., 296; Edward W. Gifford, "Pomo Lands on Clear Lake," *UCPAAE*, vol. 20, no. 5 (1923), 80: Edward W. Gifford, "Clear Lake Pomo Society," *UCPAAE*, vol. 18, no. 2 (1926), 328; Omer C. Stewart, "Notes on Pomo Ethnogeography," *UCPAAE*, vol. 40, no. 2 (1943), 35–44, 48, 52, 56; Kroeber, "Nature of Landholding Groups in Aboriginal California," 96–97, 112–113.

30. Alfred L. Kroeber, *Handbook of the Indians of California,* Bureau of American Ethnology Bulletin no. 78 (Washington, D.C., 1925), 3, 351; Kroeber, "Nature of Landholding Groups in Aboriginal California," 113.

31. Lowell John Bean and Florence C. Shipek, "Luiseño," in Heizer, *California,* 551; Lowell John Bean and Charles R. Smith, "Serrano," in ibid., 572; Lowell John Bean, "Cahuilla," in ibid., 580, 582; Florence C. Shipek, "History of Southern California Mission Indians," in ibid., 613; Edward Gifford, "Miwok Lineages," 328–329; Kroeber, "The Nature of Landholding Groups in Aboriginal California," 93; William D. Strong, "Aboriginal Society in Southern California," *UCPAAE,* vol. 26, no. 1 (1929), 248–249, 330–331, 342; Driver, *Indians of North America,* 276–277; Raymond White, "Luiseño Social Organization," *UCPAAE,* vol. 48, no. 2 (1963), 123. For a recent summary of Southern California Indian land tenure at the time of Spanish contact, see Florence C. Shipek, *Pushed Into the Rocks: Southern California Indian Land Tenure, 1769–1986* (Lincoln, 1987), 1–18. Shipek maintained that the native peoples of Southern California densely populated the area and practiced intensive land use "including plant husbandry and planting of domesticates." The emphasis of Shipek's book was on contemporary land use and tenure of Southern California Indians.

32. Alfred L. Kroeber, "Nature of the Landholding Group," *Ethnohistory* 2 (1955): 312; Driver, *Indians of North America,* 276–277; Carrol Riley, "The Makah Indians: A Study of Political and Economic Organization," *Ethnohistory* 15 (1968): 57–95.

33. Driver, *Indians of North America,* 273.

34. Ibid.

35. George Snyderman, "Concepts of Land Ownership Among the Iroquois and Their Neighbors," in *Symposium on Local Diversity in Iroquois Culture,* ed. William N. Fenton, Bureau of American Ethnology Bulletin no. 149 (Washington, D.C., 1951), 20–23; William N. Fenton, "Locality as a Basic Factor in the Development of Iroquois Social Structure," in ibid., 41–44; Driver, *Indians of North America,* 278–279.

36. John R. Swanton, "Aboriginal Culture of the Southeast," *Forty-Second Annual Report of the Bureau of American Ethnology* (Washington, D.C., 1928), 696; Driver, *Indians of North America,* 278; Anthony Wallace, "Political Organization and Land Tenure Among the Northeastern Indians, 1600–1830," *Southwestern Journal of Anthropology* 13 (1957): 306, 312.

37. Ruth Underhill, *Red Man's America: A History of Indians in the United States* (Chicago, 1953), 66; G. Melvin Herndon, "Indian Agriculture in the Southern Colonies," *North Carolina Historical Review* 44 (1967): 288–290.

38. Wallace, "Political Organization and Land Tenure," 312; Paul Radin, "The Winnebago Tribe," *Thirty-Seventh Annual Report of the Bureau of American Ethnology* (Washington, D.C., 1923), 109–115.

39. John M. Cooper, "Is the Algonquian Family Hunting Ground System Pre-Columbian?" *American Anthropologist,* n.s. 41 (1939): 66–90; See Vernon Kinietz, "Notes on the Algonquian Family Hunting Ground System," ibid., n.s. 42 (1940): 179; Frank G. Speck and Loren Eiseley, "Significance of Hunting Territory Systems of the Algonkian in Social Theory," ibid., n.s. 41 (1939): 269–280; A. Irving Hallowell, "The Size of Algonkian Hunting Territories: A Function of Ecological Adjustment," ibid., n.s. 51 (1949): 35–45.

40. C. Darryl Forde, *Habitat, Economy and Society: A Geographic Introduction to Ethnology* (New York, 1934), 254–255; Alfred Bowers, *Hidsatsa Social and Ceremonial Organization,* Bureau of American Ethnology Bulletin no. 194 (Washington, D.C., 1965), 72, 79; Driver, *Indians of North America,* 277.

41. Edwin T. Denig, "Indian Tribes of the Upper Missouri," ed. J. N. B. Hewitt, *Forty-Sixth Annual Report of the Bureau of American Ethnology* (Washington, D.C., 1930), 476–77; Albert Jenks, "The Wild Rice Gatherers of the Upper Lakes," *Nineteenth Annual Report of the Bureau of American Ethnology* (Washington, D.C., 1900), 1073; Melvin Herskovits, *Economic Anthropology: The Economic Life of Primitive Peoples* (New York, 1952), 364.

42. Spicer, *Perspectives in American Indian Culture Change,* 104–105; Julian Steward, *Theory of Culture Change* (Urbana, 1955), 169.

43. Forde, *Habitat, Economy, and Society,* 233–237; Herskovits, *Economic Anthropology,* 363–364; C. Darryl Forde, "Hopi Agriculture and Land Ownership," *Royal Anthropological Institute Journal* 61 (1931): 370–379.

44. Herskovits, *Economic Anthropology,* 362–363.

45. William W. Hill, "Notes on Pima Land Law and Tenure," *American Anthropologist,* n.s. 38 (1936): 586–589.

46. Driver, *Indians of North America,* 280.

47. John R. Swanton, "Social and Religious Beliefs and Usages of the Chickasaw Indians," *Forty-Fourth Annual Report of the Bureau of American Ethnology* (Washington, D.C., 1928), 240; John R. Swanton, *Indians of the Southeastern United States,* Bureau of American Ethnology Bulletin no. 137 (Washington, D.C., 1946), 309; John R. Swanton, "Social Organization and Social Usages of the Indians of the Creek Confederacy," *Forty-Second Annual Report of the Bureau of American Ethnology* (Washington, D.C., 1928), 337–338; Swanton, "Aboriginal Culture of the Southeast," 696.

48. Swanton, *Indians of the Southeastern United States,* 309; Swanton, "Social Organization of the Creek Confederacy," 336, 443–444; Swanton, "Social and Religious Beliefs of the Chickasaw Indians," 216.

49. Swanton, "Social Organization of the Creek Confederacy," 336, 443; Swanton, *Indians of the Southeastern United States,* 137; Underhill, *Red Man's America,* 30, 33.

50. Swanton, *Indians of the Southeastern United States,* 717.

Chapter 3

1. *Journals of the Continental Congress, 1774–1789,* 34 vols. (Washington, D.C., 1904–1937), 25:680–694 (hereafter cited as *CCJ*); *CCJ* 32:66–69; *CCJ* 34:124–126; Kappler, Charles, comp., *Indian Affairs, Laws and Treaties,* 5 vols. (Washington, D.C., 1904–1941), 2:18–25; *American State Papers: Indian Affairs,* 2 vols. (Washington, D.C., 1832–1834), 1:8, 13. For an excellent survey of Indian affairs see Arrell M. Gibson, *The American Indian: Prehistory to the Present* (Lexington, 1980).

2. *American State Papers: Indian Affairs* 1:8, 13, 53, 61, 65–68; Clarence Carter, ed., *Territorial Papers of the United States,* 26 vols. (Washington, D.C., 1934–1956), 4:35; *The Works of Thomas Jefferson,* ed. Paul Ford, 12 vols. (New York, 1904),

6:55–56. See also Bernard W. Sheehan, *Seeds of Extinction: Jeffersonian Philanthropy and the American Indian* (New York, 1973).

3. Carter, *Territorial Papers* 2:47.

4. *Register of Debates in Congress,* 14 vols. (Washington, D.C., 1825–1837), vol. 6, pt. 2, 1031 (hereafter cited as *CD*); Carter, *Territorial Papers,* 6:107; *The Congressional Globe,* 46 vols. (Washington, D.C., 1834–1873), 27th Cong., 3d sess., app., 74 (hereafter cited as *CG*); John Sevier to James Ore, 12 May 1798, in *Messages of the Governors of Tennessee,* ed. Robert White, 5 vols. (Nashville, 1952), 1:58; Lewis Cass, "Removal of the Indians," *North American Review* 30 (1830): 77.

5. *CCJ* 4:111; *American State Papers: Indian Affairs* 1:53–54, 235; ibid. 2:200–221; James D. Richardson, comp., *A Compilation of the Messages and Papers of the Presidents,* 10 vols. (Washington, D.C., 1896–1899), 1:104–105, 127, 185; 1 Stat. 330 (1793); 1 Stat. 472 (1796); 1 Stat. 746 (1799); 2 Stat. 143 (1802); 3 Stat. 516–517 (1819).

6. Jefferson to Harrison, 27 Feb. 1803, *Messages and Letters of William H. Harrison,* ed. Logan Esarey, 2 vols. (Indianapolis, 1922), 1:69–73; 2 Stat. 283–289 (1804); *American State Papers: Indian Affairs* 1:684–685; Jefferson to Benjamin Hawkins, 18 Feb. 1803, *Works of Thomas Jefferson* 9:445. For a discussion of Jefferson's ideas on removal see Annie Abel, "The History of Events Resulting in Indian Consolidation West of the Mississippi," *Annual Report of the American Historical Association for the Year 1906,* 1:241–249.

7. Kappler, *Laws and Treaties* 2:5–6, 39–45.

8. *CCJ* 19:219, 223; *CCJ* 24:264; *CCJ* 25:602, 844–845; 1 Stat. 137–138 (1790); 1 Stat. 329–332 (1793); 1 Stat. 472 (1796); 1 Stat. 746 (1799); 2 Stat. 143 (1802).

9. Jack Campisi, "New York–Oneida Treaty of 1795: A Finding of Fact," *American Indian Law Review* 4 (1976): 71–82.

10. *Joint Tribal Council of the Passamaquoddy Tribe v. Morton,* 528 F.2d 370; Francis Paul Prucha, *American Indian Policy in the Formative Years: The Indian Trade and Intercourse Acts, 1790–1834* (Cambridge, Mass., 1962), 37; SH13, 31.

11. *American State Papers: Indian Affairs* 1:776, 806–807, 826–837. See generally R. David Edmunds, *Tecumseh and the Quest for Indian Leadership* (Boston, 1984); R. David Edmunds, *The Shawnee Prophet* (Lincoln, 1983).

12. Arrell M. Gibson, *The Kickapoos: Lords of the Middle Border* (Norman, 1963), 58–72.

13. Kappler, *Laws and Treaties* 2:8–16, 25–29, 51–54, 56–59, 63, 69, 73, 79, 82–88, 90–92, 107–110; *American State Papers: Indian Affairs* 1:826, 837–861.

14. *American State Papers: Indian Affairs* 1:154–162; Kappler, *Laws and Treaties* 2:203.

15. *American State Papers: Indian Affairs* 2:124–126, 129–130; Kappler, *Laws and Treaties* 2:95–99, 124–126, 129–130, 140–144, 167–168, 217–221, 288–291.

16. *American State Papers: Indian Affairs* 2:180; Kappler, *Laws and Treaties* 2:11–14, 87–88, 137, 160–161, 191–195, 210–214.

17. *American State Papers: Indian Affairs* 2:569, 611–614; Kappler, *Laws and Treaties* 2:25–29, 58–59, 85–86, 107–110, 155–156, 195–197, 214–216, 264–268, 284–286.

18. *American State Papers: Indian Affairs* 2:279–281, 541–544; Richardson, *Messages and Papers of the Presidents* 2:415–416, 456–459; *CD,* vol. 6, pt. 2, 1017–1018; Ronald Satz, *American Indian Policy in the Jacksonian Era* (Lincoln, 1974), 5–6, 10.

19. Wilson Lumpkin, *The Removal of the Cherokee Indians from Georgia,* ed. Wymberly Jones De Renne, 2 vols. (New York, 1907); *CD,* vol. 6, pt. 2, 1016–1037. For a psychohistorical study of Jackson, see Michael Rogin, *Fathers and Children: Andrew Jackson and the Subjugation of the American Indian* (New York, 1975).

20. Richardson, *Messages and Papers of the Presidents* 2:458–459; Dale Van Every, *Disinherited: The Lost Birthright of the American Indian* (New York, 1966), 279–284; *CD,* vol. 6, pt. 2, app., 15.

21. *American State Papers: Indian Affairs* 2:543–544, 653–654; *CD,* vol. 6, pt. 2, 1064–72.

22. *CD,* vol. 6, pt. 2, 994–1015, 1019–1022, 1037–1078, 1103–1117. For a discussion of humanitarian response to removal see Satz, *American Indian Policy,* 39–63; Sheehan, *Seeds of Extinction,* 243–275.

23. See for example, act of 20 Dec. 1828, *Acts of the General Assembly of the State of Georgia* (1828), 88–89.

24. *Johnson v. McIntosh,* 21 US Reports (8 Wheat.) 543; *CD,* vol. 6, pt. 2, 1032.

25. *Cherokee Nation v. Georgia,* 30 US Reports (5 Pet.) 1.

26. *Worcester v. Georgia,* 31 US Reports (6 Pet.) 515. Jackson did not have the legal authority or means to enforce the Supreme Court decision. However, the quoted statement undoubtedly reflected Jackson's attitude.

27. Kappler, *Laws and Treaties* 2:910, 915, 918–937, 942–950.

28. *CG,* 32d Cong., 2d sess., 80, 559, 1113–1117; *CG,* 33d Cong., 1st sess., app., 222.

29. *CG,* 32d Cong., 2d sess., 556–559, 1020; *CG,* 33d Cong., 1st sess., app., 159, 540.

30. *CG,* 32d Cong., 2d sess., 560–562; *CG,* 33d Cong., 1st sess., app., 800.

31. Kappler, *Laws and Treaties* 2:608–646, 677–681; Commissioner of Indian Affairs, *Annual Report, 1853,* in S. Doc. 1, 33d Cong., 1st sess., 1:247 (hereafter cited as CIAA Report).

32. Secretary of the Interior, *Annual Report, 1857–1858,* S. Ex. Doc. 11, pt. 1, 35th Cong., 1st sess., 2:63; ibid., 1861, S. Ex. Doc. 1, pt. 1, 37th Cong., 2d sess., 676–686; CIAA Report, 1866, 19, 53; Kappler, *Laws and Treaties* 2:609, 612–613, 619–621, 797, 801, 804, 808, 814–827, 835–838, 937, 939, 961, 971; 10 Stat. 277–290 (1854); George W. Manypenny, *Our Indian Wards* (Cincinnati, 1880), 116. See Annie Abel, "Indian Reservations in Kansas and the Extinguishment of Their Title," *Kansas Historical Society Transactions,* vol. 8 (Topeka, 1904), 72–109; Paul Gates, *Fifty Million Acres: Conflicts over Kansas Land Policy, 1854–1890* (Ithaca, 1954).

33. Kappler, *Laws and Treaties* 2:796–799, 803, 807, 811–828, 937–942, 951–955, 960–974.

34. Ibid. 2:772–775, 875–883; CIAA Report, 1877, p. 96; *Executive Orders Relating to Indian Reservations,* 2 vols. (Washington, D.C., 1912, 1922; reprint, 2 vols. in 1, Wilmington, Delaware, 1975), 145–146; Grant Foreman, *The Last Trek of the Indians* (Chicago, 1946), 240–243, 280; 21 Stat. 422 (1881); SED5.

35. 17 Stat. 159–160 (1872); 23 Stat. 91 (1840); *Executive Orders Relating to Indian Reservations,* 143–144, 146; Kappler, *Laws and Treaties* 1:190.

36. *CG,* 32d Cong., 1st sess., pt. 2, 1120–1122; ibid., pt. 3, 2103, 2172–2173; ibid., app., 1082; C. Hart Merriam, "The Indian Population of California," *American Anthropologist,* n.s. 7 (1905): 600; SED2, 296.

37. Kappler, *Laws and Treaties* 2:603–607, 654–660, 665–669, 714–719, 741, 865–868, 876–878, 908–909; Francis Paul Prucha, *The Great Father,* abr. ed. (Lincoln, 1986), 133. See Stephen Beckham, *Requiem for a People: The Rogue Indians and the Frontiersmen* (Norman, 1971).

38. Kappler, *Laws and Treaties* 2:661–664, 669–677, 682–685, 694–698, 719–721; Alvin Josephy, *The Indian Heritage of America* (New York, Bantam edition, 1969), 328.

39. Kappler, *Laws and Treaties* 2:702–706, 843–847; CIAA Report, 1877, 212–213.

40. CIAA Report, 1877, 81, 212–214; ibid., 1885, 57; Secretary of War, *Annual Report, 1877,* H. Ex. Doc. 1, 45th Cong., 2d sess., 15; Chief Joseph, "American Indian's View of Indian Affairs," *North American Review,* 128 (1879): 431–433; 20 Stat. 74, 76 (1878); 23 Stat. 90 (1884); 23 Stat. 378 (1885). For a detailed study see Alvin Josephy, *The Nez Perce Indians and the Opening of the Northwest* (New Haven, 1965).

41. Kappler, *Laws and Treaties* 2:722–725, 848–853, 1020–1023.

42. Ibid., 865–868; HED1; *Executive Orders Regarding Indian Reservations,* 144–145; 18 Stat. 447 (1875). For a detailed study of Modoc War, see Keith Murray, *The Modocs and Their War* (Norman, 1959).

43. Secretary of War, *Annual Report, 1883,* in H. Ex. Doc. 1, 48th Cong., 1st sess., 160, 173–178; ibid., 1886, H. Ex. Doc. 1, 49th Cong., 2d sess., 12–15, 73–74, 144–146, 170–181; Kappler, *Laws and Treaties* 2:1015–1020; *Executive Orders Regarding Indian Reservations,* 1–9, 31–36, 116, 128; CIAA Report, 1913, 34; CIAA Report, 1914, 56–57; Britton Davis, *The Truth About Geronimo,* ed. M. M. Quaife (New Haven, 1929; Lincoln, 1976), 144–158.

44. Kappler, *Laws and Treaties* 2:990–996; *Executive Orders Regarding Indian Reservations,* 66–67; CIAA Report, 1879, 16–19, 82–97; CIAA Report, 1880, xxiv–xxv, 14–18, 193–198; SH7, 30; Prucha, *The Great Father,* 173. Extensive information is found in SED4; and Marshall Sprague, *Massacre: The Tragedy at White River* (Boston, 1957).

45. See John F. Martin, "From Judgment to Land Restoration: The Havasupai Land Claims Case," in *Irredeemable America: The Indians' Estate and Land Claims,* ed. Imre Sutton (Albuquerque, 1985).

46. Kappler, *Laws and Treaties* 2:594–595, 887–895, 997–999; SED3; SR1. See also Stan Hoig, *The Sand Creek Massacre* (Norman, 1961).

47. Douglas Jones, *The Treaty of Medicine Lodge: The Story of the Great Treaty Council As Told by Eyewitnesses* (Norman, 1966); William Leckie, *The Military Conquest of the Southern Plains* (Norman, 1963).

48. Josephy, *Indian Heritage,* 336; Arrell M. Gibson, *The West in the Life of the Nation* (Lexington, Mass., 1976), 422.

49. Kappler, *Laws and Treaties* 2:998–1007, 1012–1015.

50. Robert Utley, *Frontier Regulars: The United States Army and the Indian, 1866–1891* (New York, 1973), 240–242; Gibson, *The West,* 439.

51. CIAA Report, 1875, 184–200; *Executive Orders Regarding Indian Reservations,* 157.

52. 15 Stat. 539 (1867); 23 Stat. 26 (1884); 26 Stat. 1100 (1891); 30 Stat. 409 (1898); 31 Stat. 321, 330 (1900); 72 Stat. 339 (1958).

53. 49 Stat. 1250 (1936); Angie Debo, *A History of the Indians of the United States* (Norman, 1970), 323.

54. 72 Stat. 339 (1958); 85 Stat. 688 (1971); SH3, 499; SR4, 82; *Alaska v. Udall,* 420 F.2d 938; 34 *Federal Register* 1025 (1969). For discussion of the role of oil companies, see Mary Berry, *The Alaska Pipeline: The Politics of Oil and Native Land Claims* (Bloomington, 1975).

55. 16 Stat. 566 (1871); 24 Stat. 388 (1887). Before the General Allotment Act, Congress had sporadically passed legislation providing for allotment on certain reservations or had approved treaties containing allotment provisions; see Paul W. Gates, "Indian Allotments Preceding the Dawes Act," in *The Frontier Challenge,* ed. John G. Clark (Lawrence, Kan., 1971), 141–170. For a discussion of Palouse Indian allotments that resulted from the Indian Homestead Act of 1874, see Clifford E. Trafzer and Richard D. Scheuerman, *Renegade Tribe: The Palouse Indian and the Invasion of the Inland Pacific Northwest* (Pullman, Wash., 1986), 122–135.

56. HR1, 10. See also D. S. Otis, *The Dawes Act and the Allotment of Indian Lands,* ed. Francis Paul Prucha (Norman, 1973).

57. 24 Stat. 391 (1888); 26 Stat. 749–750 (1891); Kappler, *Laws and Treaties* 1:330, 344.

58. 25 Stat. 957, 1004 (1889); 26 Stat. 563 (1890); 26 Stat. 749 (1891); 27 Stat. 640, 643 (1893); 28 Stat. 907 (1895); 34 Stat. 539 (1906); Kappler, *Laws and Treaties* 1:409, 709, 766–767.

59. Kappler, *Laws and Treaties* 1:646–656; 27 Stat. 645 (1893); 30 Stat. 495–519, 567–569 (1898); 31 Stat. 861–873 (1901); 32 Stat. 716–727 (1901).

60. Angie Debo, *And Still the Waters Run* (Princeton, 1973), 53–60.

61. 25 Stat. 888, 894 (1889); 33 Stat. 207 (1904); 33 Stat. 254, 319 (1904); 34 Stat. 1049, 1230 (1907); 36 Stat. 440, 448 (1910).

62. 26 Stat. 795 (1891); CIAA Report, 1900, 13; Board of Indian Commissioners, *Annual Report, 1898,* 25; Debo, *And Still the Waters Run,* 92–102. For an example of leasing practices used by white ranchers who leased trust lands from individual Crows in Montana, see *Stray Calf v. Scott Land and Livestock Co.,* 549 F.2d 1209.

63. Board of Indian Commissioners, *Annual Report, 1898,* 15; *Lake Mohonk Conference Proceedings,* 1890, 146.

64. 31 Stat. 229 (1900); 32 Stat. 245, 275 (1902); 34 Stat. 182 (1906); 34 Stat. 1018 (1907). Congressional provisions for the removal of restrictions on alienation of allotments varied somewhat for the Five Civilized Tribes; see 32 Stat. 500 (1902); 33 Stat. 204, 218 (1904); 33 Stat. 1072 (1905); 34 Stat. 137, 144–145 (1906).

65. CIAA Report, 1917, 3–5; ibid., 1920, 49, 172; ibid., 1921, 23; Board of Indian Commissioners, *Annual Report, 1922,* 67–68; Harold Fey and D'Arcy

McNickle, *Indians and Other Americans Two Ways of Life Meet,* rev. ed. (New York, Perennial Library edition, 1970), 88. In the 1980s several lawsuits were filed to set aside fee patents issued before the expiration of the twenty–five year trust period without the consent of the allottees. The actions sought either recovery of allotments lost after the issuance of these forced fee patents or the current monetary value of the allotments. In *United States v. Mottaz,* 106 S.Ct. 2224, the U.S. Supreme Court held that the expiration of the federal statute of limitations in the Quiet Title Act barred the claims against the United States. The former allotment in the case had passed to federal ownership. The court implied that allottees or their heirs might have a valid claim against private owners. However, the Eighth Circuit Court of Appeals subsequently affirmed lower court decisions dismissing fourteen lawsuits, which were consolidated on appeal, for recovery of allotments and trespass damages from individual land owners; *Nichols v. Rysavy,* 809 F.2d 1317. See LeAnn LaFave, "South Dakota's Forced Fee Indian Land Claims: Will Landowners Be Liable for Government's Wrongdoing?" *South Dakota Law Review* 30 (1985): 60.

   66. *Muskogee Phoenix,* 14 June 1911, 8 May 1913, 22 Apr. 1915; *Daily Oklahoman,* 1 Jan. 1911; *Vinita Weekly Chieftain,* 3 Sept. 1903; Kirke Ducheneaux and Karen Ducheneaux, *One Hundred Million Acres* (New York, 1973), 22–23; Debo, *A History of the Indians of the United States,* 285; Debo, *And Still the Waters Run,* 103–112, 181–202, 305–312.

   67. Debo, *And Still the Waters Run,* 76–77; *AKN* 2 (Apr. 1970): 31.

   68. *New York Times,* 15 July 1985; Edward Michael Peterson, "That So-Called Warranty Deed: Clouded Land Titles on the White Earth Indian Reservation in Minnesota," *North Dakota Law Review* 59 (1983): 158.

   69. HR6, 2–3; Peterson, "That So-Called Warranty Deed," 167.

   70. SH18, 29–43, 102–115.

   71. Ibid.; Peterson, "That So-Called Warranty Deed," 170–176.

   72. *New York Times,* 15 July 1985; *AKN* 17 (Fall 1985): 13.

   73. 100 Stat. 61 (1986); *New York Times,* 14 Dec 1985.

   74. See note 73.

   75. Fey and McNickle, *Indians and Other Americans,* 44; D'Arcy McNickle, *Native American Tribalism: Indian Survivals and Renewals* (New York, 1973), 84; Indian Land Consolidation Act of 1982, 96 Stat. 2517 (1983), 25 *USCA* sec. 2201–2211. One section provided for escheat to the tribe for heirship interests that consisted of less than 2 percent of the allotment and that earned less than $100 annually. This escheat provision as originally enacted was declared unconstitutional by the U.S. Supreme Court; *Hodel v. Irving,* 107 S.Ct. 2076. For examples of legislation for specific tribes, see 96 Stat. 2515 (1983); 98 Stat. 2411 (1984).

   76. Lewis Meriam, et al., *The Problem of Indian Administration* (Baltimore, 1928), 41–42; 48 Stat. 984 (1934). See also Kenneth Philp, *John Collier's Crusade for Indian Reform, 1920–1954* (Tucson, 1977).

   77. For a detailed study see Gary Orfield, *A Study of the Termination Policy* (Denver, 1966); Donald L. Fixico, *Termination and Relocation: Federal Indian Policy, 1945–1960* (Albuquerque, 1986).

   78. 68 Stat. 250, 795 (1954); *AKN* 2 (Apr. 1970): 1; *Wassaja* 4 (June 1976):

17; James S. Olson and Raymond Wilson, *Native Americans in the Twentieth Century* (Urbana, 1984).

79. *AKN* 4 (Summer 1972): 15; *AKN* 5 (Early Autumn 1973): 20; *AKN* 8 (Early Summer 1976): 29; *Wassaja* 4 (June 1976): 17.

Chapter 4

1. Debo, *History of the Indians of the United States,* 324–325, 332–333.

2. Ibid., 326, 329–330, 338–339.

3. Federal Water Power Act of 1920, 41 Stat. 1063, codified as pt. 1 of the Federal Power Act, 16 *USC* sec. 791a; Federal Power Act, 41 Stat. 1066, 16 *USC* sec. 797. Since 1901 allotted lands have been subject to condemnation by eminent domain in the same manner as non-Indian lands; 25 *USC* sec. 357. In 1977 licensing authority was transferred to the Federal Energy Regulatory Commission.

4. 39 Stat. 123, 157–158; *Federal Power Commission Reports* 50 (1973): 753, 756. See also *Escondido Mutual Water v. La Jolla,* 466 US Reports 765.

5. *AKN* 3 (Late Summer 1971): 7; *AKN* 5 (Late Summer 1973): 40; *AKN* 5 (Early Autumn 1973): 22; *Federal Power Commission Reports* 50 (1973): 753, 757–758. In the 1870s, allotment was started on the reservation. By 1970, about 4,000 acres remained in tribal ownership and approximately 26,000 acres of allotments remained in trust status. About 26,000 acres had passed into non-Indian ownership. Six years later the amount of tribal trust land increased substantially when 13,000 acres of federal surplus lands was returned to the tribe; SH9, 17, 20.

6. *Lac Courte Oreilles Band of Lake Superior Chippewa Indians v. Federal Power Commission,* 510 F.2d 198.

7. *Federal Energy Regulatory Commission Reports,* vol. 1, par. 63,041 (1977); ibid., vol. 13, par. 61,055 (1980); ibid., vol. 25, par. 63,044 (1983); ibid., vol. 27, par. 63,068 (1984); ibid., vol. 28, par. 61,398 (1984). The Chippewa based their tribal consent argument on provisions of their 1854 treaty, section 16 of the Indian Reorganization Act, and the 1935 Federal Power Act. A subsequent decision by the U.S. Supreme Court in *Escondido Mutual Water v. La Jolla,* 466 US Reports 765, supported the commission's decision. The court declared that the commission was not required to obtain tribal consent before it could license a project on land of three bands of Mission Indians.

8. *Federal Power Commission v. Tuscarora Indian Nation,* 362 US Reports 99, 115, 117; *AKN* 2 (Apr. 1970): 31. See Laurence M. Hauptman, *The Iroquois Struggle for Survival: World War II to Red Power* (Syracuse, 1986), 123–178 for Tuscarora and Mohawk opposition to the taking of their land for the construction of Tuscarora Reservoir and the Saint Lawrence Seaway project.

9. 32 Stat. 389 (1902); 33 Stat. 189, 225 (1904); William Veeder, "Greed and Bigotry: Hallmark of American Indian Law," *American Indian Journal* 3 (Dec. 1977): 13–14; 36 Stat. 1063 (1911).

10. *AKN* 2 (Apr. 1970): 31; Alvin Josephy, Jr., *Now That the Buffalo's Gone: A Study of Today's American Indians* (Norman, 1984), 139–150; Hauptman, *Iro-*

quois Struggle for Survival, 85–122; Washburn, *Red Man's Land, White Man's Law,* 148–149.

11. David H. Getches and Charles F. Wilkinson, *Federal Indian Law: Cases and Materials,* 2d ed. (St. Paul, 1986), 203–209; *Seneca Nation of Indians v. Brucker,* 262 F.2d 27. See also *Seneca Nation of Indians v. United States,* 338 F.2d 55. A few courts, such as the Eighth Circuit Court of Appeals in *United States v. Winnebago Tribe,* 542 F.2d 1002, have refused to allow the Army Corps of Engineers to condemn Indian lands absent clear congressional authorization. The court held that the federal agency could not take by eminent domain certain Winnebago lands for the Oxbow Recreation Lakes, Snyder Winnebago Complex, and Missouri River Recreation Lakes Project. There was insufficient evidence to show clear congressional intent to abrogate the treaty of March 8, 1865, in which the United States had guaranteed that the tribal lands would be "set apart for the occupation and future home of the Winnebago Indians, forever."

12. Michael L. Lawson, *Dammed Indians: The Pick-Sloan Plan and the Missouri River Sioux, 1944–1980* (Norman, 1982), xxi, 18–20, 27, 180.

13. Ibid., 29, 47–58.

14. Ibid., 27, 59–61; Vine Deloria, Jr., *Of Utmost Good Faith* (New York, Bantam edition, 1972), 310–321; Roy Meyer, "The Fort Berthold Reservation and the Garrison Dam," *North Dakota History* 35 (1968): 217–264.

15. Lawson, *Dammed Indians,* 19, 199.

16. *AKN* 6 (Early Winter 1974): 38. For a discussion of the impact of Priest Rapid Dam upon the Wanapum Indians, see Margery Sharkey, "Revitalization and Change: A History of the Wanapum Indians, Their Prophet, Smowhala, and the Washani Religion" (Master's thesis, Washington State University, 1984), 98–112.

17. HR8, 4; SH20, 43.

18. HR8, 4–5, 7.

19. Ibid., 6.

20. Ibid.; 96 Stat. 1274 (1982).

21. 100 Stat. 1798 (1986); HR8, 10.

22. 100 Stat. 1800 (1986); SH20, 43, 50–54, 60–62, 75–79; HR8, 8–9.

23. HR9, 3–5. The Sells Reservation consists of 2,774,390 acres.

24. HR9, 5–7. SH20, 62–66, 79–83; 100 Stat. 1196 (1986).

25. *Wassaja* 4 (Mar. 1976): 1, 18; ibid. 4 (June 1976): 1; ibid. 4 (Aug. 1976): 11; ibid. 4 (Sept. 1976): 1, 17; ibid. 4 (Oct. 1976): 1, 18–19; ibid. 4 (Nov.–Dec. 1976): 12; ibid. 5 (Mar. 1977): 14; *AKN* 5 (Late Summer 1973): 14; *Weekly Compilation of Presidential Documents,* 13 (25 Apr. 1977): 557–559; SR5, 518.

26. *Arizona Republic,* 24 Mar. 1983.

27. *Arizona Republic,* 25 July 1981, 24 Mar. 1983, 31 Jan. 1986.

28. *Winters v. United States,* 207 US Reports 564, 576–577; *Arizona v. California,* 373 US Reports 546; *United States v. Cappaert,* 426 US Reports 128.

29. 373 US Reports 598, 600–601.

30. 426 US Reports 128, 138, 143.

31. 305 US Reports 527, 531–533.

32. *Colville Confederated Tribes v. Walton,* 647 F.2d 42; see also *Colville Confederated Tribes v. Walton,* 752 F.2d 397.

33. 424 US Reports 800.

34. Ibid.

35. Ibid.

36. 463 US Reports 545.

37. *United States v. Adair,* 723 F.2d 1394.

38. SH19, 27, 33, 43, 64–65, 118–20, 199–202.

39. Ibid., 79, 65–66.

40. Ibid., 2–20, 25, 62–77; SR6.

41. *Escondido Mutual Water v. La Jolla,* 466 US Reports 765.

42. *AKN* 2 (Apr. 1970): 31; *Wassaja* 4 (Apr. 1976): 1, 3; *Wassaja* 5 (May 1977): 1, 10.

43. 373 US Reports 546, decree of 9 Mar. 1964, 376 US Reports 340, supplemental decree of 9 Jan. 1979, 439 US Reports 419.

44. In 1979 the Supreme Court in a supplemental decree qualified the state "present perfected rights," but referred the tribal intervention and allocation issues to a Special Master. His decision substantially supported the tribes' and the United States' position. *Arizona v. California,* 439 US Reports 419; *Arizona v. California,* 460 US Reports 605.

45. *Metropolitan Water District of Southern California v. United States,* 628 F.Supp. 1018; *Metropolitan Water District of Southern California v. United States,* 14 *Indian Law Reporter* 2182 (14 Oct. 1987).

46. *AKN* 5 (Late Summer 1973): 2. The Middle Rio Grande Conservancy District, a state political subdivision, was formed in 1925 to provide irrigation and flood control protection to the Rio Grande Basin in central New Mexico. Approximately 75 percent of the water supply in the Upper Rio Grande Basin is used for irrigated agriculture; Charles T. DuMars, Marilyn O'Leary, and Albert E. Utton, *Pueblo Indian Water Rights* (Tucson, 1984), 84–85, 108.

47. *New Mexico v. Aamodt,* 537 F.2d 1102; *AKN* 2 (Apr. 1970): 5; *AKN* 2 (July–Aug. 1970): 23; *AKN* 2 (Sept. 1970): 7; *AKN* 5 (Late Summer 1973): 20–21.

48. 537 F. 2d 1111–1113.

49. *New Mexico ex rel. Reynolds v. Aamodt,* 618 F.Supp. 993, 1010.

50. *Jicarilla Apache Tribe v. United States,* 601 F.2d 116.

51. Lloyd Burton, Jr., "American Indian Water Rights in the Western United States: Litigation, Negotiation, and the Regional Planning Process" (Ph.D. diss., University of California, Berkeley, 1984), 55–60; *AKN* 5 (Early Summer 1973): 23.

52. Dumars, O'Leary, and Utton, *Pueblo Indian Water Rights,* 86; *AKN* 8 (Early Summer 1976): 22–23; *Wassaja* 4 (June 1976): 8.

53. *Oklahoma Journal,* 1 July 1969; *AKN* 5 (Early Summer 1973): 23; *AKN* 8 (Early Summer 1976): 22–23; Monroe Price and Gary D. Weatherford, "Indian Water Rights in Theory and Practice: Navajo Experience in the Colorado River Basin," *Law and Contemporary Problems* 40 (1976): 97–131.

54. *Wassaja* 5 (Jan. 1977): 13; *Wassaja* 5 (Feb. 1977): 13; *AKN* 11 (Late Winter 1979): 23.

55. 43 Stat. 475 (1924); American Indian Policy Review Commission, Task Force One, *Final Report on Trust Responsibilities and the Federal-Indian Relationship Including Treaty Review* (Washington, D.C., 1976), 210–214; Monroe Price, *Law*

and the American Indian (New York, 1973), 328; *Wassaja* 4 (Nov.–Dec. 1976): 9; *AKN* 5 (Early Summer 1973): 21; *Wassaja* 8 (Early Summer 1976): 23.

56. *Arizona v. San Carlos Apache Tribe*, 463 US Reports 545; *United States v. Superior Court in and For Maricopa County*, 697 P.2d 658; *White Mountain Apache Tribe v. Hodel*, 784 F.2d 921; *United States v. White Mountain Apache Tribe*, 784 F.2d 917; *Matter of Determination of Conflicting Rights to the Use of Water From the Salt River Above Granite Reef Dam*, 484 F.Supp. 778. The Navajo also opposed state court adjudication of their water rights in the Little Colorado River. The case was one of three consolidated cases decided by the Supreme Court in *Arizona v. San Carlos Apache*.

57. SH20, 43, 45–46, 71; HR5, 5–6.

58. 96 Stat. 1274 (1982); 92 Stat. 409 (1978); 98 Stat. 2698 (1984).

59. *AKN* 9 (Summer 1977): 18–20; *AKN* 11 (Late Winter 1979): 23; William H. Veeder, "Water Rights in the Coal Fields of the Yellowstone River Basin," *Law and Contemporary Problems* 40 (1976): 77–96; HH6, 255–256; Lawson, *Dammed Indians*, 191–192.

60. *AKN* 9 (Summer 1977): 20.

61. *Wassaja* 7 (Jan.–Feb. 1979): 5; *Wassaja* 7 (May 1979): 4, 9, 12; *AKN* 11 (Late Winter 1979): 23; HH6, 255–257.

62. *Arizona v. San Carlos Apache Tribe*, 463 US Reports 545. In 1939 the Supreme Court in *United States v. Powers*, 305 US Reports 527, had upheld the *Winters* doctrine for the Crow Indians' rights to water from the Big Horn River.

63. *Wassaja* 7 (Jan.–Feb. 1979): 5; *Wassaja* 7 (May 1979): 4, 9, 12; *AKN* 11 (Late Winter 1979): 23; *Montana Code Annotated* sec. 2-15-212, 85-2-211 to 85-2-608, 85-2-701 to 85-2-705 (Montana Legislative Council, 1987).

64. *Arizona v. San Carlos Apache Tribe*, 463 US Reports 545; *State ex rel. Greely v. Confederated Salish and Kootenai Tribes of the Flathead Reservation*, 712 P.2d 754; *Blackfeet Indian Nation v. Hodel*, 634 F.Supp. 646.

65. *Montana Code Annotated* sec. 85-20-201, 85-2-701(2).

66. *United States v. Ahtanum Irrigation District*, 330 F.2d 897, 899, 915; *AKN* 9 (Autumn 1977): 29; *Wassaja* 7 (Mar. 1979): 6.

67. *Colville Confederated Tribes v. Walton*, 647 F.2d 42.

68. *United States v. Anderson*, 736 F.2d 1358.

69. *Holly v. Confederated Tribes and Bands of Yakima Indian Nation*, 655 F.Supp. 557.

70. *United States v. Anderson*, 736 F.2d 1358; *Colville Confederated Tribes v. Walton*, 647 F.2d 42.

71. *AKN* 2 (Apr. 1970): 31; *AKN* 2 (Sept. 1970): 7; *Wassaja* 4 (June 1976): 13. See Josephy, *Now That the Buffalo's Gone*, 151–176; Martha Knack and Omer Stewart, *As Long As the River Shall Run: An Ethnohistory of Pyramid Lake Indian Reservation* (Berkeley and Los Angeles, 1984).

72. *Pyramid Lake Paiute Tribe of Indians v. Morton*, 354 F.Supp. 252; *Truckee-Carson Irrigation District v. Secretary of the Interior*, 742 F.2d 527; Getches and Wilkinson, *Federal Indian Law*, 240–243, 673–674. For a related case see *Carson-Truckee Water Conservancy District v. Clark*, 741 F.2d 257.

73. *Nevada v. United States*, 463 US Reports 110.

74. Ibid.; *Arizona v. California*, 460 US Reports 605, 627–628 and dissenting

opinion at 649–652; *Blackfeet Indian Nation v. Hodel*, 634 F.Supp. 646; *White Mountain Apache Tribe v. Hodel*, 784 F.2d 921.

75. See Getches and Wilkinson, *Federal Indian Law*, 701–705.

76. Edgar S. Cahn and David W. Hearne, eds., *Our Brother's Keeper: The Indian in White America* (New York, 1969), 85, 88–91; *Wassaja* 4 (Aug. 1976): 3; Kevin Gover, "Oklahoma Tribes: A History," *American Indian Journal* 3 (June 1977): 12–13.

77. *AKN* 2 (Apr. 1970): 31; Wendell H. Oswalt, *This Land Was Theirs: A Study of North American Indians*, 4th ed. (Mountain View, Calif., 1988), 175.

78. *AKN* 4 (Summer 1972): 14; Cahn and Hearne, *Our Brother's Keeper*, 88–91.

79. Gary Jones, "Enforcement Strategies for Indian Landlords," *American Indian Law Review* 2 (1974): 45–48; *Yavapai–Prescott Indian Tribe v. Watt*, 707 F.2d 1072.

80. SH8, 32–44.

81. Ibid., 32–46 and generally; 25 *Code of Federal Regulations* sec. 171.9; 94 Stat. 1701 (1980).

82. Government Accounting Office, *Oil and Gas Royalty Collections—Serious Financial Management Problems Need Congressional Attention* (Washington, D.C., 1979): 6–22. The 1982 report by the Commission on Fiscal Accountability of the Nation's Energy Resources is discussed in Barbara McLennan, "Federal Policy With Respect to Collection of Royalties From Oil and Gas Leases on Federal and Indian Lands," *Oil & Gas Tax Quarterly* 87 (1983): 95–98; *Weekly Compilation of Presidential Documents*, 19 (12 Jan. 1983), 24; Government Accounting Office, *Indian Natural Resources—Part II: Coal, Oil, and Gas—Better Management Can Improve Development and Increase Indian Income and Employment* (Washington, D.C., 1976), 28–38. See generally SH10; SH11.

83. 96 Stat. 2447 (1983); *Los Angeles Times*, 5 Oct. 1987. In 1986 the Bureau of Indian Affairs issued a policy decision that it would obtain assistance from the private sector to improve management of nonmineral trust accounts. The private sector's involvement would be in the areas of collecting funds, accounting and reporting status of accounts to beneficiaries, and investing trust funds. Although the Bureau of Indian Affairs' management of tribal and individual trust funds undoubtedly needed to be reformed, the question was whether a new Pandora's box would be opened by involving the private sector in the management of the nonmineral trust accounts. 51 *Federal Register* 16001 (1986).

84. *Assiniboine and Sioux Tribes of the Fort Peck Indian Reservation v. Board of Oil and Gas Conservation of State of Montana*, 792 F.2d 782.

85. 96 Stat. 1938 (1982); HR4, 3–4.

86. 96 Stat. 1938–1940 (1982).

87. 25 *USC* sec. 415, 416a. For a discussion of policy considerations involved in long-term leasing see Reid Peyton Chambers and Monroe E. Price, "Regulating Sovereignty: Secretarial Discretion and the Leasing of Indian Lands," *Stanford Law Review* 26 (1974): 1061.

88. *AKN* 4 (Summer 1972): 14; Cahn and Hearne, *Our Brother's Keeper*, 88–91.

89. Getches and Wilkinson, *Federal Indian Law*, 233.

90. Cahn and Hearne, *Our Brother's Keeper*, 89–90. In 1966 Congress passed legislation establishing a statute of limitations for filing monetary damage claims for

trespass on Indian trust lands occurring before 1966. Congress extended the statute of limitations deadline several times. In 1982 Congress directed the secretary of the interior to follow certain administrative procedures for the resolution of remaining claims. 28 *USC* sec. 2415; 48 *Federal Register* 13698, 51204 (1983); 49 *Federal Register* 518 (1984).

91. *AKN* 2 (June 1970): 22; Cahn and Hearne, *Our Brother's Keeper,* 74–75, 117; Warren Cohen and Philip Mause, "The Indian: The Forgotten American," *Harvard Law Review* 81 (1968): 1826; *Tooahnippah v. Hickel,* 397 US Reports 598; 25 *USC* sec. 372, 373.

92. Cahn and Hearne, *Our Brother's Keeper,* 74.

93. For a discussion of the heirship problem see Ethel J. Williams, "Too Little Land, Too Many Heirs—The Indian Heirship Land Problem," *Washington Law Review* 46 (1971): 709.

Chapter 5

1. James Cook and James King, *A Voyage to the Pacific Ocean* . . . , 3 vols. (London, 1784).

2. For a listing of the ships with their respective national registry see Bernice Judd, *Voyages to Hawaii Before 1860* . . . , enl. and rev. by Helen Younge Lind (Honolulu, 1974). John Ledyard, *A Journal of Captain Cook's Last Voyage* . . . , ed. Kenneth Munnford (London, 1783; Corvallis, Ore., 1963), 67–68, 103–104, 109; George Dixon, *A Voyage Round the World* . . . , 2d ed. (London, 1789), 89–113; Nathaniel Portlock, *A Voyage Round the World* . . . (London, 1789), 58–91 passim, 146–197 passim; George Vancouver, *A Voyage of Discovery to the North Pacific Ocean, and Round the World* . . . *in the Years 1790, 1791, 1792, 1794, and 1795* . . . , 3 vols. (London, 1798), 1:154, 157–158, 172, 179; Joseph Ingraham, *The Log of the "Brig Hope"* . . . , Hawaiian Historical Society Reprint no. 3 (Honolulu, 1918), 3–35 passim.

3. Ralph Kuykendall, *The Hawaiian Kingdom,* 3 vols. (Honolulu, 1938), 1:21; Harold Bradley, *The American Frontier in Hawaii, the Pioneers, 1789–1842* (Stanford, 1942), 52.

4. John Meares, *Voyages Made in the Years 1788 and 1789 From China to the North West Coast of America* (London, 1790; Amsterdam and New York, 1967), xcv; Campbell, *Voyage Round the World,* 114–115; Letter by George Vancouver, printed in *Sandwich Island Gazette,* 7 Oct. 1837; Vancouver, *Voyage of Discovery* 3:29–32, 48, 54–57; Kuykendall, *Hawaiian Kingdom* 1:21; Bradley, *American Frontier in Hawaii,* 52.

5. Peter Corney, *Early Voyages in the Northern Pacific, 1813–1818,* ed. Glen C. Adams (London, 1821; Honolulu, 1896; Fairfield, Wash., 1965), 132, 156–159, 184–185; Otto von Kotzebue, *A Voyage of Discovery* . . . , 3 vols. (London, 1821; reprinted in 2 vols., Amsterdam and New York, 1967), 1:303–305. For a detailed study see Richard Pierce, *Russia's Hawaiian Adventure, 1815–1817* (Berkeley and Los Angeles, 1965).

6. See note 5.

7. See note 5.

8. See note 5.

9. Vancouver, *Voyage of Discovery* 1:157–158, 179, 2:186, 198, 3:67, 71; Ledyard, *Journal of Captain Cook's Last Voyage*, 109; Meares, *Voyages*, 354–356; Campbell, *Voyage Round the World*, 105; Corney, *Early Voyages*, 185; *Missionary Herald* 23 (1827): 273 (hereafter cited as *MH*); Gabriel Franchere, *Narrative of A Voyage to the Northwest Coast of America in the Years 1811, 1812, 1813, and 1814 . . . ,* ed. Milo M. Quaife (Redfield, N.Y., 1854; Chicago, 1954), 36.

10. Campbell, *Voyage Round the World,* 95, 98, 103–106, 111–112, 120, 126–128, 160; Kotzebue, *Voyage of Discovery* 1:292, 302, 309, 345; Vancouver, *Voyage of Discovery* 3:17, 66–68, 140; Ross H. Gast and Agnes C. Conrad, *Don Francisco de Paula Marin and the Letters and Journal of Francisco de Paula Marin* (Honolulu, 1973), 199–242 passim (hereafter cited as Marin, *Journal*).

11. Vancouver, *Voyage of Discovery* 2:122, 140; Kotzebue, *Voyage of Discovery* 1:333.

12. Campbell, *Voyage Round the World,* 107–109.

13. Vancouver, *Voyage of Discovery* 2:181, 3:67–68; Franchere, *Narrative of a Voyage,* 41; Meares, *Voyages,* 350; Marin, *Journal,* 214–215, 242–243; Campbell, *Voyage Round the World,* 126; Corney, *Early Voyages,* 133; *MH* 17 (1821): 283.

14. Malo, *Hawaiian Antiquities,* 195; Campbell, *Voyage Round the World,* 137; Ii, *Fragments of Hawaiian History,* 16, 69–70, 116; Hiram Bingham, *A Residence of Twenty-One Years in the Sandwich Islands . . . ,* 3d ed. rev. (Hartford, 1849; New York, 1969), 49; John Jones to John Q. Adams, 31 Dec. 1822, U.S. Department of State, Dispatches from United States Consuls in Honolulu, 1820–1903, vol. 1 (hereafter cited as USDS Consul Dispatches); Ellis, *Narrative of A Tour Through Hawaii,* 306; Kotzebue, *Voyage of Discovery* 2:191.

15. Kotzebue, *Voyage of Discovery* 1:333, 2:191; Jarves, *History of the Hawaiian Islands,* 86.

16. Jarves, *History of the Hawaiian Islands,* 122; Kuykendall, *Hawaiian Kingdom* 1:119–120.

17. Kotzebue, *Voyage of Discovery* 3:199–200; Marin, *Journal,* 201; Ingraham, *Log of the "Brig Hope,"* 18–20; Campbell, *Voyage Round the World,* 152; Corney, *Early Voyages,* 133, 157, 180–181, 188, 191, 194, 215, 228; Kuykendall, *Hawaiian Kingdom* 1:88–89; John Hussey, ed., *The Voyage of the Racoon: A "Secret" Journal of a Visit to Oregon, California, and Hawaii, 1813–1814* (San Francisco, 1958), 36.

18. See note 17.

19. John Jones to John Q. Adams, 31 Dec. 1822, USDS Consul Dispatches, vol. 1; Ellis, *Narrative of A Tour Through Hawaii,* 49, 309–310; *MH* 19 (1823): 184; *MH* 25 (1829): 116; Jarves, *History of the Hawaiian Islands,* 193; Levi Chamberlain Journal, 25, 30, 31 July 1823, Hawaiian Mission Children's Society Library, Honolulu; Charles S. Stewart, *A Residence in the Sandwich Islands,* 5th ed. and enl. (Boston, 1839), 104. For an examination of the transformation occurring in land use and the impact on the maka'āinana living in the Anahulu Valley, O'ahu after 1795, see Kirch, *Feathered Gods and Fishhooks,* 310–314.

20. Franchere, *Narrative of a Voyage,* 41; Kotzebue, *Voyage of Discovery* 1:333; *MH* 18 (1822): 249, 278; *MH* 20 (1824): 282; *MH* 21 (1825): 40; Interior Department Letter Book 2, 25 Jan., 10 Mar. 1849, Archives of Hawaii, Honolulu (hereafter cited as AH).

21. The *Missionary Herald* and *Polynesian* were filled with remarks by missionaries and commercialists about the need for alteration of the land tenure system. For example see *MH* 25 (1829): 209; *Polynesian,* 6 July 1844, 8 July 1948. Also see note 22.

22. Quote from editorial, *Polynesian,* 25 Oct. 1845; *Polynesian,* 6 July 1844, 24 Apr. 1847; *Sandwich Island Gazette,* 2 Dec. 1837; Stewart, *Residence in the Sandwich Islands,* 117–118.

23. John Colcord Journal, 28–29, AH; James Hunnewell to Levi Chamberlain, 25 Apr. 1832, Hunnewell Papers, Hawaiian Mission Children's Society Library; Chamberlain Journal, 31 Aug., 26, 27 Oct. 1826; *Sandwich Island Gazette,* 16, 23 Sept., 15 Apr. 1837; *MH* 22 (1826): 173–174; *MH* 25 (1829): 209.

24. *Polynesian,* 13 Mar. 1841, 8 June 1850, 25 Jan. 1851, 8 Feb. 1851. Foreigners urging alteration of the land tenure system used this argument until Kamehameha III changed the method of land ownership. For example see R. C. Wyllie to William Lee, 24 July 1849, Foreign Office and Executive File, AH (hereafter cited as F.O.EX).

25. Colcord Journal, 54; *MH* 17 (1821): 246; *MH* 25 (1829): 184, 248; Stewart, *Residence in the Hawaiian Islands,* 139; *Sandwich Island Gazette,* 21 Apr. 1838; *Polynesian,* 6 July 1844. Many early traders remarked about the industriousness of the Native Hawaiians. For example see Dixon, *Voyage Round the World,* 131; Campbell, *Voyage Round the World,* 94–95, 129.

26. *Polynesian,* 8 July 1848.

27. For example see Chamberlain Journal, 18 Mar. 1833.

28. Stewart to J. Evarts, 14 July 1827, in Stewart, *Residence in the Hawaiian Islands,* app., 337; Kuykendall, *Hawaiian Kingdom* 1:119–120.

29. Jones to John Q. Adams, 31 Dec. 1822, USDS Consul Dispatches, vol. 1; Jones to Henry Clay, 1 July 1827, ibid.; Jones to Louis M. Lane, 31 Dec. 1834, ibid.; SED6, 4. In 1829 and 1832, Hawaiian leaders reassured the commanders of the U.S.S. *Vincennes* and the U.S.S. *Potomac* that they would pay the trade debts. Actually they were not paid in full until the 1840s; Kuykendall, *Hawaiian Kingdom* 1:434–436.

30. Chamberlain Journal, 7 Oct. 1836; John Jones to Henry Clay, 8 Feb. 1826, USDS Consul Dispatches, vol. 1; treaty in HED3, 276–277.

31. Chamberlain Journal, 4, 7 Oct. 1836; W. S. Ruschenberger, *A Voyage Round the World . . . in 1835, 1836, 1937* (Philadelphia, 1838), 495–497. Kamehameha III also stated this view in his letter to King William IV, in Proposed Treaty with England, 1836, F.O.EX.

32. Chamberlain Journal, 7 Oct. 1836; Kennedy to Kaukeauli [sic], 7 Oct. 1836, F.O.EX.

33. C. K. Stribling to Kenou, 1 Oct. 1836, F.O.EX; *Sandwich Island Gazette,* 8 Oct. 1836.

34. John C. Jones to Kamehameha III, 23 May, 24 May, 16 June 1837, F.O.EX; Kamehameha III to Jones, 14 June 1837, F.O.EX.

35. Kamehameha III to William IV, 16 Nov. 1836, William Richards manuscript, AH; Charlton to Kamehameha III, 17 Jan. 1836, F.O.EX; Kauikeaouli Proclamation, 16 Nov. 1836, F.O.EX; Statement of Chiefs, Nov. 1836, F.O.EX; Charlton to Kamehameha III, 7 Nov. 1836, F.O.EX; Chamberlain Journal, 8, 12, 15, 16 Nov. 1836; *Sandwich Island Gazette,* 19 Nov. 1836; treaty, in HED3, 278;

Emma Lyons Doyle, comp., *"Makua Laiano," The Story of Lorenzo Lyons, Compiled from Manuscript Journals, 1832–1886,* 2d ed. (Honolulu, 1953), 92; Kuykendall, *Hawaiian Kingdom* 1:153.

36. The *Sandwich Island Gazette* and F.O.EX files for 1837 contained extensive information on the persecution of Catholics in Hawaii. See also Colcord Journal, 30; Chamberlain Journal, 9, 13 July 1839; Peter Brinsmade to John Forsyth and enclosures, 17 July 1839, Notice by Brinsmade to American residents, 9 July 1839, and Laplace to Brinsmade, 10 July 1839, USDS Consul Dispatches, vol. 1.

37. Hunter Miller, *United States Treaties and Other International Acts of the United States of America,* 8 vols. (Washington, D.C., 1937), 5:626–627.

38. Charlton to Kamehameha III, 26 Sept. 1842, F.O.EX; William Hooper to Daniel Webster and enclosures, 7 Mar. 1843, Paulet to Kamehameha III, 16, 17 Feb. 1943, and Kamehameha III to Paulet, 17 Feb. 1843, USDS Consul Dispatches, vol. 1; Charles Kanaina to Timothy Haalilio, 5 Mar. 1843, F.O.EX.

39. Chamberlain Journal, 17 Feb. 1843; Kekūanaōʻa to Simpson, 30 Sept. 1842, F.O.EX; Kamehameha III and Kekāuluohi to Simpson, 8 Oct.1842, F.O.EX; Paulet to Kamehameha III, 17 Feb. 1843, enclosures with Hooper to Webster, 7 Mar. 1843, USDS Consul Dispatches, vol. 1.

40. Kuykendall, *Hawaiian Kingdom* 1:222; Chamberlain Journal, 24 Feb. 1843; Richard Armstrong to Reuben Chapman, 3 Mar. 1843, photostat copy in Richard Anderson Papers, AH; Paulet's proclamation establishing the provisional government and other documents concerning cession in enclosures with Hooper to Webster, 7 Mar. 1843, USDS Consul Dispatches, vol. I.

41. Haalilio and Richards to Aberdeen, 6, 21 Mar., 3 Apr. 1843, F.O.EX; Aberdeen to Haalilio and Richards, 12 Sept. 1843, F.O.EX; Haalilio and Richards to Aberdeen, 20 Sept. 1843, F.O.EX.

42. Aberdeen to Haalilio and Richards, 12 Sept. 1843, F.O.EX; Haalilio and Richards to Kamehameha III, 30 Sept. 1843, F.O.EX.

43. Kekūanaōʻa to Haalilio, 6 Mar. 1843, F.O.EX; Kekūanaōʻa to Richards, 6 Mar. 1843, F.O.EX; Aberdeen to Haalilio and Richards, 30 Sept. 1843, F.O.EX; Kuykendall, *Hawaiian Kingdom* 1:225.

44. Judd to Wyllie, 15 Feb. 1845, F.O.EX; John Ricord, "An Award Upon the Meaning of Lord Aberdeens's Letter," 23–76, in USDS Consul Dispatches, vol. 2; *Polynesian,* 22 Aug. 1846 (Report of Minister of Foreign Relations to Hawaiian Legislature of 1 Aug. 1846); *Polynesian,* 22 Aug. 1846 (Letter of H. W. Addington, Foreign Office, H.B.M., 27 Dec. 1845, and William Miller to R. C. Wyllie, 12 Aug. 1845); *Polynesian,* 5 June 1847 (R. C. Wyllie to G. F. Seymour, 1 Sept. 1846); *Polynesian,* 5 June 1847 (Report of Minister of Foreign Relations to Hawaiian Legislature, 4 May 1847); *Polynesian,* 5 June 1847 (Wyllie to Seymour, 3 Sept. 1846). The *Polynesian* on 11, 18 Sept. 1847, published a number of letters between Wyllie and William Miller concerning the Charlton case. The Privy Council also discussed the Charlton controversy; Privy Council Records, vol. 2 passim.

45. John Tyler, 30 Dec. 1842, in Richardson, *Messages and Papers of the Presidents* 4:211–214; Chamberlain Journal, 20, 24 Feb. 1843; Judd to Haalilio, 10 Mar. 1843, F.O.EX; Hooper to Webster, 7 Mar. 1843, USDS Consul Dispatches, vol. 1; Kamehameha III to President of the United States, enclosure with Hooper to Webster, 11 Mar. 1843, USDS Consul Dispatches, vol. 1.

46. Colcord Journal, 49–50; Chamberlain Journal, 27, 29 July 1843; Thomas'

Declaration, 31 July 1843 and copy of treaty, enclosures with Hooper to Webster, 15 Aug. 1843, USDS Consul Dispatches, vol. 2; Judd to Richards, 1 Aug. 1843, F.O.EX; John Ii to Haalilio, 4 Aug. 1843, F.O.EX.

47. Hooper to Webster, 10 Oct. 1842, USDS Consul Dispatches, vol. 1; Hooper to Webster, 15 Aug. 1843, ibid., vol. 2; Hooper to Secretary of State, Sept. 1843, ibid.

Chapter 6

1. See chapter 5, 98–100.

2. Marshall Sahlins and Dorothy Barrère, eds., "William Richards on Hawaiian Culture and Political Conditions of the Islands in 1841," *Hawaiian Journal of History* 7 (1973): 3 n. 11; *Polynesian,* 4 July 1840, 8 May, 6 Feb., 28 Aug., 18 Sept., 16 Oct. 1841.

3. Constitution, published in *Polynesian,* 6 Feb. 1841.

4. Kamehameha III to American Consul, 22 July 1841, Notes from the Hawaiian Legation in the United States to the Department of State, 1841–1899, vol. 1 (hereafter cited as Hawaiian Legation Notes); Proclamation by Kamehameha III and Kekauluohi, 31 May 1841, F.O.EX; Judd to Secretary of ABCFM, 5 Sept. 1844, F.O.EX; Privy Council Records, 2:146, AH; *Polynesian,* 15 Aug. 1846 (Report of the Attorney General to the Legislature, 1 Aug. 1846); Judd, Remarks on Ten Eyck's Draft of a New Treaty with the United States, 20 Feb. 1848, F.O.EX; *Polynesian,* 17 June 1841.

5. Edward Joesting, *Kauai: the Separate Kingdom* (Honolulu, 1984), 129–141; Colcord Journal, 55; Ruschenberger, *Voyage Round the World,* 497; *Polynesian,* 17 June, 17 July, 13 Nov. 1841, 3 July 1847; Bradley, *American Frontier in Hawaii,* 236–240.

6. Thurston, Lorrin, ed., *The Fundamental Law of Hawaii* (Honolulu, 1904), 121; Hooper to Kekūanaōʻa, 19 Feb. 1845, USDS Consul Dispatches, vol. 2.

7. Ruschenberger, *Voyage Round the World,* 497; Judd to Richards, 2 Aug. 1842, F.O.EX; Judd to Secretaries of American Board of Commissioners for Foreign Missions, 5 Sept. 1844, F.O.EX; *Polynesian,* 31 May 1845, 8 Aug. 1846; Hooper to Secretary of State, 28 Aug. 1845, USDS Consul Dispatches, vol. 2; Legislature Records, AH, 2:95–96, 21 March 1846; *Polynesian,* 1 May 1847.

8. J. P. Judd to R. C. Wyllie, 22 Aug. 1844, F.O.EX; *Polynesian,* 12 Oct. 1844.

9. *Polynesian,* 31 May 1845, 11 July 1846, 8, 29 May, 19 June, 3 July 1847, 1 July 1848, 24 June 1854; Privy Council Records 2:432; Kuykendall, *Hawaiian Kingdom* 1:281; Jon J. Chinen, *Original Land Titles in Hawaii* (Honolulu, 1961), 9–12; Chinen, *Great Mahele,* 8–14.

10. The *Polynesian* published "The Principles . . ." on 19 June 1847; many letters in the Interior Department Letter Book 2 reveal the sale and leasing of lands to non-Hawaiians.

11. *Polynesian,* 29 May, 25 Sept. 1847; Privy Council Records 2:308 and passim; Legislature Records, vol. 2, 15 Oct. 1846–24 May 1847 passim; Judd to Kamehameha III and Privy Council, 17 Dec. 1847, F.O.EX; Wyllie, Suggestions on the Proposed Division of Lands, 13 Dec. 1847, F.O.EX; Lee to Wyllie, 14 Dec. 1847,

F.O.EX; Lee to Kamehameha III, 14 Dec. 1847, F.O.EX; Lee, Suggested Four Principles on Division of Lands Delivered in Privy Council, 13 Dec. 1847, F.O.EX; Judd, Memo of Resolutions of Discussion in Legislature, 11 Dec. 1847, F.O.EX; Privy Council Records 4:250–260, 264–277, 280–290.

12. Privy Council Records 3:219–220, 231–234, 687, 761–763; Interior Department Letter Book 3, 19 Aug. 1850; *Polynesian,* 26 June 1852; *Pacific Commercial Advertiser,* 13 Sept. 1860; Kuykendall, *Hawaiian Kingdom* 1:288; Chinen, *Great Mahele,* 15–28; Chinen, *Original Land Titles,* 12–14, 24. Chinen provided sample land commission awards, royal patents on the awards, Kamehameha deeds, royal patent grants and land patents.

13. Quote from Wyllie, Report on Land, Capital, and Labor, 1 Dec. 1847, F.O.EX; Wyllie to Judd, 19 Nov. 1849, F.O.EX. When the government sold lands to Hawaiian citizens, it reserved the rights of the commoners; for example see Kalama to Henry Swanton, 13 Mar. 1849, Interior Department Letter Book 2; Privy Council Records 3:384, 404, 415–418, 711–712, 741–743, 755–773.

14. Privy Council Records 3:417–418; Act of 6 Aug. 1850, published in *Polynesian,* 7 Sept. 1850; Interior Department Letter Book 3, 25 Sept., Dec. 1851; *Polynesian,* 2 Feb., 14 Dec. 1850; Chinen, *Original Land Titles,* 15–24; Chinen, *Great Mahele,* 29–31.

15. *Polynesian,* 15 Aug. 1846, 2 June 1849; J. S. Green to editor, *Polynesian,* 26 Sept., 3 Oct. 1846; G. M. Robertson to John Richardson, 17 Nov. 1848, Interior Department Letter Book 2.

16. Quote in Thurston to D. B. Lyman, 8 Jan. 1852, Department of Interior Letter Book 3; Chinen, *Great Mahele,* 29–31; *Polynesian,* 17 May 1851, 9 Apr. 1853, 3 July 1857; Alexander, "Brief History of Land Titles in the Hawaiian Kingdom," 123–124; Hobbs, *Hawaii: A Pageant of the Soil,* 62; Kuykendall, *Hawaiian Kingdom* 1:293. For example of survey, see Edward Perkins, *Na Motu: Or, Reef-Rovings in the . . . Hawaiian . . . Islands* (New York, 1854), 149–155.

17. *Polynesian,* 15 May 1852; *Polynesian,* 3 May 1851; Isabella Lucy (Bird) Bishop, *The Hawaiian Archipelago; Six Months Among . . . the Sandwich Islands,* 1st Am. ed. (London, 1894; reprint from 5th English ed., New York, 1903), 270.

18. Chinen, *Great Mahele,* 31.

19. *Polynesian,* 23 Mar. 1850; Kuykendall, *Hawaiian Kingdom* 1:292.

20. Armstrong and Lee's letters printed in *Polynesian,* 16 Feb. 1850; *Polynesian,* 2 June 1849, 2 Feb. 1850.

21. The act allowing aliens to purchase and convey land was published in *Polynesian,* 13 July 1850; Judd, Remarks on Ten Eyck's Draft of a New Treaty with the United States, 20 Feb. 1848, F.O.EX; *Polynesian,* 16 Sept., 25 Nov. 1848.

22. Kekūanaōʻa to Hooper, 18, 24 Feb. 1845, USDS Consul Dispatches, vol. 2; Hooper to Secretary of State, 28 Aug. 1845, ibid.; Hooper to Kekūanaōʻa, 19, 25 Feb. 1845, F.O.EX.

23. Ten Eyck to Secretary of State, 1 Oct., 21 Dec. 1846, 27 Mar., 25 May, 2 June 1847, USDS Consul Dispatches, vol. 3; Wyllie to Joel Turrill, 15 Dec. 1848, ibid., vol. 4; Turrill to Buchanan, 22 Dec. 1848, ibid.; Judd, Remarks on Ten Eyck's Draft of a New Treaty with the United States, 20 Feb. 1848, F.O.EX.

24. *Polynesian,* 3 July 1847; Kuykendall, *Hawaiian Kingdom* 1:296.

25. Ten Eyck to Secretary of State, 3 Nov. 1847, USDS Consul Dispatches, vol.

3; Judd, Remarks on Ten Eyck's Draft of a New Treaty with the United States, 20 Feb. 1848, F.O.EX; Buchanan to Ten Eyck, in HED3, 310–311; Kuykendall, *Hawaiian Kingdom* 1:297.

26. *Polynesian,* 26 Feb., 8 July, 16, 30 Sept., 7 Oct., 25 Nov. 1848, 16 Feb. 1850, 8 Oct. 1853, 30 Oct. 1858.

27. Lee to Wyllie, 8 Dec. 1847, F.O.EX. Wyllie, Report on Land, Capital, and Labor, 1 Dec. 1847, F.O.EX.

28. Privy Council Records 3:681, 689; law printed in *Polynesian,* 13 July 1850.

29. *Polynesian,* 14 Dec. 1850, 2 Mar. 1861.

30. Kali Watson, comp., "Adverse Possession," prepared for Alu Like (Honolulu, n.d.) (testimony before Hawaii Constitutional Convention, 1978); *Hawaii Revised Statutes* sec. 657-31. For a discussion of adverse possession and quiet title law in Hawaii see John Montague Steadman, "The Statutory Elements of Hawaii's Adverse Possession Law," *Hawaii Bar Journal* 14 (1978): 67; Naomi Hirayasu, "Adverse Possession and Quiet Title Actions in Hawaii—Recent Constitutional Developments," *Hawaii Bar Journal* 19 (1985): 59; Keith Steiner, "Adverse Possession Against Unknown Claimants Under Land Court and Quiet Title Procedures," *Hawaii Bar Journal* 2 (1964): 4. Steadman maintained that the running of the statute of limitations transferred title to the adverse possessor, while Hirayasu argued that it only limited the true owner's remedy for recovery; Steadman, 70 and Hirayasu, 70–71, 66 n. 61. See also Neil M. Levy, "Native Hawaiian Land Rights," *California Law Review* 63 (1975): 869–870.

31. For a brief discussion of the taxation issue see *Lai v. Kukahiko,* 569 P.2d 352, 356.

32. *Poka v. Holi,* 357 P.2d 100, 110; *Yin v. Midkiff,* 481 P.2d 109, 112.

33. *City and County of Honolulu v. Bennett,* 57 Haw. 195, 209–211. For cases involving the *Bennett* good faith test see *Smart v. Luiki,* 640 P.2d 1172; *Hana Ranch v. Kanakaole,* 623 P.2d 885; *Hana Ranch v. Kanakaole,* 672 P.2d 550.

34. From 1870 to 1898 the statute of limitations was twenty years. For the next seventy-five years it was ten years.

35. Hawaii Constitution, art. 16, sec. 12; *Hawaii Revised Statutes* sec. 657-31.5; *Hawaii Revised Statutes* sec. 669-1; *Honolulu Advertiser,* 11 Nov. 1977.

36. Watson, "Adverse Possession," (testimony of Kali Watson).

37. Hawaii Constitution Convention File, 1978, AH (testimony of Kali Watson); *Honolulu Advertiser,* 11 Nov. 1977; HH3, 200.

38. Watson, "Adverse Possession," (testimony of Kali Watson).

39. *Hustace v. Kapuni,* 718 P.2d 1109, 1115–1116.

40. For a case showing the importance of genealogical documentation see *Hana Ranch Inc. v. Kanakaole,* 623 P.2d 885. Within the last decade organizations such as the Native Hawaiian Legal Corporation have provided legal assistance to kuleana owners, which in some instances has resulted in judicial decisions making it more difficult for adverse possessors to acquire Native Hawaiian land; see *Hustace v. Kapuni,* 718 P.2d 1109, 1115–1116.

41. HH3, 200.

42. Standing Committee Report no. 57, Hawaii Constitutional Convention Files, 1978.

43. *Honolulu Advertiser,* 11 Nov. 1977; HH3, 200. For a discussion of heirship,

access rights, and adverse possession, see Levy, "Native Hawaiian Land Rights," 868–870. Levy discussed available remedies for dealing with these matters.

44. HH3, 161, 172; SH4, 188; *Honolulu Advertiser,* 11 Nov. 1977.

45. Thomas M. Spaulding, *The Crown Lands of Hawaii,* University of Hawaii Occasional Papers, no. 1 (Honolulu, 1923), 15–16; Hobbs, *Hawaii,* 73–74.

46. *Polynesian,* 16 Feb. 1850, 8 Oct. 1853, 30 Oct. 1858; S. B. Dole, "The Problem of Population and Our Land Policy," *Pacific Commercial Advertiser,* 26 Oct. 1872; P. Nahaolelua, "Biennial Report of the Minister of Finance to the Legislative Assembly of 1872," 7–8, in Hawaiian Legation Notes, vol. 2.

47. Dole, "Problem of Population," *Pacific Commercial Advertiser,* 10 Sept. 1863.

48. Ralph Kuykendall and A. Grove Day, *Hawaii: A History,* rev. ed. (Englewood, N.J., 1961), 205–206; HH1, 36.

49. 30 Stat. 750 (1898); 31 Stat. 141 (1900).

50. Robert Horwitz and Judith Finn, *Public Land Policy in Hawaii: Major Landowners,* Hawaii Legislative Reference Bureau Rept. 3 (Honolulu, 1967), 13–15, 35–43.

51. *Hawaii Housing Authority v. Midkiff,* 467 US Reports 229; *Hawaii Housing Authority v. Lyman,* 704 P.2d 888. Private parties unsuccessfully challenged the monopoly power of the large landowners in Hawaii on the basis of alleged violations of the Sherman Antitrust Act and the Hawaii fair trade statutes; *Sousa v. Estate of Bishop,* 594 F.Supp. 1480.

52. *Hawaii Housing Authority v. Midkiff,* 467 US Reports 229; *Hawaii Housing Authority v. Lyman,* 704 P.2d 888.

53. *San Francisco Examiner,* 24 Mar. 1985; *New York Times,* 1 June 1984; *Hawaii Housing Authority v. Midkiff,* 467 US Reports 229; *Hawaii Housing Authority v. Lyman,* 704 P.2d 888. The Bishop Estate owned almost 20 percent of the residential land on O'ahu and approximately 25 percent of the unimproved residential land on the island; *Hawaii Housing Authority v. Lyman,* 704 P.2d 894 n. 7. For an examination of the Bishop Estate trust for Native Hawaiians, see Levy, "Native Hawaiian Land Rights," 870–875.

54. *Hawaii Housing Authority v. Midkiff,* 467 US Reports 229; *Hawaii Housing Authority v. Lyman,* 704 P.2d 888. The U.S. Supreme Court further ruled that the condemnation plan was within the state's police powers. For analysis of the constitutionality of the Hawaii Land Reform Act see Graig S. Harrison and Tom Grande, "*Midkiff v. Tom:* The Constitutionality of Hawaii's Land Reform Act," *University of Hawaii Law Review* 6 (1984): 561; Thomas J. Coyne, "Hawaii Housing Authority v. Midkiff: A Final Requiem for the Public Use Limitation on Eminent Domain?" *Notre Dame Law Review* 60 (1985): 388; James P. Conahan, "Hawaii's Land Reform Act: Is it Constitutional?" *Hawaii Bar Journal* 6 (1969): 31. Just compensation provisions of the land act have also been at issue; *Hawaii Housing Authority v. Lyman,* 704 P.2d 888. In a recent case the Hawaii Supreme Court held that a section of the Hawaii Land Reform Act that applied to leases in effect at the time of the act's amendment in 1975 was an unconstitutional impairment of contractual rights. It ruled that the provision requiring all residential lessors in the state, not just those subject to the land conversion act, to pay the fair market value of property improvements when the lessee wanted to sell them to the lessor at the

termination of a lease was not an exercise of the state's eminent domain power; *Anthony v. Kualoa Ranch, Inc.*, 736 P.2d 55.

55. *Carter v. Territory of Hawaii*, 14 Haw. 465, rev'd 194 US Reports 154; *Territory v. Trustee of Estate of Kanoa*, 41 Haw. 358.

56. *Damon v. Hawaii*, 194 US Reports 154, 158, 159; Richard Kosaki, *Konohiki Fishing Rights*, Hawaii Legislative Reference Bureau Rept. no. 1 (Honolulu, 1954), 1, 2, 31.

57. Hawaii Organic Act sec. 95, 96, 48 *USCA* sec. 506, 507; *Bishop v. Mahika*, 35 Haw. 608; *Damon v. Hawaii*, 194 US Reports 154; *Carter v. Hawaii*, 200 US Reports 255; *State v. Hawaiian Dredging Company*, 397 P.2d 593; Richard Kosaki, *Konohiki Fishing Rights*, Hawaii Legislative Reference Bureau Rept. no. 1 (Honolulu, 1954), 9, 10, 13–14, and generally.

58. *Hawaii Revised Statutes* sec. 187A-21 to 187A-23, 190D-24 (1986).

59. Ellis, *Narrative of a Tour Through Hawaii*, 223. Hawaiians had also expressed this fear in 1820, *MH* 17 (1821): 118, 172.

60. Brown to Calhoun, 18 Jan. 1845, USDS Consul Dispatches, vol. 2; Petition, 12 June 1845, F.O.EX; Legislature Records 2:20–22; *Polynesian*, 2 Aug. 1945; John Young to residents of Lahaina, 7 Aug. 1855, Interior Department Letter Book 6.

61. Theodore Morgan, *Hawaii: A Century of Economic Change, 1778–1876* (Cambridge, Mass., 1948), 138–139; *Yoshimoto v. Lee*, 634 P.2d 130.

62. Henry Peirce to Hamilton Fish, 10 Feb., 5 July 1873, U.S. Department of State, Dispatches From U.S. Ministers in Hawaii, 1843–1900, vol. 15 (hereafter cited as USDS Minister Dispatches); Charles Bishop to Peirce, 14 Nov. 1873, enclosure with Peirce to Fish, 18 Nov. 1873, ibid.; *Hawaiian Gazette*, 9 July 1873.

63. Quote from Peirce to Fish, 26 May 1873, USDS Minister Dispatches, vol. 15; Peirce to Fish, 28 Feb., 7 July, 24 Nov. 1873, ibid.; Peirce to Fish, 25 Feb. 1871, ibid., vol. 13; *Pacific Commercial Advertiser*, 10 Aug., 7 Dec. 1867, 1, 4 Jan. 1868, 12 Mar., 2 July 1870, 8 Feb., 5, 12, 26 July, 27 Sept., 22 Nov. 1873; *Hawaiian Gazette*, 26 Feb., 3 July, 19 Nov. 1873.

64. Bishop to Peirce, 14 Nov. 1873, enclosures with Peirce to Fish, 18 Nov. 1873, USDS Minister Dispatches, vol. 15; Peirce to Fish, 24 Nov. 1873, ibid.; resolutions, *Pacific Commercial Advertiser*, 5 July 1873; *Pacific Commercial Advertiser*, 4 Jan., 28 Oct. 1868, 9, 16 Aug., 13 Sept., 22 Nov., 13 Dec. 1873; *Hawaiian Gazette*, 26 Mar. 1873.

65. 19 Stat. 625 (1875).

66. 25 Stat. 1400 (1887). For detailed studies of reciprocity and annexation see Merze Tate, *Hawaii: Reciprocity or Annexation* (East Lansing, 1968); Sylvester Stevens, *American Expansion in Hawaii, 1842–1898* (Harrisburg, Pa., 1945).

67. George Merrill to James Blaine, 1, 6 Aug. 1879, in HED3; John Stevens to Blaine, 7, 10 Feb. 1890, in HED3; Peirce to Fish, 5 Feb. 1874, USDS Minister Dispatches, vol. 16; Bishop, *Hawaiian Archipelago*, 421; see generally Ralph Kuykendall, *The Hawaiian Kingdom, 1874–1893: The Kalakaua Dynasty*, vol. 3 (Honolulu, 1967).

68. Native Hawaiian opposition to annexation existed throughout the second half of the nineteenth century; see *Pacific Commercial Advertiser*, 14 Mar. 1868; Peirce to Fish, 17 Mar., 28 Apr., 18 Nov. 1873, USDS Minister Dispatches, vol. 15; Emma to Peter, 6 Jan. 1874, in Alfons Korn, ed., *News From Molokai: Letters*

Between Peter Kaeo and Queen Emma, 1873–1876 (Honolulu, 1976), 169; Proclamation by Kamehameha III and Keoni Ana, 10 Mar. 1851, in HED3; Luther Severance to Daniel Webster, 11 Mar. 1851, in HED3; Webster to Severance, 14 July 1851, in HED3; W. L. Marcy to John Mason, 16 Dec. 1853, in HED3; Marcy to Gregg, 4 Apr. 1854, 31 Jan. 1855, in HED3; Gregg to Marcy, 26 July, 7 Aug., 15 Sept., 2 Oct., 29 Dec. 1854, in HED3.

69. *Pacific Commercial Advertiser,* 28 Dec. 1867, 1 Jan., 8, 22 Feb., 4 Mar., 24 Oct. 1868, 2 July, 19 Nov. 1870, 15, 22 Feb., 1, 8, 15, 29 Mar., 5, 12 Apr., 7 June 1873; *Hawaiian Gazette,* 5 Mar. 1873; Peirce to Fish, 26 May 1873, USDS Minister Dispatches, vol. 15; William Seward to Edward McCook, 12 Sept. 1867, in HED3; Seward to Z. S. Spaulding, 5 July 1868, in HED3.

70. Quote in Peirce to Fish, 26 May 1873, USDS Minister Dispatches, vol. 15; Peirce to Fish, 28 Feb., 7 July, 24 Nov. 1873, ibid.; Peirce to Fish, 25 Feb. 1871, ibid., vol. 13; Seward to Edward McCook, 12 Sept. 1867, in HED3; Seward to Z. S. Spaulding, 5 July 1868, in HED3.

71. Blaine to Comly, 1 Dec. 1881, Department of State, *Papers Relating to the Foreign Relations of the United States for 1881* (Washington, D.C., 1882), 635–636, 638–639.

72. Stevens to Blaine, 8 Mar. 1892, in HED3.

73. HED2.

74. Stevens to John Foster, 1 Feb. 1893 (telegram), in HED3; Stevens to Foster, 1 Feb. 1893, in HED3; Foster to Stevens, 14 Feb. 1893, in HED3.

75. HED2, xii–xiii; Blount Report in ibid.; see also SR2. Many congressional reports and letters on the overthrow of the monarchy and on United States–Hawaii relations were collected in Department of State, *Papers Relating to the Foreign Relations of the United States for 1894,* app. 2 (Washington, D.C., 1895).

76. Since the 1970s, a small segment of the Native Hawaiian population has publicly advocated restoration of Hawaiian sovereignty.

Chapter 7

1. 60 Stat. 1049 (1946); 90 Stat. 1990 (1976).

2. Nancy Lurie, "The Indian Claims Commission," *The Annals of the American Academy of Political and Social Science* 436 (1978): 99. For an examination of Indian land claims, including claims resolved by the Indian Claims Commission, see Imre Sutton, ed., *Irredeemable America: The Indians' Estate and Land Claims* (Albuquerque, 1985).

3. Lurie, "Indian Claims Commission," 100; *Indian Claims Commission, August 13, 1946–September 30, 1978: Final Report* (Washington, D.C., 1978).

4. Lurie, "Indian Claims Commission," 99–100, 103; 39 *Federal Register* 1835 (1974); Monroe Price, *Law and the American Indian,* 497–498; 87 Stat. 466 (1973), 25 *USCA* sec. 1401.

5. Lurie, "Indian Claims Commission," 104–105; William Brophy and Sophie D. Aberle, comps., *The Indian: America's Unfinished Business: Report of the Commission on the Rights, Liberties, and Responsibilities of the American Indian* (Norman, 1966), 199–206.

6. HH3, 66, 109, 133, 156, 164, 168–171, 174, 226, 261, 279, 280, 311;

SH4, 83, 108, 133, 135, 154–155, 184, 192, 214, 258–259, 266–268; HH–SH1, 137, 172–173, 177, 180–182, 221, 224, 225, 257.

7. HH3, 46–51; SH4, 40–41, 80–82, 90–93, 112, 189; HH–SH1, 83, 136, 165, 220, 257; 124 *CR* 15050-57 (1978).

8. 120 *CR* 21705-08 (1974); 121 *CR* 1192-94 (1975); HH3.

9. SH4, 62–75, 83, 95, 100–101, 156, 189, 266; HH–SH1, 67–70, 220; 121 *CR* 41541 (1975).

10. 124 *CR* 15050-57 (1978); SH4, 108, 124–125, 180, 229, 246, 254, 332, 410; HH–SH1, 75, 80, 163–167, 188, 212, 218, 225, 266–272, 335–336; 94 Stat. 3324 (1980).

11. SH17, 3, 7, 603.

12. See generally SH17; HH5; *Native Hawaiians Study Commission Report on the Culture, Needs and Concerns of Native Hawaiians,* 2 vols. (Washington, D.C., 1983).

13. HED2, xiii.

14. *Hawaii Revised Statutes* sec. 10-2(4)(5) (Supp. 1984); see generally Hawaii Constitutional Convention File, 1978, AH.

15. For example, during the 1980s land was added to reservations under the authority of section 7 of the Indian Reorganization Act. Some of the land restorations included 139 acres to the Coushatta Indian Reservation in Louisiana, 46 *Federal Register* 1040 (1981); 55 acres to the Lower Elwha Reservation in Washington, 46 *Federal Register* 9788 (1981) and 47 *Federal Register* 31753 (1982); 1,500 acres to Grand Portage Reservation in Minnesota, 47 *Federal Register* 23813 (1982); 750 acres to St. Croix Chippewa Reservation in Wisconsin, 48 *Federal Register* 30764 (1983); 500 acres to the Mescalero Apache in New Mexico, 50 *Federal Register* 3979 (1985); creation of reservation for the Wisconsin Winnebago, 49 *Federal Register* 1431 (1984). Theodore H. Haas, "The Indian Reorganization Act in Historical Perspective," in *Indian Affairs and the Indian Reorganization Act: The Twenty Year Record,* ed. William Kelly (Tucson, 1954), 22.

16. *City of Sault Ste. Marie v. Andrus,* 532 F.Supp. 157; *City of Tacoma v. Andrus,* 457 F.Supp. 342.

17. 89 Stat. 577 (1975). The exact boundaries of the submarginal lands returned to the tribes were published in the *Federal Register*; for example see 43 *Federal Register* 18049 (1978), 18,749 acres to the Cherokee in Oklahoma. Before 1975 Congress occasionally passed legislation transferring submarginal land title to individual tribes; for example see 86 Stat. 795 (1972), 13,077 acres to the Stockbridge Munsee Community, Wisconsin; 86 Stat. 806 (1972), 762 acres to the Burns Indian Colony, Oregon.

18. 88 Stat. 1954 (1975). The Bureau of Indian Affairs published notices in the *Federal Register* indicating the return of surplus federal lands to individual tribes; for example see 50 *Federal Register* 49620 (1985), 345 acres to the Cherokee in Oklahoma; 47 *Federal Register* 31325 (1982), 10 acres to the Assiniboine and Sioux Tribes, Fort Peck Indian Reservation, Montana; 40 *Federal Register* 50732 (1975), 1,600 acres to the Oglala Sioux, Pine Ridge Reservation, South Dakota.

19. Reagan and the Bureau of Indian Affair's policy was expressed at congressional hearings on many of the land restitution bills; for example see SH12, 9–12.

20. Walter J. Hickel to Senator Henry M. Jackson, 8 July 1970, SR5; *AKN* 2 (Sept. 1970): 9; 43 Stat. 636–637 (1924); 48 Stat. 108 (1933).

21. Hickel to Jackson, 8 July 1970, SR5; *AKN* 2 (July–Aug. 1970): 18; *AKN* 2 (Sept. 1970): 8–9.

22. See note 21.

23. See note 21.

24. See note 21.

25. 84 Stat. 1437 (1970).

26. 92 Stat. 244 (1978), 618 acres to the Zuñi; 98 Stat. 1533 (1984), 11,050 acres to the Zuñi; 92 Stat. 1679 (1978), 4,850 acres to the Zia; 100 Stat. 3356 (1986), 1,840 acres to the Zia; 98 Stat. 315 (1984), 25,000 acres to the Cochiti; 98 Stat. 179 (1984), 80 acres to the Makah; SH14, 20–34; SH6; SH15; SH16; HR7.

27. *Lyng v. Northwest Indian Cemetery Protective Association,* 108 S.Ct. 1319 (1988) (Yurok, Karok, and Tolowa); *Wilson v. Block,* 708 F.2d 735 (Hopi); *Badoni v. Higginson,* 638 F.2d 172 (Navajo); *Crow v. Gullet,* 706 F.2d 856 (Sioux).

28. 92 Stat. 1672 (1978), 16,000 acres to Santa Ana Pueblo; 86 Stat. 719 (1972), 61,000 acres to Warm Springs; 94 Stat. 1067 (1980), 14,400 acres to Tule River; 94 Stat. 2565 (1980), 3,000 acres to Ute Mountain Ute. See also 96 Stat. 1946 (1982), 570 acres to Pascua Yaqui; 97 Stat. 1121 (1983), 133 acres to Kaw; 98 Stat. 11 (1984), 4,770 acres to Paiutes in Utah; 100 Stat. 828 (1986), 1,950 acres to Reno Sparks Indian Colony, Nevada; 97 Stat. 1383 (1983), 3,800 acres to Las Vegas Paiutes.

29. 88 Stat. 2091 (1975); *AKN* 3 (June 1971): 20; *AKN* 5 (Late Summer 1973): 15; *AKN* 6 (Early Summer 1974): 38–39; *AKN* 7 (Early Spring 1975): 36.

30. 85 Stat. 688 (1971). In January 1976 Alaska Natives residing in Oregon organized a thirteenth regional corporation. The courts and Congress upheld this action; *Alaska Native Association of Oregon v. Morton,* 459 F.Supp. 459; 89 Stat. 1145, 1149 (1976).

31. For example see *Koniag v. Kleppe,* 405 F.Supp. 1360; *Aleut Corporation v. Arctic Slope Regional Corporation,* 417 F.Supp. 900; *Tyonek Native Corporation v. Secretary of the Interior,* 629 F.Supp. 554. In the latter case the village of Tyonek in 1974, pursuant to the terms of the Alaska Native Claims Settlement Act, claimed certain lands within its vicinity only to find that they had already been claimed by Alaska under the Mental Health Enabling Act of 1956. As a result the Bureau of Land Management rejected Tyonek's application for the acreage. Tyonek filed suit claiming that Alaska did not have valid title to the land. But in 1986 the U.S. District Court ruled in favor of Alaska stating that the language of A.N.C.S.A. did not allow native claims to nullify state interest in the property.

32. *AKN* 2 (Apr. 1970): 12; *AKN* 9 (Early Spring 1977): 10–11; *AKN* 10 (Autumn 1978): 21; see generally Berry, *The Alaska Pipeline.*

33. 15 Stat. 539 (1867); 23 Stat. 26 (1884); 31 Stat. 321, 330 (1900); 72 Stat. 339 (1959).

34. *AKN* 3 (Late Autumn 1971): 6; *AKN* 3 (Early Winter 1971): 4; *AKN* 9 (Early Spring 1977): 10–11; *AKN* 10 (Autumn 1978): 21.

35. Thomas Berger, *Village Journey: The Report of the Alaska Native Review Commission* (New York, 1985), 59–70; Alaska National Interest Lands Conservation Act, 94 Stat. 2371 (1980).

36. 742 F.2d 1145.

37. *Village of Gambell v. Hodel,* 774 F.2d 1414; *Amoco Production Co. v. Village of Gambell,* 107 S.Ct. 1396.

38. 803 F.2d 1016; *Juneau Empire,* 23 May 1986.

39. Patricia Barcott, "The Alaska Native Claims Settlement Act: Survival of a Special Relationship," *University of San Francisco Law Review* 18 (1981): 157; John F. Walsh, "Settling the Alaska Native Claims Settlement Act," *Stanford Law Review* 38 (1985): 244–245. For a detailed study on the legal rights of Alaska Natives see David S. Case, *Alaska Natives and American Laws* (Fairbanks, 1984).

40. *Anchorage Daily News,* 30 Oct. 1987; Alaska Native Claims Settlement Act Amendments of 1987, 101 Stat. 1788 (1988).

41. Executive Order 11670, *Weekly Compilation of Presidential Documents,* 8 (22 May 1972): 880–881; *AKN* 2 (Nov.–Dec. 1970): 9; *AKN* 3 (Jan.–Feb. 1971): 15; *AKN* 3 (Late Spring 1971): 43; *AKN* 4 (Late Spring 1972): 8.

42. *Wassaja,* 5 (May 1977): 17; *Choctaw Nation v. Oklahoma,* 397 U.S. 620; *AKN* 8 (Early Autumn 1976): 18; *AKN* 10 (Late Spring 1978): 15; *United States v. Dann,* 105 S.Ct. 1058.

43. *United States v. Dann,* 105 S.Ct. 1058.

44. *United States v. Gemmill,* 535 F.2d 1145; *AKN* 2 (July–Aug. 1970): 1, 2, 4; *AKN* 2 (Sept. 1970): 28, 31–32; *AKN* 2 (Nov.–Dec. 1970): 12, 13, 16, 17; *AKN* 3 (Mar. 1971): 44; *AKN* 3 (Early Summer 1971): 12; *AKN* 3 (Late Summer 1971): 21; *AKN* 4 (Early Spring 1972): 8; *AKN* 4 (Late Spring 1972): 12; *AKN* 4 (Late Autumn 1972): 13; *AKN* 6 (Late Spring, 1974): 38; *Wassaja* 5 (Feb. 1977): 20.

45. *Narragansett Tribe of Indians v. Southern Rhode Island Land Development Corp.,* 418 F.Supp. 798; *Narragansett Tribe of Indians v. Murphy,* 426 F.Supp. 132; 92 Stat. 813 (1978); *Wassaja* 7 (Apr. 1979): 13; *AKN* 10 (Autumn 1978): 11; *Norman Transcript,* 19 Aug. 1979.

46. *Joint Tribal Council of the Passamaquoddy v. Morton,* 528 F.2d 370, 376–377, 380; *Wassaja* 4 (Jan. 1976): 3; *Wassaja* 4 (June 1976): 15.

47. William B. Gunter, "Recommendation to President Carter From William B. Gunter," *American Indian Law Review* 5 (1977): 427–430; Telegram, "Passamaquoddy and Penobscot Tribes to Carter," 26 July 1977, *American Indian Law Review* 5 (1977): 430; *AKN* 9 (Autumn 1977): 18–19.

48. 123 *CR* 5692-99 (1977); *Wassaja* 5 (Apr. 1977): 1, 3.

49. *AKN* 10 (Early Spring 1978): 22; *Wassaja* 7 (Mar. 1979): 8.

50. Maine Indian Claims Settlement Act, 94 Stat. 1785 (1980).

51. HR3; *AKN* (Late Spring 1980): 24.

52. *Oneida Indian Nation v. New York,* 649 F.Supp. 420.

53. *County of Oneida v. Oneida Indian Nation (Oneida II),* 105 S.Ct. 1245; see *Oneida Indian Nation v. County of Oneida (Oneida I),* 414 US Reports 661. The Court's decision should make it easier for tribes to win in other cases involving state violations of the Trade and Intercourse Act.

54. *New York Times,* 5 Mar. 1985, 13 Apr. 1986, 29 Dec. 1986.

55. *South Carolina v. Catawba Indian Nation,* 106 S.Ct. 2039.

56. *Mashpee Tribe v. Secretary of Interior,* 820 F.2d 480; *Mashpee Tribe v. New Seabury Corp.,* 592 F.2d 575.

57. HR10.

58. Wampanoag Tribal Council of Gay Head Inc. Indian Claims Settlement Act of 1987, 101 Stat. 704 (1987); Native American Rights Fund, *News Release,* 31 Aug. 1987. The Miccosukee and Mashantucket Pequot also obtained land claims settlements for state violations of the Trade and Intercourse Act; Florida Indian Land Claims Settlement Act (Miccosukee), 96 Stat. 2012 (1982), 25 *USCA* sec. 1741; Connecticut Indian Land Claims Act (Mashantucket Pequot), 97 Stat. 851 (1983), 25 *USCA* sec. 1751.

59. 59 *CR* 7453 (1920); Hawaiian Homes Commission Act, 42 Stat. 108 (1921).

60. Bureau of the Census, *Fourteenth Census of the United States,* 1920, vol. 3, *Population* (Washington, D.C., 1922), 1172–73; Carey McWilliams, *Brothers Under the Skin* (Boston, 1948), 182.

61. HR2, 6; Gavan Daws, *Shoal of Time: A History of the Hawaiian Islands* (New York, 1968), 297.

62. See note 61.

63. SH2, 118.

64. 42 Stat. 108 (1921); Theon Wright, *The Disenchanted Isles* (New York, 1972), 32–35; Ralph Kuykendall and Lorin Gill, *Hawaii in the World War* (Honolulu, 1928), 403.

65. SH1, 38.

66. HH2, 121–122, 127–128.

67. Ibid.; HR2, 6; 42 Stat. 108 (1921).

68. 42 Stat. 108 (1921).

69. 42 Stat. 1221 (1923); Hawaii Department of Hawaiian Home Lands, *Annual Report, 1976–1977,* 13.

70. Hawaii Department of Hawaiian Home Lands, *Annual Report, 1976–1977,* 13, 26–27. Since statehood, the Department of Hawaiian Home Lands, a state agency, has managed the homelands program. The Hawaiian Homes Commission, an executive committee, heads the department.

71. Diana Hansen, *The Homestead Papers: A Critical Analysis of the Management of the Department of Hawaiian Home Lands* (Honolulu, 1971), 5, 13.

72. Ibid., 37.

73. Ibid., 3–4; SH4, 21; HH-SH1, 278; Hawaii Department of Hawaiian Home Lands, *Annual Report, 1976–1977,* 14.

74. Hansen, *Homestead Papers,* 4–7; SH4, 23, 149. During the 1976 hearings, Chairman of the Department of Hawaiian Home Lands Billie Beamer noted that the 112,000 acres leased to business had a total rental price of $730,000.

75. Hansen, *Homestead Papers,* 11–18; SH4, 281; Herman S. Doi, *Legal Aspects of the Hawaiian Homes Program,* Hawaii Legislative Reference Bureau Rept. no. 1A (Honolulu, 1964), 14–16, discussed the question of contracts to pineapple companies. He quoted Hawaii attorney generals' opinions that such arrangements were not considered subleases. In 1960 a state court decision upheld such contracts but would not allow a Hawaiian homesteader to divide her tract and sublease part of it to her daughter.

76. SH4, 258; Hansen, *Homestead Papers,* 4, 7–10, 38, 54; Donald Clegg and Richard Bird, *Program Study and Evaluation of the Department of Hawaiian Home Lands, State of Hawaii* (Honolulu, 1971), 51–52; Hawaii Constitutional Conven-

tion File, 1978, AH (testimony of Ginger Wurdeman and Kaipo Prejean). The Department of Hawaiian Home Lands *Annual Report 1976–1977,* listed thirty-one executive orders by the governor for almost 17,000 acres.

77. Hansen, *Homestead Papers,* 10, 36–37, 51.

78. 73 Stat. 4-6 (1959), sec. 4, 5; Hawaii Constitution art. 12, sec. 2. In every bill providing for statehood, Congress had included a provision requiring the perpetuation of the homelands program; for example, see SR3.

79. 113 *CR* 13465 (1967); 114 *CR* 7120 (1968).

80. 103 *CR* 4706 (1957); 105 *CR* 55 (1959).

81. Hawaii Constitutional Convention File, 1978 (testimony of Kaipo Prejean, Winona Freitas, Keoni Agard, and Merwyn Jones).

82. Ibid.; Hawaii Constitution art. 12; *Hawaii Revised Statutes,* Organic Laws, titles 1–5, chp. 1–42 (1985); 100 Stat. 3143 (1986).

83. Commission on Civil Rights, Hawaii Advisory Committee, *Breach of Trust? Native Hawaiian Homelands* (Washington, D.C., 1980), 15–17; *Keaukaha-Panaewa Community Association v. Hawaiian Homes Commission (Keaukaha I),* 588 F.2d 1216.

84. *Keaukaha I,* 588 F.2d 1216; *Keaukaha-Panaewa Community Association v. Hawaiian Homes Commission (Keaukaha II),* 739 F.2d 1467; *Honolulu Advertiser,* 22 Mar. 1987; SH17, 809–814.

85. SH17, 345–348; Federal-State Task Force on the Hawaiian Homes Commission Act, *Report to United States Secretary of the Interior and the Governor of the State of Hawaii* (Honolulu, 1983).

86. SH17, 253–254, 276–279, 475, 797–805.

87. *Honolulu Advertiser,* 1, 3, 30 Sept. 1986; *Los Angeles Times,* 20 Apr. 1986; *San Francisco Chronicle,* 29 Sept. 1985.

88. See note 87.

89. 73 Stat. 4-6, sec. 5; Hawaii Constitution art. 12, sec. 4.

90. The constitutionality of the Office of Hawaiian Affairs has been upheld; *Hoohuli v. Ariyoshi,* 631 F.Supp. 1153. See also John Van Duke, "The Constitutionality of the Office of Hawaiian Affairs," in HH17, 142–207; James Dannenberg, "The Office of Hawaiian Affairs and the Issue of Sovereign Immunity," *University of Hawaii Law Review* 7 (1985): 95–105.

91. *Trustees of the Office of Hawaiian Affairs v. Yamasaki,* 737 P.2d 446; *Price v. Hawaii,* 764 F.2d 623; Note, "Hawaii's Ceded Lands," *University of Hawaii Law Review* 3 (1981): 101–146.

92. For example see SH17, 250–253, 261–270, 783–785, 788–792.

93. See chapter 7, 135–137.

94. HH3, 274–275.

95. HH-SH1, 282 (statement of Dorothea Whittle).

96. Hawaii Constitution art. 12, sec. 5.

97. HH-SH1, 29, 242; SH4, 104, 149, 259; Hawaii Constitutional Convention File, 1978 (testimony of Nina Bowman, Anne N. Kauaihilo, Benson K. Lee, and Alfred Wong).

98. Myra Jean F. Tuggle, "The Protect Kaho'olawe 'Ohana: Cultural Revitalization in a Contemporary Hawaiian Movement" (Master's thesis, University of Hawaii, 1982), 59–61; *San Francisco Chronicle,* 11 June 1984; *New York Times,* 25 Apr. 1982.

99. See note 98; *San Diego Union,* 26 Oct. 1986.

100. *Honolulu Star-Bulletin,* 4 July 1919. This attitude was reflected throughout the hearings held in Hawaii and in statements made at the 1978 Hawaii constitutional convention; for example see HH-SH1, 242–243; SH4, 148–149; Hawaii Constitutional Convention File, 1978 (testimony of Joyce Kainoa).

101. *Dedman v. Board of Land and Natural Resources,* 740 P.2d 28; *Honolulu Advertiser,* 23 Apr. 1987.

102. *Dedman v. Board of Land and Natural Resources,* 740 P.2d 28.

103. See generally Hawaii Constitutional Convention File, 1978 (testimony on adverse possession); *Honolulu Advertiser,* 8 Sept. 1978.

104. *Hawaii Revised Statutes* sec. 560, 2-105.5 (1987).

Chapter 8

1. Privy Council Minutes, 13 July 1850, quoted in *Kalipi v. Hawaiian Trust Co.,* 656 P.2d 745; Hawaii Constitution art. 12, sec. 8; Levy, "Native Hawaiian Land Rights," 868–869. Section 7-1 of the *Hawaii Revised Statutes* provides: Where the landlords have obtained, or may hereafter obtain, allodial titles to their lands, the people on each of their lands shall not be deprived of the right to take firewood, house-timber, aho cord, thatch, or ki leaf, from the land on which they live, for their own private use, but they shall not have a right to take such articles to sell for profit. The people shall also have a right to drinking water, and running water, and the right of way. The springs of water, running water, and roads shall be free to all, on all lands granted in fee simple; provided that this shall not be applicable to wells and watercourses, which individuals have made for their own use.

2. Article 12, section 7 provides: The State reaffirms and shall protect all rights, customarily and traditionally exercised for subsistence, cultural and religious purposes and possessed by ahupua'a tenants who are descendants of Native Hawaiians who inhabited the Hawaiian Islands prior to 1778, subject to the right of the State to regulate such rights.

3. *Kalipi v. Hawaiian Trust Co.,* 656 P.2d 745, 749. For purposes of section 1-1, ancient Hawaiian usage or custom has been defined as usage that existed prior to November 25, 1892; *State v. Zimring,* 479 P.2d 202.

4. *Hawaii Revised Statutes* 174C-101 (1987).

5. Tuggle, "Protect Kaho'olawe 'Ohana," 40–41, 90. In 1968 the state supreme court ruled that the boundary between public and private land was the "upper reaches of the wash of waves, usually evidenced by the edge of vegetation or by the line of debris left by the wash of waves"; *In Re Ashford,* 440 P.2d 76, 77. Five years later the court added that "where the wash of waves is shown by both debris line and vegetation line further inland, the latter is the boundary"; *County of Hawaii v. Sotomura,* 517 P.2d 57.

6. *Hawaii Revised Statutes* sec. 115-1 to 115-8; *Akau v. Olohana Corp.,* 652 P.2d 1130. For a legal analysis of the public access issue, see Michael Anthony Town and William Wai Lim Yuen, "Public Access to Beaches in Hawaii: 'A Social Necessity'," *Hawaii Bar Journal* 10 (1973): 5; Michael D. Tom, "Hawaiian Beach Access: A Customary Right," 26 *Hastings Law Journal* 26 (1975): 823.

7. *Palama v. Sheehan,* 440 P.2d 95; *Rogers v. Pedro,* 642 P.2d 549.

8. See *McBryde Sugar Co. v. Robinson,* 504 P.2d 1330.

9. *Hawaii Revised Statutes* sec. 7-1 (1985); *McBryde Sugar Co. v. Robinson,* 504 P.2d 1330. The McBryde decision was appealed to the federal district court, who ruled in favor of the appellant sugar companies, holding that the state supreme court's decision had deprived them of private property without just compensation. The state appealed to the Ninth Circuit Court of Appeals and then to the U.S. Supreme Court. The Supreme Court vacated the lower court's opinion and remanded the case for consideration in light of *Williamson County Regional Planning Commission v. Hamilton Bank,* 473 U.S. 172; *Robinson v. Ariyoshi,* 441 F.Supp. 559, aff'd 753 F.2d 1468, vacated and remanded 106 S.Ct. 3269. See also *Robinson v. Ariyoshi,* 658 P.2d 287; and *Reppun v. Board of Water Supply,* 656 P.2d 57, where the court ruled that a Hawaii landowner with riparian rights could not maintain an action for diversion unless he could show that it caused actual harm to his own reasonable use of the stream water.

10. *Hawaii Revised Statutes* 174C-101 (L 1987 c. 45, pt. of 2).

11. Ibid. See also *Hawaii Revised Statutes* 7-1 (1985); Hawaii Constitution art. 12, sec. 7 (1985).

12. 198 US Reports 371, 381 (1905).

13. *Maison v. Confederated Tribes of Umatilla Indian Reservation,* 314 F.2d 169; *United States. v. Oregon,* 302 F.Supp. 899.

14. *Confederated Tribes of the Umatilla Indian Reservation v. Maison,* 262 F.Supp. 871, 873; *Kimball v. Callahan,* 493 F.2d 564; *Oregon Department of Fish and Wildlife v. Klamath Indian Tribe,* 105 S.Ct. 3420.

15. *Puyallup Tribe v. Department of Game (Puyallup I),* 391 US Reports 392, 398.

16. *Department of Game v. Puyallup (Puyallup II),* 414 US Reports 44, 48; *Antoine v. Washington,* 420 US Reports 194, 207.

17. *United States v. Washington,* 496 F.2d 620, 621; *Department of Game v. Puyallup Tribe,* 548 P.2d 1058.

18. *Puyallup Tribe v. Department of Game (Puyallup III),* 433 U.S. 165.

19. *Sohappy v. Smith,* 302 F.Supp. 899, 907.

20. *Sohappy v. Smith,* 529 F.2d 570. The Columbia River Fishery Management program is discussed in *United States v. Oregon,* 14 *Indian Law Reporter* 3151 (1987).

21. *Settler v. Lameer,* 507 F.2d 231; *Oregon v. Jim,* 725 P.2d 365; *Oregon v. Settler,* 726 P.2d 410; *United States v. Sohappy,* 770 F.2d 816.

22. *United States v. Washington,* 384 F.Supp. 312, 340–343; For an examination of the Northwest fishing controversy, see American Friends Service Committee, *UnCommon Controversy: Fishing Rights of the Muckleshoot, Puyallup, and Nisqually Indians* (Seattle, 1970); and Fay G. Cohen, *Treaties on Trial: The Continuing Controversy over Northwest Indian Fishing Rights* (Seattle, 1986). *Akwesasne Notes* also included numerous articles on the controversy.

23. 573 F.2d 1123, 1126.

24. Ibid., 1128; *Wassaja* 4 (July 1976): 7.

25. *Puget Sound Gillnetters Association v. United States,* 573 F.2d 1123.

26. Judge Boldt remarked that the state had failed to produce "any credible evidence showing any instance" of Indian destruction or depletion of the fish supply, *United States v. Washington,* 384 F.Supp. 312, 338–339, 420 n. 26; *Puget Sound*

Gillnetters Association v. United States District Court, 573 F.2d 1123, 1126, 1129. Ralph Johnson, "The States Versus Indian Off-Reservation Fishing: A United States Supreme Court Error," *Washington Law Review* 47 (1972): 207–236, discussed the detrimental effects of state conservation laws on Indian fisherman.

27. 573 F.2d 1123; Cohen, *Treaties on Trial,* 107–109.

28. *Wassaja* 4 (Feb. 1976): 10; *Wassaja* 5 (May 1977): 19.

29. John Echohawk, et. al. to Griffin Bell, 19 Aug. 1978, 5 *Indian Law Reporter* M45-55 (1978).

30. Ibid., M48-49.

31. *Washington v. Washington State Commercial Passenger Fishing Association,* 443 US Reports 658.

32. *United States v. Washington,* 759 F.2d 1353; *United States v. Washington,* 761 F.2d 1404; *United States v. Washington,* 774 F.2d 1470. The U.S. Court for the Western District of Washington retained jurisdiction. A compilation of the court's major post-trial substantive orders issued from July 1978 through 31 Dec. 1985 is found in *United States v. Washington,* 626 F.Supp. 1405.

33. *People v. Jondreau,* 384 Mich. 539; *Wassaja* 4 (July 1976): 17; *Wassaja* 5 (Feb. 1977): 13; *People v. LeBlanc,* 248 N.W.2d 199; HH4, 209–210, 212.

34. *United States v. Michigan,* 471 F.Supp. 192, remanded 623 F.2d 448; *United States v. Michigan,* 520 F.Supp. 207.

35. *United States v. Michigan,* 520 F.Supp. 209.

36. Ibid., 210.

37. *United States v. Michigan,* 653 F.2d 277, 278–79.

38. Ibid., 279; *United States v. Michigan,* 520 F.Supp. 207; *United States v. Michigan,* 534 F.Supp. 668.

39. HH4, 190–194.

40. *United States v. Michigan,* 520 F.Supp 210 n. 5; Getches and Wilkinson, *Federal Indian Law,* 751.

41. *State v. Coffee,* 556 P.2d 1185; *In Re Wilson,* 634 P.2d 363.

42. *Menominee Tribe of Indians v. United States,* 391 US Reports 404.

43. *Klamath and Modoc Tribes v. Maison,* 139 F.Supp. 634; *Klamath and Modoc Tribes v. Maison,* 338 F.2d 620.

44. *Kimball v. Callahan (Kimball I),* 493 F.2d 564.

45. *Kimball v. Callahan (Kimball II),* 590 F.2d 768.

46. 105 S.Ct. 3420.

47. 576 F.2d 145.

48. 334 F.Supp. 1001; see discussion of litigation's background in *Minnesota v. Forge,* 262 N.W.2d 341. In 1983, the U.S. Supreme Court in *Solem v. Bartlett,* 465 US Reports 463, discussed the factors that a court should analyze in determining whether a reservation had been disestablished.

49. *Minnesota Statutes Annotated* sec. 97A.151, 97A.155, 97A.161 (West, 1986). For other successful Indian fishing rights cases in Minnesota, see *White Earth Band of Chippewa v. Alexander,* 683 F.2d 1129; *State v. Clark,* 282 N.W.2d 902.

50. *Cheyenne-Arapaho Tribes v. Oklahoma,* 618 F.2d 665.

51. *Confederated Tribes of the Colville Indian Reservation v. Washington,* 412 F.Supp. 651, rev'd 591 F.2d 89; *Arnett v. Five Gill Nets,* 121 Cal. Reptr. 906.

52. *Wassaja* 7 (Mar. 1979): 11; *Wassaja* 7 (Apr. 1979): 3; *Wassaja* 4 (Aug. 1976): 17; *Wassaja* 4 (Oct. 1976): 15; *AKN* 10 (Autumn 1978): 17.

53. *United States v. Eberhardt*, 789 F.2d 1354; *Mattz v. California*, 14 *Indian Law Reporter* 5088 (Cal.Ct.App. 7 Oct. 1987).

54. *Montana v. United States*, 450 US Reports 544.

55. *New Mexico v. Mescalero Apache Tribe*, 462 US Reports 324; *White Mountain Apache Tribe v. Bracker*, 448 US Reports 136.

GLOSSARY

aboriginal title   The legal title to land claimed by an indigenous group based upon their ancestors' use and occupancy.

adverse possession   Acquiring title to land by occupying it for a period of time. The conditions and length of the occupancy required vary among the different states.

alienation of land   The transfer from one person to another of title or other rights to land.

ahupua'a   Ideally, a pie-shaped unit of land with the apex at the top of a mountain or in high country. The wide range of elevations provides a variety of flora and fauna that helps make the land unit self-sufficient.

'āina   Land.

ali'i   Hawaiian royalty.

ali'i 'ai moku   Hawaiian royalty who govern a *moku* (district).

extinguish title   To abolish rights to land.

fee simple   Absolute, unrestricted ownership of an estate, which the owner may unconditionally alienate or dispose of as he wishes.

geothermal development   Establishment of a method to convert the natural heat of the earth's interior into useful energy.

haku   A master, owner, or employer.

haole   A white person, Caucasian.

heiau   Place of worship; shrine.

hui   A transitional form of Hawaiian land tenure in which communally owned tracts of land are allotted to individual families to farm.

'ili   A subdivision of an *ahupua'a.*

'ili kūpono   An independent subdivision of land within an *ahupua'a*. The administrators pay tribute directly to the king instead of to the *ahupua'a* overseer.

kahuna   A ritual specialist, sorcerer, or priest.

kālaimoku   The chief's political and military administrator in precontact times.

229

Kāne   One of the four major Hawaiian deities; associated with maleness.

kapus   Religious prohibitions often observed during certain days of the month.

kīhāpai   Field.

koa   *(Acacia koa)* The largest and most economically important tree native to the Hawaiian islands. Its wood was used for canoes, containers, and housing.

kō'ele   A small piece of land cultivated by a commoner for the exclusive use of the *ali'i*.

konohiki   The manager of an *ahupua'a,* who worked under supervision of the *ali'i* but retained some fishing and land rights.

kuhina nui   The King's prime minister during the monarchy.

kuleana   The right or authority to possess a small piece of land within an *ahupua'a;* farm.

lele   A detached parcel of land belonging to an *'ili* but located within another tract of land.

Lono   One of four major Hawaiian deities; associated with fertility, medicine, and other attributes.

maka'āinana   A commoner who usually tilled the soil.

Makahiki festival   An ancient celebration beginning in the middle of October and lasting until the middle of February. The god Lono presided over the festival, which included religious rituals, games, a taboo on war, and payment of tribute to the *ali'i*.

mō'ī   Sovereign kings or queens who were second in the ruling hierarchy, ranking below the chiefs descended from the god Kāne.

moku   A district, island, or section.

mo'o'āina   A land unit farmed by extended family households.

'ohana   Family or kin group.

olonā   *(Touchardia latifolia)* A native shrub whose bark contained a durable fiber that was used for making fishnets.

pili grass   *(Heteropogon contortus)* A grass used to make thatch houses.

tapa (kapa)   Clothing or quilts made from the bark fibers of *wauke* or *mamaki* plants.

taro   *(Colocasia esculenta)* A plant whose starchy rhizome was a major food source for pre-Cook Hawai'i.

usufruct   The right to use and enjoy the benefit of land or property that belongs to someone else.

wauke   *(Broussonetia papyrifera)* A small tree whose bark was used to make *tapa*.

BIBLIOGRAPHY

Manuscript Collections

Anderson, Richard. Papers. Archives of Hawaii, Honolulu.

Chamberlain, Levi. Journal. Hawaiian Mission Children's Society Library, Honolulu.

Colcord, John. Journal. Archives of Hawaii, Honolulu.

Foreign Office and Executive File. Archives of Hawaii, Honolulu.

Hawaii Constitutional Convention File, 1978. Archives of Hawaii, Honolulu.

Hunnewell, James. Papers. Hawaiian Mission Children's Society Library, Honolulu.

Interior Department Letter Books. Archives of Hawaii, Honolulu.

Legislature Records. Archives of Hawaii, Honolulu.

Privy Council Records. Archives of Hawaii, Honolulu.

Richards, William. Manuscript. Archives of Hawaii, Honolulu.

U.S. Department of State. Dispatches From United States Consuls in Honolulu, 1820–1903. National Archives. Record Series M-144.

U.S. Department of State. Dispatches From United States Ministers in Hawaii, 1843–1900. National Archives. Record Series T-30.

U.S. Department of State. Notes From the Hawaiian Legation in the United States to the Department of State, 1841–1899. National Archives. Record Series T-160.

U.S. Congressional Documents and Publications

CD. *Register of Debates in Congress*. 14 vols. Washington, D.C., 1825–1837.

CG. *Congressional Globe*. 46 vols. Washington, D.C., 1834–1837.

CR. *Congressional Record*. Vols. 59–124. Washington, D.C., 1920–1978.

CCJ. *Journals of the Continental Congress, 1774–1789*. 34 vols. Washington, D.C., 1904–1937.

House Executive Documents

HED1. *Message of President, Transmitting Copies of Correspondence in War with Modoc Indians.* 43d Cong., 1st sess., 1874. H. Ex. Doc. 122.
HED2. *Presidential Message on Hawaiian Islands.* 53d Cong., 2d sess., 1893. H. Ex. Doc. 47.
HED3. *Correspondence, Diplomatic and Naval, Relating to Hawaii.* 53d Cong., 2d sess., 1893. H. Ex. Doc. 48.

House Hearings

HH1. Committee on the Territories. *Leasing of Land in Hawaii: Hearings on H.R. 17599.* 62d Cong., 2d sess., 1912.
HH2. ———. *To Amend An Act to Provide Government for Hawaii, as Amended, to Establish Hawaiian Homes Commission, and for Other Purposes: Hearings on H.R. 13500.* 66th Cong., 2d sess., 1920.
HH3. Committee on Interior and Insular Affairs. Subcommittee on Indian Affairs. *Hawaiian Native Claims Settlement Act: Hearings on H.R. 1944.* 94th Cong., 1st sess., 1975. Committee Serial No. 94-2.
HH4. Committee on Merchant Marine and Fisheries. Subcommittee on Fisheries and Wildlife Conservation and the Environment. *Indian Fishing Rights: Hearings on the Question of the Extent to which the Federal Government May Help Resolve Conflicts Among Competing Users of the Great Lakes Fishery Resources.* 95th Cong., 2d sess., 1978. Committee Serial No. 95-27.
HH5. Committee on Interior and Insular Affairs. *Native Hawaiian Study Commission Report: Oversight Hearing.* 98th Cong., 2d sess., 1984. Committee Serial No. 98-44.
HH6. Committee on Interior and Insular Affairs. Subcommittee on Water and Power Resources. *Recommendations of the Garrison Diversion Unit Commission, Hearing on H.R. 1116.* 99th Cong., 1st sess., 1985. Committee Serial No. 99-1.

House and Senate Hearings

HH-SH1. House Committee on Interior and Insular Affairs. Subcommittee on Indian Affairs and Public Lands. Senate Committee on Energy and Natural Resources. Subcommittee on Public Lands and Resources. *Hawaiian Native Claims Settlement Commission: Joint Hearings on S.J. Res. 4 and H.J. Res. 526.* 95th Cong., 1st sess., 1977. Publication No. 95-83.

House Reports

HR1. *Report on Lands in Severalty to Indians.* 46th Cong., 2d sess., 1880. H. Rept. 1576.
HR2. *Rehabilitation of Native Hawaiians: Report to Accompany H.R. 13500.* 66th Cong., 2d sess., 1920. H. Rept. 839.
HR3. Committee on Interior and Insular Affairs. *Providing for the Settlement of*

Land Claims of Indians in the State of Maine: Report to Accompany H.R. 7919. 96th Cong., 2d sess., 1980. H. Rept. 96-1353.

HR4. ———. *Permitting Indian Tribes to Enter into Certain Agreements for the Disposition of Tribal Mineral Resources: Report on S. 1894.* 97th Cong., 2d sess., 1982. H. Rept. 97-746.

HR5. ———. *Water Rights of the Ak-Chin Indian Community: Report to Accompany H.R. 6206.* 98th Cong., 2d sess., 1984. H. Rept. 98-1026.

HR6. ———. *Settling Unresolved Claims Relating to Certain Allotted Indian Lands on the White Earth Indian Reservation, to Remove Clouds from the Titles to Certain Lands.* 99th Cong., 2d sess., 1986. H. Rept. 99-489.

HR7. ———. *Declaring that the United States Holds Certain Public Domain Lands in Trust for the Pueblo of Zia: Report to Accompany H.R. 5167.* 99th Cong., 2d sess., 1986. H. Rept. 99-819.

HR8. ———. *Providing for the Settlement of Certain Claims of the Papago Tribe Arising from the Operation of Painted Rock Dam, and for Other Purposes: Report to Accompany H.R. 4216.* 99th Cong., 2d sess., 1986. H. Rept. 99-851.

HR9. ———. *Providing for the Settlement of Certain Claims of the Papago Tribe of Arizona Arising from the Construction of Tat Momolikot Dam, and for Other Purposes: Report to Accompany H.R. 4217.* 99th Cong., 2d sess., 1986. H. Rept. 99-852.

HR10. ———. *Settling Indian Land Claims in the Town of Gay Head, Massachusetts, and for Other Purposes: Report to Accompany H.R. 2868.* 99th Cong., 2d sess., 1986. H. Rept. 99-918.

Senate Executive Documents

SED1. *Hawaii, Its Natural Resources and Opportunities for Home-Making.* 60th Cong., 2d sess., 1909. S. Doc. 668.

SED2. *Copy of Correspondence Between Interior Department and Indian Agents and Commissions in California.* 33d Cong., Spec. sess., 1853. S. Ex. Doc. 4.

SED3. *Evidence Taken at Denver and Fort Lyon, on Sand Creek Massacre.* 39th Cong., 2d sess., 1867. S. Ex. Doc. 26.

SED4. *Message of President on Agreement with Ute Indians.* 46th Cong., 2d sess., 1880. S. Ex. Doc. 114.

SED5. *Message of President on Report of Commission Appointed to Ascertain Fact in Regard to Removal of Ponca Indians.* 46th Cong., 3d sess., 1881. S. Ex. Doc. 30.

SED6. *Message From the President of the United States Transmitting Correspondence Respecting Relations Between the United States and the Hawaiian Islands from September, 1820, to January, 1893.* 52d Cong., 2d sess., 1893. S. Ex. Doc. 77.

Senate Hearings

SH1. Committee on the Territories. *Hawaiian Homes Commission Act: Hearings on H.R. 13500.* 66th Cong., 3d sess., 1920.

SH2.   ———. *Proposed Amendments to the Organic Act of the Territory of Hawaii, Rehabilitation and Colonization of Hawaiians . . . : Hearings on H. R. 7257,* 67th Cong., 1st. sess., 1921.

SH3.   Committee on Interior and Insular Affairs. *Hearings . . . on a Bill to Authorize the Secretary of the Interior to Grant Certain Lands to Alaska Natives, Settle Alaska Native Land Claims and for Other Purposes.* Pt. 1, Appendix C, 90th Cong., 2d sess., 1968.

SH4.   ———. *Establishing the Hawaiian Aboriginal Claims Settlement Study Commission: Hearings on S.J. Res. 155.* 94th Cong., 2d sess., 1976.

SH5.   Select Committee on Indian Affairs. *Water for Five Arizona Indian Tribes for Farming Operations: Hearings on S. 905.* 95th Cong., 1st sess., 1977.

SH6.   ———. *Pueblo Trust Lands: Hearing on S. 2358 and S. 2588.* 95th Cong., 2d sess., 1978.

SH7.   ———. *Conveyance of Federal Land to the Ute Mountain Ute Tribe: Hearing on S. 2066.* 96th Cong., 2d sess., 1980.

SH8.   ———. *Leases Involving the Secretary of the Interior and the Northern Cheyenne Indian Reservation: Hearing on S. 2126.* 96th Cong., 2d sess., 1980.

SH9.   ———. *Disbursal of Lac Courte Oreilles Band Trust Funds: Hearing on S. 1890.* 97th Cong., 1st sess., 1981.

SH10.   ———. *Hearing on Federal Supervision of Oil and Gas Leases on Indian Lands, Pts. 1–3.* 97th Cong., 1st sess., 1981.

SH11.   ———. *Hearing on Oil Removal from Blackfeet Lease.* 97th Cong., 1st sess., 1981.

SH12.   ———. *To Declare That the United States Holds in Trust for the Pascua Yaqui Tribe of Arizona Certain Land in Pima County, Arizona: Hearing on H.R. 4364.* 97th Cong., 2d sess., 1982.

SH13.   ———. *Mashantucket Pequot Indian Land Claims: Hearing on S. 1499.* 98th Cong., 1st sess., 1983. S. Hrg. 98-877.

SH14.   ———. *A Bill to Declare that the United States Holds Certain Lands in Trust for the Makah Indian Tribe, Washington: Hearing on H.R. 3376.* 98th Cong., 2d sess., 1984. S. Hrg. 98-798.

SH15.   ———. *Pueblo de Cochiti Lands Bill: Hearing on S. 2403.* 98th Cong., 2d sess., 1984. S. Hrg. 98-880.

SH16.   ———. *Zuni Indian Tribe Lands Bill: Hearing on S. 2201.* 98th Cong., 2d sess., 1984. S. Hrg. 98-892.

SH17.   Committee on Energy and Natural Resources. *Hearings on the Report of the Native Hawaiians Study Commission.* 98th Cong., 2d sess., 1984. S. Hrg. 98-1257, pt. 1.

SH18.   Select Committee on Indian Affairs. *White Earth Indian Land Claims Settlement: Hearing on S. 1396.* 99th Cong., 1st sess., 1985. S. Hrg. 99-261.

SH19.   Select Committee on Indian Affairs and Committee on Energy and Natural Resources. *Indian Water Claims in San Diego County, CA: Joint Hearings on S. 2676.* 99th Cong., 2d sess., 1986. S. Hrg. 99-930.

SH20.   Select Committee on Indian Affairs. *Settlement of Certain Land and Water Rights Claims of the Papago Tribe of Arizona: Hearing on S. 2105, S. 2106, S. 2107.* 99th Cong., 2d sess., 1986. S. Hrg. 99-935.

Senate Reports

SR1. "The Chivington Massacre." In *Condition of the Indian Tribes: Report of the Joint Special Commission*. 39th Cong., 2d sess., 1867. S. Rept. 156.

SR2. *Report on Inquiry into Whether Irregularities Have Occurred in Diplomatic or Other Intercourse Between United States and Hawaii in Relation to Recent Political Revolution in Hawaii*. (Morgan Report). 53d Cong., 2d sess., 1893. S. Rept. 227.

SR3. *Statehood for Hawaii: Report to Accompany H.R. 49*. 81st Cong., 2d sess., 1950. S. Rept. 1928, pt. 2.

SR4. *Alaska Native Claims Settlement Act of 1970: Report to Accompany S. 1830*. 91st Cong., 2nd sess., 1970. S. Rept. 925.

SR5. *Taos Indian Land Act: Report on H.J. Res. 471*. 91st Cong., 1st sess., 1970. S. Rept. 1345.

SR6. *Providing for the Settlement of Water Rights Claims of the La Jolla, Rincon, San Pasqual, Pauma, and Pala Bands of Mission Indians in San Diego County, California*. 100th Cong., 1st sess., 1987. S. Rept. 47.

Other Government Documents and Publications

Acts of the General Assembly of the State of Georgia. 1828.

American Indian Policy Review Commission. Task Force One. *Final Report on Trust Responsibilities and Federal-Indian Relationship Including Treaty Review . . .* Washington, D.C., 1976.

American State Papers: Indian Affairs. 2 vols. Washington, D.C., 1832–1834.

Board of Indian Commissioners. *Annual Report, 1898, 1922*.

Bureau of the Census. *Fourteenth Census of the United States, 1920*. Vol. 3, *Population*. Washington, D.C., 1922.

Carter, Clarence, ed. *Territorial Papers of the United States*. 26 vols. Washington, D.C., 1934–1956.

Code of Federal Regulations.

Commission on Civil Rights. Hawaii Advisory Committee. *Breach of Trust? Native Hawaiian Homelands*. Washington, D.C., 1980.

Commissioner of Indian Affairs. *Annual Report, 1853*. In S. Doc. 1, 33d Cong., 1st sess., vol. 1.

Commissioner of Indian Affairs. *Annual Report, 1854–1921*.

Department of State. *Papers Relating to the Foreign Relations of the United States for 1881*. Washington, D.C., 1882.

Department of State. *Papers Relating to the Foreign Relations of the United States for 1894*. Appendix 2. Washington, D.C., 1895.

Executive Orders Relating to Indian Reservations. 2 vols. Washington, D.C., 1912, 1922; Reprint, in 1 vol., Wilmington, Delaware, 1975.

Federal Energy Regulatory Commission Reports.

Federal Power Commission Reports.

Federal Register. Vols. 34–52. Washington, D.C., 1969–1987.

Federal-State Task Force on the Hawaiian Homes Commission Act. *Report to*

United States Secretary of the Interior and the Governor of the State of Hawaii. Honolulu, 1983.

Government Accounting Office. *Indian Natural Resources—Part II: Coal, Oil, and Gas—Better Management Can Improve Development and Increase Indian Income and Employment.* Washington, D.C., 1976.

Government Accounting Office. *Oil and Gas Royalty Collections—Serious Financial Management Problems Need Congressional Attention.* Washington, D.C., 1979.

Hawaii Constitution.

Hawaii Department of Hawaiian Home Lands. *Annual Report, 1976–1977.* Honolulu, 1977.

Hawaii Revised Statutes.

Indian Claims Commission. *Indian Claims Commission, August 13, 1946–September 30, 1978: Final Report.* Washington, D.C., 1978.

Kappler, Charles, comp. *Indian Affairs, Laws and Treaties.* 5 vols. Washington, D.C., 1903–1938.

Miller, Hunter, ed. *United States Treaties and Other International Acts of the United States of America.* 8 vols. Washington, D.C., 1937.

Minnesota Statutes Annotated.

Montana Code Annotated. Montana Legislative Council, 1987.

Native Hawaiians Study Commission. *Native Hawaiian Study Commission Report on the Culture, Needs and Concerns of Native Hawaiians.* 2 vols. Washington, D.C., 1983.

Richardson, James, comp. *A Compilation of the Messages and Papers of the Presidents.* 10 vols. Washington, D.C., 1896–1899.

Secretary of the Interior. *Annual Report, 1857–1858.* In S. Ex. Doc. 11, pt. 1, vol. 2, 35th Cong., 1st sess.

Secretary of the Interior. *Annual Report, 1861.* In S. Ex. Doc. 1, pt. 1, 37th Cong., 2d sess.

Secretary of War. *Annual Report, 1877.* In H. Ex. Doc. 1, 45th Cong., 2d sess.

Secretary of War. *Annual Report, 1883.* In H. Ex. Doc. 1, 48th Cong., 1st sess.

Secretary of War. *Annual Report, 1886.* In H. Ex. Doc. 1, 49th Cong., 2d sess.

Territory of Hawaii. *Indices of Awards Made by the Board of Commissioners to Quiet Land Titles in the Hawaiian Islands.* Honolulu, 1929.

United States Code.

United States Code Annotated.

United States Statutes at Large.

Weekly Compilation of Presidential Documents. Washington, D.C., 1965–.

Court Cases

Akau v. Olohana Corp. 652 P.2d 1130 (Haw. 1982).

Alaska v. Udall. 420 F.2d 938 (D.C. Cir. 1969).

Alaska Native Association v. Morton. 459 F.Supp. 459 (D.C. Cir. 1974).

Aleut Corp. v. Arctic Slope Regional Corp. 417 F.Supp. 900 (D.Alaska 1976).

Amoco Production Co. v. Village of Gambell. 107 S.Ct. 1396 (1987).

Anthony v. Kualoa Ranch, Inc. 736 P.2d 55 (Haw. 1987).

Antoine v. Washington. 420 US Reports 194 (1975).

Arizona v. California. 373 US Reports 546 (1963); final decree, 376 US Reports 348 (1964); supplemental decree, 439 US Reports 419 (1979); 460 US Reports 605 (1983).

Arizona v. San Carlos Apache Tribe. 463 US Reports 545 (1983).

Arnett v. Five Gill Nets. 121 Cal. Reptr. 906 (1975), cert. denied 425 US Reports 907 (1976).

Assiniboine and Sioux Tribes of the Fort Peck Indian Reservation v. Board of Oil and Gas Conservation. 792 F.2d 782 (9th Cir. 1986).

Badoni v. Higginson. 638 F.2d 172 (10th Cir. 1980), cert. denied 452 US Reports 954 (1981).

Bishop v. Mahika. 35 Haw. 608 (1940).

Blackfeet Indian Nation v. Hodel. 634 F.Supp. 646 (D.Mont. 1986).

Cappaert v. United States. 426 US Reports 128 (1976).

Carson-Truckee Water Conservancy District v. Clark. 741 F.2d 257 (9th Cir. 1984), cert. denied 105 S.Ct. 1842 (1985).

Carter v. Territory of Hawaii. 14 Haw. 465 (1902), rev'd 194 US Reports 154 (1904) and 200 US Reports 255 (1906).

Cherokee Nation v. Georgia. 30 US Reports (5 Pet.) 1 (1831).

Cheyenne-Arapaho Tribes v. Oklahoma. 618 F.2d 665 (10th Cir. 1980).

Choctaw Nation v. Oklahoma. 397 US Reports 620 (1970).

City of Angoon v. Hodel. 803 F.2d 1016 (9th Cir. 1986).

City and County of Honolulu v. Bennett. 57 Haw. 195 (1976).

City of Sault Ste. Marie v. Andrus. 532 F.Supp. 157 (D.D.C. 1980), aff'd 672 F.2d 893 (D.C. Cir. 1981), cert. denied 459 US Reports 825 (1982).

City of Tacoma v. Andrus. 457 F.Supp. 342 (D.D.C. 1978).

Colorado River Water Conservation Dist. v. United States. 424 US Reports 800 (1976).

Colville Confederated Tribes v. Walton. 460 F.Supp. 1320 (E.D.Wash. 1978), rev'd 647 F.2d 42 (9th Cir. 1981), cert. denied 454 US Reports 1092 (1981); 752 F.2d 397 (9th Cir. 1985).

Confederated Tribes of the Colville Indian Reservation v. Washington. 412 F.Supp. 651 (E.D.Wash. 1976), rev'd 591 F.2d 89 (9th Cir. 1979).

Confederated Tribes of the Umatilla Indian Reservation v. Maison. 262 F.Supp. 871 (D.Ore. 1966).

County of Hawaii v. Sotomura. 517 P.2d 57 (Haw. 1973).

County of Oneida v. Oneida Indian Nation (Oneida II). 105 S.Ct. 1245 (1985).

Crow v. Gullet. 706 F.2d 856 (8th Cir. 1983).

Damon v. Hawaii. 194 US Reports 154 (1904).

Dedman v. Board of Land and Natural Resources. 740 P.2d 28 (Haw. 1987).

Department of Game v. Puyallup Tribe (Puyallup II). 414 US Reports 44 (1973).

Department of Game v. Puyallup Tribe. 548 P.2d 1058 (Wash. 1976).

Escondido Mutual Water v. La Jolla. 466 US Reports 765 (1984).

Federal Power Commission v. Tuscarora Indian Nation. 362 US Reports 99 (1960).

Hana Ranch v. Kaholo. 632 P.2d 293 (Haw.Ct.App. 1981).

Hana Ranch v. Kanakaole. 623 P.2d 885 (Haw.Ct.App. 1981).

Hana Ranch v. Kanakaole. 672 P.2d 550 (Haw. 1983).

Hawaii Housing Authority v. Lyman. 704 P.2d 888 (Haw. 1985).

Hawaii Housing Authority v. Midkiff. 467 US Reports 229 (1984).

Hodel v. Irving. 107 S.Ct. 2076 (1987).

Holly v. Confederated Tribes and Bands of Yakima Indian Nation. 655 F.Supp. 557 (E.D.Wash. 1986).

Hoohuli v. Ariyoshi. 631 F.Supp. 1153 (D.Haw. 1986).

Hustace v. Kapuni. 718 P.2d 1109 (Haw.Ct.App. 1986).

In Re Ashford. 440 P.2d 76 (Haw. 1968).

In Re Wilson. 634 P.2d 363 (Cal. 1981).

Jicarilla Apache Tribe v. United States. 601 F.2d 116 (10th Cir.), cert. denied 444 US Reports 995 (1979).

Johnson v. McIntosh. 21 US Reports (8 Wheat.) 543 (1823).

Joint Tribal Council of the Passamaquoddy Tribe v. Morton. 528 F.2d 370 (1st Cir. 1975).

Kalipi v. Hawaiian Trust Co. 656 P.2d 745 (Haw. 1982).

Keaukaha-Panaewa Community Association v. Hawaiian Homes Commission (Keaukaha I). 588 F.2d 1216 (9th Cir. 1978), cert. denied 444 US Reports 826 (1979).

Keaukaha-Panaewa Community Association v. Hawaiian Homes Commission (Keaukaha II). 739 F.2d 1467 (9th Cir. 1984).

Kimball v. Callahan (Kimball I). 493 F.2d 564 (9th Cir.), cert. denied 419 US Reports 1019 (1974).

Kimball v. Callahan (Kimball II). 590 F.2d 768 (9th Cir.), cert. denied 444 US Reports 826 (1979).

Klamath and Modoc Tribes v. Maison. 139 F.Supp. 634 (D.Ore. 1956).

Klamath and Modoc Tribes v. Maison. 338 F.2d 620 (9th Cir. 1964).

Koniag v. Kleppe. 405 F.Supp. 1360 (D.D.C. 1975).

Kunaknana v. Clark. 742 F.2d 1145 (9th Cir. 1984).

Lac Courte Oreilles Band of Lake Superior Chippewa Indians v. Federal Power Commission. 510 F.2d 198 (D.C. Cir. 1975).

Lai v. Kukahiko. 569 P.2d 352 (Haw. 1977).

Leech Lake Band of Chippewa Indians v. Herbst. 334 F.Supp. 1001 (D.Minn. 1971).

Lyng v. Northwest Indian Cemetery Protective Association. 108 S.Ct. 1319 (1988), rev'd *Northwest Indian Cemetery Protective Association v. Peterson,* 795 F.2d 688 (9th Cir. 1986).

McBryde Sugar Co. v. Robinson. 504 P.2d 1330, aff'd upon reh'g 517 P.2d 26 (1973), cert. denied 417 US Reports 976, appeal dismissed 417 US Reports 962 (1974).

Maison v. Confederated Tribes of Umatilla Indian Reservation. 314 F.2d 169 (9th Cir.), cert. denied 375 US Reports 829 (1963).

Mashpee Tribe v. New Seabury Corp. 592 F.2d 575 (1st Cir. 1979), cert. denied 444 US Reports 866 (1979).

Mashpee Tribe v. Secretary of Interior. 820 F.2d 480 (1st Cir. 1987).

Matter of Determination of Conflicting Rights to the Use of Water From the Salt River Above Granite Reef Dam. 484 F.Supp. 778 (D.Ariz. 1980).

Mattz v. State of California. 14 *Indian Law Reporter* 5088 (Cal.Ct.App. 1987).

Menominee Tribe of Indians v. United States. 391 US Reports 404 (1968).

Metropolitan Water District of Southern California v. United States. 628 F.Supp. 1018 (1986), rev'd 14 *Indian Law Reporter* 2182 (9th Cir. 1987).

Minnesota v. Forge. 262 N.W.2d 341 (Minn. 1977).

Montana v. United States. 450 US Reports 544 (1981).

Narragansett Tribe of Indians v. Murphy. 426 F.Supp. 132 (D.R.I. 1978).

Narragansett Tribe of Indians v. Southern Rhode Island Land Development Corp. 418 F.Supp. 798 (D.R.I. 1976).

Nevada v. United States. 463 US Reports 110 (1983).

New Mexico v. Aamodt. 537 F.2d 1102 (10th Cir. 1976), cert. denied 429 US Reports 1121 (1977).

New Mexico v. Mescalero Apache Tribe. 462 US Reports 324 (1983).

New Mexico ex rel. Reynolds v. Aamodt. 618 F.Supp. 993 (D.N.M. 1985).

Nichols v. Rysavy. 809 F.2d 1317 (8th Cir. 1987).

Oneida Indian Nation v. County of Oneida (Oneida I). 414 US Reports 661 (1974).

Oneida Indian Nation v. New York. 649 F.Supp. 420 (N.D.N.Y. 1986).

Oregon v. Jim. 725 P.2d 365 (Ore.Ct.App. 1986).

Oregon v. Settler. 726 P.2d 410 (Ore.Ct.App. 1986), cert. denied 107 S.Ct. 2461 (1987).

Oregon Department of Fish and Wildlife v. Klamath Indian Tribe. 105 S.Ct. 3420 (1985).

Palama v. Sheehan. 440 P.2d 95 (Haw. 1968).

People v. Jondreau. 384 Mich. 539 (1971).

People v. LeBlanc. 248 N.W.2d 199 (Mich. 1976).

Poka v. Holi. 357 P.2d 100 (Haw. 1960).

Price v. State of Hawaii. 764 F.2d 623 (9th Cir. 1985), cert. denied 474 US Reports 1055, reh'g denied 475 US Reports 1091 (1986).

Puget Sound Gillnetters v. United States District Court. 573 F.2d 1123 (9th Cir. 1978).

Puyallup Tribe v. Department of Game (Puyallup I). 391 US Reports 392 (1968).

Puyallup Tribe v. Department of Game (Puyallup III). 433 US Reports 165 (1977).

Pyramid Lake Paiute Tribe of Indians v. Morton. 354 F.Supp. 252 (D.D.C. 1972 and 1973).

Reppun v. Board of Water Supply. 656 P.2d 57 (Haw. 1982).

Robinson v. Ariyoshi. 441 F.Supp. 559 (D.Haw. 1977), aff'd 753 F.2d 1468 (9th Cir. 1985), vacated and remanded 106 S.Ct. 3269 (1986).

Robinson v. Ariyoshi. 658 P.2d 287 (Haw. 1982), reh'g denied 726 P.2d 1133 (1983).

Rogers v. Pedro. 642 P.2d 549 (Haw.Ct.App. 1982).

Sac and Fox Tribe of the Mississippi in Iowa v. Kicklider. 576 F.2d 145 (8th Cir.), cert. denied 439 US Reports 955 (1978).

Seneca Nation of Indians v. Brucker. 262 F.2d 27 (D.C. Cir.), cert. denied 360 US Reports 909 (1959).

Seneca Nation of Indians v. United States. 338 F.2d 55 (2d Cir. 1964), cert. denied 380 US Reports 952 (1965).

Settler v. Lameer. 507 F.2d 231 (9th Cir. 1974).

Smart v. Luiki. 640 P.2d 1172 (Haw.Ct.App. 1982).

Sohappy v. Smith. 302 F.Supp. 899 (D.Ore. 1969).

Sohappy v. Smith. 529 F.2d 570 (9th Cir. 1976).

Solem v. Bartlett. 465 US Reports 463 (1983).

Sousa v. Estate of Bishop. 594 F.Supp. 1480 (D.Haw. 1984).

South Carolina v. Catawba Indian Tribe. 106 S.Ct. 2039 (1986).

State v. Clark. 282 N.W.2d 902 (Minn. 1979).

State v. Coffee. 556 P.2d 1185 (Idaho 1976).

State v. Hawaiian Dredging Company. 397 P.2d 593 (Haw. 1964).

State v. Zimring. 479 P.2d 202 (Haw. 1970).

State ex. rel. Greely v. Confederated Salish and Kootenai Tribes of the Flathead Reservation. 712 P.2d 754 (Mont. 1985).

Stray Calf v. Scott Land and Livestock Co. 549 F.2d 1209 (9th Cir. 1977).

Territory v. Trustee of Estate of Kanoa. 41 Haw. 358 (1956).

Tooahnippah v. Hickel. 397 US Reports 598 (1970).

Truckee-Carson Irrigation District v. Secretary of the Interior. 742 F.2d 527 (9th Cir. 1984), cert. denied 105 S.Ct. 2701 (1985).

Trustees of the Office of Hawaiian Affairs v. Yamasaki. 737 P.2d 446 (Haw. 1987).

Tyonek Native Corporation v. Secretary of Interior. 629 F.Supp. 554 (D.Alaska 1986).

United States v. Adair. 723 F.2d 1394 (9th Cir. 1984).

United States v. Ahtanum Irrigation District. 330 F.2d 897 (9th Cir. 1964).

United States v. Anderson. 736 F.2d 1358 (9th Cir. 1984).

United States v. Cappaert. 426 US Reports 128 (1976).

United States v. Dann. 105 S.Ct. 1058 (1985).

United States v. Eberhardt. 789 F.2d 1354 (9th Cir. 1986).

United States v. Gemmill. 535 F.2d 1145 (9th Cir. 1976).

United States v. Michigan. 471 F.Supp. 192 (W.D.Mich. 1979).

United States v. Michigan. 520 F.Supp. 209 (W.D.Mich. 1981).

United States v. Michigan. 534 F.Supp. 668 (W.D.Mich. 1982).

United States v. Michigan. 653 F.2d 277 (6th Cir. 1981).

United States v. Montana. 457 F.Supp. 599 (D.Mont. 1978).

United States v. Mottaz. 106 S.Ct. 2224 (1986).

United States v. Oregon. 14 *Indian Law Reporter* 3151 (D.Ore. 1987).

United States v. Powers. 305 US Reports 527 (1939).

United States v. Sohappy. 770 F.2d 816 (9th Cir. 1985).

United States v. Superior Court in and for Maricopa City. 697 P.2d 658 (Ariz. 1985).

United States v. Washington. 496 F.2d 620 (9th Cir. 1974), cert. denied 419 US Reports 1032 (1976).

United States v. Washington. 384 F.Supp. 312. (W.D.Wash. 1974), aff'd 520 F.2d 676 (9th Cir. 1975), cert. denied 423 US Reports 1086 (1976).

United States v. Washington. 626 F.Supp. 1405 (1985).

United States v. Washington. 759 F.2d 1353 (9th Cir. 1985).

United States v. Washington. 761 F.2d 1404 (9th Cir. 1985).

United States v. Washington. 774 F.2d 1470 (9th Cir. 1985).

United States v. White Mountain Apache Tribe. 784 F.2d 917 (9th Cir. 1986).

United States v. Winans. 198 US Reports 371 (1905).

United States v. Winnebago Tribe of Nebraska. 542 F.2d 1002 (8th Cir. 1976).

Village of Gambell v. Hodel. 774 F.2d 1414 (9th Cir. 1985).

Washington v. Washington State Commercial Passenger Fishing Vessels. 443 US Reports 658 (1979).

White Earth Band of Chippewa v. Alexander. 683 F.2d 1129 (8th Cir. 1982).

White Mountain Apache Tribe v. Bracker. 448 US Reports 136 (1980).

White Mountain Apache Tribe v. Hodel. 784 F.2d 921 (9th Cir. 1986).
Williamson County Regional Planning Commission v. Hamilton Bank. 473 US Reports 172 (1985).
Wilson v. Block. 708 F.2d 735 (D.D.C. 1983), cert. denied 464 US Reports 1056 (1984).
Winters v. United States. 207 US Reports 564 (1908).
Worcester v. Georgia. 31 US Reports (6 Pet.) 515 (1832).
Yavapai-Prescott Indian Tribe v. Watt. 707 F.2d 1072 (9th Cir. 1983), cert. denied 464 US Reports 1017 (1983).
Yin v. Midkiff. 481 P.2d 109 (Haw. 1971).
Yoshimoto v. Lee. 634 P.2d 130 (Haw.Ct.App. 1981).

Newspapers

Akwesasne Notes (Mohawk Nation, N.Y.).
Anchorage Daily News.
Arizona Republic (Phoenix).
Daily Oklahoman (Oklahoma City).
Hawaiian Gazette (Honolulu).
Honolulu Advertiser.
Honolulu Star-Bulletin.
Juneau Empire.
Los Angeles Times.
Muskogee Phoenix (Okla.).
New York Times.
Norman Transcript (Okla.)
Oklahoma Journal (Oklahoma City).
Pacific Commercial Advertiser (Honolulu).
Polynesian (Honolulu).
San Diego Union.
Sandwich Island Gazette (Honolulu).
San Francisco Chronicle.
San Francisco Examiner.
Tulsa World.
Vinita Weekly Chieftain (Okla.).
Wassaja (San Francisco).

Books, Articles, Letters, Theses, Dissertations

Abel, Annie. "The History of Events Resulting in Indian Consolidation West of the Mississippi." *Annual Report of the American Historical Association for the Year 1906.*
———. "Indian Reservations in Kansas and the Extinguishment of Their Title." *Kansas Historical Society Transactions* 8 (1904): 72–109.

Alexander, William D. "A Brief History of Land Titles in the Hawaiian Kingdom." *Hawaiian Annual* (1891): 105–124.

American Friends Service Committee. *Uncommon Controversy: Fishing Rights of the Muckleshoot, Puyallup, and Nisqually Indians.* Seattle, 1970.

Barcott, Patricia. "The Alaska Native Claims Settlement Act: Survival of a Special Relationship." *University of San Francisco Law Review* 16 (1981): 157–178.

Bean, Lowell John. "Cahuilla." In *California,* vol. 8, *Handbook of North American Indians,* edited by Robert F. Heizer, 575–587. Washington, D.C., 1978.

Bean, Lowell John, and Florence C. Shipek. "Luiseño." In *California,* vol. 8, *Handbook of North American Indians,* edited by Robert F. Heizer, 550–563. Washington, D.C., 1978.

Bean, Lowell John, and Charles R. Smith. "Serrano." In *California,* vol. 8, *Handbook of North American Indians,* edited by Robert F. Heizer, 570–574. Washington, D.C., 1978.

Bean, Lowell John, and Dorothea Theodoratus. "Western Pomo and Northeastern Pomo." In *California,* vol. 8, *Handbook of North American Indians,* edited by Robert F. Heizer, 289–305. Washington, D.C., 1978.

Beckham, Stephen. *Requiem for A People: The Rogue Indians and the Frontiersmen.* Norman, 1971.

Beckwith, Martha W. "The Hawaiian Romance of Laieikawai." In *Thirty-Third Annual Report of the Bureau of American Ethnology,* 285–666. Washington, D.C., 1919.

Berger, Thomas. *Village Journey: The Report of the Alaska Native Review Commission.* New York, 1985.

Berry, Mary. *The Alaska Pipeline: The Politics of Oil and Native Land Claims.* Bloomington, 1975.

Bingham, Hiram. *A Residence of Twenty-one Years in the Sandwich Islands.* . . . 3d ed., rev. New York, 1969.

Bishop, Isabella Lucy (Bird). *The Hawaiian Archipelago; Six Months Among the Palm Groves, Coral Reefs and Volcanoes of the Sandwich Islands.* London, 1894. Reprint from 5th English ed. New York, 1903.

Bowers, Alfred. *Hidsatsa Social and Ceremonial Organization.* Bureau of American Ethnology Bulletin no. 194. Washington, D.C., 1965.

Bradley, Harold. *The American Frontier in Hawaii: The Pioneers, 1789–1843.* Stanford, 1942.

Brophy, William, and Sophie D. Aberle, comps. *The Indian: America's Unfinished Business: Report of the Commission on the Rights, Liberties, and Responsibilities of the American Indian.* Norman, 1966.

Burton, Lloyd. "American Indian Water Rights in the Western United States: Litigation, Negotiation, and the Regional Planning Process." Ph.D. diss., University of California, Berkeley, 1984.

Cahn, Edgar S., and David W. Hearne, eds. *Our Brother's Keeper: The Indian in White America.* New York, 1969.

Campbell, Archibald. *A Voyage Round the World, From 1806 to 1812.* . . . 4th American ed. Rosbury, Mass., 1825.

Campisi, Jack. "New York–Oneida Treaty of 1795: A Finding of Fact." *American Indian Law Review* 4 (1976): 71–82.

Case, David. *Alaska Natives and American Laws*. Fairbanks, 1984.

Cass, Lewis. "Removal of the Indians." *North American Review* 30 (1830): 62–121.

Chambers, Reid Payton, and Monroe E. Price. "Regulating Sovereignty: Secretarial Discretion and the Leasing of Indian Lands." *Stanford Law Review* 26 (1974): 1061–1096.

Chief Joseph. "American Indian's View of Indian Affairs." *North American Review* 128 (1879): 412–433.

Chinen, Jon J. *The Great Mahele: Hawaii's Land Division of 1848*. Honolulu, 1958.

――――. "The Hawaiian Land Revolution." *Hawaii Bar Journal* 5 (1967): 11–16.

――――. *Original Land Titles in Hawaii*. Honolulu, 1961.

Clegg, Donald, and Richard Bird. *Program Study and Evaluation of the Department of Hawaiian Home Lands, State of Hawaii*. Honolulu, 1971.

Cohen, Fay G. *Treaties on Trial: The Continuing Controversy Over Northwest Indian Fishing Rights*. Seattle, 1986.

Cohen, Felix S. *Handbook of Federal Indian Law*. Edited by R. Strickland. Rev. ed. Charlottesville, 1982.

Cohen, Warren, and Philip Mause. "The Indian: The Forgotten American." *Harvard Law Review* 81 (1968): 1818–1858.

Conahan, James P. "Hawaii's Land Reform Act: Is It Constitutional?" *Hawaii Bar Journal* 6 (1969): 31–53.

Cook, James, and James King. *A Voyage to the Pacific Ocean . . . in the Years 1776, 1777, 1778, 1779, and 1780*. 3 vols. 2d ed. London, 1785.

Cooper, John M. "Is the Algonquian Family Hunting Ground System Pre-Columbian?" *American Anthropologist*, n.s. 41 (1939): 66–90.

Corney, Peter. *Early Voyages in the Northern Pacific, 1813–1818*. Edited by Glen C. Adams. London, 1821; Honolulu, 1896; Fairfield, Washington, 1965.

Coyne, Thomas J. "*Hawaii Housing Authority v. Midkiff*: A Final Requiem for the Public Use Limitation on Eminent Domain?" *Notre Dame Law Review* 60 (1985): 388–404.

Dannenberg, James. "The Office of Hawaiian Affairs and the Issue of Sovereign Immunity." *University of Hawaii Law Review* 7 (1985): 95–105.

Davis, Britton. *The Truth About Geronimo*. Edited by M. M. Quaife. New Haven, 1929; Lincoln, 1976.

Daws, Gavan. *Shoal of Time: A History of the Hawaiian Islands*. New York, 1968.

Debo, Angie. *And Still the Waters Run*. Princeton, 1973.

――――. *Geronimo*. Norman, 1976.

――――. *A History of the Indians of the United States*. Norman, 1970.

Deloria, Vine, ed. *Of Utmost Good Faith*. San Francisco, 1971; New York, 1972.

Denig, Edwin. "Indian Tribes of the Upper Missouri." In *Forty-Sixth Annual Report of the Bureau of American Ethnology*, edited by J. N. B. Hewitt., 375–628. Washington, D.C., 1930.

Dixon, George. *A Voyage Round the World; But More Particularly to the Northwest Coast of America: Performed in 1785, 1786, 1787, and 1788, in the King George and Queen Charlotte, Captains Portlock and Dixon*. 2d ed. London, 1789.

Doi, Herman S. *Legal Aspects of the Hawaiian Homes Program*. Hawaii Legislative Reference Bureau Report no. 1A. Honolulu, 1964.

Dole, Sanford. "Hawaiian Land Policy." *Hawaiian Annual* (1898): 125–128.

Doyle, Emma Lyons, comp. *"Makua Laiano," The Story of Lorenzo Lyons, Compiled From Manuscript Journals, 1832–1886.* 2d ed. Honolulu, 1953.

Driver, Harold. *The Indians of North America.* 2d ed., rev. Chicago, 1969.

Ducheneaux, Kirke, and Karen Ducheneaux. *One Hundred Million Acres.* New York, 1973.

DuMars, Charles T., Marilyn O'Leary, and Albert E. Utton. *Pueblo Indian Water Rights.* Tucson, 1984.

Echohawk, John, et al. "John Echohawk, et al. to Griffin Bell," 19 Aug. 1978. In *Indian Law Reporter* 5 (1978): M45–55.

Edmunds, R. David. *The Shawnee Prophet.* Lincoln, 1983.

———. *Tecumseh and the Quest for Indian Leadership.* Boston, 1984.

Ellis, William. *A Narrative of a Tour Through Hawaii.* . . . London, 1827; Honolulu, 1963.

Fenton, William N. "Locality As a Basic Factor in the Development of Iroquois Social Structure." In *Symposium On Local Diversity in Iroquois Culture.* Bureau of American Ethnology Bulletin no. 149, edited by William N. Fenton, 35–54. Washington, D.C., 1951.

Fey, Harold E., and D'Arcy McNickle. *Indians and Other Americans: Two Ways of Life Meet.* New and rev. ed. New York, 1970; Perennial Library, 1970.

Fixico, Donald. *Termination and Relocation: Federal Indian Policy, 1945–1960.* Albuquerque, 1986.

Forde, C. Darryl. "Ethnology of the Yuma Indians." *UCPAAE* 28, no. 4 (1931): 83–278.

———. *Habitat, Economy and Society: A Geographic Introduction to Ethnology.* New York, 1934.

———. "Hopi Agriculture and Land Ownership." In *Royal Anthropological Institute Journal* 61 (1931): 357–405.

Foreman, Grant. *The Last Trek of the Indians.* Chicago, 1946.

Fornander, Abraham. *An Account of the Polynesian Race: Its Origin and Migrations and the Ancient History of the Hawaiian People to the Times of Kamehameha I.* 3 vols. London, 1878–1885; Rutland, Vermont, 1969.

Franchere, Gabriel. *Narrative of a Voyage to the Northwest Coast of America in the Years 1811, 1812, 1813, and 1814 or the First American Settlement on the Pacific.* Translated and edited by J. V. Huntington. Redfield, New York, 1854. Reprint edited by Milo M. Quaife. Chicago, 1954.

Fuchs, Lawrence. *Hawaii Pono: A Social History.* New York, 1961.

Gast, Ross H., and Agnes C. Conrad. *Don Francisco de Paula Marin and the Letters and Journal of Francisco de Paula Marin.* Honolulu, 1972.

Gates, Paul W. *Fifty Million Acres: Conflicts over Kansas Land Policy, 1854–1890.* Ithaca, 1954.

———. "Indian Allotments Preceding the Dawes Act." In *The Frontier Challenge: Responses to the Trans-Mississippi West,* edited by John G. Clark, 141–170. Lawrence, 1971.

Gerard, Forrest. "Indian Water Policy Review." 24 May 1978. In *Indian Law Reporter* 5 (1978): M40–42.

Getches, David H. "Alternative Approaches to Alaska Land Claims." In *Irredeemable America: The Indians' Estate and Land Claims,* edited by Imre Sutton, 301–335. Albuquerque, 1985.

Getches, David H., and Charles F. Wilkinson. *Federal Indian Law: Cases and Materials.* 2d ed. St. Paul, 1986.

Gibson, Arrell M. *The American Indian: Prehistory to the Present.* Lexington, 1980.

———. *The Chickasaws.* Norman, 1971.

———. *The Kickapoos: Lords of the Middle Border.* Norman, 1963.

———. *The West in the Life of the Nation.* Lexington, 1976.

Gifford, Edward Winslow. "Clear Lake Pomo Society." *UCPAAE* 18, no. 2 (1926): 287–390.

———. "Miwok Lineages and the Political Unit in Aboriginal California." In *The California Indians: A Source Book,* edited by Robert F. Heizer and M. A. Whipple, 326–335. Berkeley and Los Angeles, 1951.

———. "Pomo Lands on Clear Lake." In *UCPAAE* 20, no. 5 (1923): 77–92.

Gilbert, William, and John Taylor. "Indian Land Questions." *Arizona Law Review* 8 (1966): 102–133.

Gover, Kevin. "Oklahoma Tribes: A History. *American Indian Journal* 3 (June 1977): 2–19.

Gray, Francine du Plessix. *Hawaii: The Sugar-Coated Fortress.* New York, 1972.

Gunter, William B. "Recommendation to President Carter From William B. Gunter." *American Indian Law Review* 5 (1977): 427–430.

Haas, Theodore H. "The Indian Reorganization Act in Historical Perspective." In *Indian Affairs and the Indian Reorganization Act: The Twenty Year Record,* edited by William Kelly, 8–25. Tucson, 1954.

Hallowell, A. Irving. "The Size of Algonkian Hunting Territories: A Function of Ecological Adjustment." *American Anthropologist,* n.s. 51 (1949): 35–45.

Handy, Edward Smith Craighill, and Mary Kawena Pukui. *The Polynesian Family System in Ka'u, Hawaii.* Wellington, New Zealand, 1958.

Handy, Edward Smith Craighill, Elizabeth Green Handy, and Mary Kawena Pukui. *Native Planters in Old Hawaii: Their Life, Lore, and Environment.* Bernice P. Bishop Museum Bulletin 233. Honolulu, 1972.

Hanke, Lewis. *All Mankind Is One: A Study of the Disputation Between Bartolomé de Las Casas and Juan Ginés de Sepúlveda on the Religious and Intellectual Capacity of the American Indians.* Dekalb, Illinois, 1974.

Hansen, Diana. *The Homestead Papers: A Critical Analysis of the Management of the Department of Hawaiian Home Lands.* Honolulu, 1971.

Harrison, Graig S., and Tom Grande. "*Midkiff v. Tom:* The Constitutionality of Hawaii's Land Reform Act." *University of Hawaii Law Review* 6 (1984): 561–600.

Harrison, William H. *Messages and Letters of William H. Harrison.* Edited by Logan Esarey. 2 vols. Indianapolis, 1922.

Hauptman, Laurence M. *The Iroquois Struggle for Survival: World War II to Red Power.* Syracuse, 1986.

"Hawaii's Ceded Lands." *University of Hawaii Law Review* 3 (1981): 101–146.

Heizer, Robert F., ed. *California.* Vol. 8 of *Handbook of the North American Indians.* Washington, D.C., 1978.

Herndon, G. Melvin. "Indian Agriculture in the Southern Colonies." *North Carolina Historical Review* 44 (1967): 283–297.

Herskovits, Melville. *Economic Anthropology: The Economic Life of Primitive Peoples.* New York, 1952.

Hill, William W. "Notes on Pima Land Law and Tenure." *American Anthropologist,* n.s. 38 (1936): 586–589.

Hirayasu, Naomi. "Adverse Possession and Quiet Title Actions in Hawaii—Recent Constitutional Developments." *Hawaii Bar Journal* 19 (1985): 59–73.

Hobbs, Jean. *Hawaii—A Pageant of the Soil.* London, 1935.

Hoig, Stan. *The Sand Creek Massacre.* Norman, 1961.

Horsman, Reginald. *Expansion and American Indian Policy, 1783–1812.* East Lansing, 1967.

Horwitz, Robert, and Judith Finn. *Public Land Policy in Hawaii: Major Landowners.* Hawaii Legislative Reference Bureau Report no. 3. Honolulu, 1967.

Hussey, John, ed. *The Voyage of the Racoon: A "Secret" Journal of a Visit to Oregon, California, and Hawaii, 1813–1814.* San Francisco, 1958.

Ii, John Papa. *Fragments of Hawaiian History.* Translated by Mary Kawena Pukui. Edited by Dorothy B. Barrère. Honolulu, 1959.

Ingraham, Joseph. *The Log of the "Brig Hope" Called the "Hope's" Trek Among the Sandwich Islands, May 20–Oct. 12, 1791.* . . . Hawaiian Historical Society Reprint no. 3. Honolulu, 1918.

Jacobs, Wilbur. *Dispossessing the American Indian: Indians and Whites on the Colonial Frontier.* New York, 1972.

Jarves, James. *History of the Hawaiian Islands.* . . . 4th ed. Honolulu, 1872.

Jefferson, Thomas. *The Works of Thomas Jefferson.* Edited by Paul Ford. 12 vols. New York, 1904.

Jenks, Albert. "The Wild Rice Gatherers of the Upper Lakes." In *Nineteenth Annual Report of the Bureau of American Ethnology,* 1013–1137. Washington, D.C., 1900.

Jennings, Francis. *The Invasion of America: Indians, Colonialism, and the Cant of Conquest.* New York, 1975.

Joesting, Edward. *Kauai: The Separate Kingdom.* Honolulu, 1984.

Johnson, Jerald Jay. "Yana." In *California,* vol. 8, *Handbook of North American Indians,* edited by Robert F. Heizer, 361–369. Washington, D.C., 1978.

Johnson, Ralph. "The States Versus Indian Off-Reservation Fishing: A United States Supreme Court Error." *Washington Law Review* 47 (1972): 207–236.

Jones, Douglas C. *The Treaty of Medicine Lodge: The Story of the Great Treaty Council as Told by Eyewitnesses.* Norman, 1966.

Jones, Gary. "Enforcement Strategies for Indian Landlords." *American Indian Law Review* 2 (1974): 41–60.

Josephy, Alvin M., Jr. *The Indian Heritage of America.* New York, 1968, 1969.

———. *The Nez Perce Indians and the Opening of the Northwest.* New Haven, 1965.

———. *Now That the Buffalo's Gone: A Study of Today's American Indians.* Norman, 1984.

Judd, Bernice, comp. *Voyages to Hawaii Before 1860; A Record Based on Historical Narratives in the Libraries of the Hawaiian Mission Children's Society and the Hawaiian Historical Society.* Enlarged and revised by Helen Younge Lind. Honolulu, 1974.

Kamakau, Samuel. *Ka Poʻe Kahiko: The People of Old.* Translated by Mary Kawena Pukui. Arranged and edited by Dorothy B. Barrère. Bernice P. Bishop Museum Special Publication 51. Honolulu, 1964.

Keesing, Felix. *Hawaiian Homesteading on Molokai.* University of Hawaii Research Publication 12. Honolulu, 1936.

Kelly, Isabel T. "Coast Miwok." In *California,* vol. 8, *Handbook of North American Indians,* edited by Robert F. Heizer, 414–425. Washington, D.C., 1978.

———. "Ethnography of the Surprise Valley Paiute." *UCPAAE* 31, no. 3 (1932): 67–210.

———. "Southern Paiute Bands." *American Anthropologist,* n.s. 36 (1934): 548–560.

Kelly, Marion. "Changes in Land Tenure in Hawaii, 1778–1850." Master's thesis, University of Hawaii, 1956.

———. "Some Problems with Early Descriptions of Hawaiian Culture." In *Polynesian Culture History: Essays in Honor of Kenneth P. Emory,* edited by Genevieve A. Highland, Roland W. Force, Alan Howard, Marion Kelly, Yosihiko H. Sinoto, 399–410. Bernice P. Bishop Museum Special Publication 56. Honolulu, 1967.

Kinietz, Vernon. "Notes on the Algonquian Family Hunting Ground System." *American Anthropologist,* n.s. 42 (1940): 179.

Kirch, Patrick Vinton. *The Evolution of the Polynesian Chiefdoms.* Cambridge, 1984.

———. *Feathered Gods and Fishhooks: An Introduction to Hawaiian Archaeology and Prehistory.* Honolulu, 1985.

Knack, Martha, and Omer Stewart. *As Long as the Rivers Shall Run: An Ethnohistory of Pyramid Lake Indian Reservation.* Berkeley and Los Angeles, 1984.

Korn, Alfons L., ed. *News From Molokai: Letters Between Peter Kaeo and Queen Emma, 1873–1876.* Honolulu, 1976.

Kosaki, Richard. *Konohiki Fishing Rights.* Hawaii Legislative Reference Bureau Report no. 1. Honolulu, 1954.

Kotzebue, Otto Von. *A Voyage of Discovery into the South Sea and Bering's Straits, for the Purpose of Exploring a North-east Passage, Undertaken in the Years 1815–1818.* 3 vols. London, 1821. Reprint ed. in 2 vols. Amsterdam and New York, 1967.

Kroeber, Alfred L. *Handbook of California Indians.* Bureau of American Ethnology Bulletin no. 78. Washington, D.C., 1925.

———. "Nature of the Land-Holding Group." *Ethnohistory* 2 (1955): 303–314.

———. "The Nature of Land-Holding Groups in Aboriginal California." In *University of California Archaeology Survey Reports,* no. 56, 87–120. Berkeley, 1956.

Kuykendall, Ralph. *The Hawaiian Kingdom, 1778–1854: Foundation and Transformation.* Vol. 1. Honolulu, 1938.

———. *The Hawaiian Kingdom, 1854–1874: Twenty Critical Years.* Vol. 2. Honolulu, 1953.

———. *The Hawaiian Kingdom, 1874–1893: The Kalakaua Dynasty.* Vol. 3. Honolulu, 1967.

Kuykendall, Ralph, and A. Grove Day. *Hawaii: A History.* Rev. ed. Englewood, N.J., 1961.

Kuykendall, Ralph, and Lorin Gill. *Hawaii in the World War.* Honolulu, 1928.

LaFave, LeAnn Larson. "Forced Fee Indian Land Claims: Will Land Owners Be Liable for Government's Wrongdoing?" *South Dakota Law Review* 30 (1985): 60–103.

Lake Mohonk Conference Proceedings, 1890.

La Pérouse, M. De. *A Voyage Round the World: Which Was Performed in the Years 1785, 1786, 1787, and 1788.* Edinburgh, 1798.

Lawson, Michael L. *Dammed Indians: The Pick-Sloan Plan and the Missouri River Sioux, 1944–1980.* Norman, 1982.

Leckie, William. *The Military Conquest of the Southern Plains.* Norman, 1963.

Ledyard, John. *A Journal of Captain Cook's Last Voyage.* . . . Edited by Kenneth Munford. London, 1783; Corvallis, Ore., 1963.

Levy, Neil M. "Native Hawaiian Land Rights." *California Law Review* 63 (1975): 848–885.

Lumpkin, Wilson. *The Removal of the Cherokee Indians From Georgia.* Edited by Wymberly Jones De Renne. 2 vols. New York, 1907.

Lurie, Nancy. "The Indian Claims Commission." *Annals of the American Academy of Political and Social Science* 436 (1978): 97–110.

Lyons, C. J. "Land Matters in Hawaii." *The Islander* 1 (1875): 103, 104, 111, 118, 119, 126, 135, 143, 150, 159, 168, 174, 182, 190.

MacKenzie, Melody K. *Sovereignty and Land: Honoring the Hawaiian Native Claim.* Honolulu, 1982.

McLendon, Sally, and Robert L. Oswalt. "Pomo: Introduction." In *California,* vol. 8, *Handbook of North American Indians,* edited by Robert F. Heizer, 274–288. Washington, D.C., 1978.

McLennan, Barbara N. "Federal Policy With Respect to Collection of Royalties From Oil and Gas Leases on Federal and Indian Lands." *Oil and Gas Tax Quarterly* (1983): 87–105.

McNickle, D'Arcy. *Native American Tribalism: Indian Survivals and Renewals.* New York, 1973.

McWilliams, Carey. *Brothers Under the Skin.* Boston, 1948.

Malo, David. *Hawaiian Antiquities.* Translated by Nathaniel Emerson. 2d ed. Bernice P. Bishop Museum Special Publications 2. Honolulu, 1903, 1951, 1971.

Manypenny, George W. *Our Indian Wards.* Cincinnati, 1880.

Martin, John F. "From Judgment to Land Restoration: The Havasupai Claims Case." In *Irredeemable America: The Indian's Estate and Land Claims,* edited by Imre Sutton. Albuquerque, 1985.

Meares, John. *Voyages Made in the Years 1788 and 1789 From China to the Northwest Coast of America.* London, 1790; Amsterdam and New York, 1967.

Meriam, Lewis, Ray A. Brown, Henry Roe Cloud, Edward Everett Dale, Emma Duke, Herbert R. Edwards, Fayette Avery McKenzie, Mary Louise Mark, W. Carson Ryan, Jr., and William J. Spillman. *The Problem of Indian Administration.* Baltimore, 1928.

Merriam, C. Hart. "The Indian Population of California." *American Anthropologist,* n.s. 7 (1905): 594–606.

Meyer, Roy. *History of Santee Sioux: United States Indian Policy on Trial.* Lincoln, 1967.

———. "The Fort Berthold Reservation and the Garrison Dam." *North Dakota History* 35 (1968): 217–264.

Meyer, William. *Native Americans.* New York, 1971.

Missionary Herald. Vols. 17–25 (1821–1829).

Morgan, Theodore. *Hawaii: A Century of Economic Change, 1778–1876.* Cambridge, Mass., 1948.

Murray, Keith. *The Modocs and Their War.* Norman, 1959.

Nash, Gary. *Red, White, and Black: The Peoples of Early America.* Englewood Cliffs, N.J., 1974.

Native American Rights Fund. *News Release,* 31 Aug. 1987.

Olson, James S., and Raymond Wilson. *Native Americans in the Twentieth Century.* Urbana, 1984.

Orfield, Gary. *A Study of the Termination Policy.* Denver, 1966.

Oswalt, Wendell H. *This Land Was Theirs: A Study of North American Indians.* 4th ed. Mountain View, Calif., 1988.

Otis, D. S. *The Dawes Act and the Allotment of Indian Lands.* Edited by Francis Paul Prucha. Norman, 1973.

Park, Willard Z., Edgar E. Siskin, Anne M. Cooke, William T. Mulloy, Marvin K. Opler, Isabel T. Kelly, and Maurice L. Zigmond. "Tribal Distribution in the Great Basin." *American Anthropologist,* n.s. 40 (1938): 622–638.

Passamaquoddy and Penobscot Tribes. "Passamaquoddy and Penobscot Tribes to Carter." Telegram, 26 July 1977. In *American Indian Law Review* 5 (1977): 427–430.

Perkins, Edward. *Na Motu: Or, Reef-Rovings in the . . . Hawaiian . . . Islands.* New York, 1854.

Peterson, Edward Michael, Jr. "That So-Called Warranty Deed: Clouded Land Titles on the White Earth Indian Reservation in Minnesota." *North Dakota Law Review* 59 (1983): 159–181.

Philp, Kenneth. *John Collier's Crusade for Indian Reform, 1920–1954.* Tucson, 1977.

Pierce, Richard. *Russia's Hawaiian Adventure, 1815–1817.* Berkeley and Los Angeles, 1965.

Porteus, Stanley. *A Century of Social Thinking in Hawaii.* Palo Alto, 1962.

Portlock, Nathaniel. *A Voyage Round the World But More Particularly to the Northwest Coast of America: Performed in 1785, 1786, 1787, and 1788, in the King George and Queen Charlotte, Captains Portlock and Dixon.* London, 1789.

Price, Monroe. *Law and the American Indian.* New York, 1973.

Price, Monroe, and Gary D. Weatherford. "Indian Water Rights in Theory and Practice: Navajo Experience in the Colorado River Basin." *Law and Contemporary Problems* 40 (1976): 97–131.

Prucha, Francis Paul. *American Indian Policy in Crisis: Christian Reformers and the Indian, 1865–1900.* Norman, 1976.

———. *American Indian Policy in the Formative Years: Indian Trade and Intercourse Acts, 1790–1834.* Cambridge, Mass., 1962.

———. *The Great Father.* Abr. ed. Lincoln, 1986.

Radin, Paul. "The Winnebago Tribe." In *Thirty-Seventh Annual Report of the Bureau of American Ethnology,* 35–550. Washington, D.C., 1923.

Riddell, Francis A. "Maidu and Konkow." In *California,* vol. 8, *Handbook of North American Indians,* edited by Robert F. Heizer, 370–386. Washington, D.C., 1978.

Riley, Carrol. "The Makah Indians: A Study of Political and Economic Organization." *Ethnohistory* 15 (1968): 57–95.

Rogin, Michael. *Fathers and Children: Andrew Jackson and the Subjugation of the American Indian*. New York, 1975.

Ruschenberger, W. S. *A Voyage Round the World . . . in 1835, 1836, 1837*. Philadelphia, 1838.

Sahlins, Marshall, and Dorothy Barrère, eds. "William Richards on Hawaii Culture and Political Conditions of the Islands in 1841." *Hawaiian Journal of History* 7 (1973): 18–41.

Satz, Ronald. *American Indian Policy in the Jacksonian Era*. Lincoln, 1974.

Sharkey, Margery. "Revitalization and Change: A History of the Wanapum Indians, Their Prophet Smowhala, and the Washani Religion." Master's thesis, Washington State University, 1984.

Sheehan, Bernard W. *Seeds of Extinction: Jeffersonian Philanthropy and the American Indian*. New York, 1973.

Shipek, Florence C. "History of Southern California Mission Indians." In *California*, vol. 8, *Handbook of North American Indians*, edited by Robert F. Heizer, 610–618. Washington, D.C., 1978.

———. *Pushed Into the Rocks: Southern California Indian Land Tenure, 1769–1986*. Lincoln, 1987.

Silverstein, Michael. "Yokuts: Introduction." In *California*, vol. 8, *Handbook of North American Indians*, edited by Robert F. Heizer, 446–461. Washington, D.C., 1978.

Snyderman, George S. "Concepts of Land Ownership Among the Iroquois and Their Neighbors." In *Symposium on Local Diversity in Iroquois Culture*, edited by William N. Fenton, 15–34. Bureau of American Ethnology Bulletin no. 149. Washington, D.C. 1951.

Spaulding, Thomas M. *The Crown Lands of Hawaii*. University of Hawaii Occasional Papers, no. 1. Honolulu, 1923.

Speck, Frank G., and Loren Eiseley. "Significance of Hunting Territory Systems of the Algonkian in Social Theory." *American Anthropologist*, n.s. 41 (1939): 269–280.

Spicer, Edward, ed. *Perspectives in American Indian Culture Change*. Chicago, 1961.

Spinden, Herbert. "The Nez Perce Indians." *American Anthropology Association Memoirs*, vol. 2, pt. 3 (1908): 165–274.

Spitz, Allan. "The Hawaiian Homes Program: A Study in Ideological Transplantation." Ph.D. diss., Michigan State University, 1964.

Sprague, Marshall. *Massacre: The Tragedy at White River*. Boston, 1957.

Steadman, John Montague. "The Statutory Elements of Hawaii's Adverse Possession Law." *Hawaii Bar Journal* 14 (1978): 67–78.

Steiner, Keith J. "Adverse Possession Against Unknown Claimants Under Land Court and Quiet Title Procedures." *Hawaii Bar Journal* 2 (1964): 4–12.

Stevens, Sylvester. *American Expansion in Hawaii, 1842–1898*. Harrisburg, Pennsylvania, 1945.

Steward, Julian. *Basin-Plateau Aboriginal Groups*. Bureau of American Ethnology Bulletin no. 120. Washington, D.C., 1938.

———. "Ethnography of the Owens Valley Paiute." *UCPAAE* 33, no. 3 (1933): 233–250.

———. "Linguistic Distributions and Political Groups of Great Basin Shoshoneans." *American Anthropologist*, n.s. 39 (1937): 625–634.

———. *Theory of Culture Change*. Urbana, 1955.

Stewart, Charles S. *A Residence in the Sandwich Islands*. 5th ed. and enl. Boston, 1839.

Stewart, Omer C. "Notes on Pomo Ethnogeography." *UCPAAE* 40, no. 2 (1943): 29–62.

Strong, William D. "Aboriginal Society in Southern California." *UCPAAE* 26, no. 1 (1929).

Sutton, Imre. *Indian Land Tenure: Bibliographical Essays and a Guide to the Literature*. New York, 1975.

———, ed. *Irredeemable America: The Indians' Estate and Land Claims*. Albuquerque, 1985.

Swanton, John R. "Aboriginal Culture of the Southeast." In *Forty-Second Annual Report of the Bureau of American Ethnology*, 673–726. Washington, D.C., 1928.

———. *Indians of the Southeastern United States*. Bureau of American Ethnology Bulletin no. 137. Washington, D.C., 1946.

———. "Social Organization and Social Usages of the Indians of the Creek Confederacy." In *Forty-Second Annual Report of the Bureau of American Ethnology*, 23–472. Washington, D.C., 1928.

———. "Social and Religious Beliefs and Usages of the Chickasaw Indians." In *Forty-Fourth Annual Report of the Bureau of American Ethnology*, 169–273. Washington, D.C., 1928.

Tate, Merze. *Hawaii: Reciprocity or Annexation*. East Lansing, 1968.

———. *The United States and the Hawaiian Kingdom: A Political History*. New Haven, 1965.

Teit, James A. "The Salishan Tribes of the Western Plateaus." Edited by Franz Boas. *Forty-Fifth Annual Report of the Bureau of American Ethnology*, 23–396. Washington, D.C., 1930.

Thurston, Lorrin A., ed. *Fundamental Law of Hawaii*. Honolulu, 1904.

Tom, Michael D. "Hawaiian Beach Access: A Customary Right." *Hastings Law Journal* 26 (1975): 823–847.

Town, Michael Anthony, and William Wai Lim Yuen. "Public Access to Beaches in Hawaii: 'A Social Necessity.' " *Hawaii Bar Journal* 10 (1973): 5–28.

Trafzer, Clifford E., and Richard D. Scheurerman. *Renegade Tribe: The Palouse Indians and the Invasion of the Inland Pacific Northwest*. Pullman, Wash., 1986.

Tuggle, Myra Jean F. "The Protect Kaho'olawe 'Ohana: Cultural Revitalization in a Contemporary Hawaiian Movement." Master's thesis, University of Hawaii, 1982.

Underhill, Ruth. *Red Man's America: A History of Indians in the United States*. Chicago, 1953.

Utley, Robert M. *Frontier Regulars: The United States Army and the Indian, 1866–1891*. New York, 1973.

Valeri, Valerio. *Kingship and Sacrifice: Ritual and Society in Ancient Hawaii*. Chicago, 1985.

Vancouver, Captain George. *A Voyage of Discovery to the North Pacific Ocean, and Round the World . . . in the Years 1790, 1791, 1792, 1793, 1794, and 1795. . . .* 3 vols. London, 1798.

Van Duke, John. "The Constitutionality of the Office of Hawaiian Affairs." In U.S. Congress. Senate. Committee on Energy and Natural Resources. *Hear-*

ings on the Report of the Native Hawaiians Study Commission. 98th Cong., 2d sess., 1984. S. Hrg. 98-1257, pt. 1.

Van Every, Dale. *Disinherited: The Lost Birthright of the American Indian*. New York, 1966.

Veeder, William. "Greed and Bigotry: Hallmark of American Indian Law." *American Indian Journal* 3 (Dec. 1977): 2–15.

———. "Water Rights in the Coal Fields of the Yellowstone River Basin." *Law and Contemporary Problems* 40 (1976): 77–96.

Wallace, Anthony. "Political Organization and Land Tenure Among the Northeastern Indians, 1600–1830." *Southwestern Anthropology* 13 (1957): 301–321.

Walsh, John F. "Settling the Alaska Native Claims Settlement Act." *Stanford Law Review* 38 (1985): 227–263.

Washburn, Wilcomb E. *Red Man's Land/White Man's Law: A Study of the Past and Present Status of the American Indian*. New York, 1971.

Watson, Kali, comp. "Adverse Possession." Prepared for Alu Like. Honolulu, n.d.

White, Raymond. "Luiseño Social Organization." *UCPAAE* 48, no. 2 (1963): 91–194.

White, Robert, ed. *Messages of Governors of Tennessee*. 5 vols. Nashville, 1952.

Williams, Ethel J. "Too Little Land, Too Many Heirs—The Indian Heirship Land Problem." *Washington Law Review* 46 (1971): 709–744.

Wright, Theon. *The Disenchanted Isles*. New York, 1972.

INDEX

Aberdeen, Lord, 102, 103
Aboriginal use and occupancy, 5, 25, 34, 46
Access rights (Hawaiian), 168–171, 225 nn.
 1–3, 5
Act: of New York, 150; of 17 May 1884, 46
Acteon (British warship), 99
Adams, John Quincy, 32
Admiralty Island, 145
Adverse possession, 115–117, 216 nn. 30,
 34, 40; restrictions on, 167; and tacking,
 117
Agua Caliente Indians, and leasing scandal,
 81
Ahupua'a, 11, 168, 169, 171; definition and
 description of, 13; of Waimea, 14
Ak-Chin Reservation, 75
Alaska Federation of Natives, 143
Alaska National Interest Lands Conservation
 Act, 144, 145
Alaska National Petroleum Reserve, 144
Alaska Native Claims Settlement Act, 47,
 134, 135, 142–146, 221 nn. 30, 31;
 amendments of 1987, 146; opposition to,
 144
Alaska Pipeline Project, 143
Alexander I (Czar of Russia), 89
Alexander VI, Pope, 2
Ali'i, 10, 88, 91, 196 n. 7; *ali'i 'aimoku,* 12
Allotment: before Dawes Act, 203 n. 55;
 Burke Act, 49; eminent domain, 205 n. 3;
 exemptions, 47; and Five Civilized Tribes,
 47, 48, 203 n. 64; general impact of, 52;
 and heirship lands, 52, 204 n. 75; Indian
 groups opposing, 48; and leasing, 48,
 203 n. 62; and litigation of forced fee
 patents, 204 n. 65; methods used by non-
 Indians to obtain, 50; and removal of trust
 restrictions, 48, 203 n. 64; and Sisseton

Sioux, 49; taxation of, 49; and White
 Earth Chippewa Reservation, 50–52. *See
 also* Dawes Act
ALOHA (Aboriginal Lands of Hawaiian
 Ancestry), 135, 136, 164
American: attitudes toward Hawaiian land
 rights, 6, 95–98, 112–114; intervention
 in Hawaii, 93, 97–103, 112, 128–131,
 137
Ancient Hawaii, 8–15; agricultural field
 systems in, 15; fish ponds in, 15; land
 tenure in, 7; social order in, 8; water rights
 in, 10
Andrus, Cecil, 162
Annexation, 121; Hawaiian resistance to,
 121, 126, 128–131, 218 n. 68
Antoine v. Washington, 184
Apache wars, 42, 43
Arapaho Indians, 76, 185
Ariyoshi, George R., 162
Arizona v. California, 66, 70, 71, 72, 73,
 207 n. 44
Arizona v. San Carlos Apache Tribe, 68, 75,
 77
Armstrong, Rev. Richard, 112
Army Corps of Engineers, 56, 59–63, 85,
 206 n. 11
Arnett v. Five Gill Nets, 185
Articles of Confederation, 150
Assimilative Crimes Act, 185

Baranov, Alexander, 88, 89
Bay Mills Indian Community, 180, 181
Beach access, 169–170
Bedford, Joseph, 113
Bell, Griffin, 178
Bishop, Bernice Pauahi (Hawaiian princess),
 122

253

ABOUT THE AUTHOR

Linda S. Parker, an associate professor of American Indian Studies at San Diego State University, writes from the vantage point of a trained historian, a Cherokee Indian, and an attorney. She is well known for her articles on Indian removal, Indian citizenship and voting rights, and federal Native Hawaiian policy in the twentieth century. Parker holds a Ph.D. and a J.D. from the University of Oklahoma.

Production Notes

This book was designed by Roger Eggers.
Composition and paging were done on the
Quadex Composing System and typesetting
on the Compugraphic 8400 by the design
and production staff of University of
Hawaii Press.

The text and display typeface is Galliard.

Offset presswork and binding were done by
Vail-Ballou Press, Inc. Text paper is Writers
RR Offset, basis 50.